Alliance
for
Biking & Walking

BICYCLING AND WALKING IN THE UNITED STATES

2014

BENCHMARKING REPORT

Funding for this report was provided by the Centers for Disease Control and Prevention.

The findings and conclusions in this report are those of the authors and do not necessarily represent the views of the Centers for Disease Control and Prevention or the Agency for Toxic Substances and Disease Registry.

This project was also made possible with support from AARP and the American Public Transportation Association.

Alliance for Biking & Walking
P.O. Box 65150
Washington, DC 20035
Phone: 202-449-9692
Benchmarking@BikeWalkAlliance.org

www.BikeWalkAlliance.org/Benchmarking.org

Cover photo by Bruce Bodjack. Traverse City, MI.

Photo by Gabriella Salary. Courtesy of Alliance for Biking & Walking

REPORT CREDITS

Author, Project Manager:
Andrea Milne, Alliance for Biking & Walking

Co-Author, Research Assistant:
Maggie Melin, Alliance for Biking & Walking

Copy Editor:
Michelle Milne

Data Quality Control:
Yolonda Weins

Research Consultants:
Ralph Buehler, PhD, Virginia Tech
John Pucher, PhD, Rutgers University

Contributing Writers:
Evan Bontrager, Friends of the Pumpkinvine Nature Trail
Ralph Buehler, PhD, Virginia Tech
Tijs Buskermolen, Goshen College
Clarrissa Cabansagan, TransForm
Brian Caulfield, Department of Civil, Structural and Environmental Engineering; Trinity College, Dublin
Alison Dewey, League of American Bicyclists
Darren Flusche, Advocacy Advance / League of American Bicyclists
Andrea Hamre, Virginia Tech
Colin Hughes, Institute for Transportation and Development Policy
Mary Lauran Hall, Alliance for Biking & Walking
Ken McLeod, Advocacy Advance / League of American Bicyclists
John Pucher, PhD, Rutgers University
Eloisa Raynault, American Public Health Association
Michael Samuelson, Alliance for Biking & Walking, Open Streets Project
Hamzat Sani, Red, Bike and Green
David Vega-Barachowitz, National Association of City Transportation Officials
Kathryn Werntz, The Sahel Calling Project
Liz Whiteley, U.S. Environmental Protection Agency
Susan Wilcox, BikeTexas

Benchmarking Review Team:
Laurie Beck, Centers for Disease Control and Prevention
Christopher Douwes, Federal Highway Administration
Darren Flusche, Advocacy Advance / League of American Bicyclists
Darnell Grisby, American Public Transportation Association
Deb Hubsmith, Safe Routes to School National Partnership
Jeffrey Miller, Alliance for Biking & Walking
Gaya Myers, Centers for Disease Control and Prevention
Robert Ping, Safe Routes to School National Partnership
Gabe Rousseau, PhD, Federal Highway Administration
Stephen Skowronski, Centers for Disease Control and Prevention
Arthur M. Wendel, MD, MPH, Centers for Disease Control and Prevention

Institute of Transportation Engineers (ITE) Review Committee:
Monica Altmaier, Fehr & Peers
Philip J. Caruso, PE, ITE
Mike Cyneki, Lee Engineering, LLC
Jennifer Donlon Wyant, Alta Planning + Design
Yung Koprowski, Lee Engineering, LLC
Jina Mahmoudi, PE, ITE
Matthew D. Ridgway, AICP, PTP, Fehr & Peers
Edward R. Stollof, AICP, ITE
Shawn M. Turner, PE, Texas Transportation Institute

ACKNOWLEDGMENTS

This report is the result of hundreds of people working together.

The Alliance for Biking & Walking extends special thanks to our partners at the Centers for Disease Control and Prevention (CDC), AARP, and the American Public Transportation Association, whose generous funding ensures the continuation and growth of the Benchmarking Project. In particular, we would like to thank Arthur Wendel and Stephen Skowronski of the CDC's National Center for Environmental Health for their guidance throughout the report development and for their continued support of the project vision. Additionally, the following agencies and organizations provided funds for the midsized cities pilot benchmarking effort included in this report for the first time:

- Bicycle Commuters of Anchorage
- Bike Chattanooga
- Bike/Walk Alliance for Missoula
- City of Albany
- City of Burlington
- Great Rivers Greenway
- Missoula in Motion
- PittsburghTODAY

Many thanks to Dr. John Pucher of Rutgers University and Dr. Ralph Buehler of Virginia Tech for contributing their expertise to the research and analysis contained in this report. Thank you to Maggie Melin for her diligent work researching, collecting, and analyzing the mounds of raw data, as well as her contributions to writing and editing text throughout the report. We thank Nicole Wynands and Bill Nesper of the League of American Bicyclists for their collaboration on integrating the benchmarking state survey with the Bicycle Friendly States survey. Additional thanks are due to Michelle Milne (primary content editor) and Yolonda Weins (data quality control) for their meticulous review of the report text and data, ensuring a high quality report.

The *Benchmarking Report* undergoes a rigorous review by a team of researchers and professionals who work with these topics daily in various fields of study. Our review team deserves much appreciation for the time and attention they give to each draft they receive. Their technical critique brings a much-needed multidisciplinary approach to the report. The team includes representatives from the Federal Highway Administration, Institute of Transportation Engineers, League of American Bicyclists, Advocacy Advance, Safe Routes to School National Partnership, Centers for Disease Control and Prevention, and American Public Transportation Association.

Lastly, but most importantly, we thank the leaders of Alliance member organizations and the many state and local officials who supported this project by tracking down data for the benchmarking surveys. This project would not have been possible without them, and it is in support of their vital work that this report has been produced.

The following people were directly involved in providing the data contained in this report. Thank you!

Activate Omaha, Julie Harris

Active Transportation Alliance / Chicago Department of Transportation, Charlie Short

Ada County Highway District, Matt Edmonds

Alabama Department of Transportation, Mary Crenshaw

Alabama Bicycle Coalition, Stan Palla

Alaska Department of Transportation, Bob Laurie

Alaska Trails, Steve Cleary

Arizona Department of Transportation, Michael Sanders and Brian Fellows

Arkansas State Highway and Transportation Department, Kim Sanders, Paul Simms, and The Governor's Bicycle Advisory Group

Atlanta Bicycle Coalition, Rebecca Serna and Leslie Caceda

Baltimore City Department of Transportation, Nate Evans

Bicycle Alliance of Minnesota, Dorian Grilley

Bicycle Coalition of Greater Philadelphia, Diana Owens Steif

Bicycle Coalition of Maine, Nancy Grant

Bicycle Coalition of New Mexico, Diane Albert

Bicycle Colorado, Dan Grunig

Bicycle Commuters of Anchorage, Brian Litmans

Bicycle Indiana, Nancy Tibbett

Bicycle Transportation Alliance, Susan Peithman, Rob Sadowksy, and Gerik Kransky

Bike Baton Rouge / Baton Rouge Advocates for Safe Streets, Mark E. Martin

Bike Cleveland, Jacob VanSickle

Bike Delaware, John Bare and James Wilson

Bike Denver, Piep Van Heuven

Bike Easy, Jamie Wine

Bike Maryland, Carol Silldorff

Bike Utah, Scott Lyttle

Bike Virginia, Kimberly Likens Perry

Bike Walk Alliance of NH, Dave Topham

Bike Walk Arkansas, Paxton Roberts

Bike Walk Connecticut, Kelly Kennedy

Bike Walk Mississippi, Melody Moody

Bike Walk Montana, Melinda Barnes

Bike Walk Tennessee, Anthony Siracusa

Bike/Walk Alliance-Wichita, Barry L. Carroll

BikeABQ, Heather Wess Arnold

Bikemore, Chris Merriam

BikePGH, Eric Boerer

BikeTexas, Robin Stallings

Boston Bikes, Alice Brown

Burlington Department of Public Works, Nicole Losch

Caltrans, April Nitsos and Paul Moore

California Bicycle Coalition, Dave Snyder

Central Dakota Cyclists, Mark Liebig

Charleston Moves, Tom Bradford and Pat Sullivan

Chattanooga-Hamilton County Regional Planning Agency, Tim Moreland

Chittenden County Regional Planning Commission, Bryan Davis

City and County of Honolulu, Chris Sayers

City of Albany, Douglas Melnick, Kate Lawrence, and William Trudeau, Jr.

City of Arlington Texas, Christina Sebastian and Alicia Winkelblech

City of Atlanta, Joshuah Mello

City of Austin, Annick Beaudet and Nadia Barrera

City of Baton Rogue/City-Parish of East Baton Rouge Planning Commission, Warren Kron and Amanda LaGrange

City of Bellingham Public Works, Kim Brown

City of Boston, Kristopher Carter

City of Boulder Public Works for Transportation, Marni Ratzel

City of Charleston, Philip Overcash

City of Charlotte Department of Transportation, Malisa Mccreedy

City of Chattanooga / Outdoor Chattanooga and Bike Chattanooga, Philip Pugliese

City of Chattanooga, Ben Taylor

City of Colorado Springs, Kristin Bennett, Anthony Pratt, and Tim Roberts

City of Columbus, Leslie Strader

City of Dallas, Max Kalhammer, Keith Manoy, and Jared White

City of Davis, Dave Kemp and Jimmy Fong

City of El Paso, Shamori Whitt, David Coronado, and Elizabeth Gibson

City of Eugene, Reed Dunbar, Lee Shoemaker, and Lindsay Selser

City of Fort Collins, Tessa Greegor

City of Fort Worth, Julia McCleeary

City of Fresno, Scott Tyler

City of Houston Department of Public Works and Engineering, Dan Raine

City of Jacksonville Planning and Development Department, James Reed

City of Kansas City, MO, Deb Ridgway

City of Las Vegas, Connie Diso, Diane Phomninh, and Greg McDermott

City of Long Beach, Allan Crawford, Nancy Villaseñor, and Paul VanDyk

City of Madison, Arthur Ross

City of Memphis, Kyle Wagenschutz

City of Mesa, James Hash and Mark Venti

City of Miami, Collin Worth

City of Minneapolis, Simon Blenski, David Peterson, and Mackenzie Turner-Bargen

City of Missoula, Ben Weiss and Dave Gray

City of New Orleans Department of Public Works, Jennifer Ruley and Louis Haywood

City of Oakland Public Works Agency, Jason Patton, and Jennifer Stanley

City of Oklahoma City, Randy Entz

City of Omaha, Carlos Morales

City of Philadelphia, Charles Carmalt

City of Phoenix, Joseph Perez

City of Pittsburgh, Stephen Patchan

City of Raleigh, Eric Lamb and Jennifer Baldwin

City of San Antonio, Julia Diana

City of San Diego, Thomas Landre

City of San Jose, John Brazil and Ryan Smith

City of Spokane, Grant Wencel

City of St. Louis, Patrick Brown and John Kohler

City of Tucson Transportation Department, Ann Chanecka

City of Tulsa Engineering Services Department, Brent Stout and Matt Liechti

Cleveland City Planning Commission, Martin Cader and Robert N. Brown

Coalition of Arizona Bicyclists, Bob Beane

Colorado Department of Transportation, Betsy Jacobsen

Connecticut Department of Energy and Environmental Protection, Laurie Giannotti

Connecticut Department of Transportation, Katherine Rattan

Consider Biking, Jeannie Martin

Davis Bicycles, Mont Hubbard

Delaware Bicycle Council, Amy Wilburn

Delaware Department of Transportation, Anthony Aglio

Denver Public Works, Emily Snyder

District Department of Transportation, Mike Goodno and Jennifer Hefferan

Florida Bicycle Association, Tim Bustos

Florida Department of Transportation, Dwight Kingsbury and DeWayne Carver

Georgia Bikes!, Brent Bulce

Georgia Department of Transportation, Tamaya Huff, Emmanuella Myrthil, and David Adams

Hawaii Bicycling League, Chad Taniguchi

Hawaii Department of Transportation, Tara Lucas and Bryan Kimura

Houston-Galveston Area Council, Chelsea Young

Houston's METRO, Meredith Alberto

Idaho Pedestrian and Bicycle Alliance, Cynthia Gibson

Idaho Transportation Department, Ted Vanegas

Illinois Department of Transportation, Gabriel Sulkes, Bola Delano, and Jeff Bell

Indian Nations Council of Governments, James Wagner

Indiana Department of Transportation, Jay Mitchell and Michael O'Loughlin

INDYCOG, Kevin Whited

Iowa Bicycle Coalition, Mark Wyatt

Iowa Department of Natural Resources, Whitney Davis

Iowa Department of Transportation, Milly Ortiz

KanBikeWalk, Inc., Dale Crawford

Kansas Department of Transportation, Becky Pepper

Kentucky Transportation Cabinet, Troy Hearn and Lynn Soporowski

Lexington-Fayette Urban County Government, Keith Lovan

League of American Bicyclists, Nicole Wynands and Bill Nesper

League of Illinois Bicyclists, Ed Barsotti

League of Michigan Bicyclists, John Lindenmayer

Local Motion, Chapin Spencer

Los Angeles County Bicycle Coalition, Eric Bruins and Benjamin Martinez

Louisiana Department of Transportation and Development, Brian Parsons

Louisville Metro Department of Public Works and Assets, Rolf Eisinger

Maine Department of Transportation, Dan Stewart

Maryland Department of Transportation, Michael Jackson

Massachusetts Department of Conservation and Recreation, Paul Jahnige

Massachusetts Department of Transportation, Josh Lehman

MassBike, David Watson

MassRIDES, Kristin Slaton

Memphis Urban Area Metropolitan Planning Organization, John Paul Shaffer

Metro Nashville Government, Laurel Creech

Michigan Department of Transportation, Josh DeBruyn

Mid-Ohio Regional Planning Commission, Juana Sandoval

Minnesota Department of Transportation, Tim Mitchell and Michelle Pooler

Mississippi Department of Transportation, Lindsey Netherland and Cookie Leffler

Missoula Bicycle and Pedestrian Advisory Board, and Bike/Walk Alliance for Missoula Bob Wachtel

Missouri Bicycle & Pedestrian Coalition, Brent Hugh

Missouri Department of Transportation, Ron Effland

Montana Department of Transportation, Mark Keeffe

Montana Fish, Wildlife and Parks, Beth Shumate

National Highway Traffic Safety Administration, National Center for Statistics and Analysis, Lorenzo Daniels

Nebraska Department of Roads, David Schoenmaker

Nevada Bicycle Coalition, Terry McAfee

Nevada Department of Transportation, Bill Story and Tim Rowe

New Hampshire Department of Transportation, Erik Paddleford and Larry Keniston

New Jersey Bicycle & Pedestrian Resource Center at Rutgers University Voorhees Transportation Center, Charles Brown

New Jersey Bike Walk Coalition, Cyndi Steiner

New Jersey Department of Transportation, Debbie Kingsland and Sheree Davis

New Mexico Department of Transportation, Anne McLaughlin, Jessica Griffin, Rosa Kozub, and Maggie Ryan

New Orleans Regional Planning Commission, Dan Jatres

New York Bicycling Coalition, Brian Kehoe and Josh Wilson

New York City Department of Transportation, Hayes Lord, Jennifer Harris-Hernandez, and Jessica Lax

New York State Department of Transportation, Eric Ophardt

North Carolina Active Transportation Alliance, Allison Carpenter

North Carolina Department of Transportation, Lauren Blackburn and Madeline Howell

North Dakota Department of Transportation, Bennett Kubischta

Ohio Bicycle Federation, Chuck Smith

Ohio Department of Transportation, Heather Bowden and Julie Walcoff

Oklahoma Bicycle Coalition, Bonnie Winslow

Oklahoma Department of Transportation, Lary Willis

Oklahoma League Cycling Instructor, Pete Kramer

Oregon Department of Transportation, Sheila Lyons and Susan Riehl

PA Walks & Bikes, Hans van Naerssen

Palmetto Cycling Coalition, Amy Johnson

Pennsylvania Department of Conservation and Natural Resources, Diane Kripas

Pennsylvania Department of Transportation, Brian Sanders and Christpher Metka

Philadelphia City Planning Commission, Deborah Schaaf

Pima Association of Governments, Gabe Thum

Rhode Island Bicycle Coalition, Matt Moritz and Sue Barker

Rhode Island Department of Transportation, Steven Church

Safe Routes to School National Partnership, Margo Pedroso

Salt Lake City Transportation Division, Becka Roolf

San Antonio-Bexar County Metropolitan Planning Organization, Lydia Kelly

San Francisco Bicycle Coalition, Marc Caswell

Seattle Department of Transportation, Doug Cox, Brian Dougherty and Craig Moore

Smart Growth America, National Complete Streets Coalition, Stefanie Seskin

South Carolina Department of Transportation, Thomas Dodds

South Dakota Bicycle Coalition, Jessica Giard

South Dakota Department of Transportation, Jerry Ortbahn and Nancy Surprenant

Southwest Pennsylvania Commission, Sara Walfoort

Tennessee Department of Environment and Conservation, Bob Richards

Tennessee Department of Transportation, Jessica Wilson

Texas Department of Transportation, Charles Riou and Teri Kaplan

Trailnet, Rhonda Smythe

University of Vermont Transportation Research Center, Brian Lee

USDOT/FHWA Fiscal Management Information System, Eric Cline

Utah Department of Transportation, Evelyn Tuddenham and Walt Steinvorth

Vermont Agency of Transportation, Gina Campoli

Vermont Agency of Transportation, Jon Kaplan

Vermont Bicycle and Pedestrian Coalition, Nancy Schulz

VIA Metropolitan Transit, Abigail Kinnison

Virginia Beach Parks & Recreation, Wayne Wilcox

Virginia Bicycling Federation, Champe Burnley

Virginia Department of Transportation, John Bolecek, Rob Williams, and Stephen Read

Walk/Bike Nashville, David Kleinfelter and Stephen Carr

WALKSacramento, Terry Preston and Jim Brown

Washington Area Bicyclist Association, Shane Farthing

Washington Bikes, Barb Chamberlain

Washington State Department of Transportation, Ian Macek and Paula Reeves

West Virginia Connecting Communities, Kasey Russell

West Virginia Department of Transportation, Perry Keller

Whatcom Council of Governments / everyoneBIKE, Mary Anderson

Whatcom Council of Governments, Ellen Barton

Wichita Area Metropolitan Planning Organization, Kristen Zimmerman

Wichita-Sedgwick County Metropolitan Area Planning Department, Scott Wadle

Wisconsin Bike Federation, Tom Klein, Sarah Gaskell and Dave Schlabowske

Wisconsin Department of Transportation, Jill Mrotek Glenzinski, Larry Corsi, and Tressie Kamp

Wyoming Department of Transportation, Talbot Hauffe and Sara Janes

Wyoming Pathways, Tim Young

CONTENTS

TABLES & GRAPHICS

Executive Summary

1: The Benchmarking Project

2: Levels of Bicycling and Walking

3: Health and Safety

4: Economic Benefits

5: Policies and Funding

6: Infrastructure and Design

7: Connecting to Transit

8: Education and Encouragement

9: People Powered Movement

ALLIANCE FOR BIKING & WALKING

The Alliance for Biking & Walking is the North American coalition of state and local bicycling and walking advocacy organizations. Our mission is to create, strengthen, and unite state/provincial and local bicycle and pedestrian advocacy organizations. Since our founding in 1996, we have grown from 12 to over 220 member organizations representing 49 U.S. states and the District of Columbia, five Canadian provinces, and two Mexican states.

In the last 18 years, we have improved the effectiveness of our organizations and expanded the state and local bicycling and walking movement by leading trainings and sharing resources in organizational development and advocacy initiatives. We are continually broadening our impact and improving the results of our member organizations through sharing best practices, replicable campaigns, campaign trainings, executive coaching, on-call support, leadership retreats, and resources, such as this report.

Alliance organizations inform and organize their communities to improve conditions for bicycling and walking, promoting these as healthy and enjoyable ways to travel. From advocating for bikeways and walkways to conducting safety courses, our member organizations are impacting the social, political, and environmental conditions for bicyclists and pedestrians across North America. The Alliance connects these grassroots forces by fostering peer networking and supporting each other in our efforts to promote bicycling and walking for a stronger economy, improved mobility options, healthy communities, healthy environment, and overall better quality of life.

Executive Summary

Making Data Count

For government officials and advocates who promote bicycling and walking in the U.S., it is clear that active transportation is gaining momentum. Protected bicycle lanes are popping up on more city streets, Open Streets initiatives are being organized in communities of all sizes, public bicycle sharing programs are finding success even in sprawling car-centric cities, and business owners are scrambling to install bicycle parking near their front door.

In order to meet the growing desire for more bicycle- and pedestrian-friendly communities, policy makers and advocates need a comprehensive analysis of current trends and trials. The Alliance for Biking & Walking's Benchmarking Project strives to meet this need by tracking and measuring these efforts across the country.

Documenting Trends

Benchmarking is a method that helps identify best practices to improve communities for bicycling and walking. It helps officials and advocates to see where their city or state measures up and where they are most in need of improvement. Through benchmarking, new goals can be set, programs evaluated, and continued progress made toward a bicycle- and pedestrian-friendly United States.

Since 2003, the Benchmarking Project has been documenting the trends in bicycling and walking in U.S. cities and states, as well as at the national level. Alliance researchers compile data from twenty-one U.S. national sources and conduct surveys with the help of state and local government officials and advocates. Updates are published biennially in this report to measure the progress of bicycling and walking over time. This is the fourth publication of *Bicycling and Walking in the United States*. Previous versions were released in 2007, 2010, and 2012.

Project Objectives

The ultimate goal of the Benchmarking Project is to provide a resource for advocates and professionals who influence the accessibility and safety of bicycling and walking. This report is made available in an effort to accomplish the following primary objectives:

Promote data collection and availability. Project researchers compile data from all 50 U.S. states, the 50 most populous U.S. cities and, for the first time in this report, 17 midsized cities. These data are summarized in the *Benchmarking Report* and are available to the public upon request.

Measure progress and evaluate results. The project began collecting data on bicycling and walking in 2003. As the project continues, it identifies trends and analyzes state and local efforts to provide bicycle- and pedestrian-friendly communities.

Support efforts to increase bicycling and walking. By providing a means for cities and states to compare themselves to one another, the *Benchmarking Report* highlights successes, encourages communities making progress, and makes communities aware of the areas where more effort is needed.

Results

Levels of Bicycling and Walking

The most recent nationwide data on bicycling and walking mode share show that only 1.0% of all trips taken in the U.S. are by bicycle, and 10.4% are on foot (NHTS 2009). Of commuters nationwide, 2.8% get to work by walking and 0.6% get to work by bicycle. These numbers are slightly higher in large cities (5.0% and 1.0%, respectively). Though these numbers are low, they represent a continuing gradual increase in bicycling and walking in the U.S.

Partially due to the current lack of data on bicycling and walking numbers, many states and cities conduct their own counts to find out their local mode share. Of the 52 most populous cities surveyed, 43 have completed counts of bicyclists and 37 have completed counts of pedestrians. Thirty-eight states have conducted counts on bicyclists and 36 states have counted pedestrians. Thirty-six states have conducted counts on bicyclists and 35 states have counted pedestrians. States and cities conduct their counts at varying times and frequencies, making it difficult to compare results consistently.

The 2014 benchmarking survey, which collected 2011/2012 data, recorded three types of counts in particular: commuter counts, household surveys, and cordon counts. Cordon counts are conducted to track the number of travelers who cross a specified line into or out of a designated area, such as a neighborhood or downtown, that is "cordoned off." To read descriptions of other types of counts recorded in the 2014 survey, see pages 59 and 61.

In addition to these, many cities have also conducted other types of counts including installing automated counters and outdoor video cameras, and other types of "spot" counts, which are included in this updated report.

Health and Safety

This report shows the relationship between bicycling and walking to work and several health indicators. Levels of diabetes, high blood pressure, and obesity are all lower in cities with higher shares of commuters bicycling or walking to work. Likewise, where commuters bicycle or walk to work in higher shares, more of the population is meeting the recommended amount of weekly physical activity.

Safety, too, has a close relationship with bicycling and walking levels. In cities where a higher percent of commuters walk or bicycle to work, corresponding fatality rates are generally lower. This is in contrast to critics who fear a higher rate of crashes when more bicyclists and pedestrians use the roadway.

Overview of U.S. Mode Share

Mode of Travel	% of Commuters		% of All Trips Nationwide [3]
	Nationwide [1]	52 Large U.S. Cities [2]	
	2.8%	5.0%	10.4%
	0.6%	1.0%	1.0%
	5.0%	17.2%	2.2%
(4)	91.6%	76.7%	86.4%
All Modes	100%	100%	100%

Sources: (1) ACS 2011 (2) ACS 2009–2011 (3) NHTS 2009 **Notes**: The term "mode share" is used to describe the percentage of all trips or percentage of trips to work by each mode of transportation. (4) This includes trips by private car and "other" means that are not public transportation, bicycling, or walking—such as taxi, motorcycle, recreational vehicle, school bus, etc.

Though bicycle and pedestrian fatalities have seen a slight increase in recent years, the long-term trend is a clear decline. Since 1980, the national pedestrian fatality rate fell from 3.6 fatalities per 100,000 people to 1.4 fatalities per 100,000 people in 2011. Though not as dramatic a drop, the bicyclist fatality rate also decreased, from 0.4 fatalities per 100,000 people in 1980 to 0.2 fatalities per 100,000 people in 2011.

However, some cities have much higher rates of bicycle and pedestrian fatalities. Both Detroit and Jacksonville have pedestrian fatality rates over 4 per 100,000 people. These two cities, as well as Fort Worth, also have the highest bicyclist fatality rates—all see more than three fatalities per 100,000 people.

Economic Benefits

Increasingly, cities and states are publishing studies that show the economic benefits of bicycling and walking. This report provides an overview of some of the most recent studies, which show the positive impact on job growth, individual transportation costs, retail sales, traffic congestion, air quality, property values and stability, health and worker productivity, and events and tourism.

Twenty-two states, ten of the 52 most populous cities, and five of the midsized cities have conducted an economic impact study. Most of these studies looked at the impact of bicycling, but other studies show the impact of walking and trails. Washington state and New York City have also studied the economic impact of car-free zones.

Policies and Funding

Since 2010, 11 states and 12 of the 52 most populous cities have added new goals to increase bicycling and walking, or to decrease bicycle and pedestrian fatalities. Overall, 88% of states and 90% of the most populous cities currently report having at least one of these goals. Nine large cities and one state (Georgia) have recently passed Complete Streets legislation or policies. Currently, 54% of states and 52% of cities now have Complete Streets policies or legislation.

For the first time, over 2% of federal transportation funding went to bicycle and pedestrian projects. Recognizing that this is still a disproportionately low level of dedicated funding, it is also a continuation of increasing funds to bicycling and walking over the years.

MAP-21, the federal transportation law passed in 2012, raised some concern that states and cities will have less access to these funds for bicycling and walking improvements. The federal Transportation Enhancements (TE) program has historically been the largest single source of dedicated funding for bicycle and pedestrian projects. However, with MAP-21, TE, Safe Routes to School (SRTS), and the Recreational Trails Program (RTP) have been consolidated into the Transportation Alternatives Program (TAP), with a specific set-aside for the RTP. Funds for TAP are 26% less in fiscal year 2014 than the combined funding for these three separate programs in 2012. However, bicycle and pedestrian projects are eligible for all Federal-aid Highway Program categories.

Infrastructure and Design

The 50 most populous cities in the U.S. (plus New Orleans and Honolulu) have a combined total of more than 8,600 miles of bicycle lanes. Combining the mileage of bicycle lanes, multi-use paths, and signed bicycle routes in these cities, they have an average of 1.6 miles of bicycle infrastructure per square mile. This is an increase from 1.3 miles per square mile in 2010 (reported in the *2012 Benchmarking Report*). San Francisco has, by far, the densest network of bicycle facilities with 7.8 miles of lanes, paths, and routes per square mile in the city.

Connecting to Transit

Over 90% of people who use public transit walk or bike to reach transit stops (Pucher, et al. 2011). In the most populous U.S. cities, 17% of commuters use public transportation to get to work. This report shows how improving facilities for bicyclists and pedestrians can help make those connections to public transit more accessible.

Providing for bicyclists and pedestrians comes in many forms including installing bicycle racks on buses, providing safe and secure bicycle parking, and ensuring safe sidewalks and crosswalks to

Disparity of Pedestrian and Bicycle Mode Share, Fatalities, and Funding

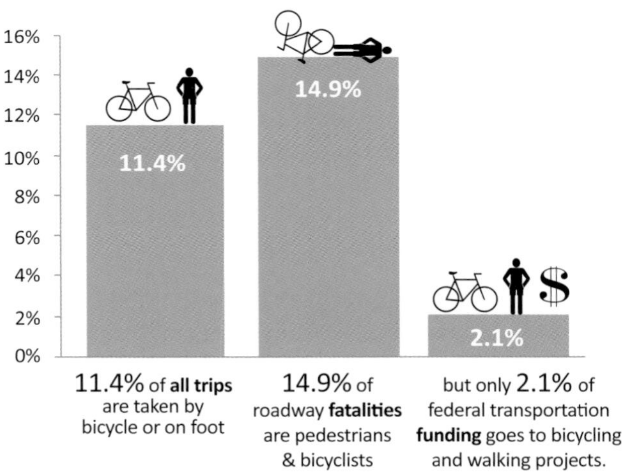

Sources: NHTS 2009, FARS 2009–2011, FHWA FMIS 2009–2012

transit stops. All of the large cities studied in this report have bicycle racks on their buses, except for New York City. Thirteen cities allow an unlimited number of bicycles on their trains. In addition, several cities in recent years have removed-restricted hours policies for bicycles on trains.

Education and Encouragement

As bicycling and walking become more viable modes of transportation, more education is needed to ensure all roadway users are aware of their rights and responsibilities. Since 2006, the number of adults participating in a bicycle education course in the most populous cities rose from just under 1,500 to over 28,000 participants in 2012. Youth participating in bicycle education courses in these cities rose from approximately 35,000 in 2006 to over 183,000 in 2012. Cities also report a total of over 168,000 youth participating in pedestrian education courses in 2012.

Similarly, bicycle- and pedestrian-themed events have gained interest over the years. Boston was the only city in the Benchmarking Project to report hosting an Open Streets initiative in 2006; the city had an estimated 2,000 participants. In 2012, Open Streets initiatives took place in 27 of the most populous cities and, combined, they reported over one million participants.

People Powered Movement

Many people are involved in bettering our communities for bicycling and walking. This report looks at both the capacity of advocacy organizations as well as the availability of state and city level staff.

On average, Alliance member organizations, both state- and city-focused, have seen an increase in membership rates (number of members per residents) since 2010, as reported in the *2012 Benchmarking Report*. Additionally, funding to these organizations has increased per capita and is more diversified. In 2012, Alliance statewide organizations averaged four cents per capita (up from two cents in 2010), and organizations representing cities in this report averaged 69 cents per capita (up from just 15 cents in 2010).

Outcome Benchmarks: Changes 2005–2012

	Years of Benchmarking				
MODE SHARE	05/06	07/08	09/10	11/12	Data Source
% of commuters who walk: national average	2.5%	2.8%	2.9%	2.8%	ACS 1 year est.
% of commuters who walk: large city average	4.5%	4.8%	4.9%	5.0%	ACS 3 year est.
% of commuters who bicycle: national average	0.4%	0.5%	0.6%	0.6%	ACS 1 year est.
% of commuters who bicycle: large city average	0.7%	0.8%	0.9%	1.0%	ACS 3 year est.
# of cities counting bicyclist trips	-	-	36/51	43/52	City Survey
# of cities counting pedestrian trips	-	-	26/51	37/52	City Survey
# of states counting bicyclist trips	-	-	24	38	State Survey
# of states counting pedestrian trips	-	-	24	36	State Survey
DEMOGRAPHICS OF COMMUTERS					
% of walking commuters who are women	-	45.8%	46.4%	46.5%	ACS 1 year est.
% of bicycling commuters who are women	-	23.3%	26.7%	26.9%	ACS 1 year est.
% of walking commuters who are non-white, non-Hispanic (1)	27.1%	28.2%	26.9%	29.0%	ACS 1 year est.
PUBLIC HEALTH					
% of U.S. adult pop. getting min. recommended aerobic physical activity	49.1%	49.5%	51.0%	51.1%	BRFSS
% of U.S. adult pop. with obesity	24.4%	26.3%	26.9%	27.7%	BRFSS
% of U.S. adult pop. with diabetes	7.3%	8.0%	8.3%	8.8%	BRFSS
% of U.S. adult pop. with high blood pressure	25.5%	27.8%	28.7%	31.6%	BRFSS
SAFETY					
% of U.S. roadway fatalities: pedestrian	11.2%	11.3%	11.7%	12.9%	FARS 3 year avg.
% of U.S. roadway fatalities: bicyclist	1.7%	1.8%	1.8%	1.9%	FARS 3 year avg.
# of pedestrian fatalities on U.S. roadways	4,892	4,699	4,109	4,432	FARS 1 year
# of bicyclist fatalities on U.S. roadways	786	701	628	677	FARS 1 year

Notes: Cells with a dash (-) mean data are unavailable. Data in each column represents the most recent data available during the benchmarking years. ACS 3-year estimates are taken from the most recent ACS data available and include two years prior. For example, the 3-year estimate covers 2009–2011 for the benchmarking years 2011/2012.
(1) ACS does not provide data for bicycling commuters by race or ethnicity.

Legend (all tables this page and next)
Increase in color shade indicates increase in value between years
Decrease in color shade indicates decrease in value between years

Input Benchmarks: Changes 2005-2012

	Years of Benchmarking				
STATE POLICIES	05/06	07/08	09/10	11/12	Data Source
# of states with goal to increase walking	16(1)	22	32	35	State Survey
# of states with goal to increase bicycling	16(1)	22	32	35	State Survey
# of states with bicycle and/or pedestrian master plan	-	25	28	32	State Survey
# of states with Complete Streets policy	9	17	26	27	NCSC
CITY POLICIES					
# of cities with goal to increase walking	25/50(1)	20/51	33/51	39/52	City Survey
# of cities with goal to increase bicycling	25/50(1)	33/51	46/51	47/52	City Survey
# of cities with bicycle and/or pedestrian master plan	-	35/51	41/51	47/52	City Survey
# of cities with Complete Streets policy	8/50(1)	13/51	19/51	27/52	NCSC
STATE FUNDING					
Per capita fed transportation $ to bike/ped(2)	$1.41	$1.58	$2.73	$3.10	FHWA FMIS
% of spending on bike/ped with fed transportation funds(2)	1.3%	1.4%	1.9%	2.1%	FHWA FMIS
CITY FUNDING					
Per capita fed transportation $ to bike/ped(2)	-	$1.80	$2.60	$2.78	FHWA FMIS
% of spending on bike/ped with fed transportation funds(2)	-	1.5%	2.4%	3.3%	FHWA FMIS
INFRASTRUCTURE IN CITIES					
Miles of bicycle facilities per sq mile	1.0	1.0	1.3	1.6	City Survey
# of bicycle parking spaces at bus stations per 10K people	1.9(4)	1.5	2.0	2.3	APTA
# of bicycle parking spaces at rail stations per 10K people	-	6.2	8.7	11.3	APTA
# of cities with bicycle racks on 100% of buses	30/50	38/51	41/51	46/52	City Survey
STATE EDUCATION & ENCOURAGEMENT					
# of states with annual state bicycle and/or pedestrian conference	-	15	24	26	State Survey
# of states with state-sponsored bike ride	-	14	17	17	State Survey
# of states with drivers test questions on bicycling	-	23	33	38	LAB(3)/State Survey
# of states with Share-the-road campaign	-	33	38	38	LAB(3)/State Survey
CITY EDUCATION & ENCOURAGEMENT					
# of cities with youth bike education courses	-	29/51	36/51	46/52	City Survey
# of cities with adult bike education courses	-	33/51	41/51	50/52	City Survey
# of cities with Bike to Work Day events	-	37/51	43/51	52/52	City Survey
# of cities with Open Streets initiatives	-	13/51	20/51	28/52	City Survey
# of cities with city-sponsored bike ride	-	23/51	31/51	33/52	City Survey
PERSONNEL					
Bike/ped city staff per 100K pop: avg of cities reporting	0.4	0.6	0.8	0.7	City Survey
Bike/ped state staff per 100K pop: avg of states reporting	0.1	0.1	0.1	0.2	State Survey
# of cities with bicycle or pedestrian advisory committee	-	33/51	36/51	39/52	City Survey
# of states with bicycle or pedestrian advisory committee	-	19	24	38	State Survey
# of cities with dedicated city-level advocacy organization	32/50	34/51	36/51	39/52	Alliance Database
# of states with dedicated statewide advocacy organization	32	35	43	43	Alliance Database

Notes: Cells with a dash (-) mean data are unavailable. Data in each column represents the most recent data available during the benchmarking years. ACS 3-year estimates are taken from the most recent ACS data available and include two years prior. For example, the 3-year estimate covers 2009–2011 for the benchmarking years 2011/2012.
(1) Walking and bicycling were combined in this survey. (2) Based on four-year averages. (3) Prior to the *2014 Benchmarking Report*, the League of American Bicyclists supplied these data from their Bicycle Friendly States surveys. (4) The calculation of bicycle parking spaces at bus stations appears inflated for 2005/2006 because fewer of the large benchmarked cities were included in the APTA data at that time.

U.S. State Rankings

Rank	Commuter Bicycling and Walking Levels [1] (Highest to Lowest)	Per Capita Spending on Bicycle/Pedestrian Projects [2] (Highest to Lowest)	Bicyclist/Pedestrian Fatality Rates [3] (Lowest to Highest)	% Getting Recommended Physical Activity [4] (Highest to Lowest)
1	**Alaska**	**Alaska**	**Vermont**	**Colorado**
2	**New York**	**Vermont**	**Nebraska**	**Oregon**
3	**Vermont**	**Delaware**	**Alaska**	**Vermont**
4	**Oregon**	**Rhode Island**	**Wyoming**	**Hawaii**
5	**Montana**	**Montana**	**New Hampshire**	**California**
6	**Hawaii**	**Wyoming**	**South Dakota**	**Alaska**
7	**Massachusetts**	**South Dakota**	**Massachusetts**	**Wisconsin**
8	**South Dakota**	**Kentucky**	**Iowa**	**Idaho**
9	**North Dakota**	**New Mexico**	**Maine**	**Maine**
10	**Maine**	**Indiana**	**Idaho**	**Massachusetts**
11	Wyoming	Minnesota	North Dakota	New Hampshire
12	Pennsylvania	Missouri	Kansas	Utah
13	Washington	Iowa	Minnesota	Montana
14	Colorado	Pennsylvania	New York	Washington
15	Idaho	North Dakota	Wisconsin	Minnesota
16	Iowa	Maine	Montana	Michigan
17	Rhode Island	Oregon	Colorado	New Jersey
18	Wisconsin	Georgia	Washington	Wyoming
19	California	Florida	Pennsylvania	Florida
20	Illinois	Washington	Connecticut	Nevada
21	Utah	Utah	Illinois	Connecticut
22	Minnesota	Tennessee	Hawaii	Virginia
23	New Jersey	Nebraska	Oregon	Arizona
24	Nebraska	Louisiana	Rhode Island	New Mexico
25	Connecticut	Mississippi	Utah	Illinois
26	Arizona	North Carolina	Virginia	Ohio
27	New Hampshire	New York	Ohio	New York
28	New Mexico	Massachusetts	West Virginia	Georgia
29	West Virginia	Connecticut	Indiana	South Carolina
30	Kansas	California	New Jersey	Missouri
31	Virginia	Colorado	Missouri	Pennsylvania
32	Michigan	Alabama	Kentucky	Nebraska
33	Maryland	Nevada	California	Maryland
34	Delaware	Michigan	Michigan	Rhode Island
35	Indiana	Arkansas	Oklahoma	Delaware
36	Ohio	Arizona	Maryland	Texas
37	Nevada	Texas	Nevada	Iowa
38	Louisiana	Wisconsin	Arkansas	North Dakota
39	South Carolina	New Hampshire	New Mexico	North Carolina
40	Kentucky	Ohio	Delaware	Kentucky
41	Missouri	Idaho	Texas	Kansas
42	Florida	Oklahoma	North Carolina	South Dakota
43	Oklahoma	Illinois	Tennessee	Indiana
44	North Carolina	Virginia	Georgia	Arkansas
45	Arkansas	West Virginia	Arizona	Oklahoma
46	Texas	Kansas	Louisiana	West Virginia
47	Mississippi	Hawaii	South Carolina	Alabama
48	Georgia	South Carolina	Mississippi	Louisiana
49	Tennessee	New Jersey	Alabama	Mississippi
50	Alabama	Maryland	Florida	Tennessee

Sources: (1) ACS 2009–2011 (2) FHWA FMIS 2009–2012 (3) FARS 2009–2011; ACS 2009–2011 (4) BRFSS 2011. **Note**: Fatality rates were calculated by dividing the number of annual pedestrian or bicyclist fatalities (between 2009–2011) by the estimated annual number of commuters walking or bicycling to work (ACS 2009–2011).

Large U.S. Cities Rankings

Commuter Bicycling and Walking Levels [1]		Per Capita Spending on Bicycle/Pedestrian Projects [2]		Bicyclist/Pedestrian Fatality Rates [3]		% Getting Recommended Physical Activity [4]	
Highest to Lowest		Highest to Lowest		Lowest to Highest		Highest to Lowest	
1	**Boston**	**1**	**Miami**	**1**	**Boston**	**1**	**Oakland**
2	**Washington, DC**	**2**	**Washington, DC**	**2**	**Seattle**	**2**	**San Francisco**
3	**San Francisco**	**3**	**Minneapolis**	**3**	**Washington, DC**	**3**	**Colorado Springs**
4	**Seattle**	**4**	**Sacramento**	**4**	**Colorado Springs**	**4**	**Denver**
5	**Portland, OR**	**5**	**Dallas**	**5**	**San Francisco**	**5**	**San Jose**
6	**Honolulu**	**6**	**Portland, OR**	**6**	**New York City**	**6**	**San Diego**
7	**New York City**	**7**	**New Orleans**	**7**	**Minneapolis**	**7**	**Portland, OR**
8	**Philadelphia**	**8**	**Philadelphia**	**8**	**Chicago**	**8**	**Sacramento**
9	**Minneapolis**	**9**	**Oakland**	**9**	**Omaha**	**9**	**Milwaukee**
10	**New Orleans**	**10**	**Albuquerque**	**10**	**Honolulu**	**10**	**Honolulu**
11	Baltimore	11	Raleigh	11	Cleveland	11	Boston
12	Chicago	12	Tucson	12	Portland, OR	12	Long Beach
13	Oakland	13	Memphis	13	Philadelphia	13	Los Angeles
14	Denver	14	Omaha	14	Oakland	14	Austin
15	Tucson	15	Atlanta	15	Baltimore	15	Minneapolis
16	Milwaukee	16	Kansas City, MO	16	Virginia Beach	16	Washington, DC
17	Atlanta	17	San Jose	17	Denver	17	Jacksonville
18	Sacramento	18	Milwaukee	18	Milwaukee	18	Seattle
19	Cleveland	19	Austin	19	New Orleans	19	Cleveland
20	Los Angeles	20	El Paso	20	Mesa	20	Tucson
21	Miami	21	Houston	21	Columbus	21	Mesa
22	Austin	22	San Antonio	22	San Diego	22	Phoenix
23	San Diego	23	Baltimore	23	Long Beach	23	Chicago
24	Long Beach	24	Charlotte	24	Arlington, TX	24	Albuquerque
25	Colorado Springs	25	Tulsa	25	Los Angeles	25	Atlanta
26	Columbus	26	Mesa	26	Austin	26	New York City
27	Detroit	27	Nashville	27	Atlanta	27	Philadelphia
28	Albuquerque	28	Jacksonville	28	San Jose	28	Houston
29	Virginia Beach	29	Long Beach	29	Wichita	29	Miami
30	Omaha	30	Los Angeles	30	Las Vegas	30	Virginia Beach
31	Mesa	31	Chicago	31	Raleigh	31	Charlotte
32	Fresno	32	Fresno	32	Tucson	32	San Antonio
33	Phoenix	33	Phoenix	33	Albuquerque	33	Las Vegas
34	San Jose	34	New York City	34	Tulsa	34	Columbus
35	Houston	35	San Francisco	35	Indianapolis	35	Raleigh
36	Raleigh	36	Denver	36	Oklahoma City	36	Omaha
37	Kansas City, MO	37	Detroit	37	Houston	37	Dallas
38	Indianapolis	38	Colorado Springs	38	Nashville	38	Kansas City, MO
39	Louisville	39	San Diego	39	Kansas City, MO	39	Detroit
40	Tulsa	40	Fort Worth	40	Miami	40	Arlington, TX
41	Charlotte	41	Wichita	41	Sacramento	41	Fort Worth
42	San Antonio	42	Arlington, TX	42	Charlotte	42	Louisville
43	Las Vegas	43	Louisville	43	Louisville	43	Baltimore
44	El Paso	44	Virginia Beach	44	San Antonio	44	Indianapolis
45	Nashville	45	Columbus	45	El Paso	45	Tulsa
46	Memphis	46	Indianapolis	46	Fresno	46	Oklahoma City
47	Dallas	47	Las Vegas	47	Dallas	47	Wichita
48	Arlington, TX	48	Seattle	48	Memphis	48	Nashville
49	Oklahoma City	49	Boston	49	Phoenix	49	New Orleans
50	Jacksonville	50	Cleveland	50	Fort Worth	50	Memphis
51	Wichita	51	Honolulu	51	Detroit	*	El Paso (no data)
52	Fort Worth	52	Oklahoma City	52	Jacksonville	*	Fresno (no data)

Sources: (1) ACS 2009–2011 (2) FHWA FMIS 2008–2011 (3) FARS 2009–2011; ACS 2009-2011 (4) BRFSS 2011. **Note**: Fatality rates were calculated by dividing the number of annual pedestrian or bicyclist fatalities (between 2009–2011) by the estimated annual number of commuters walking or bicycling to work (ACS 2009–2011)

1 The Benchmarking Project

When the first *Bicycling and Walking in the U.S.: Benchmarking Report* was released in 2007, only 16 states had a published goal to increase bicycling and walking mode share. Sharrows, a street design that indicates bicyclists share the lane with cars, were a new and innovative concept. Only a couple U.S. cities had experimented with community bike programs, but no city had the sophisticated bike share systems we see today.

Today, city and state leaders are competing for bicycle- and pedestrian- friendly status, prioritizing more of their transportation dollars to non-motorized transportation infrastructure. They are learning from and writing their own studies on economic growth in districts where bicycling and walking safety have been improved.

Public support, too, has dramatically increased as more and more people experience improved access to multiple transportation options. Property owners, parents of young children, and communities of color are demanding expanded bicycling and walking networks that will promote vibrant economies, enjoyable living environments, and social and recreational opportunities.

Chicago, IL. Photo by Todd Winters. Courtesy of Alliance for Biking & Walking

This report provides a picture of how the landscape is changing for bicycling and walking across the U.S. It shows which states and cities are making strides and which are setting the benchmarks. Most importantly, the report serves as a tool for officials, advocates, researchers, and the media to track and support continued efforts to increase investment in bicycling, walking, safety, and public health.

Introduction

The Alliance's Benchmarking Project aligns with and helps track the goals and objectives of national public health initiatives by promoting cross-sector collaboration, data-driven decision-making, and broader access to bicycling and walking opportunities.

The Project supports initiatives such as the Centers for Disease Control and Prevention's (CDC) Winnable Battles, which seeks to understand and develop policies that increase physical activity and reduce motor vehicle injuries. Further, the project supports multi-agency efforts such as Healthy People 2020 and the National Prevention Strategy, which seek to improve the health and safety of communities across the U.S.

The Project began in 2003 when Alliance leaders recognized the need for data to help advocates measure progress on bicycling and walking initiatives. Without data to measure results, Alliance organizations were missing a key tool to strengthen their efforts.

Benchmarking Project History

2003 **Benchmarking Project initiated**
Data collection on bicycling begins for 15 cities and 15 states in the U.S.

2004 **First Bicycling Benchmarking Report *Produced***

2005 Data collection on both bicycling and walking begins for all 50 states and the 50 most populous cities.

2007 **First full report published**
Bicycling and Walking in the United States: Benchmarking Report

2010 **Second full report published**
Report includes expanded content and doubled number of data sources.

2012 **Third full report published**
A new chapter on economic benefits of bicycling and walking is added.

About 10,000 copies of the *2012 Benchmarking Report* have been downloaded or distributed.
The report is cited in over 400 media stories, reports, plans, and articles.

2014 **Fourth full report published**
17 midsized cities added to analysis, along with a new chapter on connections to transit.

In 2003, the Alliance initiated a pilot benchmarking effort that collected bicycling data from 15 cities and 15 states to test methods for the project. This first report helped pave a smoother path for the collection of more comprehensive data from all 50 states and the 50 most populous U.S. cities in 2006 and 2007. The first full report on the status of bicycling and walking in the United States was published in August 2007 (under the organization's former name: Thunderhead Alliance).

Through three updated reports in 2010, 2012, and this current publication, the report continues to stay relevant by reviewing the latest tools and methods that active transportation advocates are using, and by addressing current topics of interest related to bicycling and walking.

Providing a Resource

By publishing regular updates to this report, we are pleased to deliver timely data that will help advocates and officials measure their progress and effectiveness, set new goals, and achieve greater results.

Through the ongoing Benchmarking Project, the Alliance for Biking & Walking publishes an updated edition of this report every two years, continuously refining methods and compiling new data sets as available.

As the project progresses, it will identify additional benchmarks and recommendations for advocates and government officials so that they have the data they need to improve bicycling and walking in the United States and eventually all of North America.

Report Objectives

Promote Data Collection and Availability

Historically, there has been little data available on bicycling and walking that can be compared across states and cities. Data that do exist are often not easily accessible to officials and advocates.

The Alliance Benchmarking Project facilitates the ongoing collection of bicycling and walking data and makes them available to the public through the *Benchmarking Report*. The project team collects nationwide data from a number of government and nonprofit sources and presents it in a way that is easily accessible to a variety of users. Through biennial surveys of states, cities, and advocacy organizations, the Benchmarking Project makes new data available such as miles of infrastructure, staffing levels, and advocacy capacity. These data are not available from any other source, but are crucial to understanding changes in health, safety, and mode share (the percentage of all trips or percentage of trips to work by each mode of transportation).

Measure Progress and Evaluate Results

The Benchmarking Project promotes evidence-based practices in improving bicycling and walking environments. Benchmarking is a necessary step to give communities a true picture of how they compare to other communities, the areas in which they are excelling, and where they are falling behind.

Tracking trends in this way enables advocates and officials to evaluate the results of their efforts and to see what other communities have tried. By providing a consistent and objective tool for evaluation, this report allows states and cities to determine what works and what does not. Successful models can be emulated and failed models discarded.

Support Efforts to Increase Bicycling and Walking

Access to the data, case studies, and tools presented in the *Benchmarking Report* supports the efforts by officials and advocates to increase bicycling and walking in their communities and improve bicycle and pedestrian safety across the U.S. By comparing bicycling and walking statistics across states and cities, this report highlights efforts of communities who provide effective models, encourages those making progress, and makes states and cities aware of areas where more effort is needed.

The Alliance hopes that this report will be used by communities to set goals for increasing bicycling and walking, plan strategies using best practice models, and evaluate results over time. The Alliance strives to make this report a useful tool for officials and advocates so that they can chart the best course toward more bikeable and walkable communities.

Make the Health Connection

The Centers for Disease Control and Prevention (CDC) has declared obesity an epidemic, citing unhealthy diet and sedentary lifestyles as among the top factors that contribute to this epidemic. Physical activity can improve a person's health at any weight and can help prevent obesity.

Many studies demonstrate that the design of a community's infrastructure is linked to the amount of physical activity in which its residents engage. (*Guide to Community Preventitive Services*, 2013; Frank et al., 2004; Goldberg, 2007; Salems and Handy, 2008; TRB, 2005). Where environments are built with bicyclists and pedestrians in mind, more people bicycle and walk. These environments increase opportunities for physical activity and mobility that promote healthy lifestyles.

Nearly 50% of all trips are three miles or less, and 27% are one mile or less (NHTS, 2009). These distances are considered easily bikeable or walkable for most people, but the proper infrastructure needs to exist to ensure the opportunity to safely ride or walk. As we look for answers to reversing the obesity epidemic, increasing bicycling and walking opportunities is an obvious solution.

The Alliance for Biking & Walking has partnered with the CDC for this project in an effort to highlight the connection between healthy lifestyles and bicycling and walking. This report includes data on physical activity, obesity and overweight trends, high blood pressure rates, and diabetes to illustrate the connection between bicycling and walking levels and these health indicators. Along with illustrating the correlation between bicycling and walking and health, the Alliance hopes to show, over time, that as bicycling and walking levels increase, the obesity epidemic begins to reverse.

Strengthen the Alliance Network

Lastly, the Alliance aims to strengthen its network of bicycle and pedestrian advocacy organizations by providing the data they need to evaluate their success, prove results, and gain prominence in their communities. Alliance organizations can show data from this report to their community leaders, government officials, and media to highlight areas in which their community is successful, making progress, and in need of improvements.

Alliance organizations can also use these data to prove that advocacy gets results by showing the link between advocacy capacity (the resources available to an organization that increase its power to influence) and levels of bicycling and walking. This report is a tool for Alliance member organizations to gain prominence and to achieve safe and accessible streets for bicycling and walking in their communities.

Selected Benchmarks

Research suggests that levels of bicycling and walking in a community are affected by the physical infrastructure provided, as well as through support and promotion from funding, policy, and education. Because the ultimate goals of the Benchmarking Project are to increase bicycling and walking and to improve health and safety, these are the primary benchmarks we use to measure the progress of states and cities.

We also measure a number of variables (input benchmarks), which we believe, and research shows, influence levels of bicycling, walking, health, and safety. Input benchmarks are the factors that affect the outcome benchmarks. Policies, funding, infrastructure, programs, and personnel are the primary input benchmarks measured in this report. While likely no single policy or program measured here is solely responsible for bicycling and walking levels, health, or safety, a number of them combined may influence the success a city or state sees.

This report also examines other factors that may influence bicycling and walking, such as climate, land use, and car ownership.

Study Areas and Data Collection

The *Benchmarking Report* focuses its data collection efforts on the 50 U.S. states and the 50 most populous U.S. cities. City populations for this report were determined using American Community Survey (ACS) 2011 3-year population estimates for urban areas.

With populations changing over the years, two cities (Tulsa, OK and Wichita, KS) have been added to the original 50 most populous cities included in earlier reports. Tulsa was added to the *2012 Benchmarking Report* when New Orleans's population dropped. Wichita is included in this report for the first time. Though New Orleans and Honolulu are no longer within the original 50 most populous cities, they are included in this report to provide consistency and to take advantage of the already collected data.

The most populous cities were chosen as the focus for this study because of the high percentage of the U.S. population living within these cities and, therefore, the great impact improvements in these cities can have on U.S. Americans.

Unless otherwise noted, all averages in this report are weighted. This means that calculations for the national and large city averages give appropriate weight to each state or city based on their population size. National averages stated in this report are averages of the 50 states, not including territories or the District of Columbia.

Expanded Research: 17 New Cities

The 2014 report also includes a first look at data from 17 small and midsized U.S. cities. This addition furthers the Benchmarking Project's goal to provide a broader perspective of the bicycling and walking movement by expanding our research to areas of different population sizes.

The 17 small and midsized cities were chosen based on their accomplishments and unique challenges, as well as for their leadership within the Alliance for Biking & Walking. The goal of this pilot benchmarking initiative was to include 15 cities (raised to 17) of varying populations

Primary Benchmarks in this Report

Outcome Benchmarks		
Mode Share:	Chapter 2	Share of commuters Share of all trips Demographics of trip takers
Public Health:	Chapter 3	Physical activity levels Overweight and obesity levels Hypertension (high blood pressure) levels Diabetes levels Asthma levels
Safety:	Chapter 3	Fatality rates Fatality risk Disparities in mode share and fatalities Demographics of fatalities

Input Benchmarks		
Policies and Funding:	Chapter 5	City and state funding levels Revenue generation for advocacy Legislation City and state policies Bicycle and pedestrian master plans Goals to increase bicycling and walking Goals to increase safety Bicycle Friendly Award Walk Friendly Award
Infrastructure:	Chapter 6	Existing infrastructure Planned infrastructure
Multimodal:	Chapter 7	Bicyclist and pedestrian integration with transit
Programs:	Chapter 8	Adult and youth bicycle education course participation Bike to Work Day participation Open Streets initiatives and participation City and state-sponsored bicycle ride participation Walk and Bike to School Day participation
Personnel:	Chapter 9	City and state staffing levels for bicycle and pedestrian programs Bicycle and pedestrian advisory committees Advocacy organization staffing levels Advocacy organization membership Advocacy capacity

and from diverse areas of the country. The only two requirements for selection were 1) a population over 20,000, so that data could be collected from ACS, and 2) an award at any level from the League of American Bicyclists Bicycle Friendly Community (BFC) program. A BFC designation was determined to be a good indicator of a community that would likely already have data available to contribute to the Benchmarking Project.

Other factors that influenced selection of the midsized cities included the following: presence of an active local bicycling or walking advocacy organization (preference for Alliance members), a WalkScore above 50, Complete Streets plan or policies in place, and location in an underrepresented region.

This report will highlight selected data from these cities in three groups based on population size: cities with less than 100,000 population, cities with population between 100,000 and 200,000, and cities with population over 200,000.

State and City Surveys

Many of the variables measured in this report are not currently available from other national sources. As part of the Benchmarking Project, the Alliance has developed survey tools to gather the desired data sets at the state and city levels. These surveys record locally tracked data, such as funding spent on bicycling and walking, number of staff employed by advocacy organizations, extent of bicycling and walking facilities, city and state education efforts, and policies and legislation enacted. The *2014 Benchmarking Report* city and state survey questions requested data from 2011 and 2012. The survey tools are reproduced in Appendix 3 of this report.

For the 2014 report, the Alliance for Biking & Walking collaborated with the League of American Bicyclists to develop a combined state survey, incorporating questions for the Benchmarking Project with the League's

Continued on page 30

Study Area Locations

Study Area Populations

State	Population
1 California	37,330,448
2 Texas	25,243,311
3 New York	19,389,160
4 Florida	18,849,600
5 Illinois	12,836,004
6 Pennsylvania	12,709,154
7 Ohio	11,537,266
8 Michigan	9,884,973
9 Georgia	9,716,069
10 North Carolina	9,555,403
11 New Jersey	8,792,116
12 Virginia	8,015,502
13 Washington	6,746,806
14 Massachusetts	6,553,538
15 Indiana	6,488,958
16 Arizona	6,412,940
17 Tennessee	6,355,603
18 Missouri	5,989,163
19 Maryland	5,781,451
20 Wisconsin	5,690,898
21 Minnesota	5,312,239
22 Colorado	5,045,562
23 Alabama	4,782,021
24 South Carolina	4,635,405
25 Louisiana	4,537,277
26 Kentucky	4,344,552
27 Oregon	3,839,598
28 Oklahoma	3,756,421
29 Connecticut	3,572,672
30 Iowa	3,048,461
31 Mississippi	2,969,120
32 Arkansas	2,918,803
33 Kansas	2,854,367
34 Utah	2,772,041
35 Nevada	2,704,091
36 New Mexico	2,061,645
37 West Virginia	1,852,506
38 Nebraska	1,828,488
39 Idaho	1,570,176
40 Hawaii	1,361,628
41 Maine	1,328,387
42 New Hampshire	1,317,033
43 Rhode Island	1,052,492
44 Montana	991,049
45 Delaware	899,552
46 South Dakota	815,914
47 Alaska	711,920
48 North Dakota	674,511
49 Vermont	625,717
50 Wyoming	564,188

Most Populous U.S. Cities	Population
1 New York City, NY	8,187,643
2 Los Angeles, CA	3,799,152
3 Chicago, IL	2,700,792
4 Houston, TX	2,113,639
5 Philadelphia, PA	1,526,413
6 Phoenix, AZ	1,456,892
7 San Antonio, TX	1,334,791
8 San Diego, CA	1,311,094
9 Dallas, TX	1,205,888
10 San Jose, CA	953,497
11 Jacksonville, FL	822,642
12 Indianapolis, IN	821,012
13 San Francisco, CA	806,696
14 Austin, TX	798,719
15 Columbus, OH	788,648
16 Fort Worth, TX	743,782
17 Charlotte, NC	736,586
18 Detroit, MI	716,555
19 El Paso, TX	652,123
20 Memphis, TN	649,267
21 Baltimore, MD	620,187
22 Boston, MA	618,629
23 Seattle, WA	611,783
24 Washington, DC	605,045
25 Denver, CO	604,140
26 Nashville, TN	602,611
27 Louisville, KY	597,892
28 Milwaukee, WI	595,161
29 Portland, OR	586,428
30 Las Vegas, NV	586,406
31 Oklahoma City, OK	582,210
32 Albuquerque, NM	546,429
33 Tucson, AZ	522,465
34 Fresno, CA	495,899
35 Sacramento, CA	467,750
36 Long Beach, CA	463,344
37 Kansas City, MO	460,496
38 Mesa, AZ	442,463
39 Virginia Beach, VA	438,944
40 Atlanta, GA	423,975
41 Colorado Springs, CO	417,977
42 Omaha, NE	411,067
43 Raleigh, NC	406,153
44 Miami, FL	401,188
45 Cleveland, OH	397,240
46 Tulsa, OK	393,750
47 Oakland, CA	392,304
48 Minneapolis, MN	384,178
49 Wichita, KS	382,560
50 Arlington, TX	368,070
52 New Orleans, LA (1)	345,483
53 Honolulu, HI (1)	340,195

Midsized Cities	Population
Population > 200K	
St Louis, MO	318,640
Pittsburgh, PA	307,019
Anchorage, AK	292,201
Madison, WI	234,286
Baton Rouge, LA	229,633
Spokane, WA	209,289
Population 100–200K	
Salt Lake City, UT	187,495
Chattanooga, TN	168,151
Eugene, OR	156,241
Fort Collins, CO	144,594
Charleston, SC	120,550
Population < 100K	
Boulder, CO	97,974
Albany, NY	97,825
Bellingham, WA	81,157
Missoula, MT	66,850
Davis, CA	65,755
Burlington, VT	42,448

Source: ACS 2009-2011 **Note**: (1) New Orleans and Honolulu, as the 52nd and 53rd most populous cities, continue to be included in the *Benchmarking Report* for consistency with previous reports and to continue data collection for these cities. Throughout the report, references to the "50 most populous cities" should be understood to include these two additional cities.

Overview

above national average / below national average

NATIONWIDE: 9.7% % Pop Change 2000-2010 · 88.1 People Per Square Mile · 37.3 Median Age · $50,502 Median Income · 15.9% % Pop Below Poverty Level

% Pop Change 2000-2010 (Nationwide 9.7%)

35.1%

% Pop Change	State
35.1%	Nevada
24.6%	Arizona
23.8%	Utah
21.1%	Idaho
20.6%	Texas
18.5%	North Carolina
18.3%	Georgia
17.6%	Florida
16.9%	Colorado
15.3%	South Carolina
14.6%	Delaware
14.1%	Wyoming
14.1%	Washington
13.3%	Alaska
13.2%	New Mexico
13.0%	Virginia
12.3%	Hawaii
12.0%	Oregon
11.5%	Tennessee
10.0%	California
9.7%	**NATIONWIDE**
9.7%	Montana
9.1%	Arkansas
9.0%	Maryland
8.7%	Oklahoma
7.9%	South Dakota
7.8%	Minnesota
7.5%	Alabama
7.4%	Kentucky
7.0%	Missouri
6.7%	Nebraska
6.6%	Indiana
6.5%	New Hampshire
6.1%	Kansas
6.0%	Wisconsin
4.9%	Connecticut
4.7%	North Dakota
4.5%	New Jersey
4.3%	Mississippi
4.2%	Maine
4.1%	Iowa
3.4%	Pennsylvania
3.3%	Illinois
3.1%	Massachusetts
2.8%	Vermont
2.5%	West Virginia
2.1%	New York
1.6%	Ohio
1.4%	Louisiana
0.4%	Rhode Island
-0.6%	Michigan

-0.6%

People Per Square Mile (Nationwide 88.1)

1,185.3

People Per Square Mile	State
1,185.3	New Jersey
1,007.2	Rhode Island
835.9	Massachusetts
737.4	Connecticut
591.5	Maryland
460.5	Delaware
410.7	New York
349.5	Florida
283.6	Pennsylvania
281.8	Ohio
239.4	California
230.9	Illinois
212.0	Hawaii
202.4	Virginia
196.2	North Carolina
180.9	Indiana
174.0	Michigan
167.8	Georgia
154.2	Tennessee
154.0	South Carolina
146.9	New Hampshire
109.4	Kentucky
104.8	Wisconsin
104.2	Louisiana
101.4	Washington
96.4	Texas
94.2	Alabama
88.1	**NATIONWIDE**
86.9	Missouri
76.9	West Virginia
67.6	Vermont
66.7	Minnesota
63.3	Mississippi
56.4	Arizona
56.1	Arkansas
54.7	Oklahoma
54.6	Iowa
48.6	Colorado
43.0	Maine
40.0	Oregon
34.9	Kansas
33.7	Utah
24.6	Nevada
23.8	Nebraska
19.0	Idaho
17.0	New Mexico
10.8	South Dakota
9.8	North Dakota
6.8	Montana
5.8	Wyoming
1.2	Alaska

1.2

Median Age (Nationwide 37.3)

42.9

Median Age	State
42.9	Maine
41.7	Vermont
41.3	West Virginia
41.2	New Hampshire
40.8	Florida
40.1	Connecticut
40.1	Pennsylvania
40.0	Montana
39.4	Rhode Island
39.1	Massachusetts
38.9	New Jersey
38.9	Michigan
38.8	Delaware
38.8	Ohio
38.6	Hawaii
38.5	Wisconsin
38.5	Oregon
38.1	Tennessee
38.1	Iowa
38.0	Maryland
38.0	New York
37.0	Kentucky
37.9	South Carolina
37.9	Alabama
37.9	Missouri
37.5	Virginia
37.5	Minnesota
37.4	North Carolina
37.4	Arkansas
37.3	**NATIONWIDE**
37.2	Washington
37.1	South Dakota
37.1	North Dakota
37.0	Indiana
36.8	Wyoming
36.6	Illinois
36.5	New Mexico
36.3	Nevada
36.3	Nebraska
36.2	Oklahoma
36.1	Colorado
36.0	Mississippi
36.0	Kansas
35.9	Louisiana
35.9	Arizona
35.4	Georgia
35.2	California
34.7	Idaho
33.9	Alaska
33.6	Texas
29.3	Utah

29.3

Median Income (Nationwide $50,502)

$71,294

Median Income	State
$71,294	Maryland
$69,911	New Jersey
$68,211	Alaska
$67,427	Connecticut
$64,909	Hawaii
$64,504	Massachusetts
$63,168	New Hampshire
$62,391	Virginia
$59,641	California
$58,580	Delaware
$57,742	Washington
$57,439	Minnesota
$56,610	Utah
$56,345	Colorado
$56,290	Wyoming
$55,972	New York
$55,044	Illinois
$54,525	Rhode Island
$52,941	Vermont
$52,276	Nevada
$51,016	Pennsylvania
$51,009	Wisconsin
$50,671	North Dakota
$50,502	**NATIONWIDE**
$50,365	Nebraska
$50,266	Texas
$50,028	Iowa
$49,929	Kansas
$48,518	Arizona
$48,377	Oregon
$48,208	South Dakota
$47,690	Georgia
$47,206	Maine
$46,847	Michigan
$46,815	Indiana
$46,595	Ohio
$46,123	Missouri
$45,736	Florida
$45,254	Idaho
$44,942	North Carolina
$44,392	Montana
$43,715	New Mexico
$43,530	Oklahoma
$43,484	Louisiana
$43,304	South Carolina
$42,661	Tennessee
$41,973	Alabama
$41,479	Kentucky
$39,588	Arkansas
$39,453	West Virginia
$37,813	Mississippi

$37,813

% Pop Below Poverty Level (Nationwide 15.9%)

22.2%

% Pop Below Poverty Level	State
22.2%	Mississippi
20.2%	New Mexico
19.0%	Arkansas
18.8%	Kentucky
18.7%	Louisiana
18.4%	Alabama
18.2%	South Carolina
17.9%	West Virginia
17.8%	Georgia
17.8%	Texas
17.7%	Tennessee
17.6%	Arizona
17.2%	North Carolina
16.8%	Oklahoma
16.7%	Michigan
16.1%	Florida
15.9%	**NATIONWIDE**
15.8%	Ohio
15.8%	Oregon
15.5%	California
15.3%	Idaho
15.2%	Indiana
15.2%	Missouri
15.1%	New York
14.9%	Montana
14.5%	Nevada
14.0%	South Dakota
14.0%	Illinois
13.6%	Kansas
13.5%	Rhode Island
13.3%	Washington
13.2%	Colorado
13.2%	Pennsylvania
13.0%	Maine
12.9%	Wisconsin
12.7%	Utah
12.7%	Nebraska
12.4%	North Dakota
12.4%	Iowa
11.8%	Vermont
11.7%	Delaware
11.6%	Minnesota
11.2%	Massachusetts
11.1%	Hawaii
11.1%	Virginia
10.8%	Wyoming
10.1%	Connecticut
10.0%	New Jersey
9.8%	Alaska
9.7%	Maryland
8.4%	New Hampshire

8.4%

Sources: ACS 2009–2011; ACS 2011; Census 2000, 2010

Overview

% Pop Change 2000-2010

46.3%

% Pop Change	City
46.3%	Raleigh
38.6%	Fort Worth
35.2%	Charlotte
22.0%	Las Vegas
21.8%	Albuquerque
20.4%	Austin
16.0%	San Antonio
15.7%	Fresno
15.4%	Colorado Springs
15.2%	El Paso
14.6%	Sacramento
14.6%	Oklahoma City
11.7%	Jacksonville
11.1%	Wichita
10.8%	Mesa
10.6%	Columbus
10.3%	Portland, OR
10.2%	Nashville
10.2%	Miami
9.8%	Arlington, TX
9.4%	Phoenix
9.0%	Louisville (1)
8.2%	Denver
8.0%	Seattle
7.5%	Houston
6.9%	San Diego
6.9%	Tucson
5.9%	**LARGE CITIES**
5.7%	San Jose
5.2%	Washington, DC
4.9%	Indianapolis
4.9%	Omaha
4.8%	Boston
4.1%	Kansas City, MO
3.7%	San Francisco
3.0%	Virginia Beach
2.6%	Los Angeles
2.1%	New York City
0.8%	Atlanta
0.8%	Dallas
0.6%	Philadelphia
0.2%	Long Beach
0.0%	Minneapolis
-0.3%	Tulsa
-0.4%	Milwaukee
-0.5%	Memphis
-2.2%	Oakland
-4.6%	Baltimore
-6.9%	Chicago
-9.3%	Honolulu
-17.1%	Cleveland
-25.0%	Detroit
-29.1%	New Orleans

-29.1%

People Per Square Mile

27,021.9

People Per Square Mile	City
27,021.9	New York City
17,163.7	San Francisco
12,888.1	Boston
11,845.6	Chicago
11,391.1	Philadelphia
11,144.1	Miami
9,918.8	Washington, DC
9,266.9	Long Beach
8,100.5	Los Angeles
7,656.6	Baltimore
7,283.1	Seattle
7,114.4	Minneapolis
7,005.4	Oakland
6,199.6	Milwaukee
5,577.0	Honolulu
5,387.0	San Jose
5,155.1	Detroit
5,092.8	Cleveland
4,773.0	Sacramento
4,427.7	Fresno
4,409.2	Portland, OR
4,311.8	Las Vegas
4,097.3	**LARGE CITIES**
4,034.1	San Diego
3,948.6	Denver
3,834.1	Arlington, TX
3,634.3	Columbus
3,536.3	Dallas
3,522.7	Houston
3,236.7	Omaha
3,229.7	Mesa
3,187.8	Atlanta
2,906.5	Albuquerque
2,895.4	San Antonio
2,840.2	Raleigh
2,818.1	Wichita
2,818.0	Phoenix
2,680.3	Austin
2,557.3	El Paso
2,471.8	Charlotte
2,301.6	Tucson
2,274.3	Indianapolis
2,187.6	Fort Worth
2,143.5	Colorado Springs
2,061.2	Memphis
2,044.3	New Orleans
1,998.7	Tulsa
1,839.7	Louisville
1,762.8	Virginia Beach
1,461.9	Kansas City, MO
1,268.7	Nashville
1,101.3	Jacksonville
960.7	Oklahoma City

960.7

Median Age

41.1

Median Age	City
41.1	Honolulu
39.4	Miami
38.5	San Francisco
37.2	Louisville
36.7	Cleveland
36.2	Oakland
36.1	Seattle
35.8	Portland, OR
35.7	Las Vegas
35.5	New York City
35.4	Mesa
35.4	Albuquerque
35.4	Jacksonville
35.3	San Jose
34.9	Tulsa
34.9	Kansas City, MO
34.8	Detroit
34.8	New Orleans
34.8	Virginia Beach
34.7	Colorado Springs
34.3	Baltimore
34.2	Los Angeles
34.2	Wichita
34.0	**LARGE CITIES**
33.9	Washington, DC
33.7	San Diego
33.7	Omaha
33.7	Indianapolis
33.7	Nashville
33.6	Denver
33.6	Oklahoma City
33.4	Philadelphia
33.3	Long Beach
33.3	Sacramento
33.3	Charlotte
33.2	Memphis
33.1	Atlanta
33.1	Tucson
32.9	Chicago
32.6	San Antonio
32.4	El Paso
32.2	Houston
32.2	Phoenix
32.0	Raleigh
31.9	Arlington, TX
31.7	Minneapolis
31.7	Dallas
31.4	Columbus
31.3	Fort Worth
31.0	Austin
30.8	Boston
30.5	Milwaukee
29.3	Fresno

29.3

Median Income

$78,557

Median Income	City
$78,557	San Jose
$72,033	San Francisco
$64,706	Virginia Beach
$62,214	Washington, DC
$61,785	San Diego
$61,562	Seattle
$55,925	Honolulu
$52,325	Long Beach
$52,029	Colorado Springs
$51,968	Raleigh
$51,783	Arlington, TX
$51,230	Boston
$51,224	Charlotte
$51,184	Oakland
$51,182	Las Vegas
$50,654	Austin
$50,331	New York City
$49,487	Portland, OR
$48,987	Fort Worth
$48,431	Los Angeles
$48,018	Sacramento
$47,242	Denver
$47,035	Mesa
$47,021	Minneapolis
$46,722	Jacksonville
$46,334	Omaha
$46,300	**LARGE CITIES**
$46,265	Albuquerque
$45,941	Phoenix
$45,732	Chicago
$45,203	Wichita
$45,087	Nashville
$44,559	Atlanta
$44,116	Kansas City, MO
$44,033	Oklahoma City
$43,946	San Antonio
$43,603	Houston
$42,250	Louisville
$42,085	Fresno
$41,761	Columbus
$41,399	Dallas
$40,348	Indianapolis
$39,991	Tulsa
$39,781	El Paso
$39,561	Baltimore
$36,721	New Orleans
$36,072	Memphis
$36,071	Tucson
$35,956	Philadelphia
$34,293	Milwaukee
$28,928	Miami
$26,253	Detroit
$25,997	Cleveland

$25,997

% Pop Below Poverty Level

38.3%

% Pop Below Poverty Level	City
38.3%	Detroit
34.7%	Cleveland
29.6%	Miami
29.1%	Milwaukee
27.3%	Fresno
26.9%	New Orleans
26.8%	Philadelphia
26.7%	Memphis
25.4%	Atlanta
25.3%	Tucson
24.0%	Baltimore
23.9%	Dallas
23.5%	Minneapolis
23.0%	Columbus
22.7%	Houston
22.5%	Chicago
22.1%	Boston
22.0%	Phoenix
21.8%	El Paso
21.3%	Los Angeles
21.1%	Sacramento
20.9%	Indianapolis
20.7%	**LARGE CITIES**
20.5%	Oakland
20.1%	New York City
20.0%	Long Beach
19.8%	Tulsa
19.7%	San Antonio
19.6%	Austin
19.6%	Fort Worth
19.6%	Denver
19.3%	Nashville
19.0%	Kansas City, MO
18.9%	Washington, DC
18.7%	Louisville
18.1%	Oklahoma City
18.1%	Portland, OR
17.7%	Albuquerque
17.1%	Raleigh
17.0%	Wichita
16.9%	Jacksonville
16.9%	Charlotte
16.7%	Las Vegas
16.7%	Arlington, TX
16.3%	Omaha
15.8%	San Diego
15.1%	Mesa
14.1%	Colorado Springs
13.6%	Seattle
12.9%	San Francisco
12.1%	San Jose
11.9%	Honolulu
7.5%	Virginia Beach

7.5%

above city average

below city average

Sources: Census 2000, 2010; ACS 2009–2011 **Note**: (1) The City of Louisville merged with Jefferson County in 2003. Therefore, population data between 2000 and 2010 are not comparable. ACS 2005 data was used to show population change for Louisville/Jefferson County.

Bicycle Friendly States survey. This meant that state-level survey respondents only received one survey rather than two separate forms as in previous years of the Benchmarking Project and the Bicycle Friendly States surveys.

The Alliance administered two city surveys separately—one for the 50 most populous U.S. cities (plus Honolulu and New Orleans) and one for a new set of 17 small and midsized cities chosen for the pilot benchmarking effort.

State and large city surveys were distributed to leaders of Alliance organizations, government officials, and advocates in October 2012. An abbreviated survey was sent to representatives in the small and midsized cities in May 2013. Because Alliance advocacy leaders can tap existing relationships with local government officials, they were able to help increase the survey response rate and ensure that returned surveys were as complete as possible.

Surveys were completed by department of transportation staff, metropolitan planning organization staff, city officials, and Alliance advocacy leaders. In many cases, surveys required input from multiple agencies because the requested data were not easily accessible in one place. The project team reached out to survey respondents, with the final data for the report coming in early June 2013.

All data were entered into the Benchmarking Project's data collection tool, reviewed for quality control, and analyzed over the next several months. This report relies largely on self-reported data and while the Alliance has made all efforts to verify, the accuracy cannot be guaranteed.

Alliance Member Database

Each year, member organizations of the Alliance for Biking & Walking are asked to provide their annual membership numbers, revenue, spending, and activity priorities. The Alliance compiles this information into a database, making it possible to track trends over time. The *Benchmarking Report* relies on these data to gauge advocacy capacity across the country.

Austin, TX. Courtesy of PeopleForBikes

National Data Sources

The Benchmarking Project team identified uniform national data sources from public agencies and organizations whenever possible. Sources are identified throughout the text and with tables and graphics. Reference this page for source information on the most commonly used citations and acronymns included in this report. A more detailed description of these sources can be found in Appendix 1 on pages 226–227.

In some cases, data in this report come from individual independent studies. All studies cited in this report are referenced in the bibliography, beginning on page 248.

- American Public Transportation Association (APTA)
  Public Transportation Infrastructure Database
- Bureau of Labor Statistics (BLS)
  Consumer Expenditure Survey
- Census Bureau
  American Community Survey (ACS)
  U.S. Census
- Centers for Disease Control and Prevention (CDC)
  Behavioral Risk Factor Surveillance System (BRFSS)
  Web-based Injury Statistics Query and Reporting System (WISQARS)
- Federal Highway Administration (FHWA)
  Fiscal Management Information System (FMIS)
  National Household Travel Survey (NHTS)
- Governors Highway Safety Association
  Distracted Driving Laws
  Crash Data Collection
- Institute of Education Sciences, U.S. Department of Education (USDOE)
  National Center for Education Statistics
- League of American Bicyclists (LAB)
  Bicycle Friendly Communities (BFC)
  Bicycle Friendly States (BFS)
- National Center for Safe Routes to School (NCSRTS)
  Safe Routes to School (SRTS) Tracking Report and Funding Distribution
- National Complete Streets Coalition
  Complete Streets Policy List
- National Highway Traffic Safety Administration (NHTSA)
  Fatality Analysis Reporting System (FARS)
- National Oceanic and Atmospheric Administration (NOAA)
  U.S. Climate Normals
- National Transportation Alternatives Clearinghouse (NTAC)
  Transportation Enhancements Spending Report
- Rails-to-Trails Conservancy (RTC)
  Rails-to-Trails Statistics
- Research and Innovative Technology Administration, U.S. Department of Transportation (USDOT)
  Bureau of Transportation Statistics
- Safe Routes to School National Partnership (SRTSNP)
  State of the States
- School Transportation News
  Buyer's Guide Statistics

Case Studies

This report includes a number of case studies from communities across the U.S. and around the world. These stories are intended to take a closer look at bicycling and walking initiatives from a broad perspective. Every community, every state, every country has its own unique challenges and opportunities. We hope that sharing reports of their efforts can lead to further research and inspiration for others.

Project Team

In addition to Alliance staff, the Benchmarking Project team includes a review committee of distinguished researchers and professionals from multiple specializations. These advisors guide the scope of the project and evaluate the findings for accuracy and effectiveness.

Using This Report

The Benchmarking Project is intended as a resource for government officials, bicycle and pedestrian advocates, researchers, and the media searching for comparable data and means to measure progress. We encourage you to search this report for your city or state to see how you compare to others. To make data easy to find, this report orders all data tables alphabetically by city or state. Charts and graphs are ordered by benchmark in order to most clearly see how states and cities compare with each other.

Here are some other tips for using this report:

See where you measure up: Review the report for your city or state. See how your location compares to others. Are you below or above the average for other cities / states? Note where you are leading and where you are behind.

Connect with the media: Consider issuing a press release or talking with the media about this report. Discuss how your state or city stacks up against others in bicycling and walking levels, safety, and funding. Highlight any areas where you are leading and opportunities for improvement. Use the data to support the work you are doing to promote bicycling and walking locally.

Evaluate your efforts: Think about where you have been focusing your efforts toward increasing bicycling and walking, health and safety. Are these efforts working? Look for trends in the data in this report. Look for benchmarks set by cities and states that are leading in the issues that concern you.

Set new goals: Use the data in this report to set new goals and refocus your efforts if needed. There are examples in this report of significant improvements in just a few short years. You will find which cities and states are leading in funding, safety, facilities, and other areas and will also see the national average and averages for major U.S. cities. Use these benchmarks to set goals for your city and/or state.

Use it as a reference book: The Alliance has heard from a number of government officials and advocates that the *Benchmarking Report* is a publication they reference frequently in their work. Keep this report on your office bookshelf in an accessible location or digital format. Use it when you are contacted by the media for statistics in your community, or when you need facts for a presentation or paper you are preparing. Use these data to support your work promoting bicycling and walking in your state or city.

Share it: Provide extra hard copies of the report to give to your local elected and agency officials, organization leaders, and others who can use it. The report can be a great reason to have a meeting, talk about the current status of bicycling and walking provisions, and improvements you can mutually strive for. It is always best to deliver the report in person. The report can also be downloaded from the Alliance for Biking & Walking website. Share the link with members, allies, and funders.

New York City, NY. Photo by Annette Orzechowski

www.BikeWalkAlliance.org/Benchmarking

If you have questions about the data in this report, would like to request additional data from the Benchmarking Project, have feedback for our team, or other questions or inquiries, please contact us at:

Benchmarking@BikeWalkAlliance.org

2 Levels of Bicycling and Walking

Thirty-six states and 47 of the most populous cities surveyed for this report have a published goal to increase either walking or bicycling levels (most often, both) within their jurisdiction. This is a significant increase from 2007 when the Benchmarking Project published its first report, showing only 16 states and 25 major cities with such goals. During this same time period, bicycling and walking levels have continued to show increases, both nationally and within major cities.

The ability to meet these goals requires access to accurate and consistent data that documents the changes over time. Unfortunately, availability of these much-needed data is still very limited.[(1)] This report relies on the two most consistent and dependable sources of data available on levels of bicycling and walking in the U.S.: the National Household Travel Survey (NHTS) and the American Community Survey (ACS).

Note: (1) See Appendix 2 on page 228 for a discussion of the challenges of determining accurate levels of bicycling and walking, as well as a discussion on the differences between the ACS and U.S. Census methodologies.

Austin, TX. Courtesy of Bike Texas

U.S. Trip Mode Share

The most recent data documenting mode of transportation for all trips taken in the U.S. comes from the 2009 National Household Travel Survey (NHTS). These data estimate that 1.0% of all trips taken in the U.S. are made by bicycle and 10.4% are by foot. This amounts to over 4 billion bicycle trips and nearly 41 billion walking trips in 2009 in the United States. Large cities (those with a population over 200,000) see trips made by bike or foot at slightly higher rates than the national average; 1.1% of all trips in large cities are by bicycle and 12.7% are by foot (NHTS, 2009).

Nationwide, in 2009, about 13% of U.S. travelers reported taking at least one bicycle trip per week and 2% took at least one trip per day. About 68% of travelers reported taking at least one walking trip per week and 24% took at least one walking trip per day (NHTS, 2009).

Data Sources for Mode Share

The National Household Travel Survey (NHTS) conducts phone surveys every 5–7 years across the U.S. to compile an inventory of daily and long-distance travel choices. The survey gathers data on mode of travel, as well as frequency and purpose for trips. The most recently published dataset is from 2009. This data was reweighted and rereleased by NHTS in November 2010; the updated numbers are reflected in this report. Small sample sizes make it difficult to make comparisons at the state or local level, so in this report, NHTS data are only used at the national level.

The American Community Survey (ACS) is the most consistent, reliable source of data for walking and bicycling in all U.S. states and cities. The annual survey reports yearly estimates of the share of workers who commute by bicycle or foot. ACS data are available as 1-year estimates, 3-year estimates, and 5-year estimates. Five-year estimates provide the greatest accuracy, and 1-year estimates provide the most current data. In this report, we use 3-year estimates when comparing states and cities to provide a current, yet more accurate picture of levels of biking and walking. One-year estimates are used for national averages only. The 2000 U.S. Census was the last census to record transportation to work for the whole population.

Though the ACS transportation to work data are by no means a complete look at mode share, they do offer some insight into mode share. Generally, we assume that in areas where people bicycle or walk to work at higher levels, they likely bicycle or walk for other purposes at higher levels, too.

U.S. Trips by Mode of Transportation

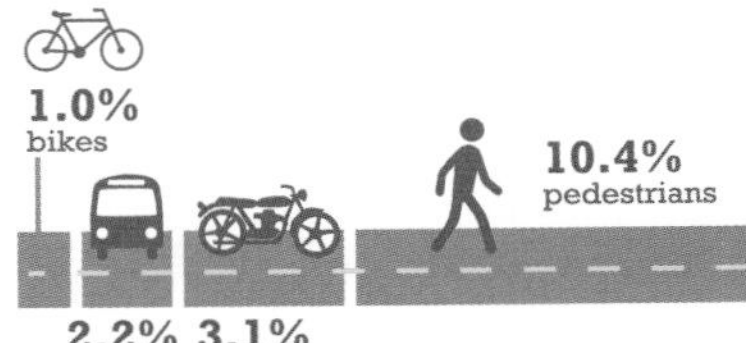

Who bicycles and walks?

Using the available data from ACS and NHTS, we can see that pedestrians are fairly diverse across gender, age, income, and ethnicity. Bicycling trips, on the other hand, are disproportionately reported by men and youth (NHTS, 2009; ACS, 2011), though the share of women commuting to work has been steadily increasing (ACS 2007–2011). In general, income does not seem to be a factor in whether a person bicycles or walks. However, in large cities, the percentage of people walking to work generally increases for households with lower annual incomes.

Throughout this report, we will look into other possible factors—the input benchmarks—that may play a part in a higher or lower bicycling and walking mode share. This section focuses on identifying who we see bicycling and walking.

Gender

A national look at pedestrian mode share shows a fairly even split between men and women. Of all trips taken, women account for 51% of walkers, which is equal to their distribution in the population overall. The gap between men and women bicyclists, however, is wide. Just 24% of all bicycle trips are taken by women, according to the 2009 NHTS.

Age

As might be expected, youth, who are not of legal driving age, make up a disproportionately high share of bicycling trips. Estimates from NHTS indicate that youth under age 16 make up 39% of bicycling trips, despite accounting for just 21% of the U.S. population. This age group also accounts for 17% of walking trips.

Adults age 65 and older represent 13% of the U.S. population and make up 10% of all walking trips and 6% of all bicycling trips. All other ages (16–64) make up 66% of the population and account for 73% of all walking trips and 54% of trips by bicycle.

Mode Share by Gender

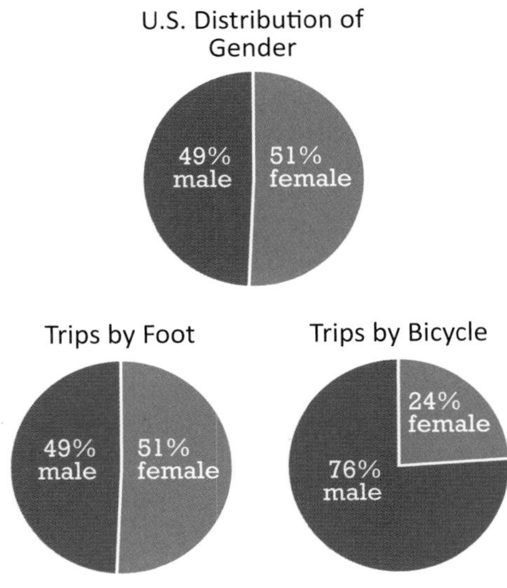

Sources: ACS 2011, NHTS 2009

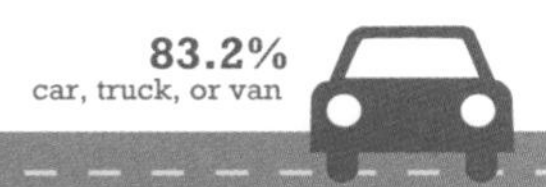

Source: NHTS 2009. **Note**: Due to rounding, some of these data do not appear to add up to 100%

Comparing NHTS data from 1969 to 2009, we see an enormous drop in the number of children bicycling and walking to school. In 1969, 48% of youth trips to school were by walking or bicycling, and only 12% were by car. By 2009, the situation had completely reversed to 45% of trips to school being taken by car and only 13% taken by foot or bicycle.

There are many reasons for the decline in bicycling by children, including their parents' fear of traffic danger and 'stranger danger.' Another contributing factor is schools' increasing consolidation into regional schools, making the trip to school longer. This increased distance to school makes walking or biking from each student's respective home more difficult (McDonald, 2012).

Chicago, IL. Photo by Josh Koonce @ Flickr

Share of Walk and Bicycle Trips by Age

Under 16 | 16-64 | 65+

= 5% of walking trips [1]
= 5% of U.S. population [2]
= 5% of bicycling trips [1]

Sources: (1) NHTS 2009 (2) ACS 2009–2011

Pedestrian trips in the U.S.
17% are children under 16 years old.
10% are adults 65 years old and older.

Bicycle trips in the U.S.
39% are by children under 16 years old.
6% are by adults 65 years old and older.

People across income groups walk and bicycle roughly proportionally to their distribution in the population.

Income Distribution for Walk and Bicycle Trips

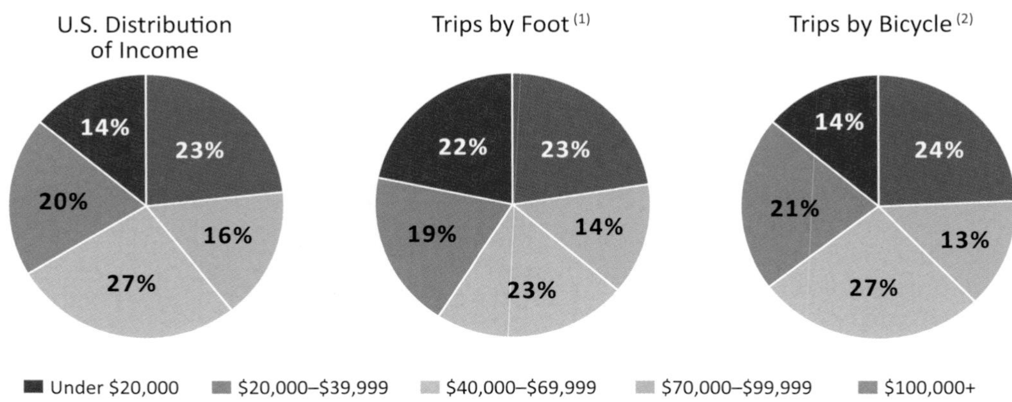

Source: NHTS 2009. **Notes**: Income data from NHTS is grouped differently depending on the analysis performed. For this reason, income categories differ among the graphics on this page. (1) Trips by Foot numbers round up and so appear to add to 101%. (2) Trips by Bicycle numbers round down and so appear to add to 99%.

Pedestrian trips make up a higher percentage of all trips taken by people with an annual income less than $20,000. The percentage of bicycle trips is similar across all income groups.

Bicyclist and Pedestrian Mode Share by Household Income

Mode of travel	Less than $20,000	$20,000 to $39,999	$40,000 to $74,999	$75,000 to $99,999	$100,000 and over	All incomes (1)
(pedestrian)	16.3%	10.3%	8.9%	8.9%	10.2%	10.4%
(bicycle)	1.0%	1.2%	1.0%	0.9%	1.1%	1.0%
All other modes	82.7%	88.5%	90.1%	90.2%	88.7%	88.5%

Source: NHTS 2009. **Notes**: Income data from NHTS is grouped differently depending on the analysis performed. For this reason, income categories differ among the graphics on this page. (1) Numbers round down and so appear to add to 99.9%.

Photo courtesy of BikeTexas

Photo courtesy of BikeTexas

Benchmarking Bicycling and Walking in Texas

by Mary Lauran Hall, Alliance for Biking & Walking

A Texas study inspired by the Alliance's *Benchmarking Report* aims to help transportation officials beef up walking and bicycling throughout the Lone Star State.

Inspired by the Alliance for Biking & Walking's national *Benchmarking Report*, the *BikeTexas 2012 Benchmark Study* examines and ranks 35 cities in Texas with a population of 90,000 or more. The report ranks these cities based on walking and bicycling mode share, health and safety statistics, policies, infrastructure, and educational programs.

BikeTexas Executive Director Robin Stallings hopes that benchmarking Texas cities on bicycling and walking issues will turn competition between similarly-sized cities into faster progress on active transportation.

"A city like Amarillo is very interested in Lovett, but is not that interested in Austin," explained Stallings. "Meanwhile, in Tyler, there's a lot more interest in Longview's progress than Dallas's progress."

BikeTexas has distributed copies to city officials around the state, to members of the Texas legislature, and to staffed bicycling and walking advocacy organizations throughout the state. Responses have been encouraging.

"One city engineer called us and requested 15 more copies," Stallings said. "The state DOT distributed 500 copies within the agency. All of the [Bicycling and Pedestrian] Coordinators, all the traffic safety people, and all the district engineers got copies."

To create the survey, researchers surveyed public officials from each of the target cities. The online survey included a glossary of bicycling and walking terms, which had the added benefit of educating city officials unfamiliar with bicycle and pedestrian planning terms.

"Now we have a lot more decision makers who know what a cycle track is," Stallings noted.

BikeTexas advocates plan to continue producing the report in future years, perhaps with more focus on smaller cities. Stallings and his colleagues also hope that fellow statewide advocacy organizations will follow suit.

"We think of this report as the beginning of a dialogue," said Stallings.

Purpose

According to responses to the 2009 NHTS, the most common reasons for walking or bicycling were either for a recreational or personal purpose. Traveling by bicycle or foot "to earn a living" only accounts for 13% and 6% of all trips, respectively.

Mode Share by Trip Purpose

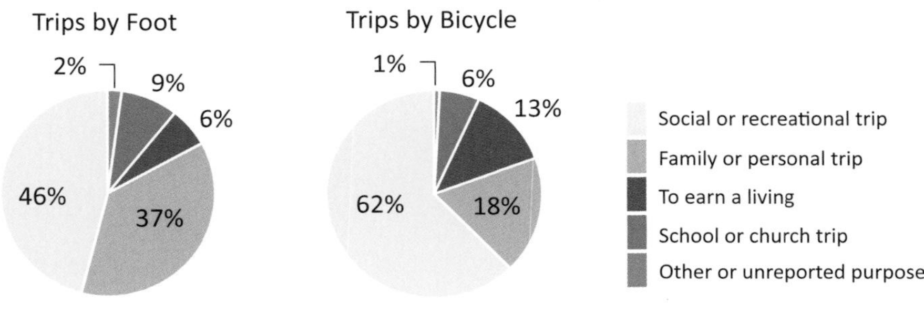

Source: NHTS 2009

Commuters

The only recent nationwide bicycling and walking data that are available to compare all states and most cities comes from the ACS. However, the ACS only tracks mode of transportation to work. As noted in the NHTS trip data by purpose, bicycling and walking trips to work make up only a small percentage of total bicycling and walking trips. Therefore, the data presented here for commuters only represent one subsection of bicyclists and pedestrians.

Recent ACS data show that, nationwide, an average of 3.4% of commuters get to work by bicycle (0.6%) or foot (2.8%). In the large U.S. cities studied in this report, the combined average share of commuters by bicycle and foot is significantly higher at nearly 6.1% (1.0% bicycling and 5.0% walking).

These data continue the very gradual trend of increasing bicycling and walking to work since 2005.

Commuters in the Most Populous Cities

Thirty-seven of the large cities studied in this report showed an increase or no change in bicycle ridership since the *2012 Benchmarking Report* was released (ACS 3-year estimates 2007–2009 compared to 2009–2011). Of the 15 cities showing a decrease in bicycle commuting, most of the decreases were slight with only six cities experiencing a drop in ridership of more than 0.1 percentage points.

Nine of the ten cities with the highest commuter bicycling rates also showed the biggest increase in those rates. Washington, DC; New Orleans; Portland, OR; and Tucson added between an additional 0.6% and 0.9% of bicycle commuters. Bicycle commuting in Washington, DC, for example, increased from an average of 2.0% in 2007–2009 to 2.9% in 2009–2011.

Forty-one cities saw an increase in commutes by foot with the greatest growth coming from Austin and Honolulu. The remaining 21 cities

Bicycling and Walking to Work in the U.S. (1990–2011)

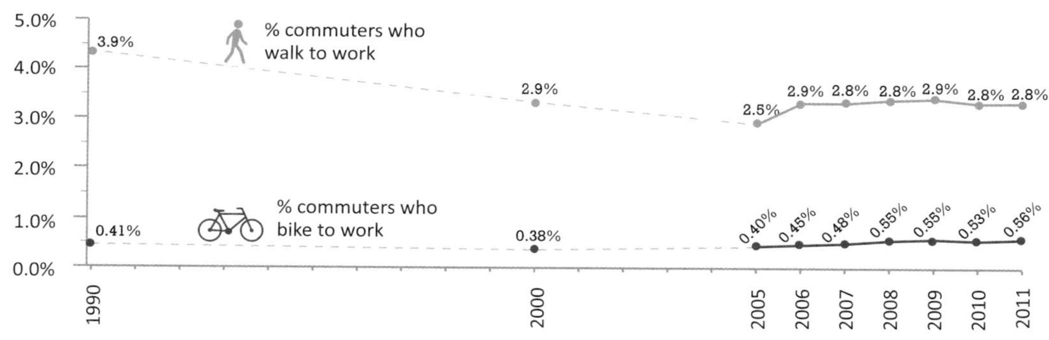

Source: US Census 1990, 2000; ACS 2005,2006, 2007, 2008, 2009, 2010, 2011

Cambridge, MA. Photo by Dan Gelinne. Courtesy of www.pedbikeimages.org.

Levels of Bicycling and Walking to Work in the U.S.

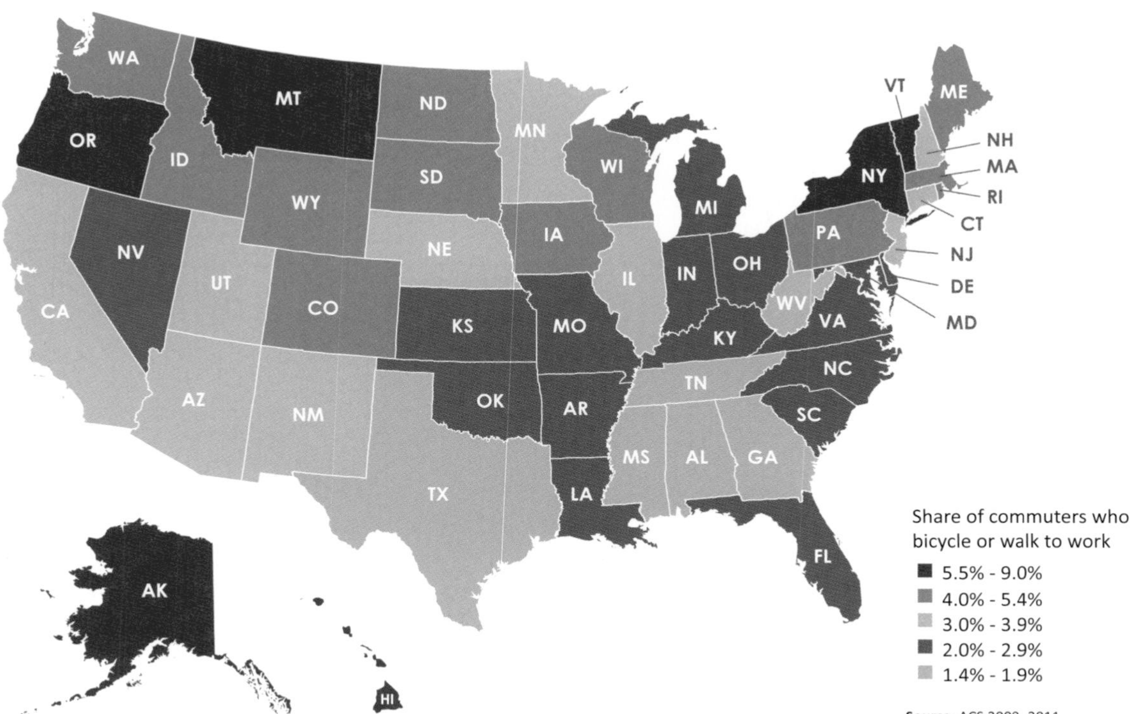

saw a slight decrease in commuters walking to work with 11 cities experiencing a drop in walking of more than 0.1 percentage points.

Commuters by State

Commuter bicycling and walking rates at the state level have changed very little in recent years. Oregon remains the state with the highest bicycle to work share at 2.3%, nearly 1% higher than the next two highest states, Montana (1.4%) and Colorado (1.3%).

The majority of states showed a decrease in commuting by foot, though most decreases were minimal. Rhode Island saw the highest increase (0.5%) since the 2007–2009 estimates. Alaska, New York, and Vermont have the highest rates for walking to work.

Commuters by Gender

Of commuting trips, women make up 46.5% of those who walk to work (ACS, 2011). This rate is equivalent to the gender distribution in the work force with women representing 46.7% of employees (DOL, 2010). However, women are less represented among bicycle commuters.

Massachusetts and New Hampshire are the only states where women walk to work at slightly higher rates than men. Men bicycle to work at higher rates than women in all states, though the gap varies among states. Wyoming has the smallest gap among men and women community bicyclists (58% and 42%). Nevada has the largest gap between men and women commuting bicyclists (85% and 15%). As an overall trend, the gap between men and women bicycle commuters has been decreasing slightly as the overall bicycle commuter rate has increased.

State Commuter Mode Share

Bicycling to Work

Highest to Lowest		
1	**Oregon**	**2.3%**
2	**Montana**	**1.4%**
3	**Colorado**	**1.3%**
4	**Idaho**	**1.1%**
5	**Alaska**	**1.0%**
6	**California**	**1.0%**
7	**Arizona**	**1.0%**
8	**Hawaii**	**0.9%**
9	**Wyoming**	**0.9%**
10	**Washington**	**0.9%**
11	Utah	0.8%
12	Vermont	0.7%
13	Wisconsin	0.7%
14	New Mexico	0.7%
15	Massachusetts	0.7%
16	Minnesota	0.7%
17	Florida	0.6%
18	Illinois	0.6%
19	North Dakota	0.5%
20	South Dakota	0.5%
21	Maine	0.5%
22	New York	0.5%
23	Nevada	0.5%
24	Iowa	0.5%
25	Nebraska	0.5%
26	Indiana	0.4%
27	Rhode Island	0.4%
28	Michigan	0.4%
29	Pennsylvania	0.4%
30	Louisiana	0.4%
31	Kansas	0.4%
32	New Jersey	0.3%
33	Virginia	0.3%
34	South Carolina	0.3%
35	Ohio	0.3%
36	Delaware	0.3%
37	Connecticut	0.3%
38	Maryland	0.3%
39	Oklahoma	0.3%
40	Texas	0.2%
41	North Carolina	0.2%
42	New Hampshire	0.2%
43	Georgia	0.2%
44	Kentucky	0.2%
45	Missouri	0.2%
46	Tennessee	0.1%
47	Alabama	0.1%
48	Arkanasas	0.1%
49	West Virginia	0.1%
50	Mississippi	0.1%

Walking to Work

Highest to Lowest		
1	**Alaska**	**7.9%**
2	**New York**	**6.4%**
3	**Vermont**	**5.8%**
4	**Hawaii**	**4.8%**
5	**Montana**	**4.8%**
6	**Massachusetts**	**4.7%**
7	**South Dakota**	**4.3%**
8	**Oregon**	**3.9%**
9	**Pennsylvania**	**3.9%**
10	**Maine**	**3.8%**
11	North Dakota	3.8%
12	Iowa	3.6%
13	Rhode Island	3.6%
14	Wyoming	3.4%
15	Washington	3.4%
16	Wisconsin	3.3%
17	New Jersey	3.2%
18	Illinois	3.2%
19	Idaho	3.1%
20	Colorado	3.0%
21	Connecticut	3.0%
22	Nebraska	2.9%
23	New Hampshire	2.9%
24	Minnesota	2.8%
25	West Virginia	2.8%
26	California	2.8%
27	Utah	2.8%
28	Kansas	2.5%
29	Virginia	2.4%
30	Maryland	2.4%
31	New Mexico	2.4%
32	Delaware	2.3%
33	Ohio	2.3%
34	Michigan	2.2%
35	Arizona	2.2%
36	Indiana	2.1%
37	Kentucky	2.1%
38	South Carolina	2.0%
39	Missouri	2.0%
40	Louisiana	2.0%
41	Nevada	2.0%
42	Arkansas	1.8%
43	Oklahoma	1.8%
44	North Carolina	1.8%
45	Mississippi	1.7%
46	Texas	1.7%
47	Florida	1.6%
48	Georgia	1.6%
49	Tennessee	1.4%
50	Alabama	1.2%

Source: ACS 2009–2011

Large City Commuter Mode Share

Bicycling to Work

Highest to Lowest		
1	**Portland, OR**	**6.1%**
2	**Minneapolis**	**3.6%**
3	**Seattle**	**3.4%**
4	**San Francisco**	**3.3%**
5	**Washington, DC**	**2.9%**
6	**Tucson**	**2.5%**
7	**Oakland**	**2.5%**
8	**New Orleans**	**2.3%**
9	**Sacramento**	**2.3%**
10	**Denver**	**2.2%**
11	Philadelphia	1.9%
12	Boston	1.7%
13	Honolulu	1.6%
14	Albuquerque	1.4%
15	Austin	1.3%
16	Chicago	1.3%
17	Long Beach	1.2%
18	Atlanta	1.1%
19	Los Angeles	1.0%
20	Mesa	1.0%
21	San Diego	0.9%
22	San Jose	0.9%
23	Baltimore	0.8%
24	Fresno	0.8%
25	Miami	0.7%
26	New York City	0.7%
27	Phoenix	0.7%
28	Virginia Beach	0.7%
29	Colorado Springs	0.7%
30	Milwaukee	0.7%
31	Cleveland	0.6%
32	Columbus	0.6%
33	Raleigh	0.5%
34	Indianapolis	0.5%
35	Tulsa	0.4%
36	Houston	0.4%
37	Louisville	0.4%
38	Las Vegas	0.4%
39	Jacksonville	0.4%
40	Nashville	0.3%
41	Kansas City, MO	0.3%
42	Wichita	0.3%
43	Detroit	0.3%
44	San Antonio	0.2%
45	Omaha	0.2%
46	Memphis	0.2%
47	Oklahoma City	0.2%
48	Dallas	0.2%
49	Charlotte	0.2%
50	El Paso	0.2%
51	Arlington, TX	0.1%
52	Fort Worth	0.1%

Walking to Work

Highest to Lowest		
1	**Boston**	**15.0%**
2	**Washington, DC**	**11.8%**
3	**New York City**	**10.3%**
4	**San Francisco**	**9.9%**
5	**Honolulu**	**9.7%**
6	**Philadelphia**	**8.8%**
7	**Seattle**	**8.6%**
8	**Baltimore**	**6.8%**
9	**Minneapolis**	**6.3%**
10	**Chicago**	**6.3%**
11	New Orleans	5.6%
12	Portland, OR	5.3%
13	Milwaukee	5.2%
14	Atlanta	4.5%
15	Cleveland	4.4%
16	Oakland	4.2%
17	Denver	4.1%
18	Miami	3.9%
19	Los Angeles	3.7%
20	Tucson	3.7%
21	Detroit	3.2%
22	Sacramento	3.0%
23	San Diego	3.0%
24	Colorado Springs	3.0%
25	Columbus	2.9%
26	Omaha	2.8%
27	Long Beach	2.8%
28	Austin	2.6%
29	Virginia Beach	2.5%
30	Kansas City, MO	2.2%
31	Charlotte	2.2%
32	Houston	2.2%
33	San Antonio	2.1%
34	Louisville	2.1%
35	Indianapolis	2.0%
36	Raleigh	2.0%
37	Fresno	2.0%
38	Phoenix	2.0%
39	Albuquerque	2.0%
40	El Paso	2.0%
41	Las Vegas	1.9%
42	Tulsa	1.9%
43	Memphis	1.9%
44	Mesa	1.8%
45	San Jose	1.8%
46	Dallas	1.8%
47	Nashville	1.8%
48	Arlington, TX	1.8%
49	Oklahoma City	1.6%
50	Wichita	1.3%
51	Jacksonville	1.3%
52	Fort Worth	1.2%

Share of Commuters Who Walk or Bicycle to Work: States

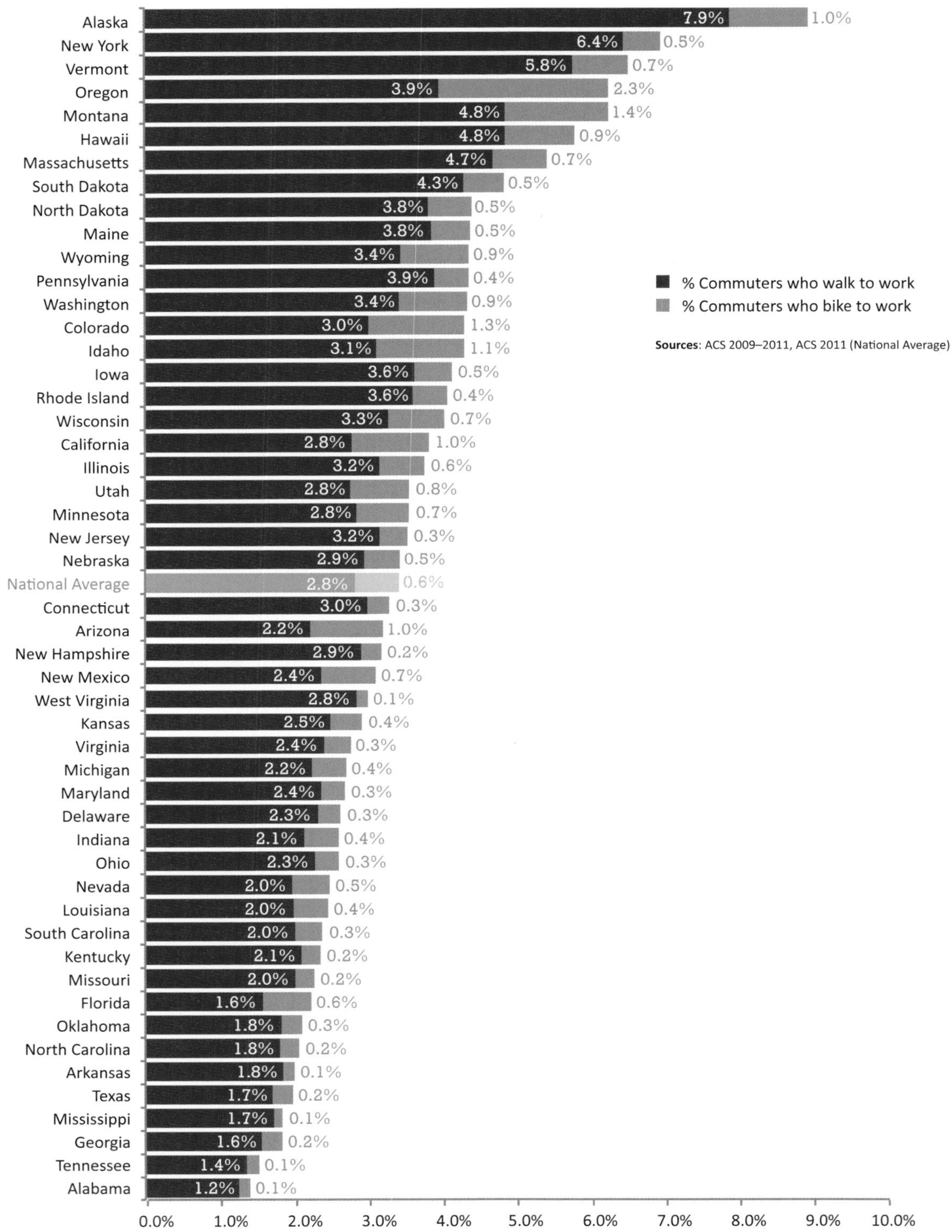

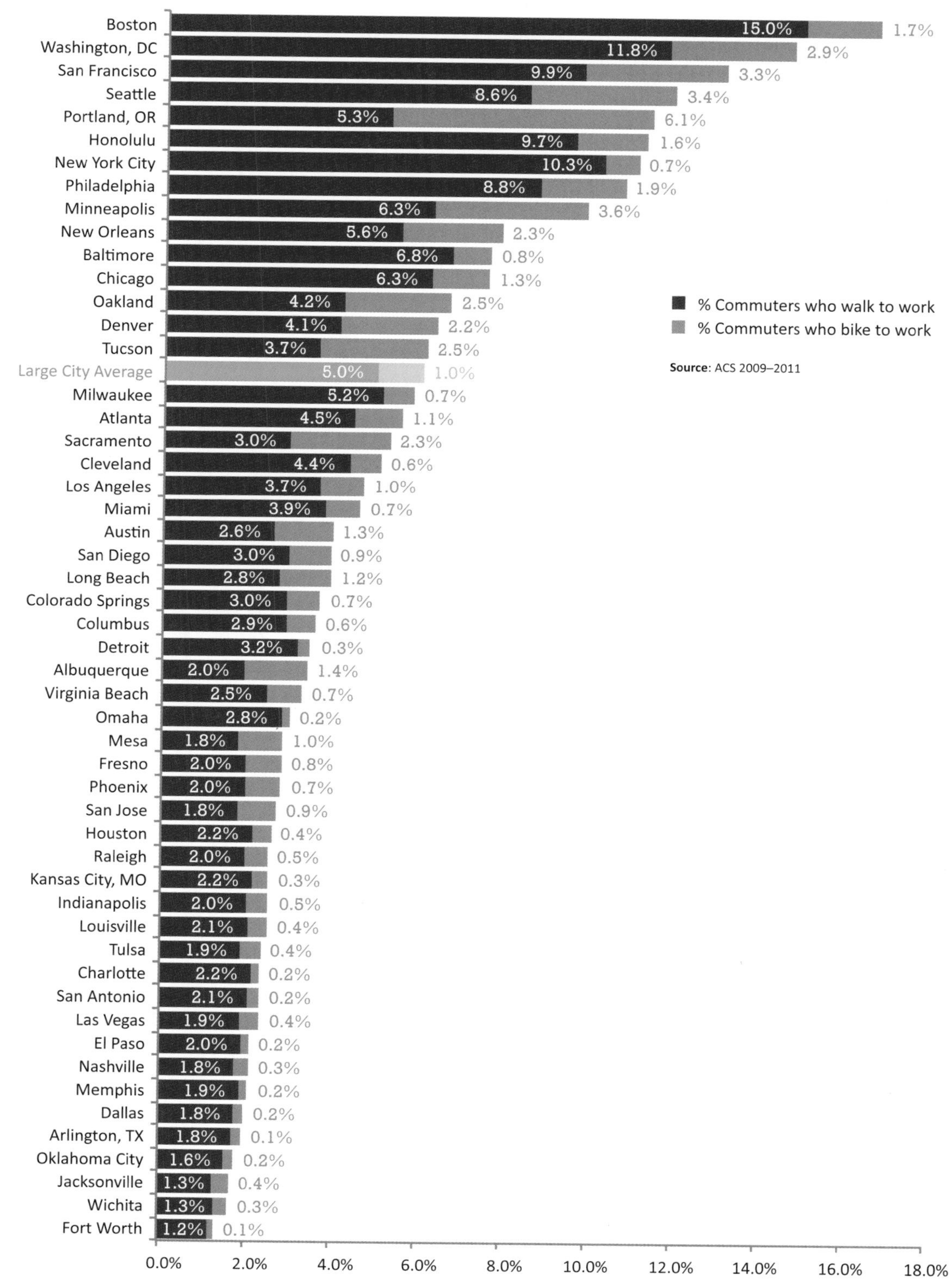
Share of Commuters Who Walk or Bicycle to Work: Large Cities
Boston 15.0% 1.7%
Washington, DC 11.8% 2.9%
San Francisco 9.9% 3.3%
Seattle 8.6% 3.4%
Portland, OR 5.3% 6.1%
Honolulu 9.7% 1.6%
New York City 10.3% 0.7%
Philadelphia 8.8% 1.9%
Minneapolis 6.3% 3.6%
New Orleans 5.6% 2.3%
Baltimore 6.8% 0.8%
Chicago 6.3% 1.3%
Oakland 4.2% 2.5%
Denver 4.1% 2.2%
Tucson 3.7% 2.5%
Large City Average 5.0% 1.0%
Milwaukee 5.2% 0.7%
Atlanta 4.5% 1.1%
Sacramento 3.0% 2.3%
Cleveland 4.4% 0.6%
Los Angeles 3.7% 1.0%
Miami 3.9% 0.7%
Austin 2.6% 1.3%
San Diego 3.0% 0.9%
Long Beach 2.8% 1.2%
Colorado Springs 3.0% 0.7%
Columbus 2.9% 0.6%
Detroit 3.2% 0.3%
Albuquerque 2.0% 1.4%
Virginia Beach 2.5% 0.7%
Omaha 2.8% 0.2%
Mesa 1.8% 1.0%
Fresno 2.0% 0.8%
Phoenix 2.0% 0.7%
San Jose 1.8% 0.9%
Houston 2.2% 0.4%
Raleigh 2.0% 0.5%
Kansas City, MO 2.2% 0.3%
Indianapolis 2.0% 0.5%
Louisville 2.1% 0.4%
Tulsa 1.9% 0.4%
Charlotte 2.2% 0.2%
San Antonio 2.1% 0.2%
Las Vegas 1.9% 0.4%
El Paso 2.0% 0.2%
Nashville 1.8% 0.3%
Memphis 1.9% 0.2%
Dallas 1.8% 0.2%
Arlington, TX 1.8% 0.1%
Oklahoma City 1.6% 0.2%
Jacksonville 1.3% 0.4%
Wichita 1.3% 0.3%
Fort Worth 1.2% 0.1%
0.0% 2.0% 4.0% 6.0% 8.0% 10.0% 12.0% 14.0% 16.0% 18.0%
% Commuters who walk to work
% Commuters who bike to work
Source: ACS 2009–2011

The gap between men and women also varies largely among major U.S. cities. As stated earlier, most cities have relatively small gaps between numbers of men and women who walk to work. In nearly ¼ of the cities studied, women walk to work at slightly higher rates than men. Philadelphia and Honolulu show the greatest percentage of pedestrian commuters who are women (both with 55%). The population of Virginia Beach is split evenly between men and women (49% and 51%, respectively), yet the city has the lowest percentage of pedestrian commuters who are women—just 28% (ACS, 2011).

Nationally, men make up 73% of bicycle commuters in the U.S. and 71% in major U.S. cities. According to ACS estimates, Fresno, Philadelphia, and Memphis have the highest percent of women commuters bicycling to work (between 40% and 41%). The vast majority of bicycle commuters in El Paso, Dallas, and Las Vegas are male (93% and higher), giving these cities the greatest gender divide among bicyclists. Low sample sizes make these estimates of gender distribution unstable and imprecise.

Chicago, IL. Photo by Steven E. Gross. Courtesy of PeopleForBikes

Gender Differences: Bicycling to Work in States and Large Cities

	% commuters by bicycle	% men	% women
Alabama	0.1%	76%	24%
Alaska	1.0%	76%	24%
Arizona	1.0%	77%	23%
Arkansas	0.1%	74%	26%
California	1.0%	74%	26%
Colorado	1.3%	71%	29%
Connecticut	0.3%	76%	24%
Delaware	0.3%	78%	22%
Florida	0.6%	73%	27%
Georgia	0.2%	79%	21%
Hawaii	0.9%	70%	30%
Idaho	1.1%	63%	37%
Illinois	0.6%	74%	26%
Indiana	0.4%	76%	24%
Iowa	0.5%	76%	24%
Kansas	0.4%	72%	28%
Kentucky	0.2%	72%	28%
Louisiana	0.4%	73%	27%
Maine	0.5%	69%	31%
Maryland	0.3%	80%	20%
Massachusetts	0.7%	72%	28%
Michigan	0.4%	71%	29%
Minnesota	0.7%	71%	29%
Mississippi	0.1%	78%	22%
Missouri	0.2%	75%	25%
Montana	1.4%	62%	38%
Nebraska	0.5%	77%	23%
Nevada	0.5%	85%	15%
New Hampshire	0.2%	77%	23%
New Jersey	0.3%	80%	20%
New Mexico	0.7%	73%	27%
New York	0.5%	76%	24%
North Carolina	0.2%	77%	23%
North Dakota	0.5%	73%	27%
Ohio	0.3%	73%	27%
Oklahoma	0.3%	78%	22%
Oregon	2.3%	66%	34%
Pennsylvania	0.4%	69%	31%
Rhode Island	0.4%	77%	23%
South Carolina	0.3%	74%	26%
South Dakota	0.5%	72%	28%
Tennessee	0.1%	75%	25%
Texas	0.2%	80%	20%
Utah	0.8%	73%	27%
Vermont	0.7%	74%	26%
Virgina	0.3%	74%	26%
Washington	0.9%	72%	28%
West Virginia	0.1%	76%	24%
Wisconsin	0.7%	69%	31%
Wyoming	0.9%	58%	42%
State average	0.6%	73%	27%
State median	0.5%	74%	26%
High	2.3%	85%	42%
Low	0.1%	58%	15%

	% commuters by bicycle	% men	% women
Albuquerque	1.4%	69%	31%
Arlington, TX	0.1%	90%	10%
Atlanta	1.1%	77%	23%
Austin	1.3%	75%	25%
Baltimore	0.8%	77%	23%
Boston	1.7%	68%	32%
Charlotte	0.2%	62%	38%
Chicago	1.3%	74%	26%
Cleveland	0.6%	81%	19%
Colorado Springs	0.7%	72%	28%
Columbus	0.6%	71%	29%
Dallas	0.2%	95%	5%
Denver	2.2%	68%	32%
Detroit	0.3%	86%	14%
El Paso	0.2%	96%	4%
Fort Worth	0.1%	84%	16%
Fresno	0.8%	59%	41%
Honolulu	1.6%	77%	23%
Houston	0.4%	78%	22%
Indianapolis	0.5%	86%	14%
Jacksonville	0.4%	78%	22%
Kansas City, MO	0.3%	67%	33%
Las Vegas	0.4%	93%	7%
Long Beach	1.2%	78%	22%
Los Angeles	1.0%	78%	22%
Louisville	0.4%	67%	33%
Memphis	0.2%	60%	40%
Mesa	1.0%	80%	20%
Miami	0.7%	69%	31%
Milwaukee	0.7%	77%	23%
Minneapolis	3.6%	65%	35%
Nashville	0.3%	70%	30%
New Orleans	2.3%	63%	37%
New York City	0.7%	75%	25%
Oakland	2.5%	66%	34%
Oklahoma City	0.2%	70%	30%
Omaha	0.2%	91%	9%
Philadelphia	1.9%	60%	40%
Phoenix	0.7%	86%	14%
Portland, OR	6.1%	63%	37%
Raleigh	0.5%	84%	16%
Sacramento	2.3%	65%	35%
San Antonio	0.2%	89%	11%
San Diego	0.9%	71%	29%
San Francisco	3.3%	68%	32%
San Jose	0.9%	82%	18%
Seattle	3.4%	70%	30%
Tucson	2.5%	70%	30%
Tulsa	0.4%	90%	10%
Virginia Beach	0.7%	62%	38%
Washington, DC	2.9%	64%	36%
Wichita	0.3%	83%	17%
Large cities average	1.0%	71%	29%
Large cities median	0.7%	75%	26%
High	6.1%	96%	41%
Low	0.1%	59%	4%

Sources: ACS 2009–2011, ACS 2011 (National Average)

Gender and Income Differences: Walking to Work in States

	% commuters by foot	% men	% women	Percent of workers who walk to work, by annual income (total = 100%) Less than $15,000	$15,000-$34,999	$35,000-$64,999	$65,000+
Alabama	1.2%	58%	42%	54%	28%	11%	7%
Alaska	7.9%	60%	40%	33%	35%	19%	13%
Arizona	2.2%	53%	47%	44%	32%	15%	8%
Arkansas	1.8%	60%	40%	52%	31%	9%	8%
California	2.8%	52%	48%	42%	31%	16%	11%
Colorado	3.0%	58%	42%	46%	29%	15%	10%
Connecticut	3.0%	56%	44%	50%	26%	15%	10%
Delaware	2.3%	53%	47%	48%	27%	15%	10%
Florida	1.6%	56%	44%	48%	33%	13%	7%
Georgia	1.6%	58%	42%	48%	32%	12%	8%
Hawaii	4.8%	52%	48%	33%	36%	22%	9%
Idaho	3.1%	58%	42%	45%	35%	13%	7%
Illinois	3.2%	53%	47%	44%	27%	16%	13%
Indiana	2.1%	55%	45%	56%	26%	12%	6%
Iowa	3.6%	55%	45%	52%	26%	16%	6%
Kansas	2.5%	56%	44%	49%	31%	14%	6%
Kentucky	2.1%	56%	44%	57%	27%	11%	5%
Louisiana	2.0%	55%	45%	50%	31%	12%	7%
Maine	3.8%	51%	49%	50%	30%	13%	7%
Maryland	2.4%	51%	49%	46%	27%	16%	11%
Massachusetts	4.7%	49%	51%	42%	25%	17%	16%
Michigan	2.2%	54%	46%	57%	24%	12%	7%
Minnesota	2.8%	56%	44%	46%	28%	17%	10%
Mississippi	1.7%	58%	42%	53%	32%	10%	4%
Missouri	2.0%	55%	45%	54%	27%	14%	5%
Montana	4.8%	56%	44%	39%	34%	18%	9%
Nebraska	2.9%	51%	49%	48%	28%	18%	6%
Nevada	2.0%	57%	43%	39%	41%	12%	7%
New Hampshire	2.9%	49%	51%	49%	27%	13%	11%
New Jersey	3.2%	53%	47%	39%	34%	16%	11%
New Mexico	2.4%	58%	42%	44%	30%	16%	10%
New York	6.4%	50%	50%	35%	28%	18%	19%
North Carolina	1.8%	63%	37%	47%	34%	12%	7%
North Dakota	3.8%	57%	43%	46%	31%	15%	8%
Ohio	2.3%	54%	46%	56%	26%	12%	6%
Oklahoma	1.8%	58%	42%	53%	30%	11%	6%
Oregon	3.9%	53%	47%	44%	32%	16%	8%
Pennsylvania	3.9%	50%	50%	47%	28%	15%	10%
Rhode Island	3.6%	54%	46%	53%	26%	12%	8%
South Carolina	2.0%	59%	41%	54%	30%	12%	4%
South Dakota	4.3%	57%	43%	42%	32%	17%	8%
Tennessee	1.4%	60%	40%	50%	30%	13%	7%
Texas	1.7%	57%	43%	50%	31%	12%	7%
Utah	2.8%	52%	48%	60%	23%	11%	6%
Vermont	5.8%	53%	47%	49%	26%	16%	9%
Virginia	2.4%	57%	43%	43%	30%	14%	12%
Washington	3.4%	55%	45%	38%	31%	18%	13%
West Virginia	2.8%	56%	44%	56%	27%	12%	6%
Wisconsin	3.3%	54%	46%	52%	27%	15%	7%
Wyoming	3.4%	59%	41%	37%	30%	23%	10%
State average	2.8%	54%	46%	45%	29%	15%	11%
State median	2.8%	55%	45%	48%	30%	15%	8%
High	7.9%	63%	51%	60%	41%	23%	19%
Low	1.2%	49%	37%	33%	23%	9%	4%

Source: ACS 2009–2011 **Note**: Due to rounding, some of these data do not appear to add up to 100%.

Gender and Income Differences: Walking to Work in Large Cities

% commuters by foot	% men	% women	Percent of workers who walk to work, by annual income (total = 100%)				
			Less than $15,000	$15,000-$34,999	$35,000-$64,999	$65,000+	
2.0%	54%	46%	48%	31%	11%	10%	Albuquerque
1.8%	66%	34%	49%	40%	9%	3%	Arlington, TX
4.5%	60%	40%	41%	29%	16%	14%	Atlanta
2.6%	57%	43%	48%	29%	14%	9%	Austin
6.8%	46%	54%	41%	30%	20%	9%	Baltimore
15.0%	51%	49%	34%	19%	21%	26%	Boston
2.2%	56%	44%	44%	24%	14%	19%	Charlotte
6.3%	48%	52%	32%	25%	22%	21%	Chicago
4.4%	49%	51%	50%	31%	14%	6%	Cleveland
3.0%	56%	44%	51%	28%	14%	7%	Colorado Springs
2.9%	55%	45%	56%	26%	12%	6%	Columbus
1.8%	51%	49%	36%	35%	19%	10%	Dallas
4.1%	54%	46%	32%	26%	25%	18%	Denver
3.2%	61%	39%	57%	26%	11%	6%	Detroit
2.0%	52%	48%	56%	31%	10%	3%	El Paso
1.2%	52%	48%	53%	27%	12%	8%	Fort Worth
2.0%	49%	51%	49%	36%	10%	4%	Fresno
9.7%	45%	55%	32%	33%	23%	11%	Honolulu
2.2%	58%	42%	46%	32%	14%	9%	Houston
2.0%	57%	43%	47%	37%	10%	6%	Indianapolis
1.3%	59%	41%	45%	40%	10%	5%	Jacksonville
2.2%	59%	41%	36%	39%	17%	8%	Kansas City, MO
1.9%	58%	42%	37%	50%	8%	5%	Las Vegas
2.8%	47%	53%	37%	44%	14%	6%	Long Beach
3.7%	51%	49%	48%	30%	13%	9%	Los Angeles
2.1%	59%	41%	51%	31%	10%	8%	Louisville
1.9%	60%	40%	55%	28%	12%	6%	Memphis
1.8%	52%	48%	46%	39%	7%	8%	Mesa
3.9%	56%	44%	38%	33%	13%	16%	Miami
5.2%	55%	45%	51%	29%	12%	7%	Milwaukee
6.3%	58%	42%	43%	25%	20%	13%	Minneapolis
1.8%	55%	45%	48%	27%	16%	9%	Nashville
5.6%	53%	47%	45%	29%	16%	10%	New Orleans
10.3%	47%	53%	27%	27%	21%	25%	New York City
4.2%	55%	45%	36%	23%	25%	16%	Oakland
1.6%	57%	43%	50%	35%	7%	8%	Oklahoma City
2.8%	52%	48%	49%	27%	17%	6%	Omaha
8.8%	45%	55%	34%	28%	21%	17%	Philadelphia
2.0%	55%	45%	40%	33%	16%	11%	Phoenix
5.3%	53%	47%	36%	33%	19%	12%	Portland, OR
2.0%	54%	46%	46%	41%	9%	4%	Raleigh
3.0%	48%	52%	32%	32%	20%	16%	Sacramento
2.1%	56%	44%	58%	27%	11%	4%	San Antonio
3.0%	57%	43%	41%	29%	20%	10%	San Diego
9.9%	49%	51%	22%	25%	26%	28%	San Francisco
1.8%	52%	48%	40%	27%	20%	14%	San Jose
8.6%	54%	46%	31%	27%	22%	20%	Seattle
3.7%	48%	52%	50%	29%	17%	4%	Tucson
1.9%	51%	49%	53%	34%	9%	4%	Tulsa
2.5%	72%	28%	41%	49%	6%	4%	Virginia Beach
11.8%	52%	48%	18%	16%	25%	41%	Washington, DC
1.3%	59%	41%	47%	35%	14%	3%	Wichita
5.0%	50%	50%	34%	28%	19%	19%	Large cities average
2.8%	54%	46%	45%	30%	14%	9%	Large cities median
15.0%	72%	55%	58%	50%	26%	41%	High
1.2%	45%	28%	18%	16%	6%	3%	Low

Source: ACS 2009–2011 **Note**: Due to rounding, some of these data do not appear to add up to 100%.

New York City, NY. Photo by Several seconds @Flickr

Commuters Walking to Work in Large Cities by Income Level

Annual income
- $65,000 +
- $35,000 - $64,999
- $15,000 - $34,999
- Less than $15,000

Highest and lowest median income among large cities
- △ Highest median income
- ▼ Lowest median income

Source: ACS 2009–2011

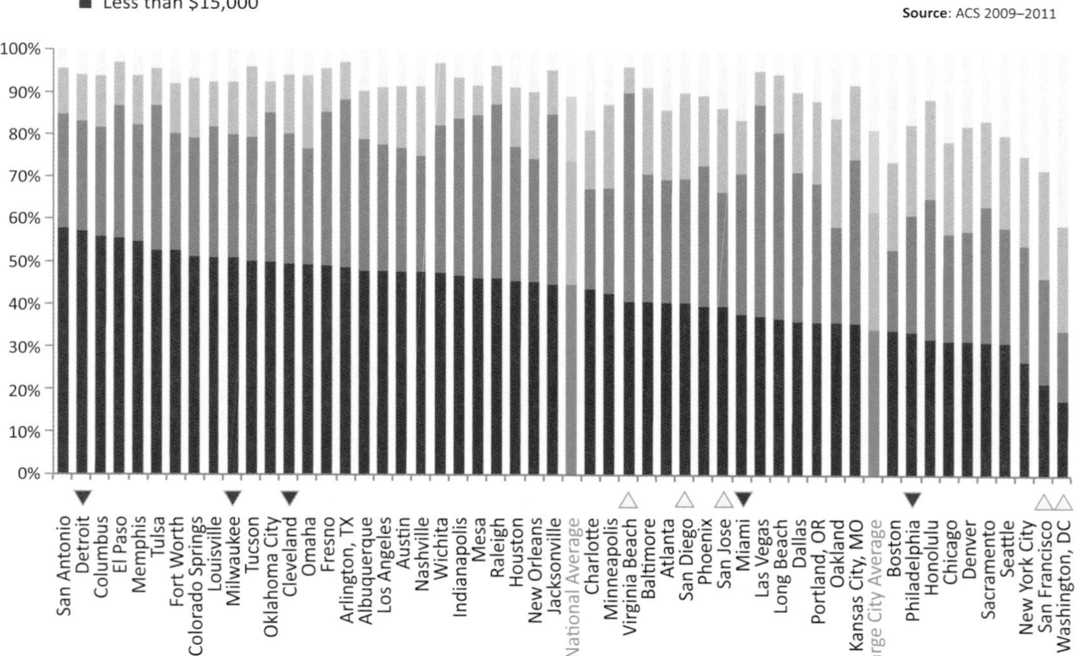

Commuters by Income

While bicycling is distributed evenly among all income groups, lower income workers make up a disproportionate share of those who walk to work. Nationwide data from ACS reveal that nearly 45% of people who walk to work earn less than $15,000 per year. On average, 62% of people who walk to work in the large cities studied for this report earn below $35,000 a year. San Francisco and New York City have the most even income distribution among people who walk to work, with all income groups well-represented.

Despite its high median income, Virginia Beach has the least equal distribution with 90% of pedestrian commuters making less than $35,000 in annual income. Washington, DC, shows an unusual concentration of higher income commuters traveling by foot, with 41% of pedestrian commuters making over $65,000.

Ethnicity

People of color are commuting to work by foot at higher rates than white workers. The ACS estimates 11% of commuters walking to work in 2011 were African American, and 18% of commuters walking to work were Hispanic. All races and ethnicities, other than those who identify as white, walk to work at disproportionally higher rates.

Commuter Mode Share by Race and Ethnicity

Distribution of U.S. Workers

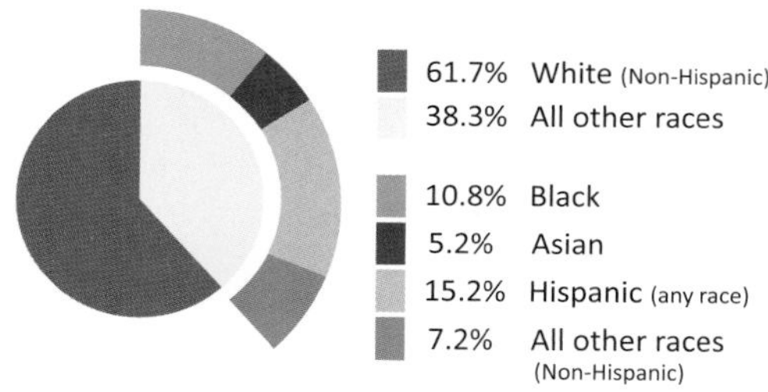

Commuters Who Walk to Work

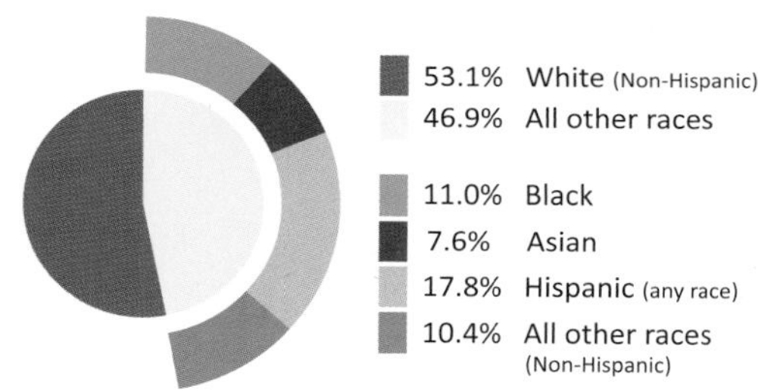

Sources: ACS 2011 **Notes**: ACS does not provide data for bicycling commuters by race or ethnicity. Due to rounding, some of these data do not appear to add up to 100%.

New York City, NY. Photo by Ed Yourdon @Flickr

Portland, ME. Photo by Jeff Scher

Victoria, BC. Photo by John Luton, Executive Director, Capital Bike and Walk

Possible Influencing Factors

Climate—Weak Relationship

Does climate influence the choice to bicycle? Montana and Alaska, for example, are among states with the coldest temperatures, yet are also among the states with the highest levels of bicycling and walking to work.

The Alliance compared thirty-year climate data (1971–2000) from the National Oceanic Atmospheric Administration (NOAA) with the percentage of work trips by bicycle and foot for the 52 most populous cities. Comparing bicycling and walking rates to average inches of precipitation and average number of days below freezing did not reveal any clear trends. However, a relationship was found between pedestrian commuting and the number of days above 90 degrees Fahrenheit. Cities experiencing a greater number of these 90-degree days were more likely to have lower walking and bicycling rates ($r = -0.44$). Both Mesa and Phoenix, for example, with over 170 days above 90 degrees per year on average, have walking and bicycling commuter rates of 2.8%. In contrast, Seattle which has a cooler, milder climate (only three days above 90 degrees per year) has a bicycling and walking rate of 11.9%.

The lack of statistically significant evidence of climate's impact on bicycling levels has been noted in other studies (Buehler and Pucher, 2011; Heinen et al., 2010; Krizek and Forsyth, 2009; Pucher and Buehler, 2006; Pucher et al., 2011), pointing out much higher rates of bicycling in countries such as Canada, which has lower average year-round temperatures than in the United States.

It seems likely that excessive cold, heat, and rainfall do indeed deter bicycling to some unknown extent, especially among less experienced bicyclists. According to a poll by the San Francisco Bicycle Coalition for their 2008 Report Card on Bicycling, 11% of respondents said that weather kept them from bicycling more than they would otherwise (down from 15% of respondents in 2006, two years earlier). Concerns about bicycle theft, safety, and insufficient carrying capacity were the other top reasons cited for not bicycling more.

Comparing Climate Indicators to Bicycling and Walking Levels

Precipitation

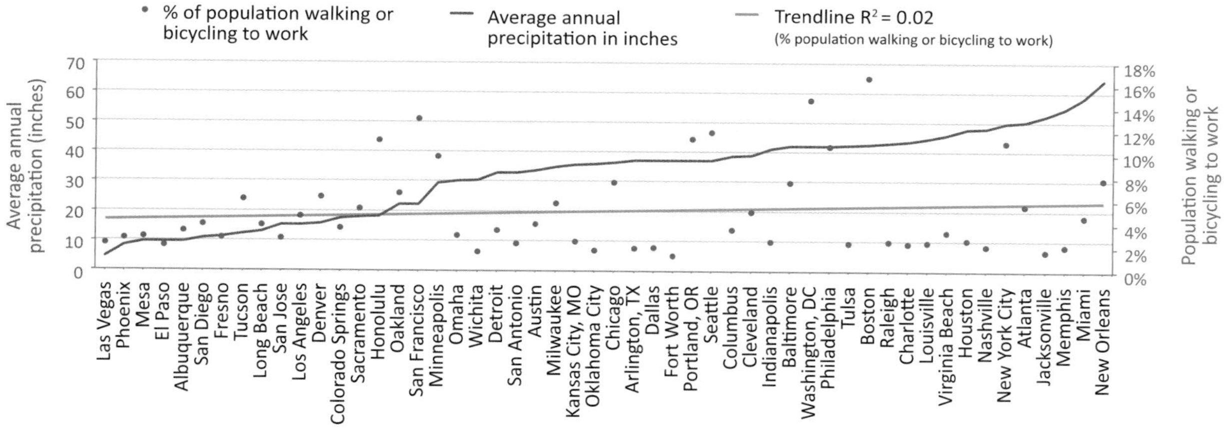

% of population walking or bicycling to work
Average annual precipitation in inches
Trendline $R^2 = 0.02$ (% population walking or bicycling to work)
Average annual precipitation (inches)
0 10 20 30 40 50 60 70
Population walking or bicycling to work
0% 2% 4% 6% 8% 10% 12% 14% 16% 18%
Las Vegas, Phoenix, Mesa, El Paso, Albuquerque, San Diego, Fresno, Tucson, Long Beach, San Jose, Los Angeles, Denver, Colorado Springs, Sacramento, Honolulu, Oakland, San Francisco, Minneapolis, Omaha, Wichita, Detroit, San Antonio, Austin, Milwaukee, Kansas City, MO, Oklahoma City, Chicago, Arlington, TX, Dallas, Fort Worth, Portland, OR, Seattle, Columbus, Cleveland, Indianapolis, Baltimore, Washington, DC, Philadelphia, Tulsa, Boston, Raleigh, Charlotte, Louisville, Virginia Beach, Houston, Nashville, New York City, Atlanta, Jacksonville, Memphis, Miami, New Orleans

Temperatures Below Freezing (32°F)

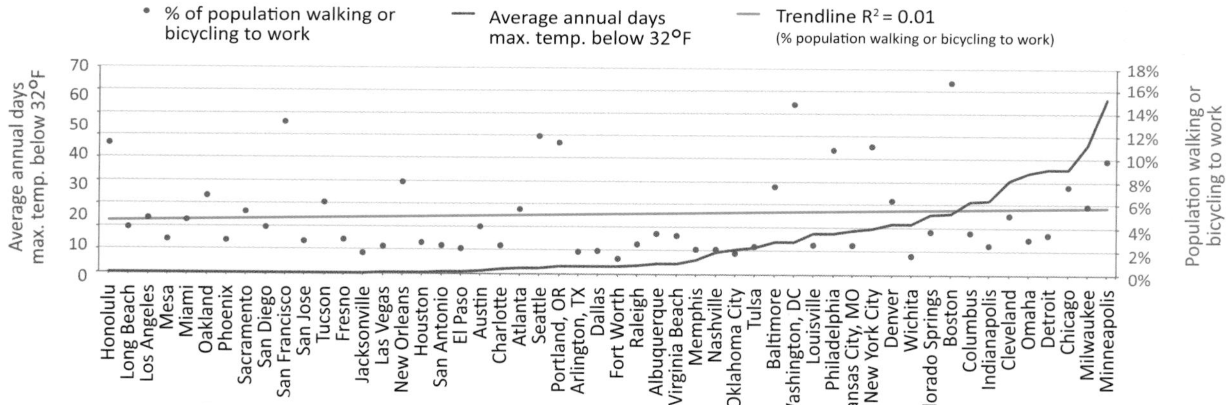

% of population walking or bicycling to work
Average annual days max. temp. below 32°F
Trendline $R^2 = 0.01$ (% population walking or bicycling to work)
Average annual days max. temp. below 32°F
0 10 20 30 40 50 60 70
Population walking or bicycling to work
0% 2% 4% 6% 8% 10% 12% 14% 16% 18%
Honolulu, Long Beach, Los Angeles, Mesa, Miami, Oakland, Phoenix, Sacramento, San Diego, San Francisco, San Jose, Tucson, Fresno, Jacksonville, Las Vegas, New Orleans, Houston, San Antonio, El Paso, Austin, Charlotte, Atlanta, Seattle, Portland, OR, Arlington, TX, Dallas, Fort Worth, Raleigh, Albuquerque, Virginia Beach, Memphis, Nashville, Oklahoma City, Tulsa, Baltimore, Washington, DC, Louisville, Philadelphia, Kansas City, MO, New York City, Denver, Wichita, Colorado Springs, Boston, Columbus, Indianapolis, Cleveland, Omaha, Detroit, Chicago, Milwaukee, Minneapolis

Temperatures Above 90°F

% of population walking or bicycling to work
Average annual days max. temp. above 90°F
Trendline $R^2 = 0.23$ (% population walking or bicycling to work)
Average annual days max. temp. above 90°F
0 20 40 60 80 100 120 140 160 180 200
Population walking or bicycling to work
0% 2% 4% 6% 8% 10% 12% 14% 16% 18%
Seattle, San Diego, Oakland, San Francisco, Cleveland, Milwaukee, Tulsa, Detroit, Portland, OR, Minneapolis, Boston, Columbus, Colorado Springs, Indianapolis, Chicago, New York City, San Jose, Long Beach, Philadelphia, Los Angeles, Baltimore, Washington, DC, Louisville, Omaha, Virginia Beach, Denver, Honolulu, Raleigh, Charlotte, Atlanta, Kansas City, MO, Nashville, Albuquerque, Wichita, Miami, Memphis, Oklahoma City, Sacramento, New Orleans, Jacksonville, Houston, Arlington, TX, Dallas, Fort Worth, Fresno, El Paso, Austin, San Antonio, Las Vegas, Tucson, Phoenix, Mesa

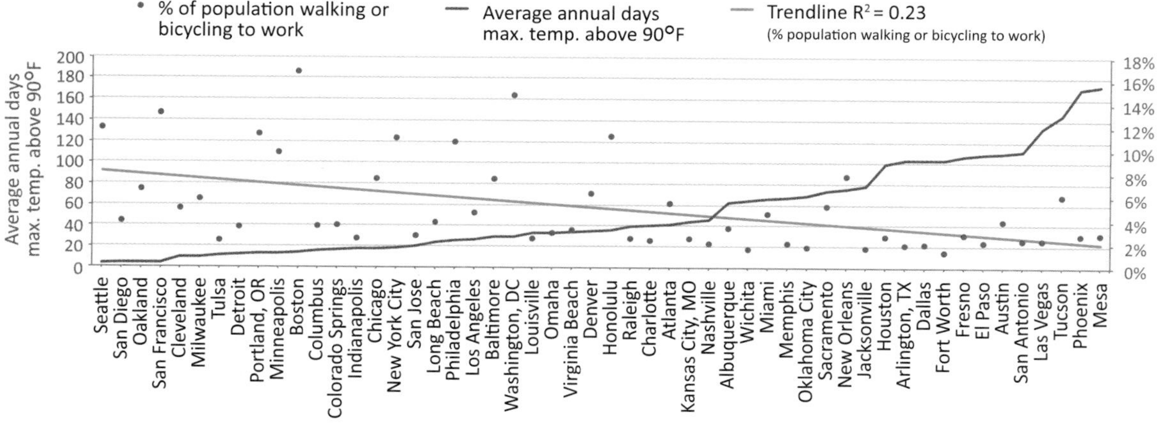

Sources: (All charts on this page) ACS 2009–2011, NOAA 1971–2000

Car Ownership—Strong Relationship

According to the 2011 ACS, cities with the highest levels of bicycling and walking have lower car ownership rates. Although the statistical relationship is strong (r = 0.77), the causation likely runs in both directions. Those who walk or bicycle a lot are less likely to need or want a car, and those who do not own a car are more likely to need to walk or bicycle for some trips.

Minority communities are less likely to have access to a car. Nineteen percent of African Americans and 13.7% of Latinos lack access to a car, compared to 4.6% of whites. The difference is even greater in low-income minority communities, where 33% of low-income African Americans and 25% of low-income Latinos lack access to a car, compared to 12.7% of low-income whites (PolicyLink, July 2009). The data suggest that these communities rely more heavily on nonmotorized transportation or public transit for daily travel, and so are likely to bicycle and walk at higher rates.

Atlanta, GA. Photo courtesy of Transportation for America

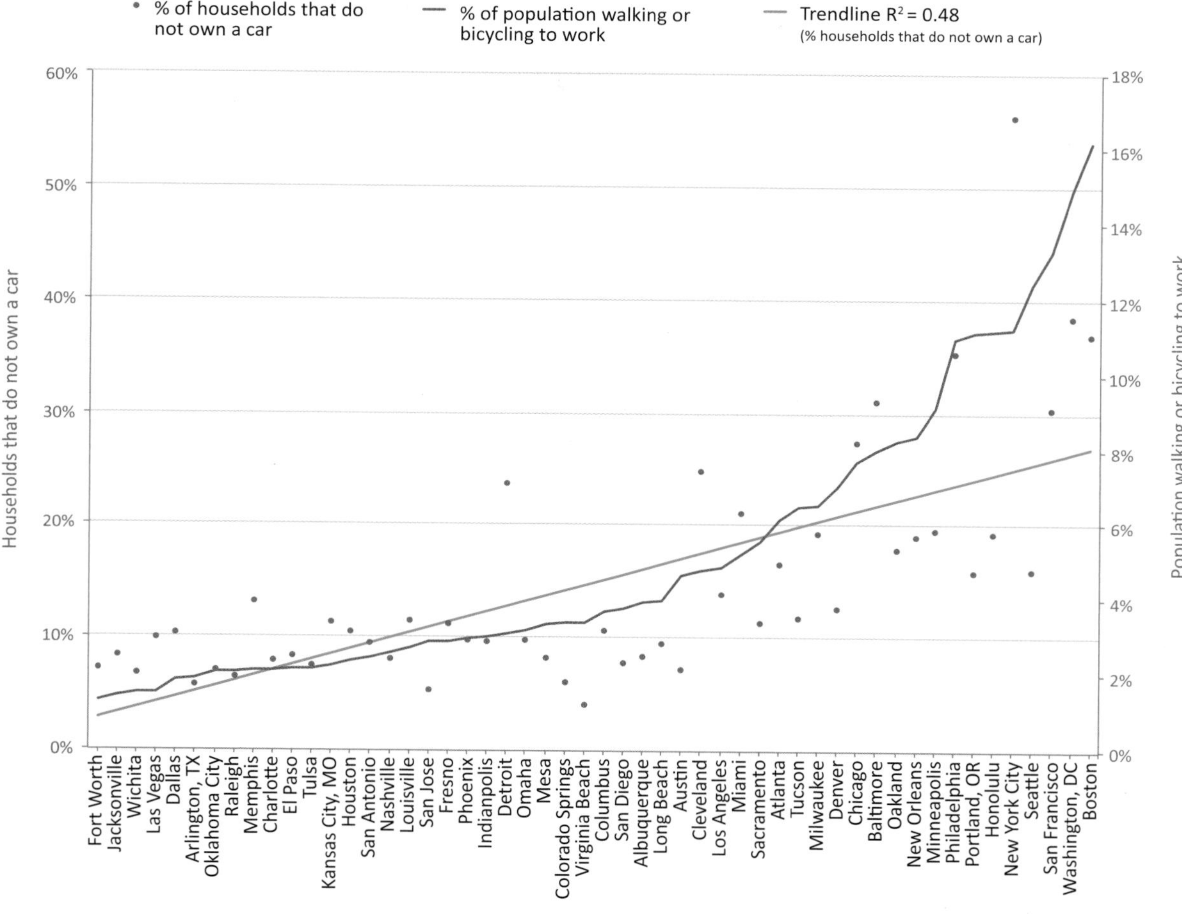

Source: ACS 2011

National Counting Efforts

by Andrea Hamre, Virginia Tech

The National Bicycle and Pedestrian Documentation Project (NBPDP), founded in 2002, is a joint effort of Alta Planning + Design and the Institute of Transportation Engineers (ITE) Pedestrian and Bicycle Council. The project addresses the lack of documentation of bicycle and pedestrian travel trends by developing and providing access to guidance materials for communities conducting nonmotorized mode share counts. All project materials are freely available on the NBPDP website (*BikePedDocumentation.org*).

This nationwide effort provides a consistent methodology for data collection that is based on screen line and intersection manual counts, as well as traveler intercept surveys. The NBPDP methodology is scalable and flexible, enabling communities to follow the methodology while adapting it to their unique capacities and needs. It can be implemented by local jurisdictions, advocacy organizations, and other interested citizens.

Los Angeles, CA. Photo by Andrew Yun @ Flickr

Resources made available through the project include count and survey training materials, sample count logs and surveys, an extrapolation workbook with supporting documentation, and additional information on bicycle and pedestrian automatic counting equipment.

The extrapolation workbook allows researchers to estimate monthly and annual travel based on two-hour manual count periods. In addition, the NBPDP offers free summary reports to those communities using Eco-Counter automatic count technology in exchange for submission of the count data to the NBPDP.

A number of communities have successfully developed estimates for long-term trends using the NBPDP methodology. The annual count and survey efforts, underway since 2006 in San Jose, CA, have helped the community document annual increases in bicycle and pedestrian travel. Data from the count showed a 12.1% increase between 2011 and 2012, and contributed to successful grant applications and budget requests.

Arlington County, VA, initially gained support for its extensive automatic counter network via quarterly manual counts beginning in 2008, and has since continued to supplement its automatic counter data with annual manual counts using the NBPDP methodology.

In addition, a research team at the University of Idaho has introduced a method to estimate directional bicycle volumes throughout a street network using NBPDP count data.

The NBPDP hopes to eventually host and make available a database of documentation submissions from across the U.S. For more information about the project and to download resources, visit *BikePedDocumentation.org*.

Seattle, WA. Photo by Seattle Department of Transportation

Local Counting Efforts

Many states and cities conduct their own surveys to find out their local mode share of bicycling and walking. Of the 52 most populous cities surveyed, 43 have completed counts of bicyclists, and 37 have completed counts of pedestrians. Approximately 40% of these cities completed counts in 2012, and 85% percent have conducted counts since 2007.

Thirty-eight states have conducted counts on bicyclists and 36 states have counted pedestrians.

The 2014 benchmarking survey (collecting data for 2011 and 2012) recorded three types of counts in particular: commuter counts, household surveys, and cordon counts. In addition to these, many cities have conducted other types of counts including those using automated counters, those using outdoor video cameras, and other types of "spot" counts, all of which are included in this updated report.

These local efforts to track mode share help decision makers and advocates understand on a deeper level who is walking and bicycling in a defined area. However, unlike counting motorized traffic, there is no standardized methodology for conducting these counts of bicyclists and pedestrians. Further, the frequency of conducting counts varies among states and cities. These discrepancies make it difficult to compare results consistently.

Types of Mode Share Counts Recorded in the Benchmarking Survey

Varying Count Methods

There are many different ways to conduct transportation counts. Some methods use powered equipment such as laser beams, heat sensors, infrared cameras, and inductive loops; others use human observers who document what they see. Often, with in-person counts, surveyors will conduct an intercept survey by stopping a percentage of passersby to gather more information about the travelers.

Commuter Counts

Counting people who bicycle or walk to work generally requires an intercept survey to identify the purpose of the trip. The survey is often completed verbally by stopping travelers to ask their destination, or completed as a questionnaire on paper or online. Sometimes commuter counts are conducted by placing the counters (human or mechanical) on routes that are known to be commuter heavy.

Cordon Counts

Cordon counts are conducted to track the number of travelers who cross a specified line into or out of a designated area, such as a neighborhood or district, that is "cordoned off."

Household Survey

These surveys record bicycling and walking habits of an entire household. Surveyors contact the households by phone, by mail, or online.

Counting Bicyclists and Pedestrians in States

	Commuter count includes:		Household survey includes:		Cordon count includes:		Other count (see page 59 for description)
	Bikes	Peds	Bikes	Peds	Bikes	Peds	
Arizona							✓
California			✓ (1)	✓ (1)			
Colorado	✓	✓					✓
Delaware			✓	✓			
Florida			✓ (1)	✓ (1)	✓	✓	✓
Georgia			✓ (1)	✓ (1)			
Hawaii	✓		✓	✓			
Idaho					✓	✓	
Illinois							✓
Indiana			✓ (1)	✓ (1)			
Iowa			✓ (1)	✓ (1)			✓
Kentucky							✓
Louisiana							✓
Maine							✓
Maryland		✓			✓	✓	✓
Massachusetts	✓	✓	✓	✓	✓	✓	
Michigan							✓
Minnesota			✓	✓	✓	✓	✓
Mississippi							✓
Missouri					✓	✓	✓
Nebraska							✓
New Jersey	✓	✓	✓	✓	✓	✓	✓
New York	✓		✓ (1)	✓ (1)	✓		✓
North Carolina			✓ (1)	✓ (1)			
Ohio			✓	✓	✓	✓	
Oregon	✓	✓	✓	✓			
Pennsylvania	✓	✓				✓	✓
Rhode Island	✓				✓	✓	✓
South Carolina			✓ (1)	✓ (1)			
South Dakota			✓ (1)	✓ (1)			✓
Tennessee			✓ (1)	✓ (1)			
Texas			✓ (1)	✓ (1)			✓
Utah	✓	✓	✓	✓			
Vermont	✓	✓	✓ (1)	✓ (1)	✓	✓	✓
Virginia	✓	✓	✓ (1)	✓ (1)			
Washington	✓	✓	✓	✓	✓	✓	✓
West Virginia					✓	✓	
Wisconsin			✓ (1)	✓ (1)			✓
Number of states conducting count	12	10	23	23	13	13	23

Source: State Survey 2011/2012. **Notes**: Unanswered survey questions, or responses of "N/A" and "unknown," were taken to mean "no." All empty cells should be understood to be a "no" response. The following states did not indicate in the benchmarking survey that any counts of bicyclists or pedestrians have been conducted: Alabama, Alaska, Arkansas, Connecticut, Kansas, Montana, Nevada, New Hampshire, New Mexico, North Dakota, Oklahoma, and Wyoming. (1) This state purchased an add-on sample for the 2009 National Household Travel Survey (NHTS). Purchasing an add-on sample means the NHTS will survey an additional number of households in that state so that data are based on a higher sample size. This provides higher quality data and allows states to better compare their counts to other states using consistent survey methodology. These states may complete household surveys in addition to the NHTS add-on data. The Benchmarking Project survey for 2014 did not track those that completed both.

Additional Counting Methods in States

	Count includes:		
	Bicycles	Pedestrians	Methodology
Arizona	✓		Inductive loop bicycle counters
Colorado	✓	✓	Electronic, 24-hour, directional counting at 30 locations around the state; monitoring devices are used on both multi-use trails and roads
Florida	✓	✓	Project-specific counts; taken in scoping phase of a given project
Illinois	✓	✓	Counts as part of individual road project design engineering
Iowa	✓		Counts on trails
Kentucky	✓		Random counts on routes known to be popular for bicycle recreation; using equipment that has been modified specifically for bicycle class counts; still in the test phases
Louisiana	✓	✓	A combination of automated counter locations and staffed cordon-count locations in the New Orleans metro area
Maine	✓	✓	Intersection turning movements and tube counts
Maryland	✓	✓	State Highway Administration conducts 13-hour counts for pedestrians at every intersection that needs improvements or upgrades; has resulted in a database of over 5,000 intersections that have been geocoded; Eco-Multi bicycle and pedestrian counter will be used along the BWI Trail
Michigan	✓	✓	Project-specific counts to determine traffic control and detours; counts to determine traffic signal needs
Minnesota	✓		Telephone interviews conducted with a random sample of Minnesota households; inquires about bicycle and pedestrian safety, laws and bicycle ridership
Mississippi	✓	✓	Turning movement counts conducted at various locations as needed
Missouri	✓	✓	Counters of various types, including volunteer counters to conduct manual counts
Nebraska	✓	✓	Human observer, typically for school crossing zones
New Jersey	✓	✓	*Bicycle Activity and Attitudes Survey* given to New Jersey households through a random-digit dialing, anonymous telephone survey
New York	✓		Intersection crossing for individual safety projects
Pennsylvania	✓	✓	Regional nonprofit rideshare program conducted a database survey of their commuter-member database; additional telephone and email surveys were oversampled for targeted areas within the region
Rhode Island	✓	✓	Three-month user survey conducted on bike paths; on-site survey gathered participants' mailing address and mailed a second, more detailed questionnaire
South Dakota	✓	✓	Individual location traffic studies
Texas	✓	✓	Research projects using both static counters and smart phone applications
Vermont	✓	✓	Combination of manual, short-term counts and longer-term (one- to two-week) counts done with automatic infrared counters
Washington	✓	✓	Local-level counts around the state, and project-specific bicyclist and pedestrian counts as needed
Wisconsin	✓	✓	Four pyro-electric counters; trail and bike lane counts of specific segments

Source: State Survey 2011/2012. **Note**: Methodology of these additional counts is self-reported by survey respondents. The Benchmarking Project did not research these methods individually. Unanswered survey questions, or responses of "N/A" and "unknown," were taken to mean "no." All empty cells should be understood to be a "no" response.

Counting Bicyclists and Pedestrians in Large Cities

	Commuter count includes:		Household survey includes:		Cordon count includes:		Other count (see page 61 for description)
	Bicycles	Pedestrians	Bicycles	Pedestrians	Bicycles	Pedestrians	
Albuquerque	✓	✓	✓	✓			
Atlanta	✓		✓	✓			✓
Austin	✓	✓	✓	✓	✓	✓	✓
Baltimore	✓	✓					
Boston					✓		
Charlotte							✓
Chicago	✓	✓	✓	✓	✓		✓
Cleveland							✓
Colorado Springs	✓	✓	✓	✓			✓
Columbus	✓	✓	✓	✓			✓
Dallas							✓
Denver	✓		✓	✓	✓	✓	✓
Detroit	(1)	(1)	(1)	(1)	(1)	(1)	(1)
Honolulu	✓						
Houston					✓		✓
Indianapolis			✓	✓	✓	✓	✓
Kansas City, MO			✓	✓			
Las Vegas		✓					✓
Long Beach	✓	✓			✓	✓	
Los Angeles	✓	✓			✓	✓	
Louisville	✓				✓	✓	✓
Mesa	✓		✓		✓	✓	✓
Miami	✓	✓			✓	✓	
Milwaukee							✓
Minneapolis	✓	✓	✓	✓	✓	✓	✓
Nashville			✓	✓			✓
New Orleans	✓				✓	✓	
New York City	✓				✓		✓
Oakland							✓
Omaha	✓	✓			✓	✓	
Philadelphia	✓	✓	✓	✓	✓	✓	✓
Phoenix							✓
Portland, OR	✓		✓	✓			✓
Raleigh							✓
Sacramento	✓						
San Antonio			✓	✓			✓
San Diego							✓
San Francisco	✓		✓		✓		✓
San Jose	✓	✓			✓	✓	✓
Seattle	✓				✓		✓
Tucson	✓	✓					
Washington, DC	✓		✓	✓	✓		✓
Wichita					✓	✓	
Number of cities conducting count	26	15	17	15	21	14	29

Source: City Survey 2011/2012. **Notes**: The following cities did not indicate in the benchmarking survey that any counts of bicyclists or pedestrians have been conducted: Arlington, El Paso, Fort Worth, Fresno, Jacksonville, Memphis, Oklahoma City, Tulsa, and Virginia Beach. Unanswered survey questions, or responses of "N/A" and "unknown," were taken to mean "no." All empty cells should be understood to be a "no" response. (1) Detroit did not submit a survey for 2011/2012.

Additional Counting Methods in Large Cities

	Count includes:		
	Bicycles	Pedestrians	Methodology
Atlanta	✓	✓	Spot counts and turning movement counts
Austin	✓	✓	Two permanent, automatic counters installed downtown; site-specific analyses of pedestrian and bicycle infrastructure projects using an Eco-Counter
Charlotte	✓		Counts of bicycle boardings on transit buses
Chicago	✓		Monthly bicycle counts at six locations around the city; bicycle counts at project-specific locations for before and after data
Cleveland	✓	✓	Annual bicycle and pedestrian counts at key intersections
Colorado Springs	✓	✓	Census counts taken in multiple locations, three times on a weekday and one time on a weekend
Columbus	✓	✓	Installed three permanent trail counters; conducts spot counts, and uses some infrared counters
Dallas	✓		Conducts counts at safety-improvement locations
Denver	✓		Video detection of movement within specified area
Houston	✓	✓	Eco-Counters
Indianapolis	✓	✓	Electronic counters on greenways
Las Vegas	✓	✓	Turning movement counts
Louisville	✓	✓	Eco-Counters on streets for two weeks at a time for bicycle counts; counters are moved to a new location biweekly for total of 30 weeks
Mesa	✓	✓	Eco-Counter Multi installed on shared use pathways
Milwaukee	✓	✓	Counts conducted as part of the National Bicycle and Pedestrian Documentation Project
Minneapolis	✓	✓	Three automatic loop detectors; annual counts at over 40 benchmark locations throughout the city
Nashville	✓	✓	Counts conducted as part of the National Bicycle and Pedestrian Documentation Project
New York City	✓	✓	Automated counter that analyzes the electromagnetic signature of each bicycle wheel, with 13 differentiation criteria; biannual commercial corridor counts at 100 locations throughout the city; spot counts for specific bicycle and pedestrian projects and locations of interest
Oakland	✓	✓	Annual turning movement counts
Philadelphia	✓	✓	Permanent count stations on trails
Phoenix	✓	✓	Long-term, outdoor video detection
Portland, OR	✓		Manual spot counts of bicycles during two-hour peak-period; 24-hour spot counts with pressure-sensitive pneumatic hoses
Raleigh	✓	✓	Turning movement counts, by request
San Antonio	✓		Bicycle travel patterns study surveyed a sample of residents and identified active bicyclists
San Diego	✓	✓	Intersection manual counts for level-of-service analysis of specific projects; automatic electronic bike counters are embedded in the asphalt at various locations throughout the city
San Francisco	✓		Intercept survey
San Jose	✓	✓	Peak-period and mid-day intersection counts
Seattle	✓	✓	Counts conducted as part of the National Bicycle and Pedestrian Documentation Project, 50 locations counted 12 times per year
Washington, DC	✓	✓	Counts conducted for specific transportation studies

Source: City Survey 2011/2012. **Note**: Methodology of these additional counts is self-reported by survey respondents. The Benchmarking Project did not research these methods individually. Unanswered survey questions, or responses of "N/A" and "unknown," were taken to mean "no." All empty cells should be understood to be a "no" response.

Bicycling and Walking in Midsized Cities

In a recent report, The Rails to Trails Conservancy used 2009 NHTS data to analyze bicycling and walking levels for rural areas compared to urban areas. They found that various community types with small populations (i.e. suburbs, towns, and isolated rural areas with population of less than 50,000) actually see bicycling levels similar to those in larger cities. Walking trips are taken less frequently in these more rural communities than in urban areas, but are still higher than bicycling trips. These areas see walking mode shares of 6.1%-8.5%, compared to 12.0% in urban core communities (Rails to Trails, 2011).

In our sample study of small and midsized cities, we found bicycling and walking levels to be generally similar to, and in some cases higher than, the levels seen in the most populous cities studied in this report. While the sample cities were handpicked for this study based on their successes improving bicycling and walking, their levels of bicycling and walking suggest they can compete with large cities. Using ACS 3-year estimates, we found a wide range of commuter walking and bicycling levels—even within similar population groups. In particular, the sample cities with populations under 100K see ranges for commuter trips by foot ranging from 2.8% in Davis to 19.6% in Burlington, and for commuter trips by bicycle ranging from 1.2% in Albany up to 19.1% in Davis.

Madison, Pittsburgh, Eugene, and all of the sample cities with populations under 100K (except for Davis) have commuter walking levels within the range of the top most populous cities studied in this report. Eugene, Fort Collins, Boulder, and Davis all show commuter bicycling rates higher than any of the most populous cities studied here, and another six cities fall within range of the commuter bicycling rates in the most populous cities studied.

As with the larger cities studied in this report, the ACS data for these midsized cities should be considered a rough estimate only. Due to small sample sizes, the margins of error for these cities are quite high, which could change the actual figures significantly.

Also, large universities have an impact on cities, particularly those with smaller resident populations. A large percentage of students and the typically dense design of university towns likely increase bicycling and walking levels.

Share of Commuters Who Walk or Bicycle to Work

	% commuters by bicycle	% commuters by foot
Population > 200K		
Anchorage, AK	1.1%	2.7%
Baton Rouge, LA	0.8%	3.9%
Madison, WI	5.2%	9.2%
Pittsburgh, PA	1.5%	11.4%
Spokane, WA	1.5%	3.6%
St. Louis, MO	0.7%	4.3%
Population 100-200K		
Charleston, SC	2.5%	4.6%
Chattanooga, TN	0.3%	2.9%
Eugene, OR	8.5%	6.4%
Fort Collins, CO	6.3%	3.3%
Salt Lake City, UT	2.5%	5.8%
Population < 100K		
Albany, NY	1.2%	9.8%
Bellingham, WA	3.9%	8.4%
Boulder, CO	10.2%	9.3%
Burlington, VT	4.5%	19.6%
Davis, CA	19.1%	2.8%
Missoula, MT	6.4%	6.5%
High value		
Midsized cities	19.1%	19.6%
52 large cites	6.1%	15.0%
Low value		
Midsized cities	0.3%	2.7%
52 large cites	0.1%	1.2%
Large cities average	1.0%	5.0%

Source: ACS 2009–2011. **Note:** Margins of error for these data range from 7.2% to 29.2% for commuter trips by foot, and from 11.1% to 56.3% for commuter trips by bicycle.

Local Counting Efforts

Many small and midsized cities are attempting to document their own mode share through local counts of bicyclists and walkers. Of the 17 sample cities surveyed, 15 conduct some type of nonmotorized traffic count. All 15 cities conducting counts include bicyclists in their counts and 11 include pedestrians.

As with larger cities, the sampled cities use a wide variety of methods and technologies to conduct their counts. A broadly accepted, standardized method of documenting mode share for an entire city is necessary for these smaller cities to understand their true bicycling and walking population.

Local Counts of Bicyclists and Pedestrians

	Count includes:		
	Bicycles	Pedestrians	Methodology
Population > 200K			
Anchorage, AK	✓		Bicycle count on Bike to Work Day
Baton Rouge, LA			None
Madison, WI	✓	✓	Monthly automated counts
Pittsburgh, PA			None
Spokane, WA	✓	✓	Online self-recording by employees
St. Louis, MO	✓	✓	Screenline counts using guidelines from the National Bicycle & Pedestrian Documentation Project
Population 100-200K			
Charleston, SC	✓	✓	12-hour spot counts every three years; peak-hour mode share counts on three downtown streets
Chattanooga, TN	✓	✓	Mix of automated and human observation counts
Eugene, OR	✓	✓	Manual counts, tube counters, and permanent counters
Fort Collins, CO	✓	✓	Counts coordinated with intersection volume counts
Salt Lake City, UT	✓		National Bicycle & Pedestrian Documentation Project; Utah Household Travel Survey
Population < 100K			
Albany, NY	✓		Biannual bicycle counts, mode share not determined
Bellingham, WA	✓	✓	Annual count augmented by surveys and trip diaries
Boulder, CO	✓	✓	Triannual travel diary of residents
Burlington, VT	✓	✓	Geocoded turning movement counts
Davis, CA	✓	✓	Peak hour counts at primary bikeways; pedestrian counts conducted for multiple locations on the 5th Street corridor (conducted by a research team at University of California, Davis)
Missoula, MT	✓	✓	Semiannual, hand-tallied counts using methodology of the National Bike Pedestrian Documentation Project

Source: Midsized City Survey 2011/2012. **Note**: Methodology of these counts is self-reported by survey respondents. The Benchmarking Project did not research these methods individually. Unanswered survey questions, or responses of "N/A" and "unknown," were taken to mean "no." All empty cells should be understood to be a "no" response.

Trails for Illinois: Making Trails Count

by Evan Bontrager, Friends of the Pumpkinvine Nature Trail

Street and highway departments have long used the results from traffic counting to influence traffic management decisions and to determine the level of service of a roadway. Traffic counting on our off-street trails can provide similar benefits. In addition, advocates and government leaders have the potential to use those counts to assign an economic value to our trail networks.

Trails for Illinois suspected the benefits of trail usage to include economic growth, improved health, and environmental stewardship. The organization used a "Triple Bottom Line" lens, sometimes summarized as Profit, People, and Planet, in the hopes of making a strong case for more communities to add non-road trails, also known as linear parks, to their regions.

In 2012, Trails for Illinois launched the project, "Making Trails Count." The project team conducted a three-month count on six non-urban Illinois trails. Rails to Trails Conservancy helped install TRAFx electronic heat-sensing counters along the trails, which would count passersby 24 hours a day, seven days a week. Rails to Trails analyzed the data using regionalized calculation models to produce annual trail traffic estimates.

In addition to the electronic traffic counts, the Trails for Illinois team enhanced their findings with human-administered surveys. A small group of volunteers stood trailside, stopping every third person to complete a survey. The team collected 789 responses over a ten-week period.

Surveys encompassed a range of questions including distance traveled to the trail, spending during trail use, spending in preparation of use, and demographics of participants.

Trail usage data was expected to support three objectives:

1. Demonstrate economic activity on trail networks.

2. Break the public perception that trails are primarily for recreation.

3. Include trail networks in the overall transportation network.

Studies on urban trails, such as in Chicago, have found data supporting all three points. Since most urban trails are in close proximity to people and their intended destinations, people can conveniently replace car trips with trail trips. In urban areas, trails are also often used for commuting to work.

Primary Reason for Trail Use by Gender

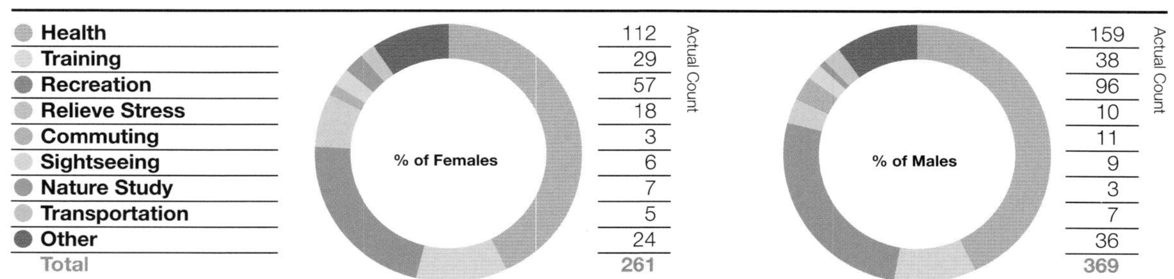

Surveys, in addition to counts, allowed researchers to learn more about the trail users and their activities.
Source: *Making Trails Count for Illinois*, Trails for Illinois, 2012. Reprinted with permission.

Photo by Steve Buchtel

The more rural study conducted by Trails for Illinois yielded a surprising result. The data did not show environmental improvements of replacing car trips with trail trips. Instead, the study found that most users drove to use the trails. The rural nature of the trails being studied showed the usage was much more recreational and much less for practical transportation. Yet the "triple bottom line" concept of Profit, People and Planet was still satisfied in the following ways.

Profit: Trails generated local economic activity and commerce. The survey captured the attitude of users on the trails, including destination and purpose. When asked, few people initially recognized they were planning on spending money. However, trails give access to commerce as a usable corridor. Bird watchers, for example, might buy coffee before or after their experience. Groups of cyclists may drive to the trailheads, but they also might stop and shop on their way there or back, as part of their group outing. These activities are in addition to the purchase of bicycles, shoes, and clothing specific to trail usage.

People: Trails improve the health and quality of life for Illinoisans. The survey tracked how much time each user spent on the trail. More time spent on trails being physically active creates health value.

Planet: Trail usage improved environmental stewardship of the users. While rural trails did not replace car trips, attitudes of trail users evolved with experience. Trail users gained new understanding of their role within the broader environment, and become more aware of their effects on the environment.

Other regions and communities can repeat the process implemented by Trails for Illinois by adapting the tool from the Making Trails Count project, which can be found along with initial results at:

www.TrailsforIllinois.tumblr.com/MakeTrailsCount

across borders

West Africa: Claiming a Place on the Road for Bicyclists

by Kathryn Werntz, The Sahel Calling Project

During a series of informal interviews with bicyclists around Sénégal, a rider recounted a recent morning commute. He had been at a complete stop, waiting for a break in traffic at a roundabout. He was there for several minutes when suddenly he was hit from behind by a taxi. The taxi driver's response to the crash: "You're a bicyclist, you shouldn't be on the road anyway."

Why Bicyclists Are On the Road

There are many reasons people choose to use bicycles as transportation in West Africa. Four main categories of bicyclists (youth, entrepreneurs, racers, and tourists) stand out and each one benefits from expanded opportunities in unique ways. Better access to education and healthcare, business ventures, competition and comraderie, and the opportunity to explore new places are all worth the potential risks of bicycling on West African roads.

1. Youth

Children and young adults (mostly girls) receive bicycles through non-government organizations who want to help improve the next generation's access to education and healthcare. In Burkina Faso alone, several local and international organizations provide bicycles to girls and young women so that they can bike the 30 kilometers often necessary to reach a junior or high school institution. Likewise, the bicycles make healthcare more accessible, reducing travel times for patients and doctors who would otherwise walk.

Sierra Leone, West Africa. Courtesy of Village Bicycle Project Africa

2. Entrepreneurs
Individuals and small business owners realized decades ago that investing in a bicycle might increase their earnings. One man, shown in the photo at the right, has ridden his bicycle every day for 17 years, delivering fresh bread from bakeries to corner stores and restaurants around his quiet town of Ziguinchor, Sénégal.

A free bicycle program in Burkina Faso sponsored by CooP-Africa (Cycling out of Poverty) collaborates with community development initiatives such as solid waste management programs. Recipients of bicycles from Bike2Clean's Solid Waste Management Program can earn money by collecting and sorting waste on their cargo bikes, then transporting the "goods" and garbage to repositories.

3. Racers
In West Africa, racers often belong to a country's national bicycle federation. These federations not only organize races, but also spearhead bicycle events for local residents. While some may see these racers as a bit elite on the streets of some of the poorest countries in the world, in Sénégal their passion drives them to engage people from all sectors of society. This commitment is evident in Dakar's bicyclist club motto: "A bicycle for everyone." Their passion has the potential to boost the number of commuting and hobby bicyclists across the region.

4. Tourists
Bicycling is now a hot tourism activity for people from many European countries, the U.S., and Canada. Bicycle tourists find an increasing range of amenities within and between West African countries. For example, Burkina Faso has a strong local bicycling culture, even in its busy capital of Ouagadougou, where most major thoroughfares have separate motorbike and bicycle lanes, some with their own traffic lights.

Sénégal, West Africa. Photo by Kathryn M. Werntz

Expanding the Possibilities

While there may be more repair shops in cities, bicyclists are seen most often in rural areas. This may be linked to the many international volunteers (such as from Peace Corps) who have been present throughout the region for 30 years. These visitors sometimes unofficially "gift" their government-issued mountain bikes to the local communities before they return to their home country. These hand-me-downs have improved the quality of bicycles available to local youth from low- and middle-income families.

Similar to other West African cities, the coastal city of Dakar, Sénégal, has undergone massive changes to its infrastructure in recent years. Grand hotels for executives and vacationers have swallowed the last stretches of open coast, increasing oceanside population density. The expansions have also triggered vast improvements to the previously dangerous roads and nonexistent sidewalks. As business and tourism continues to increase in West Africa, new thoroughfares will be built, and new opportunities will arise to make roads fair for all.

3 Health and Safety

Providing opportunities for regular physical activity, such as walking and bicycling, can make a big impact on improving public health and life expectancy (Buehler et al., 2011; Gordon-Larsen, 2009; Hamer and Chida, 2008; Oja, 2011; Pucher et al., 2010; Shephard, 2008). In fact, the quantified health benefits of active transportation can outweigh any risks associated with these activities by as much as 77 to 1, and add more years to our lives than are lost from inhaled air pollution and traffic injuries (Rojas-Rueda et al., 2011; Jacobsen and Rutter, 2012).

This chapter looks at the relationship of bicycling and walking to health and safety in U.S. cities and states.

Bicycling and Walking for Health

Our daily mode of travel has a great impact on our health as a society. Fifty percent of trips in the U.S. are three miles or shorter, and over 25% of our trips are less than one mile. Yet as many as 69% of those short trips are taken in private motorized vehicles (NHTS, 2009).[1] In comparison, only half of the U.S. population gets the recommended weekly amount of aerobic physical activity. One-third of the population is overweight and another one-third is obese (BRFSS, 2011).

In the Alliance analysis, data suggest a strong relationship between statewide percentages of bicycling and walking to work and key public health indicators. States with higher levels of bicycling and walking to work see lower levels of diabetes (r = -0.70), obesity (r = -0.55), and high blood pressure (r = -0.54), and see higher levels of the population meeting recommended weekly physical activity levels (r = 0.63).

Active transportation not only improves our physical health, but also our mental well-being and ability to focus (Garrard et al., 2012; Singh et al., 2012; Egelund, 2012; Chaddock et al., 2010; Hillman et al., 2005). A recent study of Danish children showed that those who bicycled to school were better able to concentrate. In fact, walking and bicycling to school had a stronger impact on a child's ability to focus than having breakfast and lunch. The physical activity associated with walking or bicycling to school advanced the child's mental alertness to the equivalent of a student half a year further in their studies (Egelund, 2012).

Note: (1) This percentage includes trips taken by car, van, SUV, truck, and recreational vehicles.

Comparing Health Indicators Among Adults to Bicycling and Walking Levels

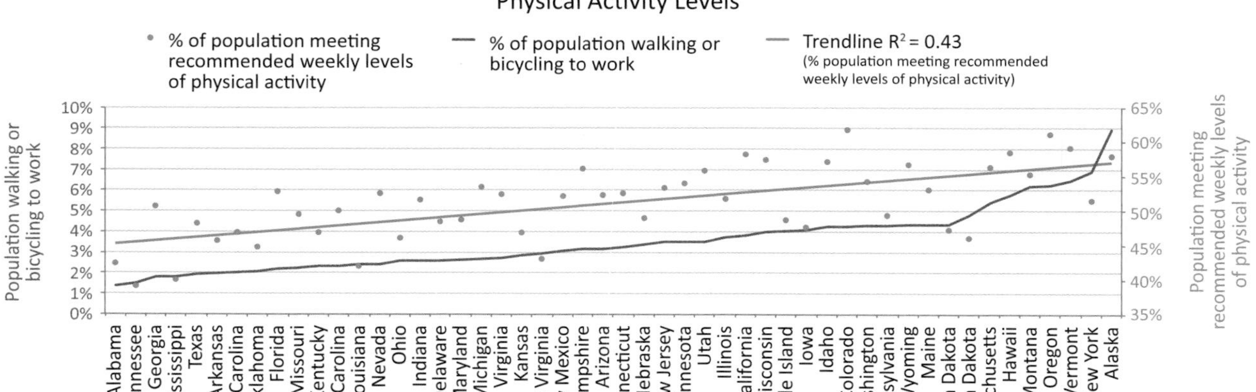

Sources: ACS 2009–2011, BRFSS 2011

Health Indicators

The Behavioral Risk Factor Surveillance System (BRFSS) provides the data used in this report to discuss key public health indicators including physical activity, obesity, high blood pressure, diabetes, and asthma.

Physical Activity

Of all states, Colorado and Oregon have the highest percentage of people meeting recommended physical activity levels, with bicycling and walking rates at 4.3% and 6.2% respectively. Tennessee, Mississippi, Louisiana, and Alabama have the lowest shares of people meeting the physical activity minimum. These states also all have bicycling and walking levels below the national average.

Obesity

According to 2011 BRFSS statistics, 64% of the U.S. population is overweight or obese. Obesity alone (BMI over 30) affects more than one-fourth (28%) of the population. Among states, the percentage of obesity varies from 21% to 35%; in the large cities studied for this report, the percentage of obesity varies from 19% to 37%.

Memphis and Detroit have the highest levels of obesity among large cities (36.8% and 33.0% respectively), and some of the lowest city bicycling and walking to work rates (Memphis at 2.1% and Detroit at 3.4%). San Francisco and Oakland, by contrast, have the lowest combined obesity rate (18.6%) and above-average bicycling and walking rates (San Francisco at 13.1% and Oakland at 6.7%).

This correlation is not seen in all cities, however. New Orleans, Baltimore, Philadelphia, and Chicago are among the top 15 cities for commuters walking and bicycling to work, but they also have above-average levels of obesity among the most populous cities (31.6%, 30.0%, 26.9%, and 26.6%, respectively).

States with higher rates of bicycling and walking to work also have a higher % of the population meeting recommended levels of physical activity, and have lower rates of obesity, high blood pressure, and diabetes.

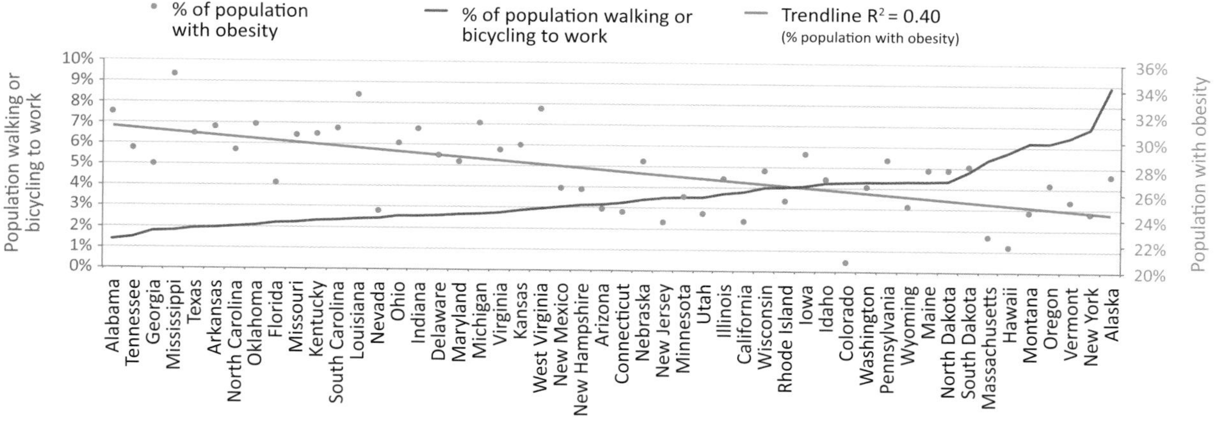

Sources: ACS 2009–2011, BRFSS 2011

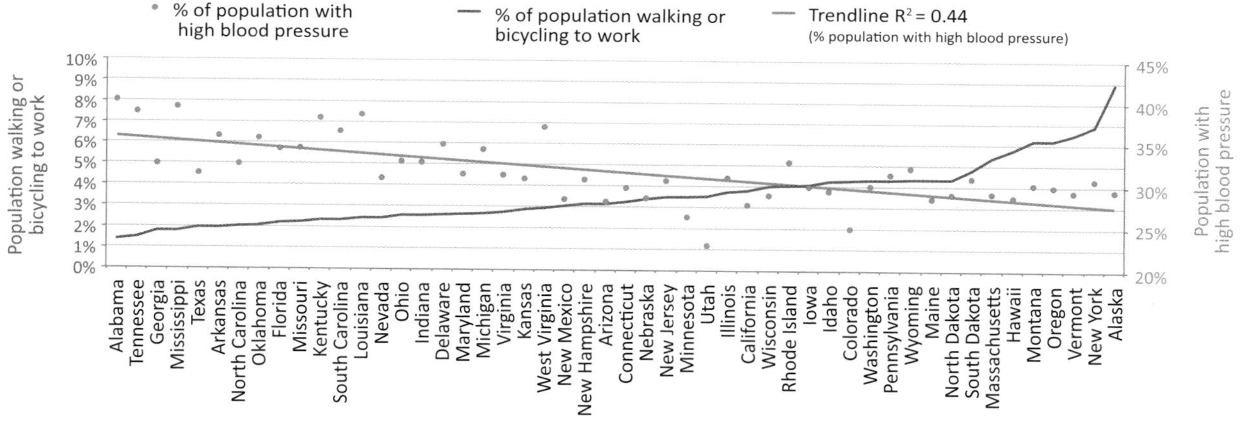

Sources: ACS 2009–2011, BRFSS 2011

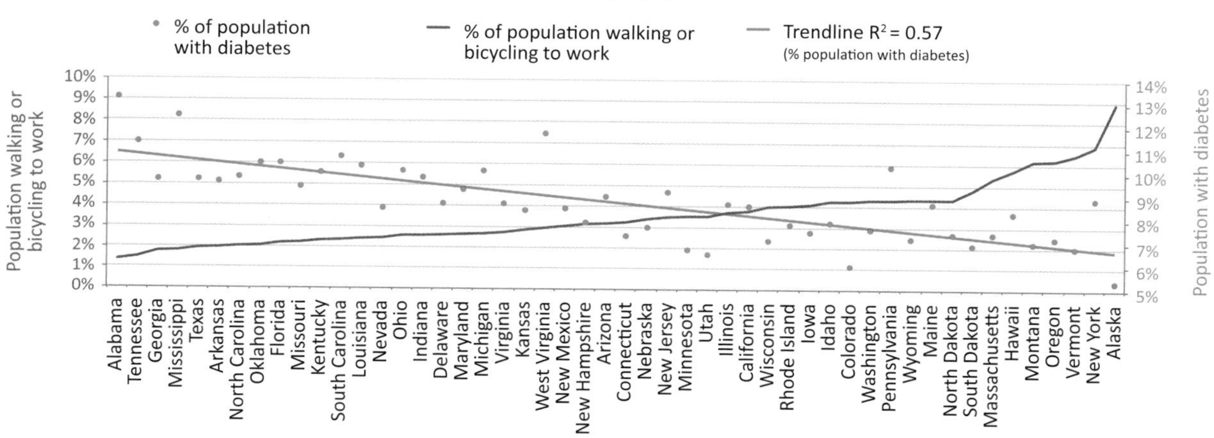

Sources: ACS 2009–2011, BRFSS 2010

High Blood Pressure and Diabetes

Nationally, 32% of Americans live with high blood pressure and 9% have diabetes. Mississippi and Alabama currently have the highest statewide levels of both high blood pressure (39% and 40%) and diabetes (12% and 13%). New Orleans and Memphis top the large city ranks for high blood pressure at 38% and 37% respectively. Memphis, El Paso, and Detroit have the highest levels of diabetes in the most populous cities, with 12-13% of residents in these cities living with diabetes.

These state and city data, as well as previous studies published in public health journals, confirm a strong and statistically significant inverse relationship between bicycling and walking commuter rates and both high blood pressure and diabetes in the United States (Bassett et al., 2009).

Asthma

There are also environmental health aspects to consider. With a car-centric transportation system, polluted air leads to higher levels of asthma, lung cancer, heart disease, respiratory illness, and premature death (Bell and Cohen, 2009). The most harmful pollutants are emitted within minutes of starting a car, meaning that short trips pollute more per mile and have a bigger impact on our overall health than longer trips (FHWA, 2012). The most recent national health data report that 9% of adults in the U.S. live with asthma (BRFSS, 2010).

Seattle, WA. Photo courtesy of Walkable and Livable Communities (WALC) Institute

Public Health Indicators in Large Cities

% commuters by bicycle or foot	% adults meeting recommended minimum weekly aerobic physical activity	% adults with obesity	% adults with diabetes [1]	% adults with high blood pressure	
3.4%	52.1%	24.8%	7.1%	25.6%	Albuquerque
1.9%	47.7%	30.0%	11.7%	29.7%	Arlington, TX
5.5%	52.1%	25.0%	8.7%	29.3%	Atlanta
4.0%	55.9%	20.7%	5.7%	23.7%	Austin
7.6%	46.1%	30.0%	9.9%	32.5%	Baltimore
16.7%	56.6%	20.9%	7.8%	27.2%	Boston
2.3%	50.3%	25.5%	9.2%	28.3%	Charlotte
7.6%	52.3%	26.6%	8.8%	29.4%	Chicago
5.1%	53.9%	26.3%	10.6%	29.7%	Cleveland
3.7%	61.7%	20.2%	5.9%	24.2%	Colorado Springs
3.5%	50.0%	27.9%	9.3%	31.6%	Columbus
2.0%	48.8%	30.6%	8.1%	29.6%	Dallas
6.4%	61.5%	21.1%	5.4%	25.1%	Denver
3.4%	48.3%	33.0%	12.1%	35.4%	Detroit
2.1%	-	28.6% [2]	12.2%	-	El Paso
-	-	-	-	-	Fort Worth
1.3%	47.7%	30.0%	11.7%	29.7%	Fresno
11.2%	57.2%	21.6%	8.5%	29.2%	Honolulu
2.6%	51.1%	28.7%	8.5%	29.8%	Houston
2.5%	46.1%	31.5%	9.6%	32.9%	Indianapolis
1.7%	54.5%	29.5%	9.3%	35.3%	Jacksonville
2.5%	48.6%	30.2%	9.1%	31.8%	Kansas City, MO
2.3%	50.2%	24.1%	9.0%	30.2%	Las Vegas
3.9%	56.0%	24.3%	8.7%	27.3%	Long Beach
4.7%	56.0%	24.3%	8.7%	27.3%	Los Angeles
2.5%	47.2%	27.8%	6.9%	34.2%	Louisville
2.1%	37.8%	36.8%	12.7%	37.3%	Memphis
2.8%	52.9%	25.0%	7.1%	26.8%	Mesa
4.6%	50.6%	24.3%	7.5%	31.1%	Miami
5.8%	58.8%	27.3%	7.6%	28.3%	Milwaukee
9.9%	55.5%	24.7%	5.3%	24.1%	Minneapolis
2.1%	43.1%	30.6%	8.7%	35.3%	Nashville
7.9%	42.4%	31.6%	11.0%	37.8%	New Orleans
11.1%	51.7%	22.0%	8.7%	29.0%	New York City
6.7%	62.4%	18.6%	7.1%	26.9%	Oakland
1.7%	44.8%	28.8%	8.7%	33.6%	Oklahoma City
3.0%	49.2%	28.4%	7.5%	27.9%	Omaha
10.8%	51.6%	26.9%	10.3%	30.1%	Philadelphia
2.7%	52.9%	25.0%	7.1%	26.8%	Phoenix
11.4%	60.3%	23.7%	6.5%	27.9%	Portland, OR
2.5%	49.7%	30.6%	7.4%	26.2%	Raleigh
5.3%	59.6%	24.3%	8.3%	27.0%	Sacramento
2.3%	50.3%	32.3%	9.2%	34.4%	San Antonio
3.9%	61.0%	24.1%	8.9%	29.1%	San Diego
13.1%	62.4%	18.6%	7.1%	26.9%	San Francisco
2.7%	61.3%	22.1%	8.6%	27.3%	San Jose
11.9%	54.5%	22.3%	6.4%	27.7%	Seattle
6.1%	53.1%	20.5%	8.0%	25.5%	Tucson
2.4%	45.7%	29.9%	10.9%	34.6%	Tulsa
3.3%	50.4%	29.4%	8.5%	33.4%	Virginia Beach
14.8%	54.9%	25.3%	8.7%	28.1%	Washington, DC
1.6%	44.0%	31.2%	7.8%	31.2%	Wichita
6.1%	52.3%	26.4%	8.6%	29.7%	Large Cities Average
3.5%	51.9%	25.9%	8.7%	29.3%	Large Cities Median
16.7%	62.4%	36.8%	12.7%	37.8%	High
1.3%	37.8%	18.6%	5.3%	23.7%	Low

Sources: ACS 2009–2011, BRFSS 2010 and 2011. **Notes**: City BRFSS data could only be calculated by averaging percentages for each city; therefore, these averages are not weighted. Cells with a dash (-) mean data were unavailable. Data for the following cities are combined in the BRFSS: Arlington/Fort Worth, San Francisco/Oakland, Los Angeles/Long Beach, Phoenix/Mesa. (1) Data on diabetes levels were not available in 2011, so 2010 data is used. (2) Data on obesity in El Paso were not available in 2011, so 2010 data is used instead.

Public Health Indicators in States

	% commuters by bicycle or foot	% adults meeting recommended minimum weekly aerobic physical activity	% adults with obesity	% adults with diabetes [(1)]	% adults with high blood pressure
Alabama	1.4%	42.4%	32.0%	13.2%	40.1%
Alaska	8.9%	57.9%	27.4%	5.3%	29.4%
Arizona	3.2%	52.3%	24.7%	9.0%	28.1%
Arkansas	2.0%	45.7%	30.9%	9.6%	35.8%
California	3.8%	58.2%	23.8%	8.6%	27.8%
Colorado	4.3%	61.8%	20.7%	6.0%	25.0%
Connecticut	3.3%	52.6%	24.5%	7.3%	29.8%
Delaware	2.6%	48.5%	28.8%	8.7%	34.8%
Florida	2.2%	52.8%	26.6%	10.4%	34.2%
Georgia	1.8%	50.7%	28.0%	9.7%	32.4%
Hawaii	5.8%	58.5%	21.9%	8.3%	28.7%
Idaho	4.3%	57.2%	27.1%	7.9%	29.4%
Illinois	3.7%	51.7%	27.1%	8.7%	31.0%
Indiana	2.6%	46.0%	30.8%	9.8%	32.8%
Iowa	4.1%	47.6%	29.0%	7.5%	29.9%
Kansas	2.9%	46.8%	29.6%	8.4%	30.8%
Kentucky	2.3%	46.8%	30.4%	10.0%	38.0%
Louisiana	2.4%	42.0%	33.4%	10.3%	38.4%
Maine	4.3%	56.7%	27.8%	8.7%	32.2%
Maryland	2.6%	48.7%	28.3%	9.3%	31.3%
Massachusetts	5.4%	56.3%	22.7%	7.4%	29.2%
Michigan	2.7%	53.5%	31.3%	10.1%	34.2%
Minnesota	3.5%	54.0%	25.7%	6.7%	26.3%
Mississippi	1.8%	40.0%	34.9%	12.4%	39.3%
Missouri	2.2%	49.5%	30.3%	9.4%	34.3%
Montana	6.2%	55.3%	24.6%	7.0%	30.2%
Nebraska	3.4%	49.0%	28.4%	7.7%	28.6%
Nevada	2.4%	52.6%	24.5%	8.5%	30.8%
New Hampshire	3.1%	56.1%	26.2%	7.9%	30.7%
New Jersey	3.5%	53.3%	23.7%	9.2%	30.6%
New Mexico	3.1%	52.2%	26.3%	8.5%	28.4%
New York	6.9%	51.5%	24.5%	8.9%	30.7%
North Carolina	2.0%	46.8%	29.1%	9.8%	32.4%
North Dakota	4.4%	47.3%	27.8%	7.4%	29.1%
Ohio	2.6%	51.6%	29.7%	10.1%	32.7%
Oklahoma	2.1%	44.8%	31.1%	10.4%	35.5%
Oregon	6.2%	61.1%	26.7%	7.2%	29.9%
Pennsylvania	4.3%	49.4%	28.6%	10.3%	31.4%
Rhode Island	4.0%	48.7%	25.4%	7.8%	32.9%
South Carolina	2.3%	50.0%	30.8%	10.7%	36.4%
South Dakota	4.8%	46.1%	28.1%	6.9%	31.0%
Tennessee	1.5%	39.0%	29.2%	11.3%	38.7%
Texas	1.9%	48.2%	30.4%	9.7%	31.3%
Utah	3.5%	55.8%	24.4%	6.5%	22.9%
Vermont	6.5%	59.2%	25.4%	6.8%	29.3%
Virgina	2.7%	52.4%	29.2%	8.7%	31.2%
Washington	4.3%	54.2%	26.5%	7.6%	30.0%
West Virginia	3.0%	43.0%	32.4%	11.7%	37.0%
Wisconsin	4.0%	57.4%	27.7%	7.1%	28.9%
Wyoming	4.3%	53.1%	25.0%	7.2%	28.6%
State Average	3.4%	51.1%	27.7%	8.8%	31.6%
State Median	3.3%	51.7%	27.8%	8.7%	30.9%
High	8.9%	61.8%	34.9%	13.2%	40.1%
Low	1.4%	39.0%	20.7%	5.3%	22.9%

Sources: ACS 2009–2011, BRFSS 2010 and 2011. **Note**: (1) Data on diabetes levels were not available in 2011, so 2010 data is used.

Pedestrian Fatality Rate (1980-2011)

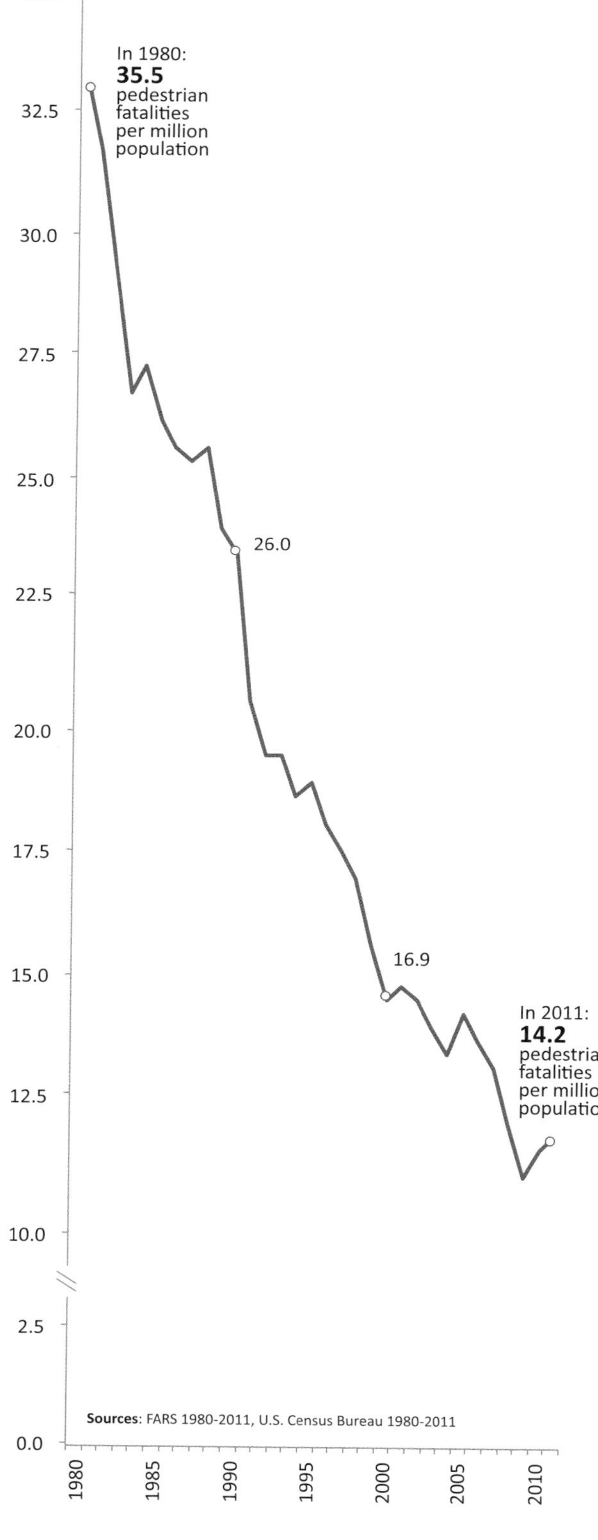

Trends in Bicycling and Walking Safety

Concern about safety is one of the most commonly stated reasons for not bicycling and walking (Jacobsen and Rutter, 2012). While there is certainly a difference between real and perceived danger for bicyclists and pedestrians, the data do show higher rates of fatalities in the U.S. than in other countries (Pucher and Buehler, 2010).

Data in this section come largely from the National Highway Traffic Safety Administration (NHTSA) Fatality Analysis Reporting System (FARS). NHTSA collects data from police reports of traffic crashes and is the authoritative national source for traffic fatalities in the United States. Data on bicycle and pedestrian injuries come from the CDC Web-based Injury Statistics Query and Reporting System (WISQARS).

Fewer fatalities occured on U.S. roadways in 2011 than in any year since 1980. The number of bicyclist and pedestrian fatalities, in particular, has also decreased significantly in the past three decades. Between 1980 and 2011, the number of pedestrians killed on U.S. roadways decreased 45% (8,070 to 4,432). During these years, the pedestrian fatality rate dropped from 35.5 to 14.2 deaths per 1 million people. Similarly, bicyclist fatalities decreased 30% (965 to 677) from 1980 to 2011 and bicyclist fatality rates dropped from 4.3 deaths per 1 million people to 2.2 deaths per 1 million people in 2011.

Bicyclist Fatality Rate (1980-2011)

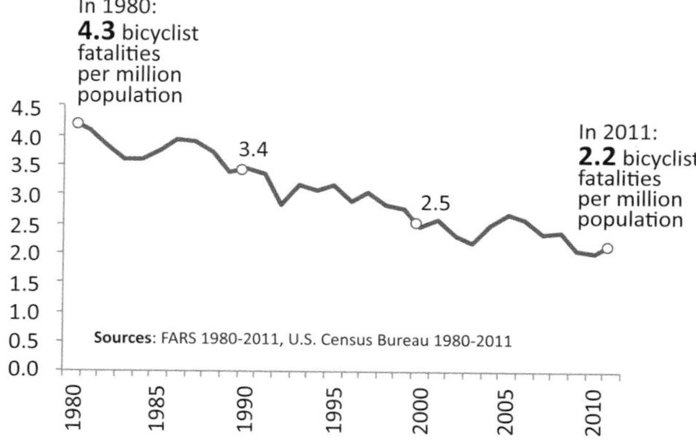

Overview of U.S. Bicycling and Bicyclist Safety

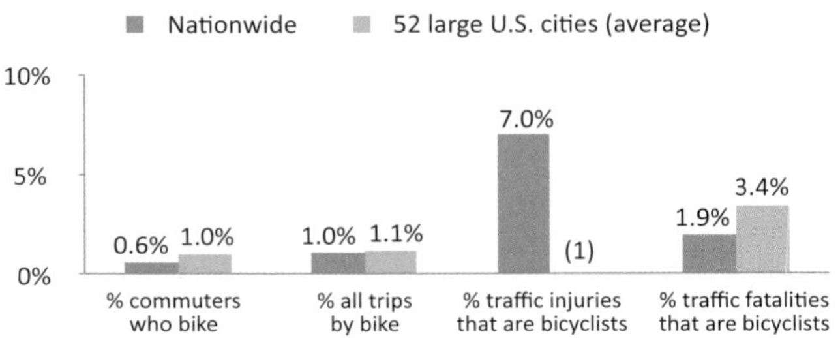

Sources: ACS 2011 (nationwide data), ACS 2009–2011 (large city average), NHTS 2009, WISQARS 2011, FARS 2009–2011. **Note:** (1) City-level data for pedestrian injuries is unavailable.

Overview of U.S. Walking and Pedestrian Safety

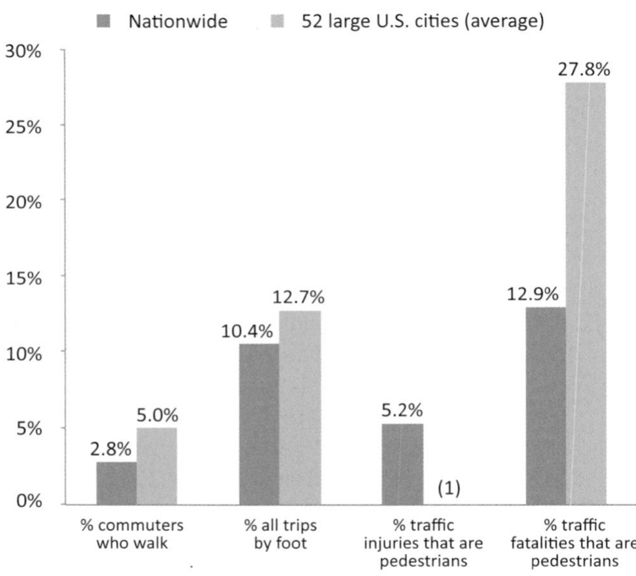

Sources: ACS 2011 (nationwide data), ACS 2009-2011 (large city average), NHTS 2009, WISQARS 2011, FARS 2009-2011. **Note:** (1) City-level data for pedestrian injuries is unavailable.

While absolute numbers of pedestrian and bicyclist fatalities have dropped, their percentage of all traffic fatalities has increased. In 2003, FARS data indicated that bicyclists and pedestrians accounted for 12.6% of all traffic fatalities. Since that time, the percentage of traffic fatalities that are bicyclists and pedestrians has gradually increased to 15.8% in 2011.

Victim Demographics

According to data from FARS, between 2009–2011, pedestrians and bicyclists aged 65 and older were killed in transportation-related collisions at a disproportionately high rate compared to their distribution in the total population. During these years, seniors represented 10% of all pedestrians and 6% of all bicyclists, yet 19% of the pedestrian fatalities and 12% of the bicyclist fatalities were people aged 65 years and older. Their level of representation of pedestrian fatalities has not changed since the *2012 Benchmarking Report*; however, senior bicyclist fatalities increased by two percentage points from 10% two years ago.

In some areas, the risk facing seniors is even greater. In Honolulu, where 42% of all traffic fatalities are pedestrians, 46% of victims are over age 65. Similarly, in Oakland, where 19% of all traffic fatalities are pedestrians, 42% of these are seniors. While cities do vary in their demographic composition, these rates of senior fatalities are still disproportionately higher than the share of trips they represent.

Roadway Fatalities in 2012

The NHTSA releases annual numbers of reported fatalities nationwide. Of the 33,561 people who died on U.S. roadways in 2012, **4,743 were pedestrians and 726 were bicyclists**. These numbers represent an increase of pedestrian and bicyclist fatalities since 2011 by both actual number and percentage of all roadway fatalities (NHTSA 2013).

Children under age 16 were involved in a smaller share of pedestrian injuries and bicyclist fatalities since the *2012 Benchmarking Report*. Representing 17% of all pedestrian trips, children under 16 represent 17% of all pedestrian injuries (WISQARS, 2011), a drop in two percentage points from 19% in 2009. Similarly, children under 16, representing 39% of all bicycle trips, were involved in only 11% of bicyclist fatalities between 2009 and 2011, a drop in three percentage points from 14% between 2007 and 2009.

A 2012 survey found that 26% of people of color said they would bicycle more, but are concerned about safety. Compare this to only 19% of white respondents who said they are concerned about safety (LAB, 2013). However, there may be good reason for this concern. Data from the CDC show that African American bicyclists are 30% more likely to be in a fatal collision than white bicyclists. Hispanic bicyclists are 23% more likely to be in a fatal collision than white bicyclists. (LAB, 2013; CDC, 2001).

What's the Risk?

To understand bicycle and pedestrian safety in a city or state, it is not enough to simply look at the number of fatalities. The level of bicycling and walking in an area also must be taken into account to determine what the risk of bicycling or walking is. For example, if a city had just 100 people who bicycled and had one bicycle fatality, and another city had 6,000 people who bicycled and had two bicycle fatalities, the first city would have a higher fatality rate and the risk in that community would be much greater, than in the second.

To measure risk to bicyclists and pedestrians, the Alliance divided the number of annual bicycle and pedestrian fatalities (an average of three years) by the number of bicycling and walking commuters as reported in the corresponding ACS 3-year estimate. This method of calculating risk is somewhat limited due to its reliance on commuter mode share, which is used as a relative measure of

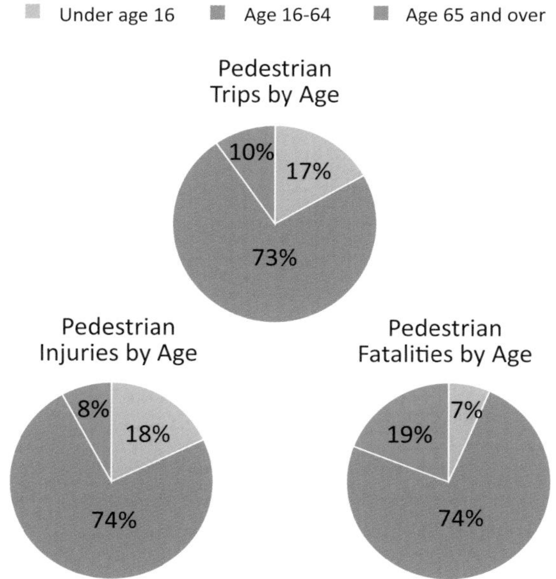

Sources: NHTS 2009, WISQARS 2011, FARS 2009–2011 **Note**: (1) Numbers round down, so appear to add to 99%

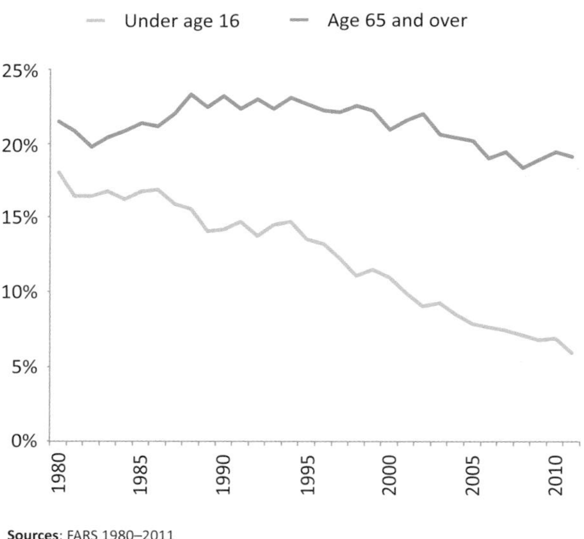

Sources: FARS 1980–2011

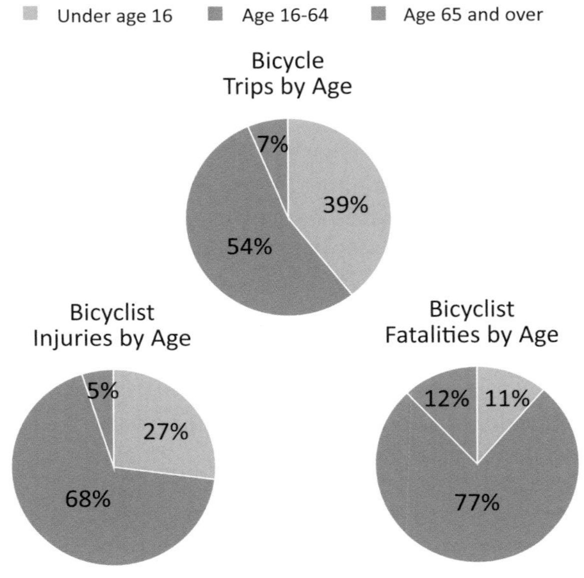

Sources: NHTS 2009, WISQARS 2011, FARS 2009–2011

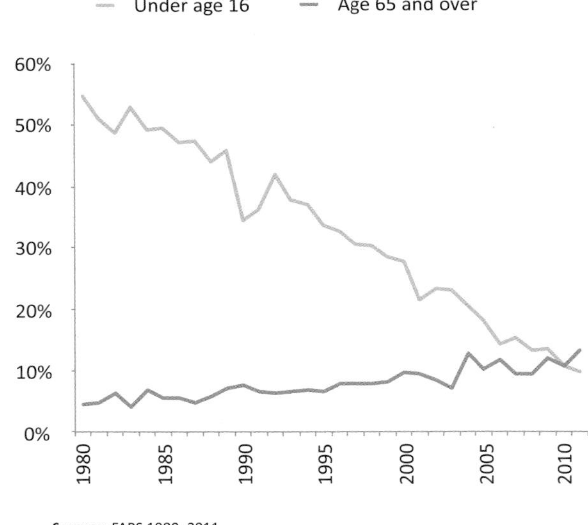

Sources: FARS 1980–2011

overall bicycling and walking. No statistical analysis has been conducted to test the significance of these rates.

FARS and ACS data indicate that between 2009 and 2011 nationwide, 8.5 bicyclists are killed per year per 10,000 daily commuter bicyclists, an improvement from 9.1 bicyclists killed per 10,000 bicycle commuters between 2007 and 2009. In large U.S. cities, bicyclists died at a lower rate (4.9 fatalities per year per 10,000 daily commuter bicyclists). These data show a slight improvement from an average of 5.3 fatalities per year reported in 2007–2009. Among states, Montana, Maine, and Vermont saw the lowest bicyclist fatality rates, with less than two deaths per 10,000 daily bicyclists. Mississippi had the highest rate of bicyclist fatalities (70.4 deaths per 10,000 daily commuter bicyclists), followed by Arkansas (29.0 deaths per 10,000 daily commuter bicyclists).

Arlington, TX, and Wichita reported no bicyclist fatalities between 2009–2011. San Francisco, Portland, and Washington, DC, saw the next lowest fatality rates of bicyclists, at 0.9, 1.1, and 1.1 deaths per 10,000 daily commuter bicyclists, respectively. Fort Worth, Detroit, and Memphis saw the highest bicyclist fatality rates with 41.9, 39.8, and 36.0 bicyclists killed per 10,000 daily commuter bicyclists, respectively.

Commuting pedestrians are similarly safer in the 52 most populous U.S. cities where 8.3 pedestrian fatalities occur each year for every 10,000 daily commuting pedestrians (an improvement from two year ago with 8.8 fatalities). In states, there are 11.0 pedestrian deaths per 10,000 daily commuter pedestrians (up slightly from 10.9 two years ago). However, states with higher pedestrian commuting rates have lower overall pedestrian fatality rates and vice versa. A strong negative relationship exists between the percentage of commuting pedestrians and the number of pedestrian fatalities per 10,000 ($r = -0.67$).

In addition to being one of the safest biking states, Vermont is also the safest state for walking, with 2.2 pedestrian deaths per 10,000 daily commuter pedestrians. Florida (38.6 deaths per 10,000 daily commuting pedestrians) and Alabama (28.1 deaths per 10,000 daily commuting pedestrians)

Pedestrian Fatality Rates

Pedestrian fatalities per 10k walking commuters

In States

1	**Vermont**	2.2
2	**Nebraska**	2.9
3	**Alaska**	3.0
4	**Wyoming**	3.7
5	**New Hampshire**	3.8
6	**South Dakota**	3.8
7	**Massachusetts**	3.8
8	**Iowa**	3.9
9	**Maine**	4.5
10	**Idaho**	4.6
11	North Dakota	4.8
12	Kansas	5.0
13	Minnesota	5.1
14	New York	5.3
15	Wisconsin	5.4
16	Montana	5.6
17	Colorado	5.8
18	Washington	5.8
19	Pennsylvania	6.4
20	Connecticut	6.4
21	Illinois	6.5
22	Hawaii	6.8
23	Oregon	6.9
24	Rhode Island	7.3
25	Utah	7.6
26	Virginia	7.9
27	Ohio	8.0
28	West Virginia	8.6
29	Indiana	9.5
30	New Jersey	11.4
31	Missouri	12.1
32	Kentucky	13.4
33	California	13.5
34	Michigan	14.1
35	Oklahoma	15.1
36	Maryland	15.7
37	Nevada	16.5
38	Arkansas	17.3
39	New Mexico	18.5
40	Delaware	19.2
41	Texas	19.7
42	North Carolina	21.2
43	Tennessee	21.6
44	Georgia	23.1
45	Arizona	23.4
46	Louisiana	23.4
47	South Carolina	24.6
48	Mississippi	25.8
49	Alabama	28.1
50	Florida	38.6

In Large Cities

1	**Boston**	0.9
2	**Seattle**	2.7
3	**Washington, DC**	3.3
4	**Colorado Springs**	3.4
5	**San Francisco**	4.0
6	**New York City**	4.0
7	**Minneapolis**	4.5
8	**Chicago**	4.5
9	**Omaha**	4.6
10	**Honolulu**	5.2
11	Cleveland	5.2
12	Portland, OR	5.8
13	Philadelphia	5.8
14	Oakland	6.3
15	Baltimore	6.7
16	Virginia Beach	6.9
17	Denver	7.6
18	Milwaukee	7.7
19	New Orleans	9.6
20	Mesa	10.6
21	Columbus	11.1
22	San Diego	11.4
23	Long Beach	12.4
24	Arlington, TX	13.9
25	Los Angeles	14.0
26	Austin	14.0
27	Atlanta	14.6
28	San Jose	15.6
29	Wichita	16.8
30	Las Vegas	17.1
31	Raleigh	17.2
32	Tucson	19.0
33	Albuquerque	19.1
34	Tulsa	19.3
35	Indianapolis	19.9
36	Oklahoma City	20.0
37	Houston	20.1
38	Nashville	20.4
39	Kansas City, MO	20.7
40	Miami	21.2
41	Sacramento	21.9
42	Charlotte	22.0
43	Louisville	24.2
44	San Antonio	24.5
45	El Paso	24.7
46	Fresno	25.6
47	Dallas	26.3
48	Memphis	29.1
49	Phoenix	29.6
50	Fort Worth	29.6
51	Detroit	40.1
52	Jacksonville	41.6

Bicyclist Fatality Rates

Bicyclist fatalities per 10k bicycling commuters

In States

1	**Montana**	1.0
2	**Maine**	1.1
3	**Vermont**	1.5
4	**Oregon**	2.6
5	**Massachusetts**	2.7
6	**Colorado**	2.8
7	**Rhode Island**	3.1
8	**Washington**	3.2
9	**Alaska**	3.7
10	**Wyoming**	4.0
11	Minnesota	4.4
12	Hawaii	4.5
13	South Dakota	4.6
14	Wisconsin	4.7
15	Idaho	4.8
16	North Dakota	5.1
17	Kansas	5.1
18	Nebraska	5.5
19	Missouri	5.5
20	Utah	6.0
21	Pennsylvania	6.3
22	California	6.3
23	Illinois	7.0
24	Iowa	7.2
25	Virginia	7.3
26	Indiana	8.0
27	New Mexico	8.2
28	Arizona	8.9
29	Nevada	9.5
30	Maryland	9.7
31	New York	9.8
32	New Jersey	10.3
33	Ohio	10.5
34	New Hampshire	10.6
35	Connecticut	11.2
36	West Virginia	11.2
37	Kentucky	11.3
38	Michigan	13.5
39	Texas	15.9
40	Oklahoma	16.7
41	Tennessee	16.9
42	Louisiana	17.0
43	Georgia	18.3
44	Florida	21.1
45	South Carolina	21.2
46	North Carolina	21.8
47	Alabama	22.1
48	Delaware	26.0
49	Arkansas	29.0
50	Mississippi	70.4

In Large Cities

1	**Arlington, TX**	0.0
2	**Wichita**	0.0
3	**San Francisco**	0.9
4	**Portland, OR**	1.1
5	**Washington, DC**	1.1
6	**Denver**	1.5
7	**Atlanta**	1.6
8	**Seattle**	1.7
9	**Minneapolis**	2.3
10	**Philadelphia**	2.3
11	Austin	2.4
12	Boston	2.5
13	Tucson	3.0
14	Oakland	3.0
15	Raleigh	3.4
16	Cleveland	3.6
17	Honolulu	3.6
18	Nashville	3.8
19	Chicago	3.9
20	Virginia Beach	3.9
21	Milwaukee	4.0
22	Los Angeles	4.3
23	San Jose	4.4
24	Baltimore	4.6
25	Colorado Springs	4.8
26	Sacramento	5.3
27	San Antonio	5.4
28	Albuquerque	5.6
29	New Orleans	5.8
30	New York City	6.4
31	San Diego	6.8
32	Columbus	7.3
33	Miami	7.9
34	Tulsa	8.2
35	El Paso	8.3
36	Long Beach	9.8
37	Kansas City, MO	10.4
38	Las Vegas	10.5
39	Houston	11.2
40	Indianapolis	11.9
41	Louisville	12.0
42	Mesa	14.5
43	Dallas	17.6
44	Charlotte	18.3
45	Omaha	18.6
46	Phoenix	19.3
47	Fresno	20.9
48	Oklahoma City	21.1
49	Jacksonville	33.1
50	Memphis	36.0
51	Detroit	39.8
52	Fort Worth	41.9

Sources: FARS 2009–2011, ACS 2009–2011 **Notes**: All fatality data are based on the 3-year average number of fatalities from 2009–2011. Because of the great fluctuations in fatality data from year to year, this rate should be seen as a rough estimate. Fatality rates were calculated by dividing the number of annual pedestrian or bicyclist fatalities (averaged between 2009–2011) by the estimated annual number of commuters walking or bicycling to work (ACS 2009–2011)

are the least safe states for walking. Boston and Seattle have the lowest pedestrian fatality rates among major U.S. cities with 0.9 and 2.7 pedestrian deaths per 10,000 daily commuting pedestrians, respectively. Jacksonville has the highest pedestrian fatality rate with 41.6 pedestrian deaths per 10,000 daily commuting pedestrians.

Overall, pedestrian fatalities have steadily declined in every age group since 1980. While bicycle fatalities among children under 16 have declined sharply during this time period, fatalities in the 16 and older age group have steadily increased. However, these charts do not take into account the change in number of people who bicycle or walk in these age groups. For example, the number of children who bicycle or walk to school has decreased 75% between 1966 and 2009. When walking and bicycling levels have declined at such rates, then reduced fatalities do not necessarily suggest safer walking and bicycling.

Safety in Numbers

To see how levels of bicycling and walking affect safety, the Alliance compared fatality rates in large cities to corresponding bicycle and pedestrian mode share. Data for the 52 cities studied in this report indicate an inverse relationship between bicycling and walking levels and fatality rates.

Cities with the highest rates of pedestrian fatalities are among those with the lowest levels of walking (r = -0.67). Similarly, cities with the highest levels of bicycling generally have lower bicycle fatality rates (r = -0.57). These results are consistent with previous research (Jacobsen and Rutter, 2012; Pucher and Buehler, 2010; Buehler and Pucher, 2012; Elvik, 2009; Jacobsen, 2003; Pucher et al., 2011; Vandenbulcke et al., 2009).

A possible explanation is that in places where more bicyclists and pedestrians are present, motorists are more used to sharing the roadways with bicyclists and are more aware of pedestrians at crossings. Environmental factors (such as signed routes, bike lanes, and sidewalks) that contribute to increased bicycling and walking also likely contribute to increased safety.

Pedestrian Injuries by Gender

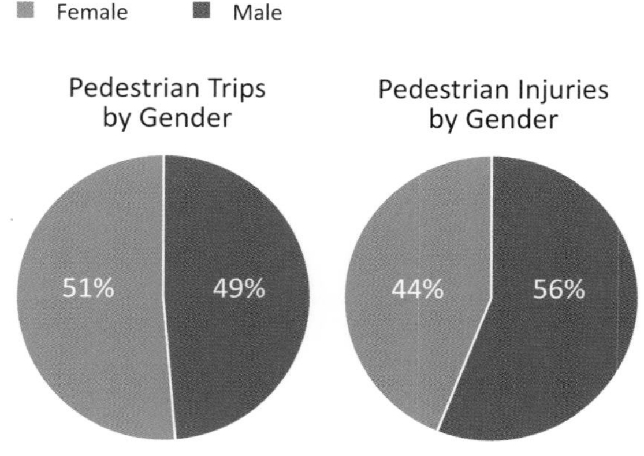

Sources: NHTS 2009, WISQARS 2011

Bicyclist Injuries by Gender

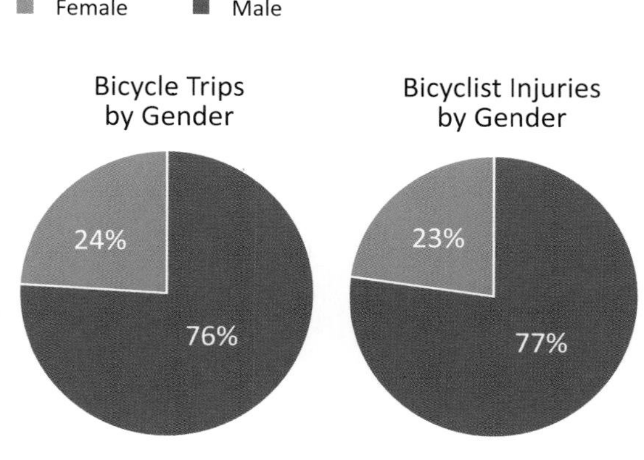

Sources: NHTS 2009, WISQARS 2011

Comparing Walking to Work and Pedestrian Fatality Rates in Large Cities

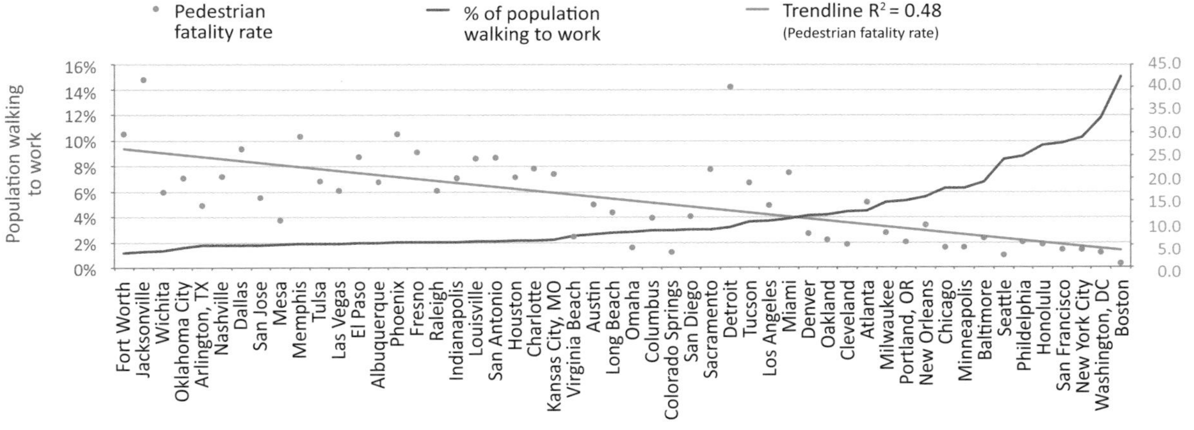

Sources: ACS 2009–2011, FARS 2009–2011

Comparing Bicycling to Work and Bicyclist Fatality Rates in Large Cities

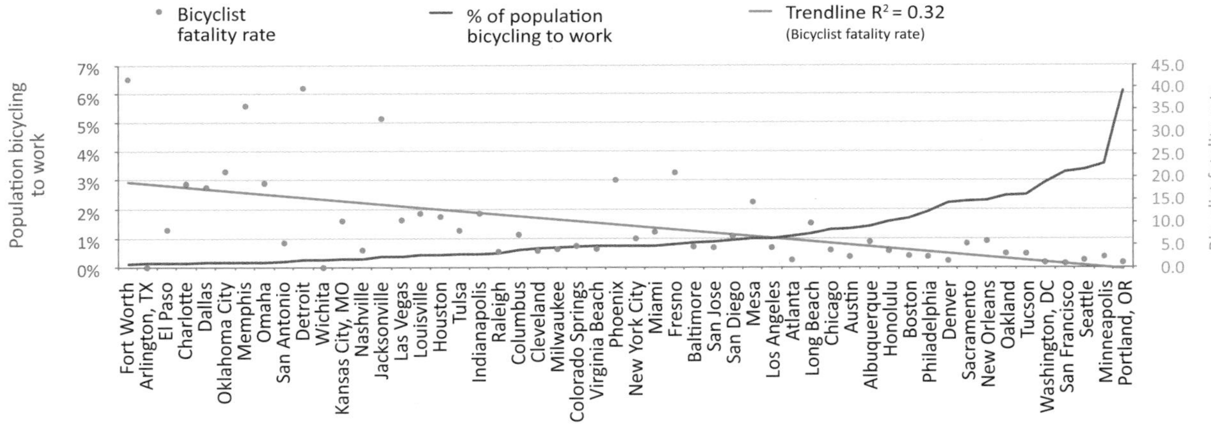

Sources: ACS 2009–2011, FARS 2009–2011

Pedestrian Safety in States

	Average annual pedestrian fatalities reported	Pedestrian fatalities per 10k walking commuters (1)	% of all traffic fatalities that are pedestrians	% of pedestrian fatalities	
				Under age 16	Over age 64
Alabama	68.0	28.1	7.8%	8.3%	16.7%
Alaska	8.0	3.0	12.5%	25.0%	16.7%
Arizona	136.7	23.4	17.2%	5.9%	17.3%
Arkansas	39.0	17.3	6.8%	6.0%	7.7%
California	597.7	13.5	20.9%	5.4%	24.9%
Colorado	42.7	5.8	9.4%	4.7%	19.5%
Connecticut	32.7	6.4	12.8%	6.1%	20.4%
Delaware	18.3	19.2	17.4%	9.1%	12.7%
Florida	481.0	38.6	19.5%	4.8%	20.7%
Georgia	150.0	23.1	12.0%	8.2%	8.7%
Hawaii	21.7	6.8	20.2%	0.0%	35.4%
Idaho	9.7	4.6	4.8%	13.8%	17.2%
Illinois	120.3	6.5	13.1%	6.1%	19.7%
Indiana	57.7	9.5	7.9%	12.7%	23.1%
Iowa	21.3	3.9	5.7%	14.1%	23.4%
Kansas	17.0	5.0	4.2%	5.9%	19.6%
Kentucky	50.7	13.4	6.7%	9.9%	17.8%
Louisiana	91.0	23.4	12.3%	8.4%	5.5%
Maine	11.0	4.5	7.2%	6.1%	33.3%
Maryland	106.0	15.7	20.8%	6.3%	16.4%
Massachusetts	57.3	3.8	16.8%	3.5%	29.1%
Michigan	128.0	14.1	14.2%	3.4%	15.6%
Minnesota	38.7	5.1	9.7%	8.6%	24.1%
Mississippi	51.7	25.8	7.9%	5.8%	11.6%
Missouri	66.0	12.1	8.0%	10.1%	14.1%
Montana	12.7	5.6	6.1%	13.2%	26.3%
Nebraska	8.0	2.9	4.0%	4.2%	16.7%
Nevada	39.0	16.5	15.7%	6.0%	20.5%
New Hampshire	7.3	3.8	6.7%	4.6%	36.4%
New Jersey	146.3	11.4	24.8%	4.8%	23.7%
New Mexico	37.7	18.5	10.6%	8.0%	11.5%
New York	299.3	5.3	25.5%	6.7%	28.6%
North Carolina	158.3	21.2	12.3%	6.7%	12.2%
North Dakota	6.7	4.8	5.1%	20.0%	15.0%
Ohio	94.0	8.1	9.0%	10.3%	18.4%
Oklahoma	45.7	15.1	6.5%	10.2%	13.1%
Oregon	45.7	6.9	13.4%	5.1%	15.3%
Pennsylvania	142.0	6.4	11.0%	7.8%	25.4%
Rhode Island	13.0	7.3	18.1%	5.1%	38.5%
South Carolina	97.3	24.6	11.5%	6.2%	13.7%
South Dakota	6.7	3.8	5.2%	5.0%	10.0%
Tennessee	79.3	21.6	8.0%	4.6%	11.3%
Texas	373.3	19.7	12.3%	7.1%	12.0%
Utah	25.7	7.6	10.5%	15.6%	15.6%
Vermont	4.0	2.2	6.0%	0.0%	58.3%
Virgina	73.3	7.9	9.7%	5.0%	16.4%
Washington	61.3	5.8	13.1%	8.7%	20.1%
West Virginia	18.0	8.6	5.4%	0.0%	5.6%
Wisconsin	49.0	5.4	8.6%	7.5%	29.9%
Wyoming	3.7	3.8	2.6%	18.2%	18.2%
State average	85.6 (2)	11.0	12.9%	6.5%	19.1%
State median	47.3	7.8	10.1%	6.3%	17.6%
High	597.7	38.6	25.5%	25.0%	58.3%
Low	3.7	2.2	2.6%	0.0%	5.5%

Sources: FARS 2009–2011, ACS 2009–2011. **Notes**: All fatality data are based on the 3-year average number of fatalities from 2009–2011. Because of the great fluctuations in fatality data from year to year, this rate should be seen as a rough estimate. (1) Pedestrian fatality rate was calculated by dividing the number of annual pedestrian fatalities (averaged between 2009–2011) by the estimated annual number of commuters walking to work (ACS 2009–2011). (2) This average is not weighted; it is an average of the state averages (annual average per state). The nationwide average (state averages totaled) annual pedestrian fatalities reported is 4,281.

Bicyclist Safety in States

Average annual bicyclist fatalities reported	Bicyclist fatalities per 10k biking commuters (1)	% of all traffic fatalities that are bicyclists	% of bicyclist fatalities		
			Under age 16	Over age 64	
5.7	22.1	0.7%	29.4%	5.9%	Alabama
1.3	3.7	2.1%	0.0%	0.0%	Alaska
22.3	8.9	2.8%	9.0%	13.4%	Arizona
4.3	29.0	0.8%	15.4%	0.0%	Arkansas
104.3	6.3	3.6%	8.9%	12.8%	California
8.7	2.8	1.9%	15.4%	11.5%	Colorado
5.3	11.2	2.1%	25.0%	18.8%	Connecticut
3.0	26.0	2.8%	55.6%	11.1%	Delaware
105.0	21.1	4.3%	6.0%	13.3%	Florida
17.7	18.3	1.4%	11.3%	5.7%	Georgia
2.7	4.5	2.5%	0.0%	25.0%	Hawaii
3.7	4.8	1.8%	9.1%	9.1%	Idaho
23.3	7.0	2.5%	15.7%	21.4%	Illinois
10.3	8.0	1.4%	9.7%	9.7%	Indiana
5.0	7.2	1.3%	6.7%	6.7%	Iowa
2.7	5.1	0.7%	12.5%	12.5%	Kansas
4.7	11.3	0.6%	35.7%	7.1%	Kentucky
14.0	17.0	1.9%	11.9%	7.1%	Louisiana
0.3	1.1	0.2%	100.0%	0.0%	Maine
7.7	9.7	1.5%	17.4%	8.7%	Maryland
6.0	2.7	1.8%	11.1%	16.7%	Massachusetts
24.0	13.5	2.7%	15.3%	16.7%	Michigan
8.0	4.4	2.0%	16.7%	20.8%	Minnesota
7.0	70.4	1.1%	19.0%	4.8%	Mississippi
3.3	5.5	0.4%	20.0%	10.0%	Missouri
0.7	1.0	0.3%	0.0%	0.0%	Montana
2.3	5.5	1.2%	0.0%	0.0%	Nebraska
5.3	9.5	2.1%	18.8%	6.3%	Nevada
1.7	10.7	1.5%	20.0%	0.0%	New Hampshire
14.3	10.3	2.4%	11.6%	14.0%	New Jersey
5.0	8.2	1.4%	0.0%	6.7%	New Mexico
40.7	9.8	3.5%	12.3%	13.1%	New York
21.3	21.8	1.7%	3.1%	9.4%	North Carolina
1.0	5.1	0.8%	33.3%	33.3%	North Dakota
15.3	10.5	1.5%	13.0%	13.0%	Ohio
7.0	16.8	1.0%	23.8%	19.0%	Oklahoma
10.0	2.6	2.9%	0.0%	13.3%	Oregon
15.7	6.3	1.2%	19.1%	2.1%	Pennsylvania
0.7	3.1	0.9%	50.0%	50.0%	Rhode Island
13.3	21.2	1.6%	5.0%	5.0%	South Carolina
1.0	4.6	0.8%	0.0%	0.0%	South Dakota
6.0	16.9	0.6%	0.0%	5.6%	Tennessee
44.3	15.9	1.5%	14.3%	12.0%	Texas
5.7	6.1	2.3%	41.2%	5.9%	Utah
0.3	1.5	0.5%	100.0%	0.0%	Vermont
9.7	7.4	1.3%	6.9%	3.4%	Virgina
8.7	3.2	1.8%	7.7%	19.2%	Washington
1.0	11.2	0.3%	33.3%	0.0%	West Virginia
9.3	4.7	1.6%	7.1%	21.4%	Wisconsin
1.0	4.0	0.7%	0.0%	0.0%	Wyoming
12.9 (2)	8.5	1.9%	11.3%	12.1%	State average
6.0	7.7	1.5%	12.4%	9.3%	State median
105.0	70.4	4.3%	100.0%	50.0%	High
0.3	1.0	0.2%	0.0%	0.0%	Low

Sources: FARS 2009-2011, ACS 2009-2011 **Notes**: All fatality data are based on the 3-year average number of fatalities from 2009-2011. Because of the great fluctuations in fatality data from year to year, this rate should be seen as a rough estimate. (1) Bicyclist fatality rate was calculated by dividing the number of annual bicyclist fatalities (averaged between 2009-2011) by the estimated annual number of commuters bicycling to work (ACS 2009-2011). (2) This average is not weighted; it is an average of the state averages (annual average per state). The nationwide average (state averages totaled) annual bicyclist fatalities reported is 643.

Pedestrian Safety in Large Cities

	Average annual pedestrian fatalities reported	Pedestrian fatalities per 10k walking commuters [(1)]	% of all traffic fatalities that are pedestrians	% of pedestrian fatalities	
				Under age 16	Over age 64
Albuquerque	9.7	19.1	22.7%	6.9%	10.3%
Arlington, TX	4.3	13.9	14.8%	30.8%	15.4%
Atlanta	12.7	14.6	28.6%	13.2%	7.9%
Austin	15.7	14.0	27.5%	2.1%	10.6%
Baltimore	11.7	6.7	33.7%	8.6%	22.9%
Boston	4.0	0.9	25.5%	0.0%	33.3%
Charlotte	17.0	22.0	32.1%	5.9%	5.9%
Chicago	34.0	4.5	24.9%	9.8%	28.4%
Cleveland	3.3	5.2	10.9%	30.0%	0.0%
Colorado Springs	2.0	3.4	10.0%	33.3%	16.7%
Columbus	12.3	11.1	22.8%	5.4%	8.1%
Dallas	26.0	26.3	23.4%	2.6%	15.4%
Denver	9.7	7.7	26.6%	6.9%	17.2%
Detroit	25.7	40.1	27.1%	2.6%	13.0%
El Paso	13.0	24.7	21.9%	2.6%	28.2%
Fort Worth	11.7	29.6	18.5%	2.9%	11.4%
Fresno	9.3	25.6	29.5%	3.6%	10.7%
Honolulu	8.7	5.2	41.9%	0.0%	46.2%
Houston	43.0	20.1	20.8%	1.6%	8.5%
Indianapolis	15.0	19.9	21.5%	15.6%	17.8%
Jacksonville	20.3	41.6	20.5%	6.6%	18.0%
Kansas City, MO	10.0	20.8	15.4%	6.7%	10.0%
Las Vegas	8.3	17.1	29.1%	4.0%	24.0%
Long Beach	7.0	12.4	24.7%	4.8%	28.6%
Los Angeles	89.0	14.0	38.9%	4.5%	24.3%
Louisville	13.3	24.2	21.9%	7.5%	22.5%
Memphis	14.7	29.1	18.0%	4.5%	6.8%
Mesa	3.7	10.6	12.6%	0.0%	9.1%
Miami	14.0	21.2	37.2%	4.8%	40.5%
Milwaukee	10.0	7.7	24.6%	16.7%	13.3%
Minneapolis	5.7	4.5	29.3%	0.0%	17.6%
Nashville	10.7	20.4	16.5%	3.1%	12.5%
New Orleans	8.0	9.6	23.8%	8.3%	4.2%
New York City	148.7	4.0	55.0%	6.3%	30.7%
Oakland	4.7	6.3	18.7%	7.1%	42.9%
Oklahoma City	8.7	20.0	11.9%	3.8%	7.7%
Omaha	2.7	4.6	13.1%	0.0%	12.5%
Philadelphia	30.3	5.8	33.1%	13.2%	17.6%
Phoenix	37.7	29.6	26.4%	6.2%	17.7%
Portland, OR	9.0	5.8	30.0%	3.7%	11.1%
Raleigh	7.0	17.2	25.0%	19.0%	19.0%
Sacramento	12.7	21.9	31.9%	0.0%	21.1%
San Antonio	30.7	24.5	24.8%	6.5%	13.0%
San Diego	21.7	11.4	30.4%	7.7%	20.0%
San Francisco	17.0	4.0	51.0%	0.0%	41.2%
San Jose	12.3	15.6	31.4%	0.0%	37.8%
Seattle	8.0	2.7	32.0%	0.0%	37.5%
Tucson	15.3	19.0	28.9%	10.9%	19.6%
Tulsa	6.7	19.3	14.0%	10.0%	20.0%
Virginia Beach	4.0	6.9	16.7%	16.7%	8.3%
Washington, DC	11.7	3.3	43.8%	8.6%	22.9%
Wichita	4.0	16.8	13.8%	8.3%	16.7%
Large cities average	17.2	8.3	27.8%	6.2%	20.8%
Large cities median	11.7	14.3	24.9%	6.1%	17.4%
High	148.7	41.6	55.0%	33.3%	46.2%
Low	2.0	0.9	10.0%	0.0%	0.0%

Sources: FARS 2009–2011, ACS 2009–2011 **Notes**: All fatality data are based on the 3-year average number of fatalities from 2009–2011. Because of the great fluctuations in fatality data from year to year, this rate should be seen as a rough estimate. (1) Pedestrian fatality rate was calculated by dividing the number of annual pedestrian fatalities (averaged between 2009–2011) by the estimated annual number of commuters walking to work (ACS 2009–2011).

Bicyclist Safety in Large Cities

Average annual bicyclist fatalities reported	Bicyclist fatalities per 10k biking commuters [1]	% of all traffic fatalities that are bicyclists	% of bicyclist fatalities		
			Under age 16	Over age 64	
2.0	5.6	4.7%	0.0%	0.0%	Albuquerque
0.0	0.0	0.0%	0.0%	0.0%	Arlington, TX
0.3	1.6	0.8%	0.0%	0.0%	Atlanta
1.3	2.4	2.3%	0.0%	0.0%	Austin
1.0	4.6	2.9%	33.3%	33.3%	Baltimore
1.3	2.5	8.5%	0.0%	25.0%	Boston
1.0	18.4	1.9%	0.0%	0.0%	Charlotte
6.0	3.9	4.4%	33.3%	22.2%	Chicago
0.3	3.6	1.1%	0.0%	0.0%	Cleveland
0.7	4.8	3.3%	0.0%	0.0%	Colorado Springs
1.7	7.3	3.1%	0.0%	20.0%	Columbus
1.7	17.6	1.5%	60.0%	20.0%	Dallas
1.0	1.5	2.8%	0.0%	33.3%	Denver
2.0	39.8	2.1%	33.3%	0.0%	Detroit
0.3	8.3	0.6%	0.0%	100.0%	El Paso
1.7	41.9	2.6%	20.0%	0.0%	Fort Worth
3.0	21.0	9.5%	11.1%	0.0%	Fresno
1.0	3.6	4.8%	0.0%	33.3%	Honolulu
4.7	11.2	2.3%	0.0%	14.3%	Houston
2.0	11.9	2.9%	0.0%	0.0%	Indianapolis
4.7	33.1	4.7%	0.0%	14.3%	Jacksonville
0.7	10.4	1.0%	0.0%	0.0%	Kansas City, MO
1.0	10.6	3.5%	0.0%	0.0%	Las Vegas
2.3	9.8	8.2%	0.0%	28.6%	Long Beach
7.3	4.3	3.2%	4.5%	4.5%	Los Angeles
1.3	12.0	2.2%	25.0%	0.0%	Louisville
1.7	36.0	2.0%	0.0%	0.0%	Memphis
2.7	14.5	9.2%	25.0%	12.5%	Mesa
1.0	7.9	2.7%	0.0%	0.0%	Miami
0.7	4.0	1.6%	0.0%	0.0%	Milwaukee
1.7	2.3	8.6%	0.0%	0.0%	Minneapolis
0.3	3.8	0.5%	0.0%	0.0%	Nashville
2.0	5.8	5.9%	0.0%	0.0%	New Orleans
17.3	6.4	6.4%	1.9%	13.5%	New York City
1.3	3.0	5.3%	0.0%	0.0%	Oakland
1.0	21.1	1.4%	0.0%	33.3%	Oklahoma City
0.7	18.6	3.3%	0.0%	0.0%	Omaha
2.7	2.3	2.9%	0.0%	0.0%	Philadelphia
9.0	19.3	6.3%	3.7%	18.5%	Phoenix
2.0	1.1	6.7%	0.0%	16.7%	Portland, OR
0.3	3.4	1.2%	0.0%	0.0%	Raleigh
2.3	5.3	5.9%	0.0%	0.0%	Sacramento
0.7	5.4	0.5%	0.0%	0.0%	San Antonio
4.0	6.8	5.6%	0.0%	8.3%	San Diego
1.3	0.9	4.0%	0.0%	0.0%	San Francisco
1.7	4.4	4.2%	0.0%	0.0%	San Jose
2.0	1.7	8.0%	0.0%	0.0%	Seattle
1.7	3.0	3.1%	0.0%	0.0%	Tucson
0.7	8.2	1.4%	0.0%	50.0%	Tulsa
0.7	4.0	2.8%	50.0%	0.0%	Virginia Beach
1.0	1.1	3.8%	0.0%	33.3%	Washington, DC
0.0	0.0	0.0%	0.0%	0.0%	Wichita
2.1	4.9	3.4%	6.3%	10.8%	Large cities average
1.3	5.4	3.0%	0.0%	0.0%	Large cities median
17.3	41.9	9.5%	60.0%	100.0%	High
0.0	0.0	0.0%	0.0%	0.0%	Low

Sources: FARS 2009–2011, ACS 2009–2011 **Notes**: All fatality data are based on the 3-year average number of fatalities from 2009–2011. Because of the great fluctuations in fatality data from year to year, this rate should be seen as a rough estimate. (1) Bicyclist fatality rate was calculated by dividing the number of annual bicyclist fatalities (averaged between 2009–2011) by the estimated annual number of commuters bicycling to work (ACS 2009–2011).

Health in Midsized Cities

The 17 midsized cities chosen for this report are facing similar health concerns as the larger cities. On average, about 26% of the population of these cities are living with obesity (the 52 large cities in this report also average 26%).

Physical activity levels, though, are higher in these small and midsized cities. Boulder sees 72.5% of its population meeting recommended levels of physical activity. On average, 56% of the population in these cities meet the weekly aerobic activity recommendations (compared to 52% in larger cities).

Public Health Indicators

	% adults meeting recommended minimum weekly aerobic physical activity	% adults with obesity	% adults with diabetes	% adults with high blood pressure
Population > 200K				
Anchorage, AK	57.4%	27.4%	-	29.0%
Baton Rouge, LA	45.1%	31.6%	10.1%	33.1%
Madison, WI	-	-	-	-
Pittsburgh, PA	50.6%	27.2%	9.2%	31.8%
Spokane, WA	55.4%	25.4%	8.3%	28.5%
St. Louis, MO	49.5%	29.8%	8.5%	33.1%
Population 100-200K				
Charleston, SC	49.6%	31.5%	11.6%	33.4%
Chattanooga, TN	36.4%	33.6%	8.8%	37.9%
Eugene, OR	65.0%	28.4%	7.0%	31.0%
Fort Collins, CO	64.8%	16.3%	4.7%	22.3%
Salt Lake City, UT	55.5%	25.1%	6.6%	22.3%
Population < 100K				
Albany, NY	-	-	-	-
Bellingham, WA	-	-	-	-
Boulder, CO	72.5%	15.1%	-	19.6%
Burlington, VT	59.1%	23.5%	6.2%	25.5%
Davis, CA	59.6%	24.3%	8.3%	27.0%
Missoula, MT	60.9%	21.0%	-	27.6%
High value				
Midsized cities	72.5%	33.6%	11.6%	37.9%
52 large cites	62.4%	36.8%	12.7%	37.8%
Low value				
Midsized cities	36.4%	15.1%	4.7%	19.6%
52 large cites	37.8%	18.6%	5.3%	23.7%
Large cities average	52.3%	26.4%	8.6%	29.7%

Source: BRFSS 2011 and 2010. **Note**: Cells with a dash (-) mean data were unavailable.

Safety in Midsized Cities

The relationship between bicycle fatalities and bicycling levels in the midsized cities follows a pattern similar to that of the most populous cities. As the percentage of trips to work by bicycle increases, the number of fatalities per 10,000 bicyclists declines. Boulder, Fort Collins, and Madison all have a cycling rate above 5% and are likewise the only three cities among the midsized cities that have a bicycling fatality rate below one per 10,000 cyclists. All of the midsized cities have low overall fatality numbers, so one additional fatality can have a large impact on the fatality rate.

Similarly, the midsized cities show the same trends for pedestrian fatalities and walking levels as the most populous cities. In general, the lower the number of pedestrian fatalities per 10,000 pedestrians in a given city, the higher the percentage of individuals walking to work. Albany, Boulder, Madison, and Pittsburgh reported the highest percentage of trips to work by foot as well as the lowest fatality rates of below four pedestrian fatalities per 10,000 pedestrians.

Pedestrian and Bicyclist Fatalities

	Total # of ped fatalities (2009–2011)	Avg annual pedestrian fatalities	% of all traffic fatalities that are pedestrians	Total # of bike fatalities (2009–2011)	Avg annual bicyclist fatalities	% of all traffic fatalities that are bicyclists
Population > 200K						
Anchorage, AK	11	3.7	25.6%	3	1.0	7.0%
Baton Rouge, LA	20	6.7	23.0%	2	0.7	2.3%
Madison, WI	12	4.0	31.6%	1	0.3	2.6%
Pittsburgh, PA	12	4.0	22.2%	1	0.3	1.9%
Spokane, WA	12	4.0	33.3%	3	1.0	8.3%
St. Louis, MO	36	12.0	28.1%	1	0.3	0.8%
Population 100-200K						
Charleston, SC	20	6.7	31.7%	5	1.7	7.9%
Chattanooga, TN	11	3.7	16.4%	3	1.0	4.5%
Eugene, OR	7	2.3	31.8%	2	0.7	9.1%
Fort Collins, CO	3	1.0	15.8%	1	0.3	5.3%
Salt Lake City, UT	10	3.3	22.7%	4	1.3	9.1%
Population < 100K						
Albany, NY	4	1.3	28.6%	1	0.3	7.1%
Bellingham, WA	-	-	-	-	-	-
Boulder, CO	5	1.7	50.0%	1	0.3	10.0%
Burlington, VT	-	-	-	-	-	-
Davis, CA	-	-	-	-	-	-
Missoula, MT	-	-	-	-	-	-
High value						
Midsized cities	36	12.0	50.0%	5	1.7	10.0%
52 large cites	446	148.7	55.0%	52	17.3	9.5%
Low value						
Midsized cities	3	1.0	15.8%	1	0.3	0.8%
52 large cites	6	2.0	10.0%	0	0.0	0.0%
Large cities	2,688	17.2	27.8%	332	2.1	3.4%

Source: FARS 2009–2011 **Note:** Cells with a dash (-) mean data were unavailable.

Quequechan River Rail Trail, Massachusetts:

Using Health Impact Assessments in Transportation Projects

by Eloisa Raynault, American Public Health Association

In recent years, the city of Fall River, Massachusetts, has been investigating the intersection of transportation and public health. The study focuses specifically on a former rail line along the Quequechan River that is being converted into a multi-purpose path for bicyclists and pedestrians.

The Quequechan River Rail Trail (QRRT) project began in 2008 with the construction of a mile-long path in Fall River's Flint and Maplewood neighborhoods (Phase One). The City of Fall River is now considering construction of a 1.6 mile extension to QRRT Phase Two that will connect Phase One to the city's downtown.

In 2012, the Metropolitan Area Planning Council (MAPC) conducted a Health Impact Assessment (HIA) of Phase Two of the QRRT in partnership with Massachusetts Department of Health (DPH), the Southeastern Regional Planning and Economic Development District (SRPEDD), and Fall River Mass in Motion. The purpose of the HIA was to evaluate the health benefits associated with construction of Phase Two, while simultaneously mitigating any potentially adverse health effects of the project.

A Health Impact Assessment (HIA) is a systematic tool used to increase the consideration of health impacts before implementing a project, plan, program, or policy. By using an array of data sources, analytic methods, and input from stakeholders, an HIA determines the potential health effects of a proposed decision on an entire population. HIAs have been conducted across a broad cross-section of transportation projects and policies in the U.S. (APHA 2011).

The HIA leveraged data from various sources, including the American Community Survey Census, the Massachusetts Behavioral Risk Factor Surveillance System, the Massachusetts Department of Transportation (MassDOT) Motor Vehicle Crash Database, and the Federal Bureau of Investigation 2010 Uniform Crime Reports. Peer-reviewed research across public health, transportation, and planning journals also helped to delineate the connections between health and trail use.

The main health determinants investigated included the following:

1. Physical activity
2. Crime and safety
3. Air quality
4. Economic development
5. Access to health-related goods and services
6. Social cohesion

These health determinants can impact health outcomes, including changes in chronic diseases such as obesity, cardiovascular disease, respiratory disease, injuries, and premature mortality (CDC, 2013).

The HIA concluded that the proposed Phase Two extension of QRRT could have positive health impacts on the city of Fall River. The extension increases opportunities for residents

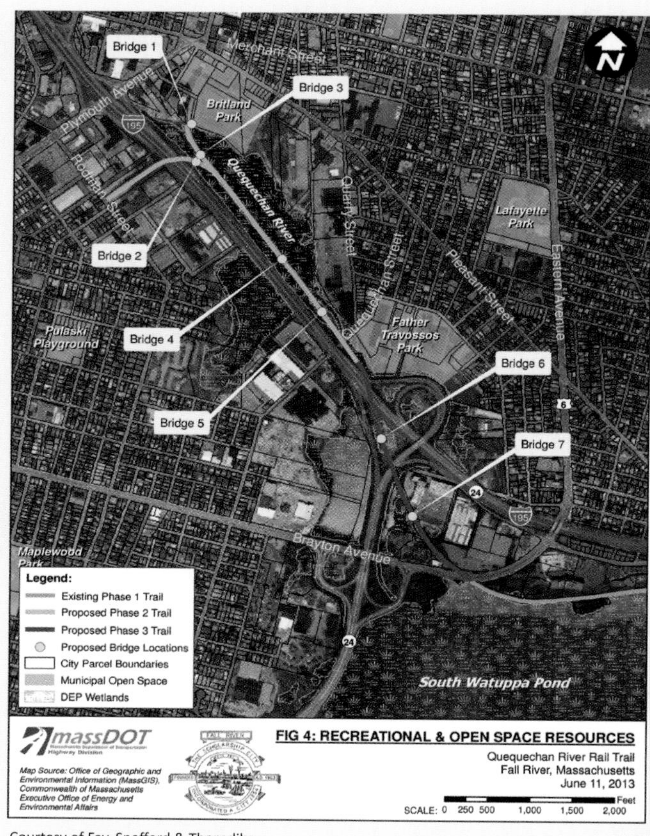

Courtesy of Fay, Spofford & Thorndike

Proposed Phase Two Trail Location
Photo courtesy of Fay, Spofford & Thorndike

Existing Phase One Trail
Photo courtesy of Fay, Spofford & Thorndike

to be physically active, which could help to reduce obesity and the risk of other chronic diseases in the community. It could help boost the local economy and positively affect health outcomes associated with socioeconomic status. Further, the extension could create safer active transportation options for residents, and help prevent injuries and crashes.

The HIA also reported that the extension could reduce crime through increased trail surveillance and outdoor lighting. Air quality in the area may improve because walking and bicycling trips would likely replace car trips. This, in turn, could reduce rates of asthma and cardiovascular disease. Lastly, the extension could improve Fall River's social environment and strengthen social cohesion by providing more opportunities for residents to interact by getting out of their homes and into their communities.

The project team has developed a plan to monitor the effectiveness of this HIA; the plan will help evaluate the outcomes of the project on the targeted health determinants and will inform next steps for future work on trails and health.

For more information, including a link to the full QRRT Phase Two HIA, visit:

www.MAPC.org/Quequechan-River-Rail-Trail-HIA

Denmark: Improving Safety Through Roadway Design

by Maggie Melin, Alliance for Biking & Walking

Over the last decade, traffic fatality rates in Denmark have dropped considerably and are among the lowest in Europe. Between 2000 and 2011, pedestrian fatalities decreased by 67% and bicyclist fatalities decreased by 48% (European Commission Statistic, 2013). In Copenhagen, as bicycling has grown, the number of seriously injured bicyclists has decreased steadily with injuries dropping from 252 in 1996 to 92 in 2010 (City of Copenhagen, 2011). Denmark's strategy to improve bicycling and pedestrian safety has been to implement a variety of initiatives to both increase physical safety and improve perceptions of safety. Strategies have included campaigning to change user behavior, and updating, and designing infrastructure to protect the most vulnerable road users.

National and local campaigns encourage bicyclists to wear helmets, use lights and reflectors, and be aware of the dangers of blind spots on right turns. The successful "Use helmets because we love you" campaign, for example, was aimed at adults in which children gave their parents helmets, and police officers handed out helmets on the streets. Additionally, schools have incorporated road safety courses into their curricula to expose children to safe bicycling at an early age. Police encouragement of basic safety habits, such as signaling when turning, using lights, and not bicycling in pedestrian crossings, have also helped improve safety conditions for all transportation users.

Infrastructure for walking and bicycling in Denmark includes cycle tracks and lanes, separated paths and greenways, road modifications aimed at slowing traffic, mixed traffic areas that prioritize pedestrians and bicyclists, specially designed intersections, pedestrian and bicyclist bridges, and bicycle parking. These infrastructure solutions not only increase the visibility and safety of bicyclists and pedestrians, they also help create a sense of security that promotes even greater participation in walking and bicycling for transportation. In 2010, 67% of bicyclists in Copenhagen reported feeling safe compared to 51% in 2008 (City of Copenhagen, 2011). On the city's street of

Copenhagen, DK. Photo by La Vitta Cita @ Flickr

Copenhagen, DK. Photo by Dylan Passmore @ Flickr

Copenhagen, DK. Photo by Dylan Passmore @ Flickr

Stormgade, a new cycle track was credited with increasing the security of bicyclists from 3.3 to 7 on a scale of 1 to 10 (City of Copenhagen, 2011).

Although building new infrastructure is cost prohibitive for many communities, municipalities in Denmark integrate some of these upgrades into planned utility construction and road renovation, much like the Complete Streets campaign in the U.S. Most often, cycle tracks are incorporated by localities when there is heavy, high-speed motorized traffic, and when there is not enough space for a bicyclist to feel secure on the road. These tracks are typically installed with a curb along the pavement to separate bicyclists and pedestrians from parked cars and other traffic. Care is taken particularly at bus stops to ensure that bus passengers do not unload directly onto a cycle track, if possible.

Similarly, bicycle lanes have also been successful in improving traffic safety across the country. Bicycle lanes are most often used on urban roads that have few shops and intersections, although, unlike cycle tracks, they do not address potential conflict areas with parked cars.

In Denmark, pothole maintenance is a priority, as is making the lanes and tracks wide enough for passing so that bicyclists do not feel the need to ride in the roadway. Roads have been slowed with speed humps, lower speeds limits, and narrowed roads to draw the attention of bicyclists and motorists to potentially dangerous situations.

In general, the national strategy has been to reduce interaction between bicyclists, pedestrians, and motorized vehicles, especially in high traffic areas, by segregating their designated spaces—or in some cases by establishing a pedestrian zone, or *woonerf*, where pedestrians have priority. See page 159 for a description of *woonerfs*.

Intersections are understood to be some of the most dangerous areas for bicyclists and pedestrians, and as a result, many Danish cities have taken steps to improve intersection flow and minimize potential dangers. Appropriate intersection design encourages bicyclists to make "box turns" by keeping them to the right of motorized traffic and guiding them to the opposite side of the road before making a left turn. In many instances stop lines for cars have been set back to allow bicyclists their own space in front of cars to wait for the light.

To help increase bicyclist and pedestrian visibility, Denmark has also established a ten-meter rule, which makes it illegal for a car to park within ten meters of a crossing. In some cases the rule has been extended to 20 or 30 meters. Some crossings have also been painted blue to further aid in increasing visibility, and green lights have been timed to give bicyclists priority over cars.

For more information on Denmark's design for safe bicycling and walking, visit the Cycling Embassy of Denmark website: *www.Cycling-Embassy.dk/*

4 Economic Benefits

Increasingly, states, cities, and individuals are realizing the many ways active transportation influences a healthy economy. Recent studies have shown that communities that invest in bicycling and walking have higher property values, create new jobs, and attract tourists. Where citizens have mobility options for more affordable transportation like bicycling and walking, they can see personal savings of thousands of dollars per year (AAA, 2013; Drennan, 2003). In addition, these communities save money for commuters, employers, and businesses by decreasing traffic congestion and commute times, and by improving air quality and public health.

This chapter highlights recent research that reveals some of the economic benefits of bicycling and walking.

Holland, MI. Photo by Dan Burden. Courtesy of *www.pedbikeimages.org*

Estimating Economic Impact

There are many ways the economic impact of bicycling and walking has been and could be measured. Some simple methods include surveys to trail users or event participants that ask them about their spending related to bicycling or walking. Others involve more complex modeling. Input-output models estimate the complete impact of bicycling or walking on the economy by including the direct, indirect, and induced effects of the activity, industry, or infrastructure.

For example, if you wanted to measure the economic impact of a specific trail, you would first quantify the direct impact, such as changes in sales, tax revenues, and jobs directly attributed to the trail. Examples might include sales at convenience stores, bicycle shops, or running stores located near the trail by trail users; food purchases by trail users; and hotel accommodations for tourists whose primary reason for coming to the area was to use the trail.

Next, you would quantify indirect impact, such as the secondary effects on suppliers to the industries directly affected—for example, businesses such as the dairies and creameries who supply ice cream to the snack stands that sell to the trail users.

Lastly, you could track induced impact, which accounts for the spending of income by people whose employment is dependent on the trail. For example, you could track the after-work spending of the person who serves the ice cream along the trail.

This model gives a comprehensive look at how money flows through the economy because of the trail.

A summary of studies estimating the economic impact of bicycling and walking can be found starting on page 98. Studies vary widely in their scope, methodology, and estimates.

Lasting Impact

After the initial economic boost from construction, pedestrian and bicycle infrastructure has lasting effects on local economies.

Years of planning and building streets for cars has left many communities severely lacking in bicycle and pedestrian infrastructure. Building new facilities for bicycling and walking can be a boost for the economy. In addition to new jobs, impacts on local economies include rising property values, increased business at local establishments, and savings from reduced traffic congestion.

Increased Sales

A study in Portland, OR, on consumer behavior by mode share addresses the concern business owners often have when asked to replace car parking with bicycle parking. According to the study, even though bicyclists and pedestrians spend less money per trip, they make more frequent visits to a business throughout a month and end up spending more on average than their car-driving counterparts (Clifton, 2013). Similar results were found in surveys of people on Polk Street in San Francisco and in Manhattan's East Village, where pedestrians in San Francisco and both pedestrians and bicyclists in Manhattan were found to spend more money over the course of a week than any other transportation mode (SFMTA, 2013; Transportation Alternatives, 2012).

New York City has employed numerous strategies to make their streets bicycle-friendly, including installing the nation's first protected bike lane in 2007. The city recently released a report, "Measuring the Street," that highlights some of the benefits seen since making improvements (NYCDOT, 2012). Though the methodology for the report has not been made available to the public, its stated findings are quite impressive. Businesses located within an improvement area saw sales increase at higher levels relative to the surrounding area, with up to 172% increase in retail sales at locally-based businesses on Pearl Street in Brooklyn after a pedestrian plaza was constructed. In Union Square North, commercial vacancies fell 49% after a protected bicycle lane was installed (NYCDOT, 2012).

Madison, WI. Photo by Eric Lowry. Courtesy of www.pedbikeimages.org

Other cities have reported similar experiences; for example, Magnolia Street in Fort Worth, TX, experienced a 163% increase in retail sales after a bicycle lane and improved bicycle parking were installed in the area (Fort Worth South, Inc., 2011). Bike share was also found to boost local retail sales in the Twin Cities. Research from the University of Minnesota estimates that during one season, customers using the Nice Ride bike share system spend an additional $150,000 at restaurants and other businesses near Nice Ride stations (Wang et al., 2012).

Property Values and Stability

Numerous studies have examined the effects proximity to trails and other bicycling and walking facilities have on property values (see table on page 99). Most recently, a 2012 study by the Brookings Institute concluded that places with higher walkability perform better commercially and have higher housing values (Brookings Institute, 2012). Their study in Washington, DC, found that office and retail spaces in areas with good walkability rented for $8.88/sq. ft. and $6.92/sq. ft. more per year, respectively, compared to places with fair walkability, holding household income levels constant. Additionally, relative to places with fair walkability, places with good walkability scores, on average, bring in $301.76 more per month in residential rents and $81.54/sq. ft. more in for-sale residential property values.

Worker Productivity

Few recent studies have been conducted in the U.S. on the impact of bicycling or walking on work productivity. A 2011 study by the London School of Economics has found that bicycling to work significantly reduces absenteeism due to illness. Regular cyclists were found to take 7.4 sick days per year on average, while non-cyclists took 8.7 sick days per year. This difference saves the U.K. economy an estimated £128 million, or $204 million, per year (London School of Economics, 2013).

Chicago, IL. Photo by Richard Pack @ *www.dickyp.com*

Decreased Traffic Congestion

In addition to the direct monetary and health benefits that can be realized through bicycling and walking, a mode shift towards nonmotorized traffic has the potential to help alleviate traffic congestion and produce major savings in time, fuel, and money.

Traffic congestion is increasingly becoming a common problem throughout the United States. According to the 2012 Urban Mobility Report from the Texas A&M Transportation Institute, which evaluated 498 urban areas, traffic congestion in 2011 caused Americans in cities to travel an additional 5.5 billion hours, purchase an additional 2.9 billion gallons of fuel, and spend an additional $121 billion in gas. On average each car commuter spent an extra 38 hours traveling as a result of congestion, costing the commuter $818 per year in delay time and wasted fuel (Texas A&M Transportation Institute, 2012).

While the effects of walking and bicycling on traffic congestion may be difficult to measure, many personal benefits are clear. By walking or bicycling, an individual no longer has to wait in bumper-to-bumper traffic, combines commuting and exercise times, renders fuel costs obsolete, and eliminates the stress of driving a car in congestion.

Cleaner Air

Reducing vehicle miles traveled also contributes to cleaner air. Communities designed to encourage safe bicycling and walking help reduce driving, and thereby reduce fuel consumption and air pollution associated with automobiles. This amounts to reduced smog that contributes to respiratory illness and asthmas, and reduced greenhouse gases that contribute to global warming. Although these savings and reductions are hard to quantify monetarily, some studies have attempted estimates, which can be found in the table on page 101.

A 2011 report from the European Cycling Federation has found that the greenhouse gas emissions built into a bicycle are over ten times lower per passenger mile than those from individual motorized transportation (Bondel et al., 2011). The study also indicates that electric bicycles (E-bikes) have a similar greenhouse gas emission range as ordinary bicycles, adding great potential to further reduce transport emissions. These findings include estimates on the average emissions required to manufacture a bicycle, as well as the food energy and additional calories required to power a bike.

Events and Tourism

Facilities like rail trails and safe places to bike and walk attract tourists. Local communities now vie for "Bicycle Friendly Community" and "Walking Friendly Community" designations, and communities with these designations report the recognition is good for business (Maus, 2006).

Numerous studies and papers have looked at the impact of bicycling on tourism, which can help boost the local economy through spending in lodging, food, travel, and entertainment. A 2012 Oregon bicycle tourism study found that

Photo courtesy of Alliance for Biking & Walking

bicycle-related expenditures amounted to nearly $400 million and supported 4,600 jobs within Oregon (Dean Runyan Associate, 2013).

A 2011 study from the University of Northern Iowa estimates that the direct and indirect economic impacts of recreational bicycling in Iowa are $365 million annually, or approximately $1 million per day (Lankford, 2011). A 2012 study by Charleston Moves and the College of Charleston further estimates that a proposed 32-mile bike route could have a $42 million economic impact on the surrounding area (Charleston Moves and the College of Charleston, 2012).

Bicycling and walking events can also stimulate local economies. The economic impact of the USA Pro-Challenge race in Colorado, which routes through 12 Colorado towns, was estimated to be $99.6 million in 2012. Charity Walk in Hawaii drew more than 14,700 walkers who raised over $1.7 million for local charities in 2013 (Charity Walk, 2014). Other estimates of the impact of bicycling and walking events can be found in the table on page 101.

The bicycling industry alone offers its own economic boost as a multi-billion dollar business in the United States. In 2012, the U.S. bicycle industry brought in $6.1 billion through retail sales, including parts and accessories (National Bicycle Dealers Association 2012). In 2010 Boulder Colorado's bicycle industry directly brought in over $52 million in revenue, as well as 330 full-time jobs through sales, repair, manufacturing, education, and advocacy (Community Cycles, 2011).

Improved Health

"The direct and indirect health costs associated with traffic collisions, pollution, and physical inactivity accounts for hundreds of billions of dollars annually" (RWJF, 2012). While nearly 80% of federal transportation dollars go towards building highways, only 2.1% is obligated for making roads more safe and accessible for bicyclists and pedestrians. A change in this ratio could lead to improved public health through active transportation, and could decrease overall public dollars spent on health costs (RWJF, 2012).

With national obesity rates predicted to grow from 28% to over 42% by 2030, a 2012 study predicts that the increase in obesity will cost the United States an estimated $550 billion between now and 2030 (Finkelstein et al., 2012). Studies show that promoting physical activity is cost-effective, and the value of health benefits can far outweigh the costs (Gotschi, 2008; Gotschi, 2011; National Governors Association, 2006; Roux et al., 2008). A 2011 study found that Portland, OR, would see between $388 and $594 million in health cost savings attributable to new bicycle infrastructure and programs by 2040 (Gotschi, 2011).

Savings

According to the Bureau of Labor Statistics, in 2011 transportation was second only to shelter for household expenditures in the U.S. The average American household spent 17% of their annual income on transportation, which is consistent across all income levels. If U.S. Americans gave up their car for just one four-mile trip each week, they would save $7.3 billion per year in avoided fuel costs (Sierra Club, 2012).

The American Automobile Association (AAA) estimated that, in 2013, the average cost of owning and operating a car increased by 2% to $9,122 a year (or 60.8 cents per mile) for a person driving 15,000 miles per year and paying $3.49 per gallon of gas (AAA, 2013). The AAA analysis considers fuel costs, routine maintenance, tire replacement, insurance, finance costs, and governmental taxes and fees that are typical for vehicle owners. Walking and bicycling create savings in all of these categories of costs.

Chicago, IL. Photo courtesy of PeopleForBikes

Highlighted Studies: Economic Impacts of Improving Bicycling and Walking

Impact on Jobs

Location	Impact
U.S. National	Pedestrian and bicycle infrastructure projects create 8–12 jobs per $1 million of spending. Road infrastructure projects create 7 jobs per $1 million of expenditures (Garrett-Peltier, 2011).
Oregon	Bicycle-related expenditures amounted to nearly $400 million statewide, and supported 4,600 jobs within Oregon (Dean Runyan Associates, 2012).
10 U.S. city case studies	Of ten cities studied that built bicycle and pedestrian facilities using federal transportaiton dollars, each of the projects profiled created between 218 and 1,050 new construction jobs (PeopleForBikes, 2010).
Iowa	The Register's Annual Great Bicycle Ride Across Iowa (RAGBRAI), a weeklong bicycle ride across the state supported 362 jobs in the state for the 2008 event (Lankford, 2008).

Impact from Increased Sales

Location	Impact
New York City	Businesses located within an improvement area saw sales increase at higher levels than the surrounding area (up to 172% increase in retail sales at locally-based businesses after a pedestrian plaza was constructed. Commercial vacancies fell 49% in one district after a protected bicycle lane was installed (NYCDOT, 2012).
Fort Worth, TX	Retail sales increased 163% between 2009–2011 after a bicycle lane and improved bicycle parking were installed (Fort Worth South, Inc., 2011, 2009).
Minnesota	Customers of the Nice Ride bike share system spent an estimated additional $150,000 in one season at restaurants and other businesses near Nice Ride stations (Wang et al., 2012).
Portland, OR	Bicyclists and pedestrians may spend less money per trip to a store, but they make more frequent visits throughout a given month, and end up spending more on average than their car-driving counterparts (Clifton, 2013).
San Francisco	Pedestrians reported spending more money over the course of a week than users of any other transportation mode (SFMTA, 2013).
New York City	Pedestrian and bicyclists reported spending more money over the course of a week than users of any other transportation mode (Transportation Alternatives, 2012).
Austin, TX	The ten-year economic impact of a downtown bicycle boulevard is estimated to be at least $1.2 million, and possibly as much as $5.6 million (City of Austin, Angelou Economics, 2010).

Impact on Property Values and Stability

Location	Impact
Washington, DC	Places with higher walkability perform better commercially and have higher housing values. Office and retail spaces in areas with good walkability rented for $8.88/sq. ft. and $6.92/sq. ft. more per year, respectively, compared to places with fair walkability, holding household income levels constant. Additionally, relative to places with fair walkability, places with good walkability scores, on average, bring in $301.76 more per month in residential rents and $81.54/sq. ft. more in for-sale residential property values (Brookings Institute, 2012).
Lodi, CA	A $4.5 million public-private, pedestrian-oriented project helped encourage residents to shop locally in their own neighborhoods. The city credits the retrofit of five street blocks with widened sidewalks, bulbed-out intersections, and other improvements for a large economic turnaround. Vacancy rates dropped from 18% to 6%. After construction was completed, the city experienced a 30% increase in downtown sales tax revenue (Local Government Commission, 2000).
Omaha, NE	Nearly two-thirds of homeowners who purchased their home after a trail was built said that the trail positively influenced their purchase decision. Eighty-one percent felt that the nearby trail's presence would have a positive effect or no effect on the sale of their homes (Greer, 2000).
Ohio	Sale prices on single-family residential properties increased by $7.05 for every foot, or over $41,000 for every mile closer that a property is located to the Little Miami Scenic Trail (Karadeniz, 2008).
U.S. National	A 5- to 10-mph reduction in traffic speeds increased adjacent residential property values by roughly 20%. Traffic calming reduced volumes on residential streets by several hundred cars per day and increased home values by an average of 18% (Local Government Commission, 2000).
U.S. National	A one-point increase in Walk Score was associated with a $500-$3,000 increase in home values (Cortright, 2009).

Impact from Decreased Traffic Congestion

Location	Impact
U.S. National	Traffic congestion in 2011 caused Americans in urban cities to travel an additional 5.5 billion hours, purchase an additional 2.9 billion gallons of fuel, and spend an additional $121 billion in gas. This means, on average, each car commuter spends roughly 40 hours and over $800 per year waiting in traffic (Texas A&M Transportation Institute, 2012).

Highlighted Studies (continued)

Impact from Improved Health and Worker Productivity

Location	Impact
Portland, OR	Portland, OR, could see between $388 and $594 million in health cost savings attributable to new bicycle infrastructure and programs by 2040. Every $1 invested in bicycling yields $3.40 in health care cost savings. When the statistical value of lives is considered, every $1 invested yields nearly $100 in benefits (Gotschi, 2011).
U.S. National	The increase in obesity among U.S. Americans could cost the United States an estimated $550 billion between 2012 and 2030 (Finkelstein et al., 2012).
Australia	Adults who commute by car on a daily basis gain significantly more weight than those who do not commute by car. Even car commuters who engage in weekly exercise gain more weight than non-car users (Sugiyama et al., 2013).
Lincoln, NE	Every $1 spent on bicycle and pedestrian trails in Lincoln, NE, (including construction, maintenance, equipment, and travel) yields $2.94 in direct medical benefits (Wang et al., 2005).
U.S. National	The national health-related cost savings of a modest increase in bicycling and walking is estimated at $420 million annually. A substantial increase in bicycling and walking could save over $28 billion per year. This estimate includes reduced health costs from an increase in physical activity by those who currently do not meet recommended levels (Rails to Trails Conservancy, 2008).
U.S. National	The total economic cost of overweight and obese citizens in the United States and Canada was roughly $300 billion in 2009. This estimate includes medical costs, disability, and excess mortality (Behan et al., 2010).
U.S. National	Obesity costs the average taxpayer $180 per year regardless of their own health status. If just one of every ten adults started a regular walking program, the United States could save $5.6 billion—the equivalent of paying the college tuition for 1,020,000 students (National Governors Association, 2006).
London, UK	Bicycling to work significantly reduces absenteeism due to illness. Regular bicyclists took 7.4 sick days per year on average, while non-bicyclists took 8.7 sick days per year. The difference saves the U.K. economy an estimated £128 million or $204 million per year (London School of Economics, 2013).

Impact from Events and Tourism

Location	Impact
Oregon	Expenditures related to bicycle tourism amounted to nearly $400 million and supported 4,600 jobs within Oregon (Dean Runyan Associates, 2012).
Iowa	The direct and indirect economic impacts of recreational bicycling in Iowa are estimated at $365 million annually, or approximately $1 million per day (Lankford, 2011).
Colorado	The economic impact of the USA Pro-Challenge race in Colorado, which routes through 12 Colorado towns, was estimated to be $99.6 million in 2012 (IFM North America, 2012).
Hawaii	More than $1.7 million was raised for local charities during the 2013 Charity Walk (Charity Walk, 2014).
Wisconsin	The annual economic impact of recreational bicycling and tourism is estimated at $924 million for the state of Wisconsin (Grabow, 2010).
North Carolina Outer Banks	The annual economic impact of bicycle tourists to North Carolina's Outer Banks is estimated at $60 million. In addition, 1,400 jobs were created or sustained annually because of these tourists (NCDOT, 2004).
Iowa	The Register's Annual Great Bicycle Ride Across Iowa (RAGBRAI), a weeklong bicycle ride across the state, contributed $16.5 million in direct spending in the state (Lankford, 2008).
Missouri	The direct economic impact of the Tour of Missouri is estimated at over $80 million over three years, with tax revenues at $38 million in 2009 (Tour of Missouri, 2010).
Virginia Creeper Trail	Every trail visitor to the Virginia Creeper Trail generated between $24 and $38 per visit. Trail visitors contributed an estimated $1.2 million annually to the local economy (Bowker, 2004).
Charleston, SC	A proposed 32-mile bicycle route could have a $42 million economic impact on the surrounding area (Charleston Moves and the College of Charleston, 2012).

Impact from Cleaner Air

Location	Impact
Europe	The built-in greenhouse gas emissions of riding a bicycle are over ten times lower than those from driving an individual driving a motorized vehicle. Electric bicycles have a similar greenhouse gas emission range as ordinary bicycles. These calculations include estimates on the average emissions required to manufacture a bicycle as well as the food energy and additional calories required to power a bicycle (European Cycling Federation, 2011).
U.S. National	A modest increase in bicycling and walking could save 3 billion gallons of gasoline and prevent the release of 28 million tons of CO_2 (Rails to Trails Conservancy, 2008).
U.S. National	With a modest increase in bicycling and walking, the national value of CO_2 reduction from the amount of avoided miles driven would be $333 million, and could be over $2.7 billion with a more substantial increase (Gotschi, 2008).

Economic Impact of Bicycling and Walking in Midsized Cities

Five of the midsized cities surveyed for this report have conducted economic impact studies of bicycling, and one completed a study on trails and their impact on reducing car miles. Their studies will help cities of varying populations gain a better understanding of how nonmotorized transportation affects more than just the bicyclist or pedestrian.

Bellingham, Washington

Whatcom Smart Trips conducted an in-depth survey and analysis to determine effects and opportunities for reducing car trips. After implementation of a follow-up marketing program, Bellingham measured a 15% reduction in the number of car trips, and an increase in the share of walking, bicycling, and bus use.

Boulder, Colorado

Community Cycles surveyed local bicycle businesses to quantify their economic impact. Results from 58 businesses found that direct economic activity exceeded $52 million in 2010, at least 33 full-time jobs existed that were associated with the bicycling industry, and retail sales and bicycle rental and repair was the largest sector of Boulder's bike economy. The survey self-reports that it does not include indirect economic activity from bicycle tourism or construction of infrastructure, and was conducted before the public bike share system was operating.

Burlington, Vermont

In 2010, the University of Vermont completed a report titled, "Estimating Tourism Expenditures for the Burlington Waterfront Path and the Island Line Trail." The conservative estimates show that the overall average tourism spending of tourist users ranges from $1 to $2.5 million over a five-month period between May and September, 2008.

Charleston, South Carolina

Charleston Moves conducted a cost-benefit analysis of the proposed Battery2Beach Route, a regional, 33-mile system of bicycle lanes linking six municipalities, two major beaches and Charleston's historic Battery.

The study was well received and led to the formation of a 15-member intergovernmental working group that continues making progress toward completing the B2B Route, as it is now called. A benefactor contributed up to $100,000 for signage, a move which will expedite completion.

Missoula, Montana

The Institute for Tourism and Recreation Research (ITRR) at the University of Montana conducts nonresident surveys year-round throughout the state of Montana. In 2012, 128,023 nonresidents took part in road/tour bicycling while in Montana and spent at least one night in Missoula County. The study showed that the possible impact of these bicyclists was $19,410,000 ($151.61 per person).

on the road

Quality Bike Products: Bicycle Friendly is Good Business

by Alison Dewey, League of American Bicyclists, Bicycle Friendly Businesses

Many businesses now recognize that it pays to encourage bicycling in the workplace. According to a recent survey and report, Quality Bicycle Products (QBP), a League of American Bicyclists' platinum-level Bicycle Friendly Business[SM] (BFB[SM]), has improved employee health and helped the company save on reduced healthcare costs through its "Health Reward" program.

Employess taking part in a bike tech class at QBP
Courtesy of League of American Bicyclists

The Bloomington, Minnesota business rewards employees who bicycle to work with incentives, such as additional contributions to an employee's Health Savings Account and credits towards QBP products. These programs are keeping QBP employees healthy, happy and productive.

According to Jason Gaikowski, QBP Marketing Director, the report "definitely shows that QBP is healthier and, as a result, more productive than the general population." It also indicates that the healthcare claim costs of the company's bicycle commuters are much lower than the claim costs of non-bicycle commuter employees.

The top bike commuters in 2012 at QBP
Courtesy of League of American Bicyclists

By encouraging their employees to commute by bicycle through 2007–2011, QBP found the following:

- Overall, from 2007 to 2011, the company experienced a 4.4% reduction in employee healthcare costs, saving an estimated $170,000 in healthcare costs over a three-year period.
- Alone, 100 employees in the "Bike to Work" program saved the company an estimated $200,000 annually.
- The company benefitted from an annual savings of $301,136 in improved employee productivity.

Learn more about the QBP Commuter Program at: *www.QBP.com/Index.php/Page/Commute*

To learn more about the Bicycle Friendly Business[SM] program, visit: *www.BikeLeague.org/Content/Businesses*

5 Policies and Funding

Increasingly, U.S. government agencies and departments are recognizing the value that bicycling and walking initiatives contribute to our communities. In 2011, the U.S. Surgeon General and a council of seventeen leaders from federal government agencies, departments, and offices presented a national strategy to improve the general health and well-being of Americans. The council drew its recommendations from the CDC's Community Preventive Services Task Force, recommending implementation of policies and practices that encourage more mixed use development and Complete Streets design to appeal to a broader range of bicyclists and pedestrians (CDC, 2012).

The percentage of federal transportation funding allocated to bicycle and pedestrian projects has gradually increased over the last four years from 1.6% (FMIS, 2006-09) to 2.1% (FMIS, 2009-12). While this increase in funding for nonmotorized transportation is a positive sign, the amount of funding provided is far from proportional to the number of bicyclists and pedestrians using the transportation network. Research shows that the cities and countries that have invested most heavily in nonmotorized transportation see the greatest share of trips by bicycle and foot (Gotschi and Mills, 2009; Pucher and Buehler, 2008; Pucher and Buehler, 2010).

As policy and funding provide more support, implementation of bicycling and walking initiatives will become more possible.

Chicago, IL. Mayor Rahm Emanuel speaking on opening day for the cycle track on Dearborn Street. Photo by Steve Vance @ Flickr

Policy and Planning

Published Goals

When states or cities publish goals to increase bicycling and walking and to decrease crashes, they are making public commitments to progress for which success can be easily measured. Since the *2012 Benchmarking Report*, several states and cities have improved in this area by adopting new goals. Florida has a goal to increase walking and Nevada has a goal to increase bicycling. Thirty-four states, an increase of five from two years ago, report they have published goals for increasing both bicycling and walking.

Similarly, more cities have now adopted goals to increase bicycling and walking. Of the 52 cities surveyed, 39 have goals to increase walking, and 47 have goals to increase bicycling. Two years ago 33 and 46 of these cities reported having such goals, respectively.

States and cities are also increasing their commitment to bicycling and walking safety. Forty-four states report having adopted goals to decrease pedestrian fatalities, and 43 have goals to decrease bicycle fatalities. Of the cities surveyed, 37 have adopted goals to reduce bicycle fatalities, and 36 have adopted goals to decrease pedestrian fatalities. Over the last two years, eight cities added new pedestrian fatality goals, and four cities reported adding a goal to reduce bicycle fatalities. In 2007, only 20 of these cities reported having goals to reduce bicycle and pedestrian fatalities.

Statewide Goals

Source: State Survey 2011/2012. **Note**: Unanswered survey questions, or responses of "N/A" and "unknown," were taken to mean "no." All uncolored cells should be understood to be a "no" response.

Measuring Goal Progress

The goals set by states and cities to increase bicycling and walking, and to improve safety for bicyclists and pedestrians, can best be achieved if those goals are measured and tracked over time.

20 states have set performance measures for the goal to **decrease bicyclist and pedestrian fatalities**:

Arizona
Arkansas
Colorado
Florida
Idaho
Iowa
Maine
Maryland
Massachusetts
Michigan
Minnesota
Missouri
Nevada
New Jersey [(1)]
New Mexico
New York
Pennsylvania
Tennessee
Texas
Washington

11 states have set performance measures for the goal to **increase walking and bicycling**:

Arizona
Colorado [(2)]
Maryland
Massachusetts
Minnesota
New Jersey
North Carolina
Pennsylvania
Rhode Island
Tennessee
Washington

19 large cities have set performance measures for the goal to **increase walking and bicycling**:

Albuquerque
Atlanta
Boston [(3)]
Chicago
Denver [(3)]
Honolulu [(3)]
Jacksonville
Memphis
Mesa [(3)]
Milwaukee [(3)]
Minneapolis
New Orleans
New York City
Oakland
Phildelphia
Portland, OR
San Jose [(3)]
Seattle
Tulsa

Sources: City Survey 2011/2012 and State Survey 2011/2012. **Notes**: Unanswered survey questions, or responses of "N/A" and "unknown," were taken to mean "no." (1) State has performance measure for decreasing pedestrian fatalities only. (2) State has performance measure for increasing bicycling only. (3) City has performance measures for increasing bicycling only.

Goals in Large Cities

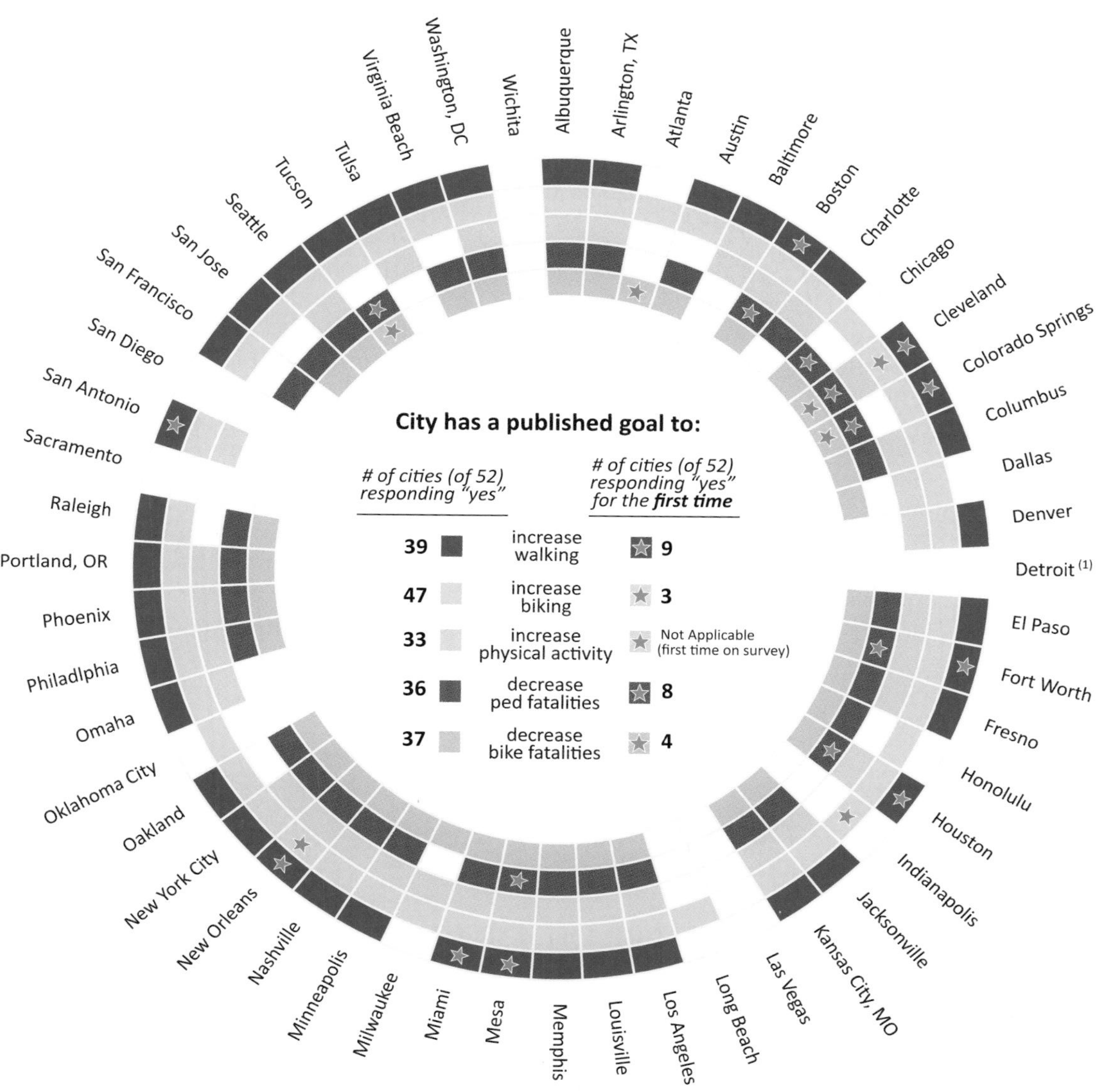

Source: City Survey 2011/2012. **Notes**: Unanswered survey questions, or responses of "N/A" and "unknown," were taken to mean "no." All uncolored cells should be understood to be a "no" response. (1) Detroit did not submit a completed survey for 2011/2012.

Master Plans

Twenty-four of the cities surveyed have either a combined bicycle and pedestrian plan or two stand-alone plans. Twenty-three more have bicycle master plans only. Many new master plans have been adopted since the *2012 Benchmarking Report*; there are nine new bicycle master plans, seven new pedestrian master plans, and three new combined bicycle/pedestrian master plans.

In addition, 32 cities have trail master plans and five cities have plans specific to mountain biking. (For links to sample bicycle and pedestrian master plans, see Appendix 6).

At the state level, trail master plans are the most common; 31 states have adopted a master plan for trails, nine of which are new since the *2012 Benchmarking Report*. Twenty-six states have either a combined bicycle/pedestrian master plan or two stand-alone plans.

Complete Streets

The bicycle and pedestrian movement, transit advocates, and advocates for accessibility have adopted the term "complete streets" because it frames the discussion to show that a street is not complete unless it accommodates all modes of transport.

A complete street provides safe access for pedestrians, bicyclists, children, the elderly, people with mobility challenges, transit users, and motorists. Complete Streets policies require that all streets are designed and built to provide safe access for all potential users. These policies ensure that provisions such as sidewalks, curb cuts, bicycle lanes, traffic calming, and inviting crossings are included in all road projects, not as optional add-ons.

According to the National Complete Streets Coalition (as of December 2013), 27 states and 27 of the 52 large cities in this report have adopted local Complete Streets policies. This

New York City, NY. Courtesy of New York City Department of Transportation.

is up slightly from 2010 when 26 states and 19 of the most populous cities had adopted Complete Streets policies.

In December 2013, the National Complete Streets Coalition announced that 607 Complete Streets policies have been adopted around the U.S. This count has more than doubled since August 2011 when the total count was at 283 local and regional Complete Streets policies.

(For links to Complete Streets resources and model policies, see Appendix 6).

Health Impact Assessments

Health Impact Assessments (HIA) can be used to evaluate a plan, project, or policy before it is implemented. Because of the many health benefits associated with physical activity, these assessments have the potential to promote bicycling and walking initiatives as part of improving the population's general health. According to the most recent survey, only six of the 50 states reported that they require HIAs to be completed. These six states are Illinois, Maine, Maryland, Massachusetts, Utah, and Washington.

Complete Streets Policies Among States and Large Cities

- Existing city policy
- New city policy (since *2012 Benchmarking Report*)
- Existing state policy
- New state policy (since *2012 Benchmarking Report*)

Source: National Complete Streets Coalition, 2013. **Note**: Only cities from the 52 large cities included in this report are noted on this map. See *www.CompleteStreets.org* for a complete list of all policies adopted.

Statewide Master Plans

	Bicycle/Pedestrian combined	Bicycle stand-alone	Pedestrian stand-alone	Trails	Mountain bikes
Alabama	✓			✓	
Alaska	✓			✓	
Arizona	✓			✓	✓
Arkansas	✓				
California					
Colorado	✓			✓	
Connecticut	✓			✓	✓
Delaware		✓	✓	✓	
Florida				✓	
Georgia		✓			
Hawaii		✓	✓		
Idaho	✓				
Illinois		✓			
Indiana		✓		✓	✓
Iowa				✓	
Kansas	✓			✓	
Kentucky					
Louisiana	✓				
Maine					
Maryland	✓			✓	
Massachusetts		✓	✓	✓	
Michigan				✓	
Minnesota		✓		✓	
Mississippi					
Missouri					
Montana		✓		✓	
Nebraska				✓	
Nevada		✓		✓	
New Hampshire	✓			✓	
New Jersey	✓			✓	✓
New Mexico					
New York	✓			✓	✓
North Carolina	✓				
North Dakota					
Ohio				✓	
Oklahoma					
Oregon	✓			✓	
Pennsylvania	✓			✓	✓
Rhode Island		✓	✓	✓	
South Carolina				✓	
South Dakota					
Tennessee	✓	✓		✓	
Texas					
Utah					
Vermont	✓			✓	
Virgina		✓	✓	✓	
Washington	✓			✓	
West Virginia				✓	
Wisconsin		✓	✓	✓	
Wyoming	✓				
# of states responding "yes"	20	13	6	30	6
# of states responding "yes" **for the first time**	2	7	3	3	5

Source: State Survey 2011/2012. **Notes**: Unanswered survey questions, or responses of "N/A" and "unknown," were taken to mean "no." All empty cells should be understood to be a "no" response.

Master Plans in Large Cities

Bicycle/Pedestrian combined	Bicycle stand-alone	Pedestrian stand-alone	Trails	Mountain bikes	
✓	✓	✓	✓	✓	Albuquerque
✓					Arlington, TX
	✓		✓		Atlanta
	✓	✓			Austin
	✓			✓	Baltimore
	✓		✓		Boston
	✓		✓		Charlotte
	✓	✓	✓		Chicago
	✓		✓		Cleveland
	✓		✓		Colorado Springs
	✓	✓	✓		Columbus
	✓		✓		Dallas
	✓	✓	✓		Denver
(1)	(1)	(1)	(1)	(1)	Detroit
					El Paso
	✓		✓	✓	Fort Worth
✓			✓		Fresno
	✓				Honolulu
	✓		✓		Houston
	✓ (2)		✓		Indianapolis
✓			✓		Jacksonville
	✓	✓	✓		Kansas City, MO
✓			✓		Las Vegas
	✓				Long Beach
	✓				Los Angeles
	✓ (3)	✓ (3)	✓		Louisville
✓			✓		Memphis
	✓				Mesa
	✓		✓		Miami
	✓		✓		Milwaukee
	✓	✓	✓		Minneapolis
✓			✓	✓	Nashville
✓					New Orleans
	✓				New York City
	✓	✓			Oakland
	✓		✓		Oklahoma City
✓			✓		Omaha
✓			✓ (2)	✓	Philadelphia
	✓		✓		Phoenix
	✓	✓	(4)		Portland, OR
	✓	✓	✓		Raleigh
					Sacramento
	✓				San Antonio
	✓				San Diego
	✓				San Francisco
	✓	✓	✓		San Jose
	✓	✓			Seattle
	✓		✓		Tucson
			✓		Tulsa
✓			✓		Virginia Beach
	✓	✓			Washington, DC
					Wichita
11	37	14	32	5	# of large cities responding "yes"
3	9	7	11	3	# of large cities responding "yes" **for the first time**

Source: City Survey 2011/2012. **Notes**: Unanswered survey questions, or responses of "N/A" and "unknown," were taken to mean "no." All empty cells should be understood to be a "no" response. (1) Detroit did not submit a survey for 2011/2012. (2) Adopted in 2013. (3) Louisville's bicycle and pedestrian master plans have not been officially adopted, but are referenced for implementation of projects. (4) Portland includes trails in the bicycle master plan.

NACTO Design Guidelines

The Urban Bikeway Design Guide and the Urban Street Design Guide, produced by the National Association of City Transportation Officials (NACTO), outline recommendations for building bicycle- and pedestrian-friendly facilities such as bicycle lanes, signage, and park elements. See page 155 for more information about these guides. Thirteen of the large cities in this report have adopted the NACTO guidelines to help them better plan for bicyclist and pedestrian traffic.

Carbon Emissions Plans

The U.S. Environmental Protection Agency (EPA) reports that in 2011 carbon dioxide (CO_2) emissions accounted for 84% of all greenhouse gases emitted as a result of human activity in the U.S. One-third of all CO_2 emissions were from the transportation sector (EPA, 2013). Many cities and states have developed plans to reduce carbon emissions over time. Some of these plans include increasing bicycling and walking activity as ways to lower vehicle miles traveled and, therefore, lower carbon emissions.

Of the 40 states that reported having a statewide carbon emissions plan, 21 include bicycling goals and 19 include walking goals. Thirty-seven of the large cities studied in this report have a carbon emissions plan; 31 include bicycling goals and 24 include walking goals.

Maximum Car Parking Requirements

The Alliance surveyed cities on policies requiring a minimum and/or maximum number of car parking spaces for new buildings. Ninety percent (47) of responding cities reported having minimum car parking requirements. These policies not only endorse, but even mandate excessive sprawl (Shoup, 2005). This inefficient use of land can inhibit the progress of bicycling and walking initiatives.

In contrast, 18 cities (up from 15 in the 2012 report and 6 in the 2010 report) reported

Equitable Transportation Policy

U.S. federal transportation policy has historically favored motorized transportation. However, many low-income and minority communities have low car ownership rates and so do not benefit from these transportation investments. In fact, these communities often suffer more from highways dividing their neighborhoods and polluting their air.

In 2009, as Congress was working on a new transportation funding bill, PolicyLink released a report (*All Aboard!* 2009) that highlighted key considerations for making federal transportation policy more equitable for marginalized communities. The report outlines the following five goals as necessary considerations for an equitable policy.

1. Create viable, affordable transportation choices. The transportation network should accomodate multiple modes of travel, providing everyone—regardless of age, income, or ability—with viable transportation opportunities and access to participate fully in the regional economy.

2. Ensure access to jobs. Transportation infrastructure should provide job access to all workers by mandating minority hiring goals and workforce training in all sectors—including construction, maintenance, and operations.

3. Invest equitably so that transportation supports all communities. Investment in transportation should reflect the local priorities and goals, and must engage all stakeholders in a transparent, accountable, and democratic way.

4. Make a positive impact on community health. Transportation policy should encourage walking and bicycling in all types of communities, improve safety conditions for active transportation, and ensure connectivity to health services.

5. Promote environmentally sustainable communities. Transportation policy should promote the reducation of vehicle miles, air pollution, and greenhouse gas emissions, and advocate conservation of energy.

Boulder, CO. Photo by Zane Selvans @Flickr

having policies that set a maximum number of car parking spaces for new buildings. These progressive policies require more dense development and land-use practices that can encourage safer and friendlier environments for bicyclists and pedestrians.

Requiring Bicycle Parking

An estimated 1.3 million bicycles are stolen in the United States each year (Johnson et al., 2008). In a 2008 survey of roughly 1,800 San Francisco bicyclists, the number one reason cited why they do not bicycle more was fear of theft (*Report Card on Bicycling: San Francisco*, 2008).

A lack of safe places to park a bicycle is a barrier to increasing bicycling (Hunt and Abraham, 2007). In fact, a recent study has shown that bicycle commuting increases when employees have access to bicycle parking as well as other amenities such as showers (Buehler, 2012). Many cities have taken steps to overcome this barrier by requiring businesses and new developments, parking garages, and public events to include bicycle parking. Of the cities surveyed for this report, 75% (39 cities) require bicycle parking in new buildings. Thirty-one cities report that they require bicycle parking in buildings and garages—up from just 25 cities reported in the 2012 report. Just nine cities require secure or valet bicycle parking at public events.

Some policies are triggered by minimum requirements such as the square footage of a building, the number of employees in a business, or the number of car parking spaces. In these cases, if the minimum is not met (such as a business having under 25 employees), a business is not required to install any bicycle parking.

Bike Parking at Schools

The Alliance also asked cities how many bicycle parking spaces were at public schools. The large cities surveyed for this report averaged 13 bicycle parking spaces per 1,000 students at public schools. Phoenix reported 16,000 bicycle parking spaces at schools—more than any other city. This equates to 56 parking spots per 1,000 students. Overall, Mesa, AZ, had the highest rate of bicycle parking at public schools with 86 spots per 1,000 students, followed by Phoenix (56 per thousand), Seattle (32 per thousand), Portland (31 per thousand), and Minneapolis (31 per thousand).

Statewide Planning & Policies

	Complete Streets policy	HIA required	Carbon emissions plan: Includes walking	Carbon emissions plan: Includes bicycling
Alabama			(1)	(1)
Alaska			✓	✓
Arizona			✓	✓
Arkansas			(1)	(1)
California	✓			✓
Colorado	✓		✓	✓
Connecticut	✓		✓ (2)	✓ (2)
Delaware	✓			
Florida	✓			
Georgia	✓			
Hawaii	✓		✓	✓
Idaho			✓	✓
Illinois	✓	✓	✓	✓
Indiana				
Iowa				✓
Kansas				
Kentucky				
Louisiana	✓			
Maine		✓	✓	
Maryland	✓	✓	✓	✓
Massachusetts	✓	✓	✓	✓
Michigan	✓		✓	✓
Minnesota	✓		✓	✓
Mississippi	✓			
Missouri				
Montana			(1)	(1)
Nebraska			(1)	(1)
Nevada				
New Hampshire			✓	✓
New Jersey	✓			✓
New Mexico			(1)	(1)
New York	✓			
North Carolina	✓			
North Dakota			(1)	(1)
Ohio				
Oklahoma				
Oregon	✓		✓	✓
Pennsylvania	✓		(1)	(1)
Rhode Island	✓		✓	✓
South Carolina	✓		✓	✓
South Dakota				
Tennessee	✓		✓	✓
Texas	✓			
Utah		✓ (3)	(1)	(1)
Vermont	✓		✓	✓
Virgina	✓		(1)	(1)
Washington	✓	✓	✓	✓
West Virginia			(1)	(1)
Wisconsin	✓			
Wyoming				
# of states responding "yes"	27	6	19	21

Source: State Survey 2011/2012. **Notes**: Unanswered survey questions, or responses of "N/A" and "unknown," were taken to mean "no." All empty cells should be understood to be a "no" response. (1) State does not have a Carbon Emissions Plan. (2) Included in state Climate Change Action Plan. (3) Utah does not have a statewide requirement for Health Impact Assessments, but the Road Respect Community Program makes HIA's mandatory for communities that participate in the program.

Planning & Policies in Large Cities

Complete Streets policy	Carbon emissions plan: Includes walking	Carbon emissions plan: Includes bicycling	Adopted NACTO design guidelines	Bicycle parking requirements: In buildings and garages	Bicycle parking requirements: In new buildings	Bicycle parking requirements: At public events	Bicycle parking requirements: At schools (# of spaces)	Max # of car spaces for new building	
	✓	✓		✓	✓				Albuquerque
	(1)	(1)			✓ (2)			✓	Arlington, TX
	✓	✓	✓	✓	✓			✓	Atlanta
✓	✓	✓	✓	✓	✓	✓			Austin
✓	(1)	(1)		✓	✓				Baltimore
	✓	✓	✓	✓	✓		864	✓	Boston
✓	(1)	(1)		✓	✓		1,700		Charlotte
✓	✓	✓	✓	✓	✓	✓	2,000		Chicago
✓	✓	✓		✓	✓				Cleveland
✓	✓	✓							Colorado Springs
✓	✓	✓			✓		1,668	✓	Columbus
									Dallas
✓	✓	✓	✓	✓	✓	✓	735		Denver
(3)	(3)	(3)	(3)	(3)	(3)	(3)	(3)	(3)	Detroit
✓	✓	✓		✓	✓			✓	El Paso
	✓	✓		✓	✓			✓	Fort Worth
					✓				Fresno
✓	(1)	(1)							Honolulu
	(1)	(1)		✓	✓			✓	Houston
✓	(1)	(1)	✓						Indianapolis
				✓	✓			✓	Jacksonville
✓	✓	✓		✓	✓		364		Kansas City, MO
	✓	✓							Las Vegas
		✓					1,600		Long Beach
	(1)	(1)		✓	✓				Los Angeles
✓		✓		✓	✓			✓	Louisville
✓	(1)	(1)		✓	✓		750		Memphis
		✓	✓	✓	✓	✓	5,700		Mesa
✓	✓	✓		✓	✓		500	✓	Miami
		✓		✓	✓		180		Milwaukee
	✓	✓	✓	✓	✓		1,000	✓	Minneapolis
✓					✓		31		Nashville
✓	(1)	(1)	✓	✓	✓				New Orleans
✓	✓	✓	✓	✓	✓		2,600	✓	New York City
✓	✓	✓			✓	✓	390		Oakland
	(1)	(1)							Oklahoma City
	(1)	(1)							Omaha
✓	✓	✓			✓		300		Philadelphia
		✓			✓		16,000	✓	Phoenix
	✓	✓		✓	✓		1,500	✓	Portland, OR
	✓	✓		✓	✓		100		Raleigh
✓									Sacramento
✓	(1)	(1)			✓			✓	San Antonio
✓		✓							San Diego
✓	✓	✓		✓	✓	✓	9	✓	San Francisco
	✓	✓	✓	✓	✓	✓			San Jose
✓	✓	✓	✓	✓	✓	✓	1,500	✓	Seattle
		✓		✓	✓	✓			Tucson
✓	✓	✓					405		Tulsa
				✓	✓		1,760	✓	Virginia Beach
✓			✓	✓	✓				Washington, DC
	(1)	(1)							Wichita
27	24	31	13	31	39	9	23	18	# of large cities responding "yes"

Source: City Survey 2011/2012. **Notes**: Unanswered survey questions, or responses of "N/A" and "unknown," were taken to mean "no." All empty cells should be understood to be a "no" response. (1) City does not have a Carbon Emissions Plan. (2) Arlington requires bicycle parking in new developments only in one zoning overlay. (3) Detroit did not submit a survey for 2011/2012.

State Legislation

Bicycles Considered Vehicles

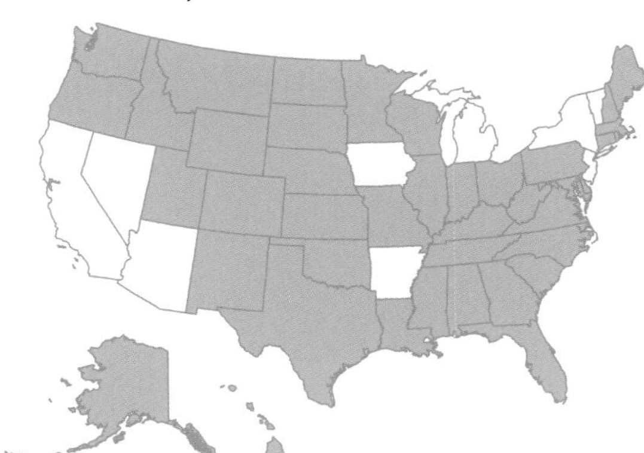

Helmet Required for Youth Bicyclists (1)

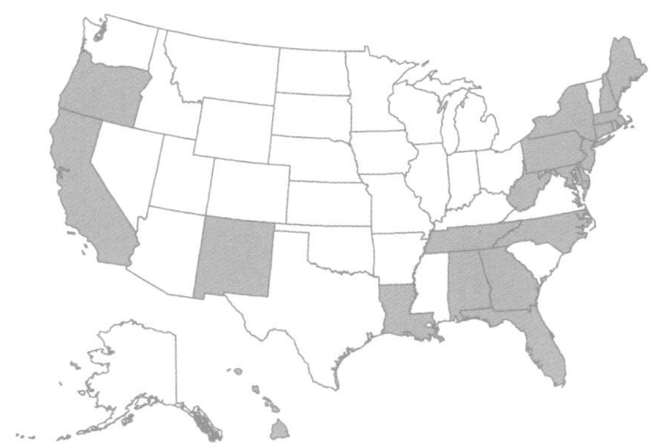

Bicyclists Can Ride Two-Abreast

Three-Foot (or Greater) Safe Passing Required

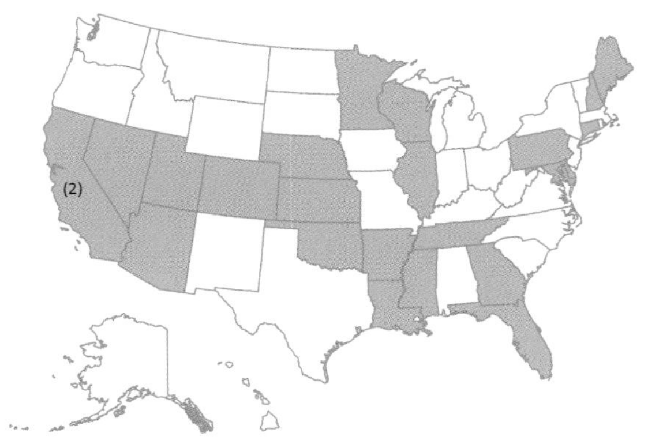

Bicyclists and Pedestrians Can Access Major Bridges and Tunnels

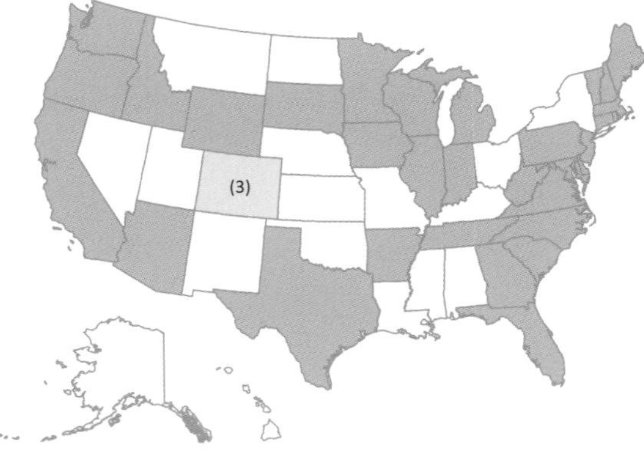

Bicyclists Can Use the Shoulder of Interstate Highways or Freeways

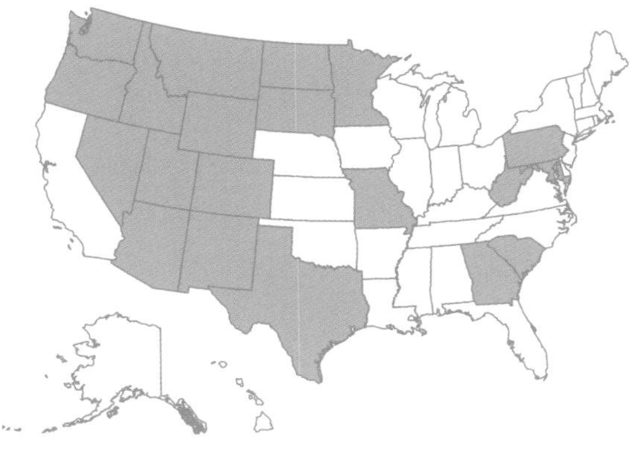

Source: State Survey 2011/2012. **Notes**: Legislation was reported as existing in states that are shaded. Wording of the actual legislation varies from state to state. For a more thorough review of bicycle laws, visit *BikeLeague.org/BikeLaws*. Unanswered survey questions, or responses of "N/A" and "unknown," were taken to mean "no." All uncolored states should be understood to be a "no" response. (1) Youth age applied varies by state. (2) California passed its three-foot passing law in 2013, after the benchmarking survey had been collected. (3) Colorado allows access only to bicyclists.

State Legislation

Bicycles are Vehicles

In most states, a bicycle is considered a vehicle on the roadway. This legislation is important on a basic level, as it acknowledges the rights of bicyclists to travel on roadways. These laws also suggest the responsibility of bicyclists to know and abide by the same road rules as motorized vehicles.

Mandatory Helmet Laws

Starting in 1987, states and local jurisdictions began passing their own laws requiring helmet use. Twenty-one states report having a mandatory youth helmet policy. Typically these policies apply to youth under age 16. No states have a helmet law applicable to all ages.

Mandatory helmet laws are controversial among bicycling advocates. For more information on these laws and the controversy around them, see Appendix 6.

Can Bicyclists Legally Ride Two-Abreast?

Most states have laws that allow bicyclists to ride side by side or "two-abreast" as long as they are not impeding traffic. Riding two abreast is often preferred for bicyclists riding with a companion and can make bicycling a more enjoyable experience, like sitting beside a friend in a bus, train, or car. Thirty-seven states reported having legislation allowing bicyclists to ride two-abreast.

Safe Passing Laws

In recent years many states have successfully pursued legislation that requires motorists to pass bicyclists at a set, "safe" distance. Twenty-one states have "3-Feet" laws, which are primarily aimed at educating motorists on how to safely pass bicyclists. Motorists may believe that just avoiding contact with bicyclists is all that is required when passing. Many motorists are unaware of the dangers of passing a bicyclist too closely, which may lead to the bicyclist being hit or startled, resulting in a collision.

Pennsylvania has enacted a four-foot passing law, and North Carolina and Virginia have a two-foot minimum. Nine states have a general requirement for "safe passing," and the remaining 18 states have no legal requirement specific to bicyclists (NCSL, 2013).

Driver Enforcement

Enforcement is one of the five Es for creating a bicycle- and pedestrian-friendly community; Engineering, Education, Encouragement, and Evaluation are the other four. Enforcement generally includes laws protecting both bicyclists and pedestrians and the enforcement of these laws. Although it is commendable to have laws that protect bicyclists, pedestrians, and other road users, these laws are not effective unless enforced. Whether by ticketing speeding motorists or reminding bicyclists to stop at traffic lights, enforcement is critical to ensuring that traffic regulations keep road users safe.

For this report, the Alliance collected data on a number of laws and policies. Forty of the large cities surveyed report that their city fines motorists for not yielding to bicyclists and pedestrians when nonmotorized users have the right of way. Of the cities that do enforce not yielding to bicycles and pedestrians, fines range from $15 to $500. The average fine for motorists is $160.

While nearly 80% of cities report enforcing these fines, it is not within the scope of this report to verify that these laws are strictly enforced in real-world practice. Advocacy groups should continue to hold city officials accountable for the rights of bicyclists and pedestrians on the road and the laws that are meant to protect them.

State Legislation

	Bicycles considered vehicles	Helmet required for youth bicyclists (1)	Bicyclists can ride two-abreast	Three-foot (or greater) safe passing required	Bicyclists and pedestrians can access major bridges and tunnels	Bicyclists can use the shoulder of interstate highways or freeways
Alabama	✓	✓	✓			
Alaska	✓		✓			
Arizona			✓	✓	✓	✓
Arkansas				✓	✓	
California	✓ (2)	✓			✓	
Colorado	✓		✓	✓	✓ (3)	✓
Connecticut	✓	✓	✓	✓	✓	
Delaware	✓	✓	✓	✓	✓	
Florida	✓	✓		✓	✓	
Georgia	✓	✓	✓	✓	✓	✓
Hawaii	✓	✓				
Idaho	✓		✓		✓	✓
Illinois	✓			✓	✓	
Indiana	✓		✓		✓	
Iowa					✓	
Kansas	✓		✓	✓		
Kentucky	✓		✓			
Louisiana	✓	✓	✓	✓		
Maine	✓	✓		✓	✓	
Maryland	✓	✓		✓	✓	✓
Massachusetts	✓	✓	✓		✓	
Michigan			✓		✓	
Minnesota	✓		✓	✓	✓	✓
Mississippi	✓		✓	✓		
Missouri	✓		✓			✓
Montana	✓		✓			✓
Nebraska	✓			✓		
Nevada			✓	✓		✓
New Hampshire	✓	✓	✓	✓	✓	
New Jersey		✓	✓		✓	
New Mexico	✓	✓	✓			✓
New York		✓	✓			
North Carolina	✓	✓			✓	
North Dakota	✓		✓			✓
Ohio	✓		✓			
Oklahoma	✓		✓	✓		
Oregon	✓	✓			✓	✓
Pennsylvania	✓	✓	✓	✓	✓	✓
Rhode Island	✓	✓	✓		✓	
South Carolina	✓		✓		✓	✓
South Dakota	✓		✓		✓	✓
Tennessee	✓	✓	✓	✓	✓	
Texas	✓		✓		✓	✓
Utah	✓		✓	✓		✓
Vermont					✓	
Virgina	✓		✓		✓	
Washington	✓		✓		✓	✓
West Virginia	✓	✓	✓		✓	✓
Wisconsin	✓		✓	✓	✓	
Wyoming	✓				✓	✓
# of states responding "yes"	42	21	37	22	33	20

Source: State Survey 2011/2012. **Notes**: Unanswered survey questions, or responses of "N/A" and "unknown," were taken to mean "no." All empty cells should be understood to be a "no" response. (1) Youth age applied varies by state. (2) California passed its three-foot passing law in 2013, after the benchmarking survey had been collected. (3) Colorado allows access only to bicyclists.

Driver Enforcement in Large Cities

Driver enforcement: For not yielding to bicyclists or pedestrians?	Driver enforcement: If yes, what is the penalty?	
✓	-	Albuquerque
✓	-	Arlington, TX
✓	-	Atlanta
✓	Prosecution	Austin
✓	$57	Baltimore
✓	$200	Boston
✓	$235	Charlotte
✓	-	Chicago
✓	$150	Cleveland
		Colorado Springs
✓	$100 and charged with minor misdemeanor	Columbus
(1)	(1)	Dallas
✓	$500	Denver
		Detroit
		El Paso
✓	$200	Fort Worth
✓	-	Fresno
✓	-	Honolulu
✓	$200	Houston
		Indianapolis
✓	$164	Jacksonville
✓	$60	Kansas City, MO
✓	Decided in court	Las Vegas
✓	-	Long Beach
		Los Angeles
✓	$20 - $200	Louisville
✓	$15	Memphis
✓	-	Mesa
✓	$179	Miami
✓	-	Milwaukee
✓	$178	Minneapolis
		Nashville
		New Orleans
✓	3-point moving violation	New York City
✓	$234	Oakland
✓	-	Oklahoma City
✓	$75	Omaha
✓	$50	Philadelphia
✓	-	Phoenix
✓	$250	Portland, OR
		Raleigh
		Sacramento
✓	$200	San Antonio
		San Diego
✓	-	San Francisco
✓	$35	San Jose
✓	$124	Seattle
✓	$115	Tucson
✓	-	Tulsa
✓	-	Virginia Beach
✓	$250	Washington, DC
		Wichita
40		# of large cities responding "yes"

Source: City Survey 2011/2012. **Note**: Unanswered survey questions, or responses of "N/A" and "unknown," were taken to mean "no." All empty cells should be understood to be a "no" response. Cells with a dash (-) mean data were unavailable or not reported. (1) Detroit did not submit a survey for 2011/2012.

Funds for Bicycling and Walking

Funds for bicycling and walking projects come from many sources. This report looks at the use of federal funds at the state and city levels. It is important to keep in mind that federal funding is not the only funding source states and cities may use for bicycle and pedestrian programs. However, looking at how states and cities use federal funds provides the most comparable analysis across varied spending practices.

Total Federal-aid highway program obligations for bicycle and pedestrian projects peaked in 2009 and 2010 because of additional funding provided under the American Recovery and Reinvestment Act (ARRA). In 2009–2010, federal aid provided $2.225 billion for bicycling and walking infrastructure projects. For 2011-2012, the total was $1.645 billion, a 26% decrease, but a 49% increase over 2007–2008 ($1.105 billion). Other than ARRA, the largest sources of Federal-aid funds since 1992 were the Transportation Enhancement (TE) activities, the Congestion Mitigation and Air Quality Improvement (CMAQ) Program, and the Surface Transportation Program (STP). From 2005 through 2012, the Safe Routes to School (SRTS) Program and High Priority Projects (HPP) funded many bicycle and pedestrian projects.

The Moving Ahead for Progress in the 21st Century Act (MAP-21), which took effect October 1, 2012, reduced funding from some of the most used programs for bicycle and pedestrian projects, although bicycle and pedestrian projects are eligible for all Federal-aid highway program funds. Funding for bicycle and pedestrian projects in 2013 totaled $676 million. For more information on the MAP-21 Act, see pages 128–129.

The Federal Highway Administration (FHWA) posts bicycle and pedestrian obligations at *www.fhwa.dot.gov/environment/bicycle_pedestrian/funding/bipedfund.cfm.*

% of Federal Transportation Dollars to Bicycle and Pedestrian Projects 2009–2012

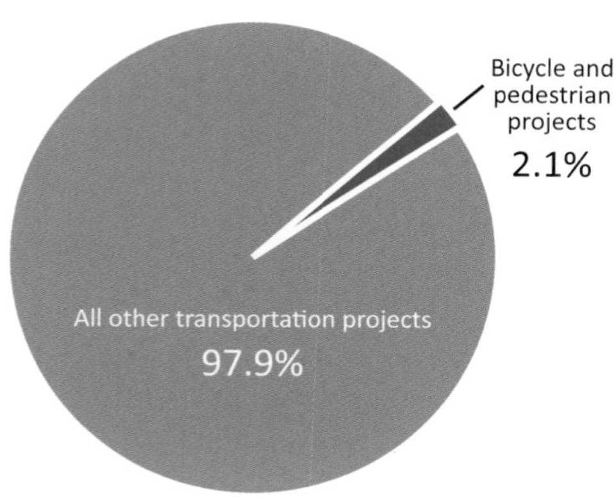

Source: FHWA FMIS 2009–2012. **Note**: Data are based on funds obligated to projects between 2009–2012 and are not necessarily the amount spent in these years.

% Bicycle and Pedestrian Dollars by Funding Program 2009–2012

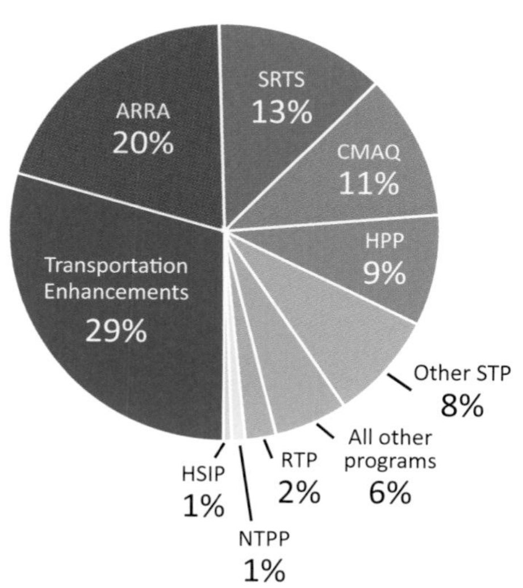

Source: FHWA FMIS 2009–2012. **Note**: Data are based on funds obligated to projects between 2009–2012 and are not necessarily the amount spent in these years. **Abbreviations**: ARRA (American Recovery and Reinvestment Act), SRTS (Safe Routes to School), CMAQ (Congestion Mitigation and Air Quality Improvement Program), HPP (High Priority Projects), other STP (Surface Transportation Program, except for Transportation Enhancements), RTP (Recreational Trails Program), NTPP (Nonmotorized Transportation Pilot Program), HSIP (Highway Safety Improvement Program).

Federal Programs to Fund Bicycling and Walking

TAP/TE: Transportation Alternatives Program / Transportation Enhancement Activities
CMAQ: Congestion Mitigation and Air Quality Improvement Program
HSIP: Highway Safety Improvement Program
STP: Surface Transportation Program
SRTS: Safe Routes to School
RTP: Recreational Trails Program
FTA: Federal Transit Administration Capital Funds
ATI: Associated Transit Improvement
NHPP: National Highway Performance Program
402: State and Community Traffic Safety Program
FLH: Federal Lands Highway Program

Funded Activity	TAP/TE	CMAQ	HSIP	STP	SRTS (1)	RTP	FTA	ATI	NHPP	402	FLH
Access enhancements to public transportation	$	$		$			$	$			$
Bicycle and/or pedestrian plans	$ (2)			$			$				$
Bicycle lanes on road	$	$	$	$	$		$	$	$		$
Bicycle parking	$	$		$	$		$	$			$
Bicycle racks on transit	$	$		$			$	$			$
Bike share	$	$		$			$	$	$		$
Bicycle storage or service centers	$	$		$			$	$			
Bridges/overcrossings	$	$	$	$	$	$	$	$	$		$
Bus shelters	$			$			$	$			$
Coordinator positions (state or local)	$ (3)	$		$	$						
Crosswalks (new or retrofit)	$	$	$	$	$	$	$	$	$		$
Curb cuts and ramps	$	$	$	$	$	$	$	$	$		$
Helmet promotion	$ (3)			$	$					$	
Historic preservation (bicycle, pedestrian, and transit facilities)	$			$			$	$			$
Landscaping, streetscaping (bicycle and/or pedestrian route; transit access)	$			$			$	$			$
Maps (for bicyclists and/or pedestrians)	$ (3)	$		$	$		$	$		$	
Paved shoulders	$	$	$	$	$				$		$
Police patrols	$ (3)			$ (3)	$					$	
Recreational trails	$			$		$					$
Safety brochures, books	$ (3)			$ (3)	$					$	
Safety education positions	$ (3)			$ (3)	$					$	
Shared use paths, transportation trails	$	$	$	$	$	$	$	$	$		$
Sidewalks (new or retrofit)	$	$	$	$	$	$	$	$	$		$
Signs/signals/signal improvements	$	$	$	$	$		$	$	$		$
Signed bicycle or pedestrian routes	$	$		$	$		$	$	$		$
Spot improvement programs	$	$	$	$	$	$	$				
Traffic calming	$		$	$	$		$		$		
Trail bridges	$	$	$	$	$	$			$		$
Trail/highway intersections	$	$	$	$	$	$			$		$
Training	$	$		$	$	$				$	
Tunnels/undercrossings	$	$	$	$	$	$	$	$	$		$

Source: FHWA 2013 **Notes**: For more information and updates go to AdvocacyAdvance.org and the "Find It Fund It Tool" (1) Until expended (2) As part of project (3) As part of SRTS

Reporting Funds for Bicycling and Walking Projects:
Inconsistencies and Varied Transparency Among States

by Ken McLeod, League of American Bicyclists and Advocacy Advance

Advocacy Advance is a partnership between the League of American Bicyclists and the Alliance for Biking & Walking, made possible by funding from the SRAM Cycling Foundation.

Reporting on funds spent for bicycling and pedestrian projects differs greatly between states, often leading to undercounted investments. Additionally, states and the federal government tend to report bicycling and walking projects together, making it difficult to identify spending on either mode individually. To understand what investments state DOTs have planned for bicycling and walking improvements, Advocacy Advance looked at one document that every state DOT is required to have—a Statewide Transportation Improvement Program (STIP).

A STIP lists at least four years of planned federally-funded transportation projects. With few exceptions, if a project is not in the STIP, it will not get built with federal transportation funds. Metropolitan Planning Organizations (MPOs) also create their own planning document, called the Transportation Improvement Program (TIP). STIPs are not required to directly include TIP projects, but those that do provide easier access to all funding information within the state. Otherwise, each MPO must be contacted individually to obtain funding information.

The Advocacy Advance team researched all 50 STIPs and many local TIPs to record every time a walking or bicycling facility was mentioned in a project description. When comparing STIPs across the country, the team found that plans differ in project detail and format, and contain other inconsistencies that limit comparing results between states.

The analysis by Advocacy Advance looked at planned projects in a systematic way that separated bicycling investments from walking investments.

Best Practices for STIP Documentation

- Show how planning and policy documents fit together
- Provide up-to-date documents and data in one place online
- Provide documents and data in many formats and guide users to appropriate formats
- Clearly identify a responsible contact for each STIP document, and provide email and phone contact information for that contact
- Include summary data in STIP documents
- Include clear explanations of information included in STIP project lists and why those elements are there
- Clearly identify whether MPO TIPs are included in the STIP document, and make MPO TIPs easy to access if they are not

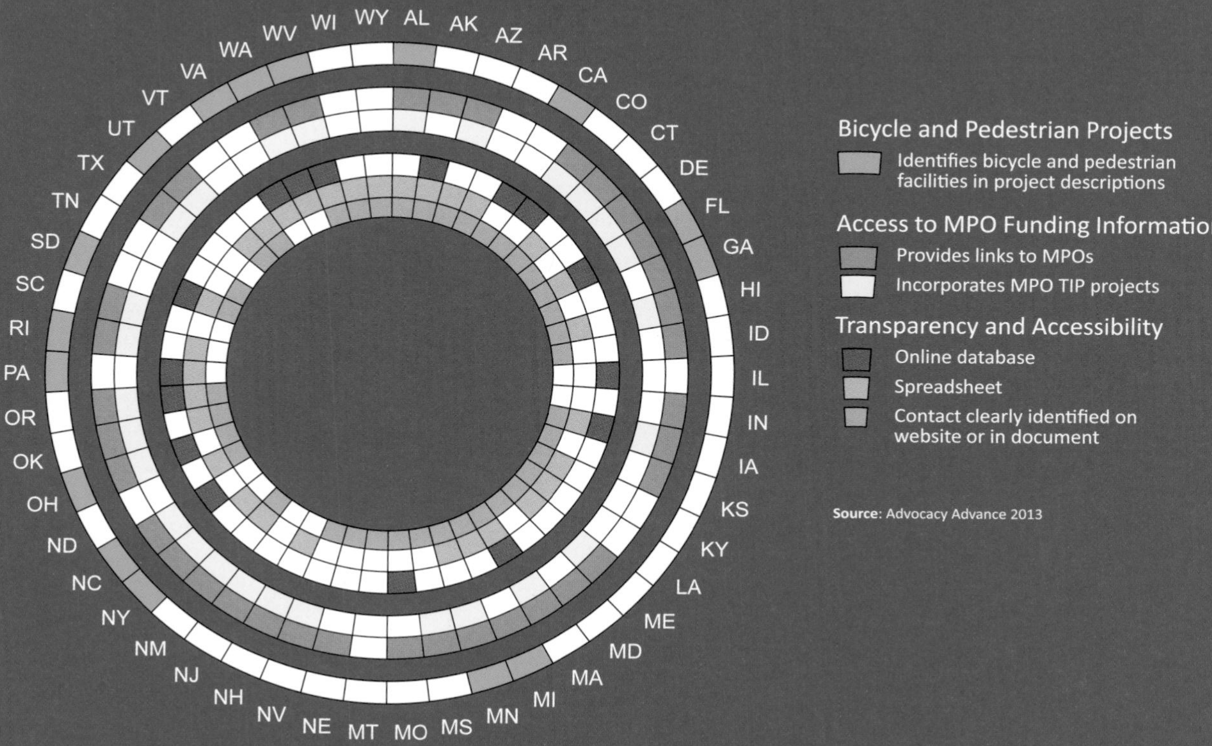

Identifying Bicycling and Walking Projects

Overall, most STIP project descriptions do not include bicycling or walking facilities, though pedestrian facilities, such as sidewalks, are more commonly mentioned than bicycle facilities. In many states, most of the bicycle and walking facilities documented were part of larger road projects. The percent of project descriptions that mention bicycling and walking projects in each state ranges from 1% of projects in Oklahoma to 27% in Washington State.

Transparency

The most comprehensive and transparent STIPs contain all the required information for a state in one place, clearly identify a contact person and email address, have narrative project descriptions, and are available to the public online or in spreadsheet format. Many states have begun to offer innovative interactive STIP tools which can help citizens understand future transportation investments.

View the full report, including best practices for transparency and Scorecards for each state at: *www.AdvocacyAdvance.org/MAP21/LiftingTheVeil*

Percent of Federal Transportation Dollars Applied to Bicycling and Walking

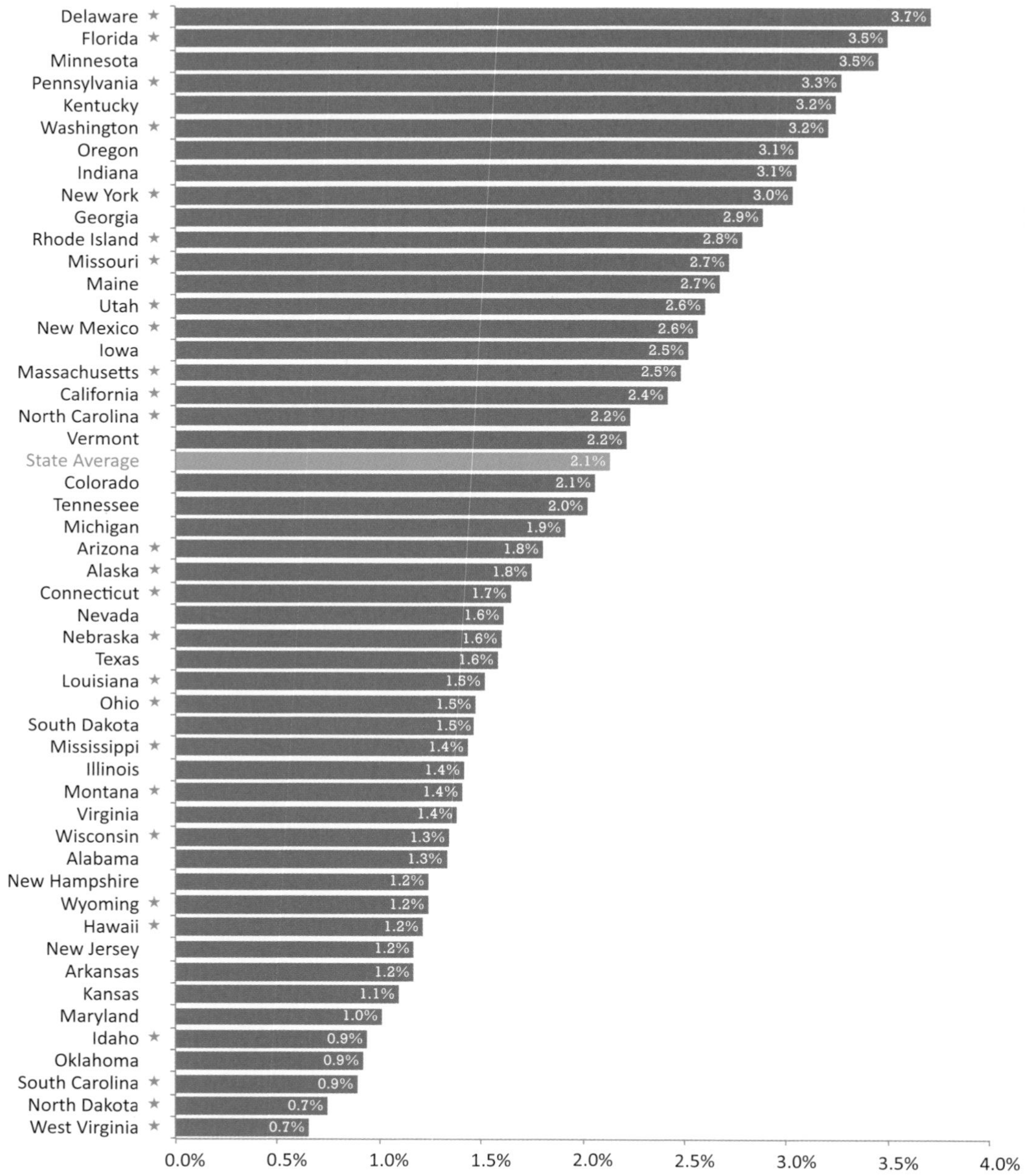

Source: FHWA FMIS 2009–2012. **Note**: Chart numbers are rounded; variation of bar length shows slight differences between states with the same percent.

Federal Funding Data

The most accurate, uniform data on federal funding for bicycling and walking comes from the Federal Highway Administration's (FHWA) FMIS accounting system. This system includes all federally-funded highway projects in the U.S. The funding data in this report (unless otherwise noted) depict a four-year average from 2009 to 2012 of federal funds obligated to projects, and are not necessarily the actual amount spent in these years. Tables on pages 126–127 show both the federal dollars per capita for each state and city, and the percentage of federal transportation dollars allocated for bicycling and walking in each state and city.

The reliability of federal funding data is limited by the way various states report transportation spending to the FHWA. Bicycle and pedestrian spending is likely underreported when a larger road project has a bicycle or pedestrian component. Often, the entire project is coded as a highway project, and therefore that state is not credited with spending the funds on bicycling and walking.

The increase in Complete Streets policies may influence tracking methods and the ability to compare spending by states. As more states include bicycling and walking elements in all transportation projects, it is increasingly difficult to track if states do not code the bicycle or pedestrian portions of the project.

When asked how their state reports projects, 28 states responded that they report standalone bicycle and pedestrian projects. Twenty-seven states responded that they report facilities that are part of larger projects. Six states did not respond or could not access this information.

Continued on page 131

Washington, D.C. Photo courtesy of Washington Area Bicyclist Association

Funding for Bicycling and Walking in States

	Annual state spending target for bicycling and walking?		Federal transportation funds (4-year average)			How state reports obligated funds to FMIS	
	Has target	% of state budget for transportation	Amount obligated to bike/ped projects per year	Amount obligated per capita	% of federal transportation $ to bike/ped	Reports stand-alone bike/ped projects?	Reports bike/ped facilities as part of larger projects?
Alabama			$12,048,861	$2.51	1.3%	✓	
Alaska			$8,711,712	$12.05	1.8%		✓
Arizona	✓	(1)	$15,414,565	$2.38	1.8%	✓	✓
Arkansas			$7,255,473	$2.47	1.2%	✓	
California			$99,003,735	$2.63	2.4%		✓
Colorado	✓	(2)	$13,428,607	$2.62	2.1%	✓	
Connecticut	✓	1.8% [3]	$9,421,083	$2.63	1.7%		✓
Delaware			$7,762,553	$8.56	3.7%		✓
Florida			$81,035,604	$4.25	3.5%	✓	✓
Georgia			$43,370,951	$4.42	2.9%		
Hawaii	✓	2.0%	$2,411,488	$1.75	1.2%	✓	✓
Idaho			$3,178,153	$2.01	0.9%	✓	✓
Illinois			$24,543,415	$1.91	1.4%	✓	
Indiana			$35,065,757	$5.38	3.1%		
Iowa			$15,257,503	$4.98	2.5%	✓	
Kansas			$5,234,337	$1.82	1.1%	✓	
Kentucky			$26,724,696	$6.12	3.2%		
Louisiana			$13,838,233	$3.02	1.5%	✓	✓
Maine	✓	1.6% [4]	$6,040,707	$4.55	2.7%	✓	
Maryland			$6,868,341	$1.18	1.0%	✓	
Massachusetts			$18,213,941	$2.76	2.5%		✓
Michigan	✓	1.0%	$24,754,904	$2.51	1.9%	✓	
Minnesota			$27,441,806	$5.13	3.5%	✓	
Mississippi			$8,755,281	$2.94	1.4%		✓
Missouri			$30,553,628	$5.08	2.7%	✓	✓
Montana			$6,584,691	$6.60	1.4%		✓
Nebraska			$5,600,097	$3.04	1.6%	✓	✓
Nevada			$6,829,969	$2.51	1.6%	✓	
New Hampshire			$2,711,785	$2.06	1.2%	✓	
New Jersey	✓	1.4%	$11,542,723	$1.31	1.2%	✓	
New Mexico			$11,205,328	$5.38	2.6%		✓
New York			$55,678,811	$2.86	3.0%		✓
North Carolina	✓	$6,600,000 [5]	$27,855,529	$2.88	2.2%		✓
North Dakota			$3,117,177	$4.56	0.7%	✓	✓
Ohio			$23,181,065	$2.01	1.5%	✓	✓
Oklahoma	✓	$6,000,000 [5]	$7,574,825	$2.00	0.9%	✓	
Oregon	✓	1.0% [6]	$17,361,586	$4.48	3.1%		
Pennsylvania			$58,582,486	$4.60	3.3%		✓
Rhode Island	✓	4.0%	$7,612,885	$7.24	2.8%		✓
South Carolina	✓	2.0%	$6,780,625	$1.45	0.9%		✓
South Dakota			$5,187,433	$6.29	1.5%		
Tennessee	✓	$15,000,000 [5]	$20,490,589	$3.20	2.0%	✓	
Texas			$55,125,274	$2.15	1.6%	✓	
Utah			$10,404,883	$3.69	2.6%		✓
Vermont	✓	2.3% [7]	$6,000,521	$9.58	2.2%	✓	
Virgina			$15,273,579	$1.89	1.4%		
Washington	✓	1.0%	$28,597,267	$4.19	3.2%	✓	✓
West Virginia			$3,485,987	$1.88	0.7%		✓
Wisconsin			$12,094,765	$2.12	1.3%	✓	✓
Wyoming			$3,730,078	$6.57	1.2%		✓
State average		1.8%	$19,178,906	$3.10	2.1%		
State median		1.7%	$11,795,792	$2.91	1.7%		
High		4.0%	$99,003,735	$12.05	3.7%		
Low		1.0%	$2,411,488	$1.18	0.7%		

Source: State Survey 2011/2012, FHWA FMIS 2009–2012, ACS 2011 (population-based averages are weighted). **Notes**: All obligations from the SRTS and NTPP programs were included as bicycle and pedestrian funding. Unanswered survey questions, or responses of "N/A" and "unknown," were taken to mean "no." All empty cells should be understood to be a "no" response. (1) Arizona bicycle and pedestrian spending level decisions are made by the ADOT State Transportation Board as well as at the regional and local levels. (2) Colorado uses Complete Streets to determine a spending target. (3) Connecticut has a target of 1% of the construction, maintenance, and repair budget per State Fiscal Year. This is accomplished across all funding programs combined. (4) This is the targeted spending amount over and above spending for bicycle and pedestrian projects as part of the Complete Streets policies. (5) North Carolina, Oklahoma, and Tennessee only provided spending target amounts. North Carolina allocates $6 million from federal funds and $600,000 from the state for bicycle and pedestrian projects. (6) Oregon spends $18–20 Million in federal dollars on bicycle and pedestrian projects in addition to its 1% target. (7) Vermont's spending target represents anticipated state fiscal year expenditures on projects identified in the bicycle and pedestrian program. The program is separate from Transportation Enhancements, but includes SRTS.

Funding for Bicycling and Walking in Large Cities

Annual city spending target for bicycling and walking?		Dedicated city budget funds in 2012	Federal transportation funds (4-year average)			
Has target	% of city budget for transportation		Obligated to bike/ped projects per year	Amount obligated per capita	% of federal transportation $ to bike/ped	
		$41,500,000	$3,423,790	$6.19	16.8%	Albuquerque
			$238,820	$0.64	2.2%	Arlington, TX
		$5,000,000	$2,171,652	$5.02	34.4% (6)	Atlanta
✓	$8,000,000 (1)	$19,000,000	$3,427,938	$4.18	4.8%	Austin
		$300,000	$1,623,421	$2.62	3.5%	Baltimore
		$1,450,000	-$319 (2)	$0.00	0.0%	Boston
✓	-	$9,500,000	$1,834,365	$2.44	2.4%	Charlotte
			$3,906,243	$1.44	1.6%	Chicago
		$2,355,243	-$98,550 (2)	-$0.25 (2)	-4.1% (2)	Cleveland
✓	-		$403,305	$0.95	0.7%	Colorado Springs
✓	5.0%	$15,715,000	$33,929	$0.04	0.1%	Columbus
			$11,224,842 (3)	$9.18	19.8%	Dallas
		$7,000,000	$646,701	$1.04	1.0%	Denver
(4)	(4)	(4)	$685,586	$0.97	0.5%	Detroit
✓	$30,000,000 (1)	$30,000,000	$1,886,160	$2.83	2.8%	El Paso
		$190,000	$558,195	$0.73	0.3%	Fort Worth
✓	-		$719,316	$1.43	1.8%	Fresno
			-$137,775 (2)	-$0.40 (2)	-2.0% (2)	Honolulu
		$46,005,046	$5,825,237	$2.71	3.3%	Houston
		$3,000,000	$1,505	$0.00	0.0%	Indianapolis
✓	34.0%	$1,500,000	$1,595,989	$1.93	1.0%	Jacksonville
✓	3.0%	$10,848,915	$2,181,112	$4.71	10.3%	Kansas City, MO
		$6,700,000	$0 (5)	$0.00	0.0%	Las Vegas
			$826,913	$1.78	0.5%	Long Beach
		$6,075,848	$6,371,971	$1.67	2.9%	Los Angeles
✓	-	$2,193,800	$79,078	$0.13	39.6% (6)	Louisville
		$2,034,620	$3,494,650	$5.36	3.3%	Memphis
		$2,560,000	$1,010,137	$2.26	2.6%	Mesa
			$5,811,712	$14.22	3.0%	Miami
			$2,581,412	$4.32	3.8%	Milwaukee
		$15,026,106	$4,246,979	$10.95	24.4%	Minneapolis
✓	20.0%	$22,000,000	$1,372,345	$2.25	2.1%	Nashville
		$100,000	$2,757,009	$7.64	4.0%	New Orleans
			$11,359,762	$1.38	5.0%	New York City
		$5,152,000	$2,554,053	$6.45	6.5%	Oakland
		$7,447,951	-$552,352 (2)	-$0.93 (2)	-0.6% (2)	Oklahoma City
✓	10.0%	$50,000	$2,194,813	$5.29	7.5%	Omaha
			$10,610,773	$6.91	5.1%	Philadelphia
✓	1.1%	$100,000	$2,082,762	$1.42	3.2%	Phoenix
✓	8.7%		$4,971,245	$8.35	9.3%	Portland, OR
		$8,891,000	$2,563,421	$6.16	8.1%	Raleigh
			$4,466,477	$9.46	7.2%	Sacramento
✓	-		$3,586,376	$2.64	5.0%	San Antonio
			$1,132,216	$0.85	3.0%	San Diego
		$5,000,000	$1,061,135	$1.31	1.2%	San Francisco
✓	7.0%	$6,000,000	$4,221,154	$4.36	22.4%	San Jose
		$8,074,986	$0 (5)	$0.00	0.0%	Seattle
		$100,000	$3,176,565	$6.04	9.5%	Tucson
		$100,617	$918,771	$2.32	0.8%	Tulsa
		$475,000	$34,129	$0.08	0.1%	Virginia Beach
✓	5.0%		$8,530,018	$13.80	4.1%	Washington, DC
		$850,000	$251,825	$0.66	3.8%	Wichita
	10.4%	$8,351,318	$2,574,362	$2.78	3.3%	Large cities average
	7.0%	$5,000,000	$1,860,263	$2.26	3.0%	Large cities median
	34.0%	$46,005,046	$11,359,762	$14.22	39.6%	High
	1.1%	$50,000	-$552,352	-$0.93	-4.1%	Low

Source: City Survey 2011/2012, FHWA FMIS 2009–2012, ACS 2011 (population-based averages are weighted). **Notes**: All obligations from the SRTS and NTPP programs were included as bicycle and pedestrian funding. Unanswered survey questions, or responses of "N/A" and "unknown," were taken to mean "no." All empty cells should be understood to be a "no" response. Cells with a dash (-) mean data were unavailable or not reported. (1) Austin and El Paso only provided spending target amounts. (2) Negative obligations are a result of more deobligated funds than new obligations between 2009 and 2012. (3) In 2009, Dallas obligated $16.7 million from ARRA toward "The Park", a major bicycle/pedestrian/open space project. (4) No data were provided for Detroit in the 2011/2012 survey. (5) Las Vegas and Seattle reported $0 in bike/ped funding to FMIS between 2009 and 2012. (6) Atlanta and Louisville's percent of bike/ped funding may appear high for this time period because of large amounts of non-bike/ped deobligated funds.

MAP-21 and Its Impact on Bicycling and Walking

by Darren Flusche, League of American Bicyclists and Advocacy Advance

Advocacy Advance is a partnership between the League of American Bicyclists and the Alliance for Biking & Walking, made possible by funding from the SRAM Cycling Foundation.

On October 1, 2012, the federal transportation law, Moving Ahead for Progress in the 21st Century Act (MAP-21), went into effect. MAP-21 maintains broad eligibility for bicycling and walking projects across transportation funding programs and puts more decision-making power in the hands of regional governments for active transportation projects. However, it also consolidated some of the most frequently used, dedicated bicycle- and walking-friendly programs and reduced total funding for them. In addition, MAP-21 makes it easier for states to divert these funds to other purposes.

Program Consolidation

Prior to MAP-21, three of the most popular sources of federal funds for bicycling and walking projects were the Transportation Enhancements (TE) Program, Safe Routes to School (SRTS), and the Recreational Trails Program (RTP). Under MAP-21, these have been consolidated into one program called the Transportation Alternatives Program (TAP). The funding for the TAP program is 26% less in fiscal year 2014 than the combined FY 2012 funding for the three programs it replaced. You can find specific funding levels for your state and region at *www.AdvocacyAdvance.org/MAP21.*

MAP-21 also created some changes in eligible activities. For example, states and regions can still use TAP funds for pedestrian and bicycling improvements, but they cannot use TAP to pay for adult bicycle education classes. There is a new activity called Safe Routes for Non-Drivers, which is meant to improve access and accommodations for older adults, children, and individuals with disabilities, and which may lend itself to creative projects. Another new use of TAP funds is that right-of-ways of former Interstates or other divided highways can be converted into walkable, low-speed thoroughfares in urban environments.

Any activity that was eligible for funding under the Safe Routes to School (SRTS) Program, including educational safety programs for K-8 students, is eligible under TAP. Some states are using a portion of TAP funds to maintain an independent SRTS project selection process; others are incorporating SRTS activities into their overall TAP process. Some states are using additional funds from the Highway Safety Improvement Program to make up for reduction in funds and to cover SRTS activities.

Every year, each state can now decide if it wants to maintain its RTP with the same agency administration and rules, or "opt-out." If the state maintains the program, the funds equal to the FY 2009 amount are taken off the top of TAP. If the state opts out, the RTP funds get absorbed into TAP. In 2013, only Florida and Kansas opted out of the RTP.

Local Control

After setting aside RTP funds, TAP funds are distributed within states in two ways. Half of the funds are controlled by the state DOT to be spent anywhere in the state. The other half is allocated to rural areas, small urban areas, and large urbanized areas based on the proportion of the population in each of those geographies.

In many places, local governments are more responsive to walking and bicycling needs than states are. In response, bicycling advocates have fought to increase the amount of control regional planning agencies—Metropolitan Planning Organizations (MPOs)—have over federal transportation dollars. The result of these efforts is that MPOs with a population of over 200,000 are now suballocated funds to run their own TAP application process and select the projects they think are most important.

Flexibility: Transferability and Opt-outs

One of the goals of MAP-21 is to increase flexibility for how states spend their federal dollars. An outcome of this flexibility, though, is that states can transfer their anywhere-in-the-state funds to other transportation programs; for example, for uses other than bicycling and walking projects. Additionally, if, on August 1, 2014, a state has an unobligated balance of available funds exceeding a full year of funding, then the state may transfer the TAP funds to any project eligible under TAP, or to any project eligible under the Congestion Mitigation and Air Quality Improvement Program (CMAQ).

Broad Eligibility

TAP is a very small part of MAP-21 and it is a small source of federal funds for walking and bicycling projects. Bicycling and walking projects are broadly eligible for funding in the vast majority of Federal-aid funding programs. CMAQ funds projects that provide alternatives to car travel, including bike share systems. The Highway Safety Improvement Program (HSIP) funds pedestrian and bicycle safety infrastructure. Section 402 State and Community Highway Safety Grants fund non-infrastructure programs, such as adult bicycle education classes and pedestrian safety trainings. Surface Transportation Program (STP) funds may be used for any bicycle and pedestrian project, for any project eligible under TAP (including any project eligible under Safe Routes to School), and for any recreational trail project eligible under the RTP. Bicycle and pedestrian projects funded under the STP and TAP may be located anywhere; they are not required to be on federal highways.

For more information about navigating MAP-21, go to *www.AdvocacyAdvance.org/MAP21*.

In the new transportation bill, Congress combined previous programs dedicated to bicycling and walking into **one smaller pot** called Transportation Alternatives Program (TAP).

Previous Bill

2011 - $1.2 billion

for bicycling and walking programs

Safe Routes to School (SRTS)
$202 million

Transportation Enhancements (TE)
$928 million

Recreational Trails Program (RTP)
$97 million

Current Bill (MAP-21)

2013 - $809 million

for bicycling and walking programs

Source: Advocacy Advance. *www.AdvocacyAdvance.org/MAP21*

State Safety Policies and Funding

	Percent of traffic fatalities that are bike/ped	State Highway Safety Funding [1]		Emphasis in state highway safety plan	
		% to bike/ped	$ per capita	on bicycling	on walking
Alabama	8.5%	0.0%	$0.00		
Alaska	14.6%	0.0%	$0.00	✓	✓
Arizona	20.0%	0.0%	$0.00		
Arkansas	7.6%	0.0%	$0.00	✓	✓
California	24.5%	0.2%	$0.01	✓	✓
Colorado	11.3%	0.8%	$0.02		✓
Connecticut	14.9%	0.0%	$0.00	✓	✓
Delaware	20.3%	0.0%	$0.00		✓
Florida	23.8%	4.3%	$0.21	✓	✓
Georgia	13.4%	0.0%	$0.00	✓	✓
Hawaii	22.7%	0.0%	$0.00	✓	✓
Idaho	6.6%	0.0%	$0.00	✓	✓
Illinois	15.6%	0.0%	$0.00	✓	✓
Indiana	9.3%	0.0%	$0.00	✓	✓
Iowa	7.0%	0.0%	$0.00		
Kansas	4.9%	0.0%	$0.00		
Kentucky	7.3%	0.0%	$0.00		✓
Louisiana	14.2%	0.1%	$0.01	✓	✓
Maine	7.5%	3.7%	$0.18	✓	✓
Maryland	22.3%	0.2%	$0.01	✓ (2)	✓
Massachusetts	18.6%	0.0%	$0.00	✓	✓
Michigan	16.9%	0.0%	$0.00	✓	✓
Minnesota	11.7%	0.2%	$0.01		
Mississippi	8.9%	0.0%	$0.00		
Missouri	8.4%	0.0%	$0.00	✓	✓
Montana	6.5%	0.0%	$0.00		
Nebraska	5.2%	0.0%	$0.00		
Nevada	17.8%	0.0%	$0.00	✓	✓
New Hampshire	8.2%	0.0%	$0.00	✓	✓
New Jersey	27.3%	0.3%	$0.00	✓	✓
New Mexico	12.0%	0.0%	$0.00	✓	✓
New York	28.9%	0.0%	$0.00		
North Carolina	14.0%	1.0%	$0.04		✓
North Dakota	5.9%	0.0%	$0.00		
Ohio	10.5%	0.1%	$0.00	✓	✓
Oklahoma	7.5%	0.0%	$0.00		
Oregon	16.3%	0.0%	$0.00	✓	✓
Pennsylvania	12.2%	0.0%	$0.00	✓	✓
Rhode Island	19.0%	0.0%	$0.00		
South Carolina	13.1%	0.0%	$0.00	✓	✓
South Dakota	6.0%	0.0%	$0.00	✓	✓
Tennessee	8.6%	0.0%	$0.00	✓	✓
Texas	13.7%	0.0%	$0.00	✓	✓
Utah	12.8%	2.5%	$0.08		✓
Vermont	6.5%	0.0%	$0.00		
Virgina	11.0%	0.8%	$0.03	✓	✓
Washington	14.9%	1.3%	$0.05	✓	✓
West Virginia	5.6%	0.0%	$0.00	✓	✓
Wisconsin	10.2%	0.0%	$0.00	✓	✓
Wyoming	3.3%	0.0%	$0.00	✓	✓
# of states responding "yes"				32	37
State average	14.9%	0.4%	$0.02		
State median	11.9%	0.0%	$0.00		
High	28.9%	4.3%	$0.21		
Low	3.3%	$0.00	$0.00		

Source: FARS 2009–2011, FHWA FMIS 2009–2012, State Survey 2011/2012, ACS 2011 (population-based averages are weighted). **Notes**: Unanswered survey questions, or responses of "N/A" and "unknown," were taken to mean "no." All empty cells should be understood to be a "no" response. (1) State Highway Safety Funding is provided by federal transportation funding from the Highway Safety Improvement Program (HSIP). (2) Bicycling was added as an emphasis area in the Maryland state highway safety plan in 2013.

The Benchmarking Project mainly tracks obligations of federal funding for bicycle and pedestrian projects; states and cities may use other sources of funding for bicycle and pedestrian programs as well. Note that federal funding amounts included in this report are not necessarily the only funding for bicycle and pedestrian programs in any particular state or city.

Funds for bicycling and walking projects come from several different federal sources. Previously, the Transportation Enhancement Surface Transportation Program (TE/STP) was the leading funding source, and was responsible for roughly one-third of all obligations to bicycle and pedestrian projects between 2009 and 2012. More than 50 additional federal funding programs have been used for bicycle and pedestrian projects, most at relatively small amounts.

Overall, states spend just 2.1% of their federal transportation dollars on bicycle and pedestrian projects (based on the four-year funding period from 2009–2012). This amounts to just $3.10 per capita for bicycling and walking each year, compared to $583.57 per capita for all federally-funded transportation projects. The variation in per capita funding and the percentage of transportation dollars spent on bicycle and pedestrian projects are great among both cities and states. States and local jurisdictions play a significant role in determining how their federal transportation dollars are spent. Generally, bicycle and pedestrian projects receive a disproportionately low percentage of the funds.

Spending Targets

Spending targets are goals set by states and cities for how much money, or what percentage of transportation spending, will be allocated to bicycling and walking. Most states and cities report that they do not have spending targets for bicycling and walking. Just 15 states report having spending targets—up from 12 states as of the *2012 Benchmarking Report*. Sixteen of the large cities report having spending targets—up from 11 cities as of the 2012 report. Some spending targets are based on percentage of transportation spending over varying time frames, while other states and cities set dollar amounts as annual spending targets.

Funding to Improve Safety

The federal Highway Safety Improvement Program (HSIP) is a federal funding program that aims to reduce traffic deaths and injuries through infrastructure-related improvements. States must have a state highway safety plan to be eligible for these funds. Thirty-two states emphasize bicycling in their state highway safety plan and 37 states emphasize walking. However, the rate at which states obligate safety funds to bicycling and walking is disproportionately low compared to the percent of traffic fatalities these modes represent. While 14.9% of traffic fatalities are bicyclists or pedestrians, just 0.4% of state highway safety funds are directed towards programs for these modes. This amounts to just two cents per capita, on average, toward national bicycle and pedestrian safety from this fund.

Safe Routes to School policies

In 2005, the federal transportation legislation called "Safe, Accountable, Flexible and Efficient Transportation Equity Act—A Legacy for Users" (SAFETEA-LU) established funding for a national Safe Routes to School (SRTS) program. As part of this legislation, all states and the District of Columbia were mandated to hire a full-time Safe Routes to School Coordinator and were apportioned no less than $1 million each per year to improve bicycling and walking routes to schools. As of September 30, 2012, nearly $1.2 billion was allocated to (set aside for) states for SRTS projects, the majority of which was allocated to providing safe and accessible infrastructure. Constructing and repairing sidewalks was the most commonly funded project (NCSRTS, 2011).

MAP-21 combined funding for Safe Routes to School (SRTS) with the Transportation Enhancement (TE) activities and Recreational Trails Program (RTP) into the Transportation Alternatives Program (TAP). No specific funds are set aside for SRTS projects. All projects, except for some that are using RTP funds, must compete for funding among other transportation projects and, are now required to contribute a 20% local match. SRTS coordinators are no longer required; however, states can decide to retain their coordinators and apportion MAP-21 funds to pay for them. The funds that were granted via SRTS prior to MAP-21 are available until the funds run out. See pages 128–129 for a full discussion on MAP-21.

As of December 2012, approximately $628 million had been obligated (awarded) to 13,863 schools or programs through the federal Safe Routes to School (SRTS) program. This amounts to $13.33 per public school student, roughly $1.67 per year, per student. In the 2014 Benchmarking Project survey, the Alliance asked states to report what percentage of their schools participated in Safe Routes to School programs during 2011–2012. Nationwide, an average of 17% of states' public schools are engaged in a Safe Routes to School program. Maine has the highest participation rate with 60% of schools involved with SRTS programs. South Dakota reported the lowest participation rate with less than 1% of schools involved with SRTS.

The National Center for Safe Routes to School (NCSRTS) also collects data to track demand for SRTS programs. Data show that, nationwide, just 37% of funding requests were awarded (based on total funds requested). States vary on how they meet the demand for SRTS programs and projects, but in almost all cases funding requests exceed available funding. Minnesota and New Jersey have the largest gaps between supply and demand, and are able to fund just 13% and 14% of the total funds requested, respectively. Kentucky and Nevada best meet demand with current funding. One hundred percent of funds requested have been awarded in these states. The Safe Routes to School National Partnership and the National Center for Safe Routes to School have leading roles in benchmarking SRTS performance and publish regular progress reports. See Appendix 6 for links to their websites and the most up-to-date statistics for Safe Routes to School.

With the recent funding changes from MAP-21, the gap between available funds and demand will likely grow considerably. The Alliance asked states if they use any additional funding sources for SRTS besides the previously available federal SRTS dollars. Twenty states reported using additional funding sources for SRTS. Other funding sources used by states include local, state, and private funds, such as state highway funds, gas taxes, sales taxes, vehicle and license registration fees, and speeding fines.

One study found that states with child poverty rates above the national median were significantly less successful in awarding their available funds for Safe Routes to Schools than states with lower levels of child poverty (Cradock et al., 2012).

Photo courtesy of Safe Routes to School National Partnership

Safe Routes to School Programs in States

	% state's schools participating in SRTS program	State provides funding for SRTS, in addition to federal funds	# funded schools/programs
Alabama	-		167
Alaska	-		116
Arizona	21.0%	✓	203
Arkansas	1.0%		56
California	12.0%	✓	3,279
Colorado	39.7%	✓	691
Connecticut	7.0%		64
Delaware	20.0%		41
Florida	46.0%	✓	1,085
Georgia	21.0%		418
Hawaii	-	✓	6
Idaho	40.0%		180
Illinois	10.7%	✓	512
Indiana	22.0%		331
Iowa	10.0%		96
Kansas	13.0%		136
Kentucky	-		127
Louisiana	2.4%	✓	88
Maine	60.0%	✓	190
Maryland	3.0%	✓	290
Massachusetts	40.0%		526
Michigan	14.3%		129
Minnesota	34.0%	✓	264
Mississippi	14.0%		87
Missouri	9.5%	✓	239
Montana	-		89
Nebraska	7.0%	✓	98
Nevada	10.0%	✓	260
New Hampshire	43.0%		143
New Jersey	13.0%	✓	348
New Mexico	-		65
New York	5.0%	✓	169
North Carolina	-		178
North Dakota	5.0%		136
Ohio	18.0%	✓	525
Oklahoma	5.0%		71
Oregon	12.0%	✓	152
Pennsylvania	3.0%		135
Rhode Island	15.0%		46
South Carolina	25.0%		26
South Dakota	1.0%		27
Tennessee	-		119
Texas	-		853
Utah	12.0%	✓	74
Vermont	21.0%		75
Virgina	13.8%		228
Washington	8.0%	✓	129
West Virginia	9.5%		74
Wisconsin	16.0%	✓	357
Wyoming	20.0%		113
State average	17.1%		276
State median	13.0%		136
High	60.0%		3,279
Low	1.0%		6

Source: State Survey 2011/2012. **Note**: Unanswered survey questions, or responses of "N/A" and "unknown," were taken to mean "no." All empty cells should be understood to be a "no" response. Cells with a dash (-) mean data were unavailable or not reported.

Safe Routes to School in Large Cities

City-sponsored SRTS program?	# pupils in public schools (K-12)	# bicycle parking spaces at public schools	# bicycle parking spaces per 1K students	City requires bicycling and walking access for students and staff	City requires bicycle parking at schools	
✓	90,000	-	-	✓	✓	Albuquerque
	-	-	-			Arlington, TX
	-	-	-	✓	✓	Atlanta
	-	-	-			Austin
✓	-	-	-			Baltimore
	56,340	864	15.3		✓	Boston
✓	135,638	1,700	12.5		✓	Charlotte
✓	379,919	2,000	5.3			Chicago
	44,000	-	-			Cleveland
✓	87,372	-	-			Colorado Springs
✓	50,000	1,668	33.4	✓	✓	Columbus
	157,000	-	-			Dallas
✓	84,500	735	8.7		✓	Denver
(1)	(1)	(1)	(1)	(1)	(1)	Detroit
	-	-	-			El Paso
	120,000	-	-		✓	Fort Worth
✓	-	-	-			Fresno
	-	-	-			Honolulu
	203,066	-	-			Houston
	127,277	-	-			Indianapolis
✓	-	-	-	✓	✓	Jacksonville
✓	44,896	364	8.1		✓	Kansas City, MO
	-	-	-			Las Vegas
✓	83,691	1,600	19.1			Long Beach
✓	662,140	-	-			Los Angeles
✓	88,000	-	-			Louisville
✓	105,000	750	7.1			Memphis
✓	66,550	5,700	85.6	✓	✓	Mesa
	37,743	500	13.2		✓	Miami
✓	78,461	180	2.3			Milwaukee
✓	32,263	1,000	31.0		✓	Minneapolis
	78,604	31	0.4			Nashville
✓	38,000	-	-			New Orleans
✓	1,100,000	2,600	2.4			New York City
✓	46,472	390	8.4			Oakland
	-	-	-			Oklahoma City
✓	75,000	-	-			Omaha
	137,512	300	2.2			Philadelphia
✓	285,700	16,000	56.0			Phoenix
✓	48,000	1,500	31.3		✓	Portland, OR
✓	143,289	100	0.7		✓	Raleigh
	-	-	-			Sacramento
✓	-	-	-			San Antonio
	-	-	-			San Diego
✓	55,000	(2)	-			San Francisco
✓	149,852	(3)	-		✓	San Jose
✓	47,000	1,500	31.9			Seattle
✓	-	-	-			Tucson
✓	41,000	405	9.9			Tulsa
✓	69,000	1,760	25.5			Virginia Beach
✓	76,752	-	-		✓	Washington, DC
	-	-	-			Wichita
	142,362	1,893	13.2			Large cities average
	81,148	932	11.2			Large cities median
	1,100,000	16,000	85.6			High
	32,263	31	0.4			Low

Source: City Survey 2011/2012. **Notes**: Unanswered survey questions, or responses of "N/A" and "unknown," were taken to mean "no." All empty cells should be understood to be a "no" response. Cells with a dash (-) mean data were unavailable or not reported. (1) No data were provided for Detroit in the 2011/2012 survey (2) Nine per school. (3) 1 space per 10 full-time employees and 6 bikes per classroom in K-8 schools, and 1 space per 10 full-time employees and 10 bikes per classroom in 9–12 schools and at colleges, universities, and vocational schools.

Funding Connections to Transit

There are many ways transit stops and stations can make access to public transportation easier for bicyclists and pedestrians. Chapter 7 of this report reviews some of the facilities that appeal to bicyclists and pedestrians (see pages 172–173) and discusses the mutual benefits of integrating a bicycle and pedestrian perspective into transit planning and design.

The U.S. Department of Transportation/ Federal Transit Administration (USDOT/FTA) has highlighted some of the federal funding programs that are available to bicycle, pedestrian, and transit integration projects. The table is reproduced below and is available online at:

http://www.FTA.DOT.gov/13747_14400.html

Federal Programs to Fund Improved Bicycle and Pedestrian Connections to Transit

Program: Metropolitan, Statewide, and Non-metropolitan Transportation Planning
Statue (Title 49): 5303, 5304, 5305; Funding Type: Formula

Eligible Recipients	Program Purpose	Eligible Bicycle Activities	Federal Share for Bicycle Activities
States, with allocation of funding to Metropolitan Planning Organizations (MPO)	Provides funding and procedural requirements for multimodal transportation planning in metropolitan areas and states that is cooperative, continuous, and comprehensive, resulting in long-range plans and short-range programs of transportation investment priorities.	Planning for bicycle facilities in a state or metropolitan transportation network	Federal share is 80% formula-based with a required 20% non-federal match.

Program: Urbanized Area Formula Program
Statue (Title 49): 5307; Funding Type: Formula

Eligible Recipients	Program Purpose	Eligible Bicycle Activities	Federal Share for Bicycle Activities
FTA (Federal Transit Administration) apportions funds to designated recipients, which then suballocate funds to state and local governmental authorities, including public transportation providers	Provides grants to Urbanized Areas (UZA) for public transportation capital, planning, job access, and reverse commute projects, as well as operating expenses in certain circumstances. These funds constitute a core investment in the enhancement and revitalization of public transportation systems in the nation's urbanized areas, which depend on public transportation to improve mobility and reduce congestion. Consolidates JARC (Job Access and Reverse Commute) eligible projects.	Bicycle routes to transit, bike racks, shelters, and equipment for public transportation vehicles	Bicycle projects can receive a 95% federal share for the first 1% of program funds in large urbanized areas.

Program: Fixed Guideway Capital Investment Grants
Statue (Title 49): 5309; Funding Type: Formula

Eligible Recipients	Program Purpose	Eligible Bicycle Activities	Federal Share for Bicycle Activities
State and local government agencies, including transit agencies	Provides grants for new and expanded rail, bus rapid transit, and ferry systems that reflect local priorities to improve transportation options in key corridors.	Bicycle racks, shelters, and equipment	Bicycle projects receive a 90% federal share.

Program: Bus and Bus Facilities Formula Grants
Statue (Title 49): 5339; Funding Type: Formula

Eligible Recipients	Program Purpose	Eligible Bicycle Activities	Federal Share for Bicycle Activities
Designated recipients and states that operate or allocate funding to fixed-route bus operators	Provides capital funding to replace, rehabilitate, and purchase buses and related equipment and to construct bus-related facilities.	Bicycle routes to transit, bike racks, shelters, and equipment for public transportation vehicles	Bicycle projects receive a 90% federal share.

Source: USDOT/FTA, *www.FTA.DOT.gov/13747_14400.html*. Reproduced with permission.

Portland, OR. Photo courtesy of PeopleForBikes

Federal Programs to Fund Improved Bicycle and Pedestrian Connections to Transit (continued)

Program: Enhanced Mobility of Seniors and Individuals with Disabilities
Statue (Title 49): 5310; Funding Type: Formula

Eligible Recipients	Program Purpose	Eligible Bicycle Activities	Federal Share for Bicycle Activities
States (for all areas under 200,000 in population) and designated recipients, state DOTs for private nonprofit agencies and public agencies that coordinate human service transportation, states or local government authorities, private nonprofit organizations, or operators of public transportation that receive a grant indirectly through a recipient	This program is intended to enhance mobility for seniors and persons with disabilities by providing funds for programs to serve the special needs of transit-dependent populations beyond traditional public transportation services and Americans with Disabilities Act (ADA) complementary paratransit services. Consolidates New Freedom eligible projects.	Bicycle improvements that provide access to an eligible public transportation facility and meet the needs of the elderly and individuals with disabilities	Bicycle projects receive an 80% federal share.

Program: Formula Grants for Rural Areas
Statue (Title 49): 5311; Funding Type: Formula

Eligible Recipients	Program Purpose	Eligible Bicycle Activities	Federal Share for Bicycle Activities
States, Indian tribes, state DOTs for local rural transit providers, including private nonprofits. Subrecipients: state or local government authorities, nonprofit organizations, operators of public transportation	This program provides capital, planning, and operating assistance to states to support public transportation in rural areas with populations less than 50,000, where many residents often rely on public transit to reach their destinations.	Bicycle routes to transit, bike racks, shelters, and equipment for public transportation vehicles	Bicycle projects receive a 90% federal share.

Program: TOD Planning Pilot Grants
Statue (Title 49): 20005(b) of MAP-21; Funding Type: Discretionary

Eligible Recipients	Program Purpose	Eligible Bicycle Activities	Federal Share for Bicycle Activities
State and local government agencies	Provides funding to advance planning efforts that support transit-oriented development (TOD) associated with new fixed-guideway and core capacity improvement projects.	Projects that facilitate multimodal connectivity and accessibility or increase access to transit hubs for pedestrian and bicycle traffic	Bicycle projects receive a 90% federal share.

What Holds us Back: Policies and Funding Choices that Limit Bicycling and Walking Initiatives

The *Benchmarking Report* focuses on the many ways states and cities have improved the transportation network for bicyclists and pedestrians. There are, however, some policies and practices that limit the impact these initiatives have.

School Siting Policies

The Alliance also asked cities and states whether they have a policy setting minimum acreage requirements for school siting. These requirements can often lead to sprawl by forcing new schools to be built far away from urban and suburban centers, and create poor conditions for bicycling and walking to school (McDonald, 2012). These same conditions may negatively influence participation in after-school and weekend activities at the school grounds (such as science club, scouts, arts, and cultural enrichment, sports, etc.).

Fifteen states reported having minimum acreage policies for school siting which is one less than two years ago. These policies vary, but on average require a minimum of 10 acres for elementary schools, 20 acres for middle schools, and 30 acres for high schools, plus one acre for every 100 students. Thirty-one cities reported having a policy that places children in schools for reasons other than proximity to their homes. Desegregation busing, the practice of assigning and busing students to schools to diversify student demographics, is one common policy that forces children to attend schools outside of their neighborhood, and which consequently makes walking and bicycling to school more difficult.

Mandatory Bike Lane and Sidepath Use Laws

Although most state laws define bicycles as vehicles with the same rights and responsibilities as other vehicles on roadways, some states and municipalities have laws that prohibit bicyclists from full use of roadways when a bicycle lane or adjacent pathway is present. These mandatory bicycle lane use and mandatory sidepath laws can make it illegal for bicyclists to navigate traffic with the best vehicular tactics (such as merging left to avoid an obstruction, merging into the left lane to turn left, or not riding to the right of traffic in a turn lane), and restrict bicyclists' access to businesses or residences.

Most states, however, do allow bicyclists full use of the lane in traffic. Forty-one states allow the full use of lanes by bicyclists when a bicycle lane is present, and 45 allow use of the full lane in the presence of a sidepath. Kentucky, New York, and West Virgina have mandatory bicycle lane use laws without exception. Six states (California, Florida, Hawaii, Maryland, Oregon, and South Carolina) have mandatory bicycle lane use laws with exceptions. States that have mandatory sidepath laws include Alabama, Kansas, and West Virginia. Nebraska and Oregon also have a mandatory sidepath law but allow some exceptions.

Rescissions to Bicycle and Pedestrian Funding

While now falling under MAP-21's Transportation Alternatives Program (TAP), the Transportation Enhancement (TE) program was previously known as the best funding source for bicycle and pedestrian infrastructure improvements. Over the last 20 years, $5.57 billion, or 51.5% of TE funding, had been allocated to bicycling and walking infrastructure and programs.

Almost $3 billion, or 21% of apportioned TE funding, has been rescinded since 1992 (NTAC, 2013). Unfortunately bicycle and pedestrian projects are disproportionately affected when states choose to rescind a greater percentage of TE funds than from other transportation funding programs.

Policies that Limit Bicycling and Walking Progress

Policy requiring minimum acreage for school-siting	Mandatory sidepath law in place	Mandatory bicycle lane use law in place	
✓	✓		Alabama
			Alaska
			Arizona
✓			Arkansas
		✓ (1)	California
			Colorado
			Connecticut
✓			Delaware
		✓ (1)	Florida
✓			Georgia
		✓ (1)	Hawaii
✓			Idaho
✓			Illinois
✓			Indiana
			Iowa
	✓		Kansas
		✓	Kentucky
			Louisiana
			Maine
		✓ (1)	Maryland
			Massachusetts
			Michigan
			Minnesota
			Mississippi
			Missouri
			Montana
	✓ (1)		Nebraska
			Nevada
✓			New Hampshire
			New Jersey
✓			New Mexico
✓		✓	New York
✓			North Carolina
			North Dakota
✓			Ohio
✓			Oklahoma
	✓ (1)	✓ (1)	Oregon
			Pennsylvania
		✓	Rhode Island
		✓ (1)	South Carolina
			South Dakota
			Tennessee
			Texas
			Utah
			Vermont
			Virgina
			Washington
✓	✓	✓	West Virginia
			Wisconsin
✓			Wyoming
15	5	10	# of states responding "yes"

Source: State Survey 2011/2012. **Note**: Unanswered survey questions, or responses of "N/A" and "unknown," were taken to mean "no." All empty cells should be understood to be a "no" response. (1) Law is in place, but allows for exceptions.

Policies and Planning in Midsized Cities

Published Goals

Among the 17 midsized cities surveyed, 11 reported having a published goal to increase walking, and 14 reported having a published goal to increase biking. Interestingly, all midsized cities that have adopted at least one of these two goals have also adopted goals to increase both pedestrian and bicycle facilities, and to increase physical activity.

A majority of these cities have published goals to decrease bicycling and pedestrian fatalities; however, such commitments are not as prevalent as the above-mentioned goals. Of the surveyed cities, ten midsized cities have committed to decreasing pedestrian fatalities, and 11 cities have committed to decreasing bicyclist fatalities.

Bicycling and Walking Goals

	City has a published goal to...						
	increase walking	increase bicycling	increase pedestrian facilities	increase bicyclist facilities	increase physical activity	decrease pedestrian fatalities	decrease bicyclist fatalities
Population > 200K							
Anchorage, AK		✓	✓	✓		✓	✓
Baton Rouge, LA	✓	✓	✓	✓	✓		✓
Madison, WI	✓	✓	✓	✓	✓	✓	✓
Pittsburgh, PA	✓	✓	✓	✓		✓	✓
Spokane, WA						✓	✓
St. Louis, MO		✓	✓	✓	✓		
Population 100-200K							
Charleston, SC	✓	✓	✓	✓	✓	✓	✓
Chattanooga, TN							
Eugene, OR	✓	✓	✓	✓	✓	✓	✓
Fort Collins, CO	✓	✓	✓	✓	✓	✓	✓
Salt Lake City, UT	✓	✓	✓	✓			
Population < 100K							
Albany, NY	✓	✓	✓	✓	✓		
Bellingham, WA			✓	✓			
Boulder, CO	✓	✓	✓	✓	✓	✓	✓
Burlington, VT	✓	✓	✓	✓	✓	✓	✓
Davis, CA		✓	✓	✓	✓		
Missoula, MT	✓	✓	✓	✓	✓	✓	✓

Source: Midsized City Survey 2011/2012. **Note**: Unanswered survey questions, or responses of "N/A" and "unknown," were taken to mean "no." All empty cells should be understood to be a "no" response.

Policies and Planning

	City has adopted...						
						Carbon emissions plan	
	NACTO design guidelines	master plan, bicycle and pedestrian combined	master plan, bicycle stand-alone	master plan, pedestrian stand-alone	master plan, trails	includes walking	includes bicycling
Population > 200K							
Anchorage, AK			✓	✓	✓		
Baton Rouge, LA			✓		✓	✓	✓
Madison, WI			✓	✓		✓	✓
Pittsburgh, PA			✓			✓	✓
Spokane, WA			✓				
St. Louis, MO							✓
Population 100-200K							
Charleston, SC						✓	✓
Chattanooga, TN	✓ (1)	✓	✓		✓	✓	✓
Eugene, OR		✓				✓	✓
Fort Collins, CO			✓	✓	✓	✓	✓
Salt Lake City, UT	✓	✓			✓	✓	✓
Population < 100K							
Albany, NY			✓			✓	✓
Bellingham, WA				✓			
Boulder, CO	✓	✓			✓	✓	✓
Burlington, VT	✓					✓	✓
Davis, CA	✓		✓			✓	✓
Missoula, MT		✓		✓	✓	✓	✓

Source: Midsized City Survey 2011/2012. **Notes**: Unanswered survey questions, or responses of "N/A" and "unknown," were taken to mean "no." All empty cells should be understood to be a "no" response. (1) Adopted in 2013.

Master Plans

Master planning for nonmotorized traffic in smaller communities is equally as important as it is for larger cities. Master plans can help link downtown areas to local amenities and improve general connectivity to address the challenges present in a specific location. A vast majority (14 out of 17) of the midsized cities have adopted some type of master plan for bicyclists and/or pedestrians.

Five have a combined bicycle and pedestrian master plan, and three have both a pedestrian-only plan and a bicycle-only plan. Five have a bicycle-only plan, and one has a pedestrian-only plan. Although Burlington, VT, has not adopted its own master plan, it does follow the NACTO design guidelines to improve its bikeway design. Seven of the midsized cities have a trail master plan; none have a mountain bike plan.

A large majority of midsized cities also reported having a plan for reducing carbon emissions. Of the 14 cities with carbon emission reduction plans, all 14 included bicycling and 13 included walking.

Funds for Bicycling and Walking Projects in Midsized Cities

Ten midsized cities reported dedicated city budget funds for bicycling and pedestrian spending. Topping the list for 2012 was Madison with $4.42 million, followed by Charleston and Burlington, both with $3.10 million. Anchorage, Davis, and Eugene reported having a city bicycle and pedestrian spending target rather than dedicated city funds, while Missoula reported both dedicated funds and a spending target of 4.5% of the city budget.

Safe Routes to School

At the time of this report, ten of the midsized cities have Safe Routes to School (SRTS) policies, and almost all of these cities receive funding through both the federal and state governments. A few cities receive private SRTS funds, including Chattanooga, Davis, and Eugene. A few more receive regional funds, including Burlington, Davis, Eugene, Fort Collins, and Madison.

Funding Bicycling and Walking

	Spending target for bicycling and walking			2012 dedicated city budget funds to bicycling and walking	2012 bicycling and walking funds budgeted per capita
	Has target	Amount of city budget	Timeline		
Population > 200K					
Anchorage, AK	✓	10.0%	5 years	-	-
Baton Rouge, LA				-	-
Madison, WI				$4,420,000	$18.87
Pittsburgh, PA				$702,000	$2.29
Spokane, WA				$13,000	$0.06
St. Louis, MO				-	-
Population 100-200K					
Charleston, SC				$3,100,000	$25.72
Chattanooga, TN				$285,000	$1.69
Eugene, OR	✓	-	-	-	-
Fort Collins, CO				$295,000	$2.04
Salt Lake City, UT				$819,000	$4.37
Population < 100K					
Albany, NY				$955,041	$9.76
Bellingham, WA				-	-
Boulder, CO				-	-
Burlington, VT				$3,100,000	$73.03
Davis, CA	✓	$140,000	1 year	-	-
Missoula, MT	✓	4.5%	32 years	1,361,120	$20.36
High value					
Midsized cities				$4,420,000	$73.03
52 large cites				$46,005,046	$75.07
Low value					
Midsized cities				$13,000	$0.06
52 large cites				$50,000	$0.07
Large cities average				$8,351,318	$11.15

Source: Midsized City Survey 2011/2012, ACS 2011. **Notes**: Unanswered survey questions, or responses of "N/A" and "unknown," were taken to mean "no." All empty cells should be understood to be a "no" response. Cells with a dash (-) mean data were unavailable or not reported.

Safe Routes to School

	City-sponsored SRTS program?	# pupils in public schools (K-12)	# bicycle parking spaces at public schools	# bicycle parking spaces per 1K students	City requires bicycle parking at schools
Population > 200K					
Anchorage, AK		-	-	-	
Baton Rouge, LA	✓	42,850	146	3.4	
Madison, WI	(1)	24,861	-	-	✓
Pittsburgh, PA		26,463	30	1.1	
Spokane, WA	✓	32,000	750	23.4	
St. Louis, MO		22,516	200	8.9	
Population 100-200K					
Charleston, SC	✓	10,800	300	27.8	✓
Chattanooga, TN	✓	42,705	-	-	
Eugene, OR	✓	21,700	-	-	✓
Fort Collins, CO	✓	23,000	2,000	87.0	
Salt Lake City, UT		22,700	-	-	
Population < 100K					
Albany, NY		10,700	130	12.1	
Bellingham, WA	✓	10,802	1,600	148.1	
Boulder, CO	✓	12,306	-	-	
Burlington, VT		3,600	-	-	
Davis, CA	✓	2,400	225 per school	-	
Missoula, MT	✓	4,873	360	73.9	
High value					
Midsized cities		42,850	2,000	148.1	
52 large cites		1,100,000	16,000	85.6	
Low value					
Midsized cities		3,600	30	1.1	
52 large cites		32,263	31	0.4	
Large cities average		142,362	1,893	13.2	

Source: Midsized City Survey 2011/2012. **Notes**: Unanswered survey questions, or responses of "N/A" and "unknown," were taken to mean "no." All empty cells should be understood to be a "no" response. Cells with a dash (-) mean data were unavailable or not reported. (1) The City of Madison does not have a formal SRTS progam. However, the Madison Metropolitan School District, which covers the majority of the city, does have a SRTS program, including a staff position for a SRTS Coordinator. School district boundaries do not match up with city boundaries—not all school districts are entirely within the City of Madison.

Nashville, Tennessee:
Building Complete Streets in Underserved Communities

by Liz Whiteley, U.S. Environmental Protection Agency

Nashville, Tennessee, is a diverse city that has grown and sprawled substantially over the past few decades. In recent years, the city has been characterized by long commutes and high rates of adult obesity and diabetes, particularly in African American and Hispanic communities. But it is also a city that has begun to recognize the importance of active transportation as a means to improved public health and sustainability. Through collaborative efforts and policy shifts at the city and regional level, Nashville is realizing the benefits from its Complete Streets policy.

The City

Mayor Karl Dean and a supportive city administration have been critical to creating change in the City of Nashville. When the Metropolitan Planning Department first raised the idea of a municipal Complete Streets policy in 2007, some departments within the city administration were wary of costs. In 2009 and 2010, however, the situation began to change. The mayor commissioned the Green Ribbon Committee on Environmental Sustainability, which recommended a Complete Streets policy in order to "provide every citizen of Davidson County at least two modes of transportation available and accessible in order to reach food, work, school, worship, and recreation" (Green Ribbon Committee on Environmental Sustainability, 2009).

At the same time, the Healthy Nashville Leadership Council was making similar recommendations and, in 2009, initiated the Nashville Livability Project. With a new Director of Healthy Living position, federal grant money tied to obesity prevention, and the mayor's appointment of a Bicycle and Pedestrian Advisory Committee, the conversation about Complete Streets was in full swing.

In October 2010, the mayor signed an executive order, requiring that transportation projects fully consider the needs of all types of users during all phases of the project. This Complete Streets policy built on the work of previous city officials, but was the first official step to changing how transportation infrastructure is implemented in Nashville. Once the mandate was in place, the city began to overhaul its outdated Major and Collector Street Plan by redesigning the roadway guidelines to reflect the new emphasis on multi-modal transportation. The plan "maps the vision for Nashville's major and collector streets, and ensures that this vision is fully integrated with the city's land use, mass transit, and bicycle and pedestrian planning efforts" (Metropolitan Nashville Planning Department, 2012).

The Region

A reoccurring theme in Nashville's progress towards Complete Streets is the explicit recognition of how transportation options affect public health. While the city was creating new committees and staff positions, the regional Metropolitan Planning Organization (MPO) was hiring a Director of Healthy Communities and collaborating with the public and elected officials. During the process to update the Regional Transportation Plan, the MPO learned from community members what they really wanted: more walkable neighborhoods with more public transit. The MPO recognized that active transportation should become a key factor in how it selected transportation projects.

Celebrating the opening of the 28th Avenue Connector, Nashville's most Complete Street.
Photo courtesy of Nashville MPO

The current 2035 Regional Transportation Plan includes updated evaluation criteria for project selection. A project is assigned up to100 points, 60 of which relate to safety, health, multi-modal, and congestion-reduction aspects of the project. In updating the Regional Transportation Plan, the MPO also recognized that obesity and other related health problems often affect underserved communities the most. It began to map low-income areas with minority and elderly populations in order to identify potential Health Impact Areas. Proposed projects are assigned additional points if they fall into one of the identified areas (Nashville Area Metropolitan Planning Organization, 2010).

Moving Forward

At both the local and regional level, Nashville now has policies in place that promote active transportation. The support for such policies has stemmed from a need to address growing health concerns, particularly in minority and low-income populations. The MPO continues to collect data on walking and bicycling. Bicycle counts, Health Impact Assessments and household travel surveys all help provide the information needed to prioritize active transportation investments where they are needed most. In 2012, Nashville was recognized as a Bronze Level Bicycle Friendly Community by The League of American Bicyclists—a great milestone in its effort to become a more sustainable and livable city.

across borders

Dublin, Ireland: Using Tax Free Loans to Purchase Bicycles

by Brian Caulfield, Department of Civil, Structural and Environmental Engineering; Trinity College, Dublin

In recent years, the Irish government has used policy and tax benefits to promote bicycling and other modes of active transportation. Implementation of these changes has been driven by the desire to reduce greenhouse gas emissions, decrease congestion, and tackle the growing national obesity problem.

Prioritizing Smarter Travel Options

In 2008, the Irish government launched the Smarter Travel Policy, a road map to increasing active transportation options. This policy presents the government's action plan to reduce national car commuting rates from 65% to 45% by 2020 (Department of Transport, 2009). The plan further intends to increase the number of people commuting by foot, bicycle, or public transit to 55% from its current level of approximately 35%.

The plan outlines 49 coordinated actions across various government departments that promote bicycling and walking through improved infrastructure, planning, education, training, enforcement, promotion, integration with public transit, and the introduction of shared bicycle programs based on the Dublin Bikes model.

Financial Incentives

The Irish government has offered financial incentives to promote sustainable modes of transport since 2000. The Taxsaver program, for example, allows commuters to purchase their monthly or annual public transport pass from their employer and save up to 51% on the cost of the ticket.

On January 1, 2009, the government expanded the Taxsaver program with the introduction of the Cycle to Work Scheme. This new program encourages employers to purchase a bicycle and/or safety equipment for their employees. The total cost, up to €1,000, is withdrawn from the employee's salary before tax deductions are made. This decrease in taxable income enables employees to save up to 51% on the total cost of their bicycle and accessories and reduces the amount employers must contribute towards Pay Related Social Insurance (PRSI). In addition, the employee can spread out their repayment to the employer through monthly salary withdrawals for up to 12 months, adding further incentive by avoiding large upfront costs.

Dublin, Ireland
Photo by Paolo Trabattoni @ Flickr

Caveats

- Each employee can take advantage of the Cycle to Work Scheme once every five years.
- The bicycle and/or safety equipment purchased through the program must be used primarily for work-related travel.
- The financial risk associated with the purchase rests with the employee. For example, if the bicycle is lost or stolen, or if the employee leaves their place of employment, they must repay any outstanding balance due from the purchase.

Leo Varadkar, Minister for Transport, Tourism, and Sport, leading the 2011 Phoenix Park bicycle ride. Dublin, Ireland. Photo courtesy of Dublin Cycling Campaign

Documented Increase in Bicycling

Caulfield and Leahy (2011) conducted a survey of program participants to evaluate the success of the Cycle to Work Scheme. The survey revealed increased levels of bicycling, particularly among individuals who had not owned a bicycle in several years. In fact, results showed that 48% of survey respondents who participated in the program did not own a bicycle prior to their Cycle to Work purchase; 36% had not owned a bicycle within four years or more of participating in the program.

Of the new bicycle owners (those who had not owned a bicycle in the past four years or more), 11% said they now bicycle to work every day, and 51% bicycle to work at least once a week. Non-work trips by bicycle also increased among the new bicycle owners; 53% said they now make at least one non-work related bicycle trip per week.

Additionally, the study found that the overwhelming majority (91%) of respondents said that if their bicycle was lost or stolen they would replace it. This finding demonstrates the benefits participants in the program derive from their bicycle, even for those who had not owned a bicycle in recent years.

For more information on the Cycle to Work Scheme, visit: *www.CitizensInformation.ie/*

To read a full report of the Caulfield and Leahy study, visit: *www.ITRN.ie/Uploads/sesD_ID119.pdf*

Potential Employee Cost and Savings

Higher rate taxpayer [1]

Cost of bicycle and accessories	€250	€500	€750	€1,000
Tax relief saving at 51%	€128	€255	€383	€510
Net cost	€123	€245	€368	€490
Payment per month	€10	€20	€31	€41

Basic rate taxpayer [1]

Cost of bicycle and accessories	€250	€500	€750	€1,000
Tax relief saving at 30%	€75	€150	€225	€300
Net cost	€175	€350	€525	€700
Payment per month	€15	€29	€44	€58

Source: Revenue 2011. **Note:** (1) See *www.Revenue.ie/en/Tax/it/Leaflets/it1.html#Section3* for more details on these tax bands.

Example: A higher rate taxpayer will save 51% (up to €510) on the purchase of a bicycle and safety equipment through decreased income tax. If this taxpayer makes the highest allowable purchase (€1,000), they can pay back the amount at €41 per month for a year.

It is worth noting that those on higher incomes receive a greater benefit from the scheme. This preferential treatment for those on higher incomes raises a number of equity issues, which could be addressed in any revision of the current program.

6 Infrastructure and Design

The Community Preventive Services Task Force, an independent panel of public health experts, recommends a focus on providing bicycle- and pedestrian-friendly infrastructure, in addition to specific policy initiatives mentioned in the previous chapter, as a way of increasing physical activity levels. The task force also recommends providing street-level urban design elements catered to bicyclists and pedestrians, such as street lighting and landscaping, to create an appealing space for these users. In particular, the task force recommends enhancing this infrastructure to make it accessible for people of all ages and physical abilities (Berrigan, 2012).

U.S. bicycle advocates commonly look to model countries, such as the Netherlands and Denmark, where cities have invested heavily in bicycling infrastructure. These investments (including bicycle lanes, separated paths, and specialized signals and traffic signs for bicyclists) may contribute to a bicycling mode share that reaches between 30% to 50% in many Dutch cities (Pucher and Buehler, 2007, 2008).

There are three aspects of the built environment that impact physical activity levels: (1) transportation infrastructure, such as roads, paths, and sidewalks; (2) land use patterns, such as residential, commercial, or open space; and (3) urban design, such as the appearance and arrangement of physical elements (Frank et al., 2003).

Portland, OR. Photo by Greg Raisman

Roads, Paths, and Sidewalks

Just as road infrastructure facilitates safe and accessible routes for motorized vehicles, so too is appropriate infrastructure critical for safe and accessible routes for bicycling and walking (Pucher and Buehler, 2010; Buehler and Pucher, 2012; Hopkinson and Wardman, 1996; McClintock and Cleary, 1996; Reynolds et al., 2009; Rietveld, 2000).

The extent and quality of bicycle and pedestrian facilities affects levels of bicycling and walking in community (Buehler and Pucher, 2012; Dill and Carr, 2003; Heinen et al., 2010; Hunt and Abraham, 2007; Moudon et al., 2005; Parkin et al., 2008; Pucher et al., 2010; Rietveld and Daniel, 2004; Vandenbulcke et al., 2011). One study found that cities with 10% more bike lanes or paths had about 2% to 3% more daily bicycle commuters (Buehler and Pucher, 2012).

Traditionally, underserved communities in particular may benefit from extended and improved bicycle and pedestrian facilities. A 2012 survey found that 60% of people of color and 59% of those with an income less than $30,000 said that more bicycle facilities would encourage them to ride more often (LAB, 2013).

Because there is no standard reporting requirement for government agencies to track bicycle and pedestrian facilities, many do not have accurate records. The quality and accessibility of facilities are equally difficult to measure and may vary greatly from place to place.

Furthermore, the usefulness of paths and trails relies on accessibility from the broader transportation network. For example, a 12-foot-wide, multi-use path on a major city bridge may be much more important for increasing bicycling and walking by providing

Bicycle Infrastructure per Square Mile in Large Cities

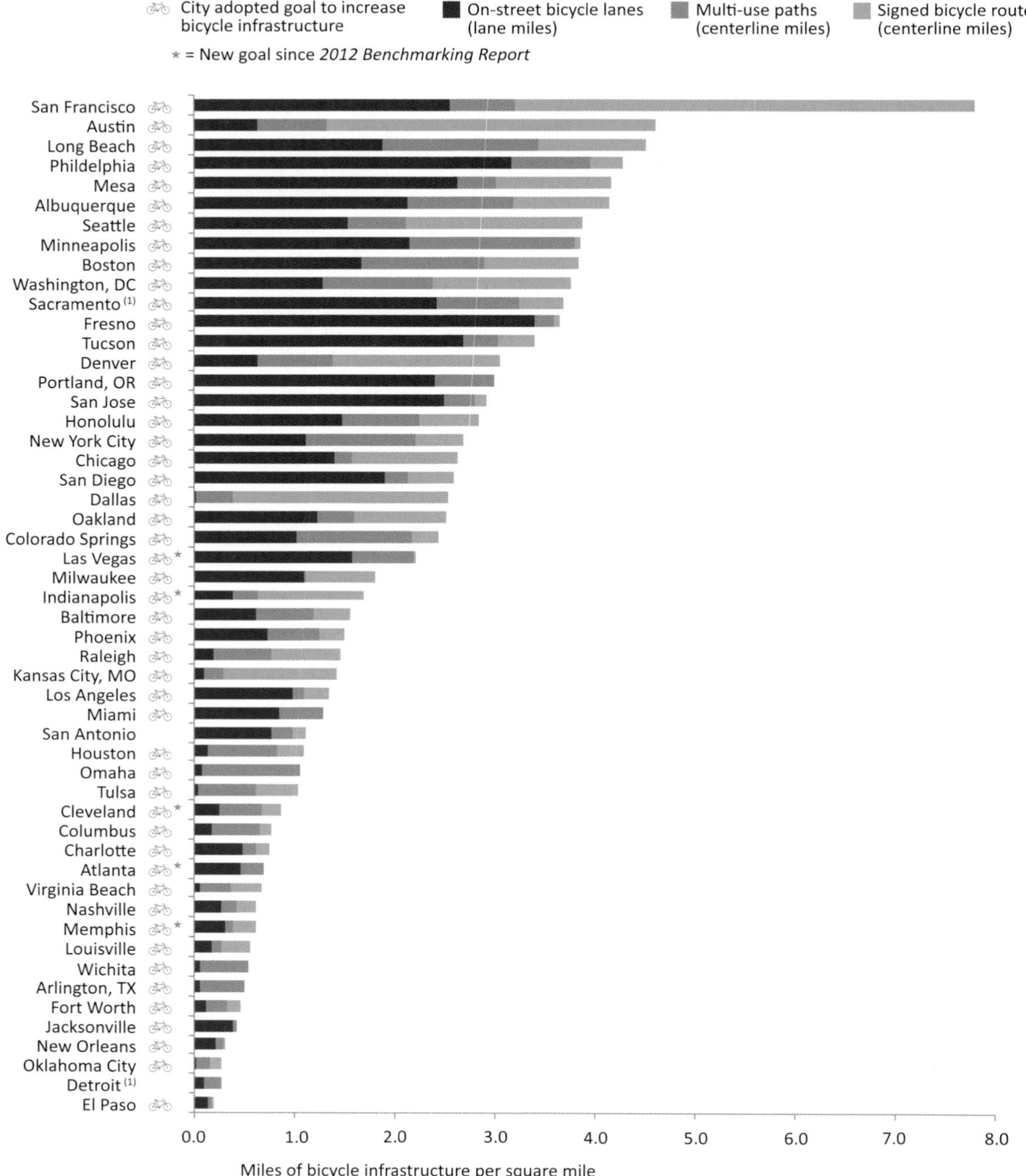

Source: City Survey 2011/2012, U.S. Census 2010 (land area). **Notes**: Data in this chart do not include specialized infrastructure such as sharrows, cycle tracks, or bicycle boulevards. (1) Data for Detroit and Sacramento are from 2008 because more recent numbers were not provided.

a network link than a four-foot-wide path through a small neighborhood. In fact, research has shown that street connectivity, specifically, has a positive impact on walking levels (Sehatzadeh et al., 2011).

Infrastructure in the 52 Largest Cities

To compare infrastructure for bicycling and walking, cities were asked to report on miles of existing and planned facilities, including on-street striped bicycle lanes, multi-use paths, and signed bicycle routes. The 52 large cities surveyed average 1.6 miles of bicycle facilities (bicycle lanes, multi-use paths, and signed bicycle routes combined) per square mile. On the high end of the range is San Francisco, with 7.8 miles of bicycle facilities per square mile. Austin and Long Beach rank second and third, with 4.6 and 4.5 miles of facilities per square mile, respectively.

Of the 34 cities that had sidewalk data available, the average amount of sidewalk was 13.4 miles per square mile. New York City reported having 12,750 miles of sidewalk, more than any other city. San Francisco reported the densest sidewalk network with 42.6 miles of sidewalk per square mile, although New York City followed closely with 42.1 miles of sidewalk per square mile. Although it is not true in every case, the general trend is that cities with higher levels of bicycling have more bicycle facilities per square mile than cities with lower bicycling levels.

Cities were also asked to report on miles of planned bicycle and pedestrian facilities. Cities who responded reported that 22,581 miles of bicycle facilities and 7,373 miles of pedestrian facilities are planned for the coming years. New York City has more planned bicycle facilities than any other city (1,800 miles). Austin has 3,500 planned miles of pedestrian facilities, more than any other city.

Washington, DC
Courtesy of Washington Area Bicyclist Association

Bicycle and Pedestrian Infrastructure in Large Cities

	Existing miles of bicycle facilities				Sidewalks		Planned facilities			
	On-street bicycle lanes	Multi-use paths	Signed routes	Total miles per sq mile	Total miles	Total miles per sq mile	For bicycles (miles)	In number of years	For peds (miles)	In number of years
Albuquerque	400	200	180	4.1	-	-	400	8	-	-
Arlington, TX	6	42	0	0.5	1,100	11.5	138	30	149	30
Atlanta	62	29	-	0.7	-	-	60	4	-	-
Austin	192	201	983	4.6	2,564	8.6	1,100	8	3,500	year 2023
Baltimore	50	47	30	1.6	-	-	150	10	-	-
Boston	80	59	45	3.8	1,733	36.1	332	8	-	-
Charlotte	142	39	45	0.8	2,023	6.8	783	25	650	year 2035
Chicago	319	42	241	2.6	-	-	640	year 2020	-	-
Cleveland	19	34	15	0.9	2,100	26.9	180	10	-	-
Colorado Springs	200	225	50	2.4	2,304	11.8	200	-	-	-
Columbus	38	102	26	0.8	1,458	6.7	73	6	31	6
Dallas	9	125	730	2.5	8,000	23.5	1,296	10	-	-
Denver	96	115	258	3.1	2,800	18.3	311	7	54	-
Detroit	14	25	0	0.3	-	-	-	-	-	-
El Paso	33	10	5	0.2	2,510	9.8	-	-	-	-
Fort Worth	38	76	44	0.5	-	-	1,000	25	-	-
Fresno	382	20	8	3.7	1,950	17.4	-	-	-	-
Honolulu	90	47	37	2.9	-	-	155	20	-	-
Houston	84	415	164	1.1	-	-	98	10	-	-
Indianapolis	142	90	381	1.7	1,466	4.1	200	12	0	0
Jacksonville	286	32	-	0.4	4,350	2.9	282	18	137	18
Kansas City, MO	28	66	352	1.4	2,200	7.0	600	15	-	-
Las Vegas	215	83	1	2.2	-	-	226	20	320	20
Long Beach	94	78	54	4.5	1,900	-	300	20	4	5
Los Angeles	463	55	109	1.3	10,750	22.9	1,680	30	-	-
Louisville	59	29	90	0.5	2,128	6.5	550	20	600	20
Memphis	96	26	70	0.6	3,600	11.4	575	25	575	25
Mesa	360	53	160	4.2	4,370	31.9	216	10	-	-
Miami	31	16	-	1.3	1,050	29.2	277	25	-	-
Milwaukee	105	3	65	1.8	3,000	31.3	394	10	-	-
Minneapolis	116	89	4	3.9	2,000	37.0	275	30	108	50
Nashville	130	69	93	0.6	1,070	2.3	490	10	540	12
New Orleans	36	14	1	0.3	2,650	15.7	996	20	-	-
New York City	338	334	146	2.7	12,750	42.1	1,800	year 2030	-	-
Oakland	69	21	52	2.5	1,120	20.0	263	20	-	-
Oklahoma City	18	75	77	0.3	1,920	3.2	212	5	35	5
Omaha	9	125	-	1.1	-	-	123	25	-	-
Philadelphia	426	104	45	4.3	4,500	33.6	400	10	60	10
Phoenix	376	275	124	1.5	-	-	5	1	-	-
Portland, OR	320	79	0	3.0	2,510	-	962	20	-	-
Raleigh	28	81	100	1.5	1,150	8.0	440	25	250	25
Sacramento	237	81	43	3.7	-	-	-	-	-	-
San Antonio	356	100	56	1.1	4,500	9.8	1,741	25	-	-
San Diego	620	75	150	2.6	-	-	595	year 2030	-	-
San Francisco	120	31	216	7.8	2,000	42.6	19	-	-	-
San Jose	443	55	20	2.9	3,200	11.3	500	7	all streets	30
Seattle	129	48	150	3.9	-	-	523	-	-	-
Tucson	610	80	81	3.4	-	-	220	27	35	20
Tulsa	9	113	83	1.0	-	-	270	5	270	5
Virginia Beach	17	75	75	0.7	-	-	300	20	-	-
Washington, DC	79	66	85	3.8	1,605	26.3	125	10	55	6
Wichita	8	64	0	0.5	-	-	107	30	-	-
Total of 52 cities	8,627	4,437	5,744		104,331		22,581		7,373	
Large cities average	166	85	120	1.6	3,069	13.4	470	16	388	17
Large cities median	96	68	68	1.6	2,164	13.7	300	17	137	18
High	620	415	983	7.8	12,750	42.6	1,800		3,500	
Low	6	3	0	0.2	1,050	2.3	5		0	

Source: City Survey 2011/2012, U.S. Census Bureau 2010 (land area). **Notes**: Data in this chart do not include specialized infrastructure such as sharrows, cycle tracks or bicycle boulevards. Cells with a dash (-) mean data were unavailable or not reported. (1) Data for Detroit and Sacramento are from 2008 because more recent numbers were not provided.

U.S. Bicycle Route System Corridor Plan

Established U.S. Bicycle Route

These routes have been designated by AASHTO (American Association of State Highway and Transportation Officials). For specific route information visit: *www.AdventureCycling.org/Routes/USBRS.*

Prioritized Corridor

These are not existing routes. These corridors are 50-mile wide areas where a route may be developed.

Alternate Corridor

These paths provide additional consideration for interstate routing. These corridors have not been assigned route numbers but may be prioritized. Corridors may be added, or existing corridors may be shifted as needed.

Private or Public Ferry

Two ferries crossing Lake Michigan are included in the U.S. route system.

Source: Map courtesy of Adventure Cycling Association, June 2013. Adapted with permission.

A National Network of Bikeways

The U.S. Bicycle Route System (USBRS) is a proposed national network of bicycle routes. These routes link urban, suburban, and rural areas with appropriate bicycle-friendly routes, including trails, bike paths, roads with shoulders, and low-traffic routes. For a route to be designated as part of the USBRS it must either connect two or more states, a state and an international border, or one or more U.S. Bicycle Routes.

The first two U.S. Bicycle Routes were designated in 1982, with no additional routes nominated for over two decades. In 2003, the American Association of State Highway and Transportation Officials (AASHTO) revived the USBRS with an official task force. An inventory of existing bicycle routes throughout the United States was created as a first step in drafting a national bicycle network plan. In 2008, AASHTO passed a resolution in support of the National Corridor Plan. An application for route designation was completed in May 2009 (Adventure Cycling Association, 2009).

According to data from Adventure Cycling Association, 34 states have an active USBRS program. Thirty-one states have identified potential USBRs in state or local bicycle plans. Routes have been officially designated as part of the USBRS in nine states, and three states have posted and signed USBRs.

Land Use

A person's choice to own a car is related to the bikeability, walkability, and accessibility to transit of the places they travel (Sehatzadeh et al., 2011). In a pedestrian- and bicyclist-friendly area, a person has less need for a car and is therefore likely to make more trips by foot or bike.

Density

To examine the role of density in the choice to bicycle or walk in the United States, the Benchmarking Project team compared residential density (persons/square mile) to the combined bicycling- and walking-to-work mode share in major cities. Data indicate that denser cities have higher levels of bicycling and walking on average than less dense cities.

Four of the five cities with the highest combined levels of bicycling and walking are also among the top seven densest cities. This finding is in line with other studies (Heinen et al., 2010; Krizek and Forsyth, 2009; Moudon et al., 2005; Parkin et al., 2008; Pucher and Buehler, 2006; Pucher et al., 2011; Reynolds et al., 2009; Rietveld and Daniel, 2004; Vandenbulck et al., 2011; Vernez-Moudon et al., 2005) that suggest a correlation between density and bicycling and walking. Dense communities have shorter trip distances, which can thus be more easily covered by walking or bicycling.

Comparing Population Density with Levels of Bicycling and Walking to Work

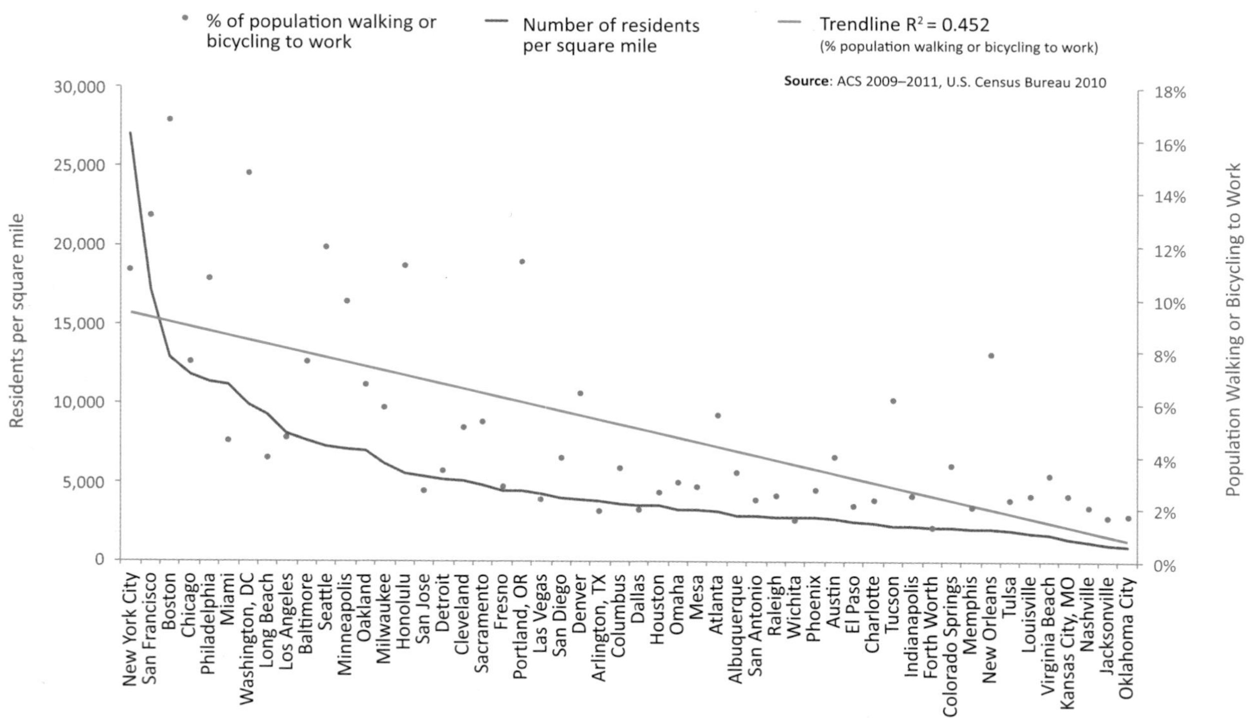

NACTO Design Guidelines

Contributions by David Vega-Barachowitz, National Association of City Transportation Officials

The National Association of City Transportation Officials' (NACTO) *Urban Bikeway Design Guide* (2012) and *Urban Street Design Guide* (2013) are paving the way towards safer, more economically vibrant streets for cities all across the U.S.

The products of collaboration of leading planners, designers, and engineers from NACTO's 26 member cities and affiliates, these guidelines forge a new blueprint for streets. From protected bikeways to parklets and plazas, the guides celebrate the unique characteristics of cities, and reinforce the notion that street design can anchor and stimulate redevelopment and investment. NACTO's *Urban Bikeway Design Guide* has been endorsed by over 40 cities. In 2013, the Federal Highway Administration announced support for the use of the NACTO guides.

All of the suggested infrastructure improvements are in use nationally and internationally; however, NACTO recognizes that each city comes with its own set of unique challenges and that implementation must be tailored to each individual setting.

Templates and suggestions for bikeway and street design are categorized into one of three levels: required, recommended, and optional. Required or critical improvements are those considered applicable across cities, to be implemented without compromise. Recommended improvements are those believed to add value to cities, while optional improvements are those that vary across cities and may add value depending on the situation.

The following chapters can be found in the design guidelines:

> *Urban Bikeway Design Guide*: Bike Lanes, Cycle Tracks, Intersections, Signs & Markings, Signals, and Bicycle Boulevards.
>
> *Urban Street Design Guide*: Streets, Street Design Elements, Interim Design Strategies, Intersections, Intersection Design Elements, and Design Controls.

Hardcopies of the NACTO design guidelines can be purchased through the NACTO website: *NACTO.org/Cities-for-Cycling/Design-Guide/*

Chicago, IL. Photo by Michelle Stenzel

Green Lanes are Spreading

by Mary Lauran Hall, Alliance for Biking & Walking

More and more cities across the United States are building next-generation bicycle lanes that physically protect bicycle riders from motor vehicle traffic. Protected bicycle lanes, or cycle tracks, are dedicated spaces for bicycling that make riding more convenient, comfortable, and safe for people of all ages and abilities.

Cycle tracks can be one-way or two-way, can be located on major two-way avenues or on one-way roads, and can exist in the middle of the street or on the side. Transportation planners use a variety of methods to protect riders from car traffic—parked cars, plastic posts, concrete curbs, and large planters have all been used around the country.

The Green Lane Project, an initiative of PeopleForBikes, has been a major proponent of protected bikeways' growth in several U.S. cities. By working closely with city departments of transportation and local advocates, the project has helped increase protected bike lanes in Austin, TX; Washington, DC; Memphis, TN; Chicago, IL; San Francisco, CA; and Portland, OR.

These futuristic lanes are clearly gaining popularity—40 brand new protected bicycle lanes were built in 2012 alone, and Green Lane Project staff predicted that the U.S. would have over 200 miles of protected green lanes by the end of 2013.

In March 2014, six new cities were selected to participate in the Green Lane Project: Atlanta, GA; Boston, MA; Denver, CO; Indianapolis, IN; Pittsburgh, PA; and Seattle, WA. Learn more at *www.PeopleForBikes.org/Green-Lane-Project*

Austin, TX. Photo courtesy of BikeTexas

Mixed Use Communities

Research has also shown that living in a community with a mix of residential and commercial uses increases the likelihood of a person choosing to make a trip by foot or bicycle (Sehatzadeh et al., 2011).

Design Elements

Traffic calming features can have a significant impact on bicycling levels. Features that have been shown to increase bicycling levels include bicycle boulevards, speed humps, curb extensions, pedestrian crossways, and separated bike lanes. Studies in Copenhagen, London, Washington, DC, and Montreal have all found that cycle tracks or protected bicycle lanes attract more bicyclists than similar streets without such features. Bicyclists were willing to reroute their paths in Portland, OR, and go the furthest out of their way to cycle on off-street bike paths followed by bicycle boulevards (Dill et al., 2013).

Studies have found that women in particular prefer facilities with less motor vehicle traffic and bicycle lanes that are separated from traffic. However, when separated lanes are lacking, bicyclists, regardless of gender, seem to prefer low-volume residential streets without bicycle lanes over high volume roads with on-street bicycle lanes (Dill et al., 2013). A study of consumer behavior in Portland, OR, for example, recently reported that for every mile of high-traffic streets within ½ mile of an establishment, the number of bicyclists frequenting that establishment dropped by 1% (Clifton et al., 2013).

While busy streets were found to deter bicycling, bicycle lanes on such roads were still found to help increase perceptions of safety. In one study, women reported feeling more uncomfortable than men on off-street paths, possibly due to personal security concerns and fears of assault. Additionally, other street features that were found to deter bicyclists are poor pavement quality, inadequate bicycle parking, and the number of stop signs and signals (Dill et al., 2013).

Research shows that the best way to get women on bicycles is to provide them with safe, comfortable, convenient bicycling facilities that are physically separated and protected from motor vehicles or low-speed, low-traffic residential streets (such as bicycle boulevards) where they can avoid the stress of fighting motor vehicle traffic (Garrard et al., 2012).

A study from Ryerson's School of Occupational and Public Health looked at how transportation infrastructure affects the potential risk of bicyclists in Canada. The study concluded that having infrastructure elements that slow down traffic and separate bicyclists from both vehicular traffic and pedestrians (for example, cycle tracks), significantly reduced the risk of injury for bicyclists. It also found that separated paths for bicycling were much safer than painted lanes or sharrows, which seemed to offer little protection (Harris et al., 2012).

An earlier report compared injury risk on cycle tracks versus on-street facilities such as bicycle lanes. The researchers found that the cycle tracks in their study were more heavily used than on-street facilities and showed 15–40% lower risk of injury (Lusk, 2011).

In a Portland, OR, study on consumer behavior, the presence of bicycle parking at an establishment showed an increase in the number of bicyclists visiting the business. The study estimated that a bicycle corral within 200 feet of a business would increase bicycle visits by 7%; and for every ten bicycle parking spaces provided, the business would see a 1% increase in bicycle consumers. However, the study also notes the possibility that businesses with bicycle parking nearby may have installed the facilities due to an already large bicycle customer base (Clifton et al., 2013).

Shared lane markings, also called "sharrows," are the most common bicycle element in use today. Although no longer considered innovative by many, forty-five cities report that they have shared lane markings, up 25% from 36 cities two years ago. Twelve cities report that they have implemented bicycle boulevards (up from nine, as reported in the *2012 Benchmarking Report*). Portland, OR, leads the way with nearly 70 miles of bicycle boulevards.

Thirteen cities have now implemented bicycle traffic lights compared to nine cities in the previous report. New York City reported the most with 190 bicycle traffic lights, followed by Long Beach with 17 bicycle traffic lights. Twenty-three cities have used colored bike lane treatments, up from sixteen cities in the *2012 Benchmarking Report*. Six cities reported implementing home zones, or "woonerfs," including Chicago, Louisville, Oakland, Philadelphia, San Antonio, and Seattle.

Twenty-two cities reported having installed bike boxes, also called advanced stop lines, which prioritize bicyclists at red lights. Most cities have no more than ten bike boxes, but New York City rises to the top with 591 bike boxes, and advanced stop lines at a majority of their additional intersections. Sixteen cities have installed cycle tracks (up from 11 two in the previous report); Chicago leads the way with 54.5 miles of protected bicycle lanes. Thirteen cities, up from ten cities in the 2012 report, have contraflow bicycle lanes.

Chicago and Seattle have implemented (or were in the process of implementing at the time of the survey) every specialized bicycling infrastructure element surveyed for this report. Austin; Minneapolis; Portland, OR; and San Francisco are close behind, each having implemented seven of the eight innovative facilities surveyed.

Specialized Infrastructure in Large Cities

	Shared lane markings ("sharrows")	Bicycle boulevards	Home zones or "woonerfs"	Colored bicycle lanes	Bike boxes	Cycle tracks or protected bicycle lanes	Contraflow lanes for bicycles	Bicycle traffic lights
Albuquerque	✓	✓			✓			
Arlington, TX								
Atlanta	✓			✓		✓		✓
Austin	✓	✓		✓	✓	✓	✓	✓
Baltimore	✓	✓		✓	✓		✓	
Boston	✓	(1)		✓	✓	✓		
Charlotte	✓			✓	✓			
Chicago	✓	(1)	✓	✓	✓	✓	✓	✓
Cleveland	✓							
Colorado Springs	✓					✓		
Columbus	✓	✓			✓			
Dallas	✓			✓	✓			
Denver	✓			✓	✓		✓	✓
Detroit	(2)	(2)	(2)	(2)	(2)	(2)	(2)	(2)
El Paso	✓							
Fort Worth	✓			✓				
Fresno								
Honolulu	✓				✓			
Houston	✓						✓	
Indianapolis	✓			✓	✓ (3)	✓		✓
Jacksonville	✓							
Kansas City, MO	✓							
Las Vegas	✓			✓		✓	✓	
Long Beach	✓	✓		✓	✓	✓		✓
Los Angeles	✓			✓				
Louisville	✓		✓		✓			
Memphis	✓							
Mesa								✓
Miami	✓			(1)				
Milwaukee								
Minneapolis	✓	✓		✓	✓	✓	✓	✓
Nashville	✓	✓		✓	✓			
New Orleans	✓							
New York City	✓			✓	✓	✓	✓	✓
Oakland	✓	✓	✓					
Oklahoma City	✓			✓				
Omaha	✓					✓		
Philadelphia	✓		✓	✓	✓		✓	
Phoenix	✓	✓			✓			
Portland, OR	✓	✓		✓	✓	✓	✓	✓
Raleigh	✓							
Sacramento	✓							
San Antonio	✓		✓			✓		
San Diego	✓							
San Francisco	✓	✓		✓	✓	✓	✓	✓
San Jose	✓			✓ (3)		✓		
Seattle	✓	✓	✓	✓	✓	(1)	✓	✓
Tucson	✓							
Tulsa	✓							
Virginia Beach								
Washington, DC	✓			✓	✓	✓	✓	✓
Wichita								
# of cities responding "yes"	45	12	6	23	22	16	13	13

Source: City Survey 2011/2012. **Notes**: Unanswered survey questions, or responses of "N/A" and "unknown," were taken to mean "no." All empty cells should be understood to be a "no" response. (1) In progress at time of survey response. (2) Detroit did not submit a survey for 2011/2012 .

Specialized Infrastructure Design

Bike Share
A public sharing system where bicycles are made available to individuals for short-term use. Bicycles can generally be picked up and dropped off at various docking stations located throughout a system's service area.

Bicycle Boulevards
A shared roadway intended to give priority to bicyclists by optimizing it for bicycle traffic and discouraging motor vehicle traffic. These routes often use "turned stop signs" allowing bicyclists to progress without stopping along the boulevard, but force cross traffic to stop.

Home Zones (Woonerfs)
These streets are designated as "shared streets," prioritizing pedestrians and bicyclists, and keeping motor vehicles at low speeds.

Colored Bicycle Lanes
Bicycle lanes that have special coloring to provide a distinct visual sign that the space is designated for bicyclists.

Shared Lane Markings
Often called "sharrows," these markings resemble a bicycle and an arrow painted on a roadway to indicate the direction of travel for bicycles as well as motorized vehicles.

Bicycle Corrals
A bicycle parking structure that converts one vehicle parking space into a parking space for ten or more bicycles. Corrals are usually located on the street along the curb.

Cycle Tracks
Also called "protected bike lanes," these exclusive bicycle facilities combine the user experience of a separated path with the on-street infrastructure of a conventional bicycle lane.

Contraflow Bicycle Lanes
A designated bicycle lane marked to allow bicyclists to travel against the flow of traffic on a one-way street.

Bicycle Traffic Lights
Lights on roadways that have specific symbols to direct bicycle traffic.

Bike Boxes
A pavement marking that utilizes two stop lines: an advanced stop line for motor vehicles, and a stop line closer to the intersection for bicyclists. This allows bicyclists to get a head start when the light turns green to more safely proceed ahead or make a left turn.

Photo credits, top to bottom: (left) Greg Griffin, courtesy of www.pedbikeimages.org; Payton Chung; La-Citta-Vita@Flickr; effelar @Flickr; John Luton (right) Jeff Miller; PeopleForBikes; John Luton; Roland Tanglao; Arthur Wendall

The Growth of Bike Share Systems

Bike share systems, which make bicycles available to the public for low-cost, short-term use, have been sweeping the nation since 2010. These systems offer many benefits: they can help replace car trips and relieve pressure on transit systems; are often more affordable than bicycle ownership to many residents; make bicycle storage more convenient; and introduce a wider audience to bicycling.

Over the last 50 years, bike share programs have evolved through three distinct stages: free programs, coin deposit systems, and automated self-serve kiosks.

Free Bike Programs—Bicycle sharing got its start in Amsterdam in the 1960s when free, unlocked bikes were placed around the city for public use. Other cities (including Portland, OR, in 1994) tried similar concepts. Unfortunately, these free bike initiatives generally failed soon after launch, mostly as a result of theft and damage.

Coin Deposit Systems—The coin deposit system began in the 1970s and 80s. Users inserted a coin deposit at a docking station to borrow a bicycle. In 1995, Copenhagen was the first major city to implement such a system, and in 1996 the Twin Cities were the first North American city to implement a coin deposit system. However, because of the anonymity and low deposits required, these systems were similarly vulnerable to theft.

Automated Self-Serve Kiosks—Today, modern bike share systems incorporate advanced information technology through automated self-serve kiosks that collect deposits and registration information, and allow for bicycle redistribution. In 2008, Washington, DC, was the first to implement this type of bike share system in the U.S.

These new systems have shown impressive results, and the systems are being implemented around the world. Today bike share programs can be found throughout Europe, North America, South America, Asia, the Middle East, and Australia.

Studies of European cities that have launched bike share programs have found substantial rises in bicycle ridership in those cities. Paris saw an increase in trips made by bicycle from 1% to 2.5%. Barcelona saw a similar rise, from 0.75% to 1.76%. Twenty-three percent of London's OYBike users reported that the city's bike share program got them to ride in instances when they previously would not have traveled at all (Dill et al., 2013).

As of December 2013, twenty of the most populous U.S. cities have a functional bike share system (up from five cities two years ago), while 22 cities reported having a bike share system that is currently in progress. Of the 20 cities with working bike share programs, a majority reported the systems were implemented by either the city government or a nonprofit. New York City's Citi Bike program has the most bicycles available at 6,000, followed by Chicago's Divvy at 4,000. Both cities have over 300 automated self-service docking stations.

New York City, NY. Photo by drpavlov @ Flickr

Chicago, IL. Photo by Anne Petersen @ Flickr

Bike Share Systems in Large Cities

Name	# operating stations	# bicycles available	# bicycles per 100K population	System implementation by: government agency	non-profit organization	other entity	Financial sponsorship from city government?
Austin B-Cycle	40	400	49	✓	✓		
(Boston) Hubway	72	1,064	170	✓		Alta Bicycle Share	✓
Charlotte B-Cycle	20	200	27			Charlotte B-Cycle	
(Chicago) Divvy	400	4,000	148			Alta Bicycle Share	
(Columbus) CoGo	30	300	38	✓			✓
Denver B-Cycle	80	800	129	✓	✓		
Fort Worth B-Cycle	30	300	39		✓		
(Honolulu) Hawaii B-Cycle	-	-	-				
Houston B-Cycle	22	182	8		✓		
Kansas City (MO) B-Cycle	12	90	18		✓		
(Long Beach) DecoBike	25	400	86				
(Minneapolis) Nice Ride	170	1,500	387		✓		✓
Nashville B-Cycle and GreenBikes	31	290	48	✓			✓
(New York City) Citi Bike	330	6,000	73				
(Oklahoma City) Spokies	7	95	16	✓	✓		✓
Omaha B-Cycle	8	43	10		✓		
San Antonio B-Cycle	52	450	33	✓	✓		✓
(San Francisco) Bay Area Bike Share	35	350	43	✓			
(San Jose) Bay Area Bike Share	16	150	16	✓		Alta Bicycle Share	
(Washington, DC) Capital Bikeshare	300	2,500	405	✓			✓
High	400	6,000	405				
Low	7	43	8				

Source: City Survey 2011/2012, ACS 2011 (population-based averages are weighted). **Notes**: Unanswered survey questions, or responses of "N/A" and "unknown," were taken to mean "no." All empty cells should be understood to be a "no" response. Cells with a dash (-) mean data were unavailable or not reported.

Additional Bike Share Systems:
In Development

	# Operating stations	# Bikes available
Atlanta	-	30
Baltimore	25	250
Cleveland	-	-
El Paso	-	-
Indianapolis	25	-
Louisville	-	-
Los Angeles	-	-
Memphis	-	-
Mesa	20	200
Miami	50	500
Milwaukee	25	250
New Orleans	-	-
Oakland	-	-
Philadelphia	150	1,000
Phoenix	-	500
Portland, OR	75	750
Raleigh	-	-
Sacramento	-	-
San Diego	-	-
Seattle	220	2,200
Tucson	-	-
Tulsa	-	-

Source: City Survey 2011/2012. **Note**: Cells with a dash (-) mean data were unavailable or not reported.

Total Bicycle Check Outs (2011–2012)

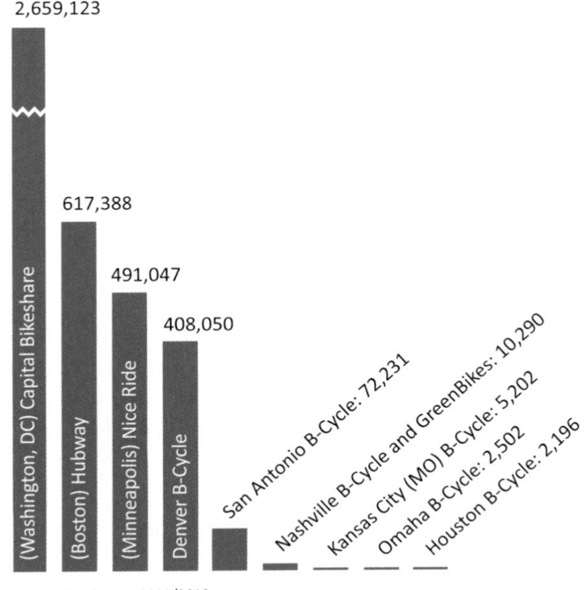

Source: City Survey 2011/2012

Infrastructure for Bicycling and Walking in Midsized Cities

All of the midsized cities have taken on the challenge of building bicycle infrastructure. Compared to the most populous cities, the midsized cities have a greater density of bicycle infrastructure, with 2.1 miles of bicycle facilties per square mile (versus 1.6 miles per square mile in the 52 largest U.S. cities). Conversely, the sidewalk density in the most populous cities (13.3 miles per square mile) is nearly twice that of the midsized cities (7.7 miles per square mile). Comparing only the midsized cities, the miles of bicycle lanes and multi-use paths per square mile are generally somewhat higher for the cities with smaller populations.

Each midsized city was asked to report on the implementation of eight specialized bicycle facilities in their city. Eugene and Madison have each implemented 7 of the 8 facilities; Missoula and Salt Lake City have both installed 6 of the 8 facilities. Sharrows were the most common form of bicycle infrastructure, with 15 of the 17 surveyed cities indicating that the shared lane symbols are in use. Bicycle boulevards and woonerfs were more rare, with

Infrastructure for Bicycling and Walking

	Existing miles of bicycle facilities				Sidewalks		City adopted goal	
	On-street bike lanes	Multi-use paths	Signed routes	Total miles per sq mile	Total miles	Total miles per sq mile	To increase bicycle facilities	To increase ped facilities
Population > 200K								
Anchorage, AK	8	166	-	1.3	-	-	✓	✓
Baton Rouge, LA	26	23	21	0.9	938	12.2	✓	✓
Madison, WI	112	52	116	3.6	-	-	✓	✓
Pittsburgh, PA	28	38	10	1.4	2,040	36.8	✓	✓
Spokane, WA	54	17	31	1.7	270	4.6		
St. Louis, MO	28	36	28	1.3	-	-	✓	✓
Population 100-200K								
Charleston, SC	16	24	32	0.7	340	3.1	✓	✓
Chattanooga, TN	35	26	48	0.8	280	2.0		
Eugene, OR	150	41	35	5.2	772	17.7	✓	✓
Fort Collins, CO	171	32	26	4.2	839	15.5	✓	✓
Salt Lake City, UT	190	33	32	2.3	965	8.7	✓	✓
Population < 100K								
Albany, NY	1	25	19	2.1	269	12.6	✓	✓
Bellingham, WA	-	-	-	-	-	-	✓	✓
Boulder, CO	73	69	44	7.5	456	18.5	✓	✓
Burlington, VT	12	12	17	3.9	150	14.6	✓	✓
Davis, CA	109	53	-	16.4	282	28.5	✓	✓
Missoula, MT	54	46	11	4.0	394	14.3	✓	✓
High value								
Midsized cities	190	166	116	16.4	2,040	36.8		
52 large cites	620	415	983	7.8	12,750	42.6		
Low value								
Midsized cities	1	12	10	0.7	150	2.0		
52 large cites	6	3	0	0.2	1,050	2.3		
Large cities average	166	85	120	1.6	3,069	13.4		

Source: Midsized City Survey 2011/2012, U.S. Census Bureau 2010 (land area). **Notes**: Unanswered survey questions, or responses of "N/A" and "unknown," were taken to mean "no." All empty should be understood to be a "no" response. Cells with a dash (-) mean data were unavailable or not reported.

Specialized Infrastructure

	Shared lane markings ("sharrows")	Bicycle boulevards	Home zones or "woonerfs"	Colored bicycle lanes	Bike boxes	Cycle tracks or protected bicycle lanes	Contraflow lanes for bicycles	Bicycle traffic lights
Population > 200K								
Anchorage, AK								
Baton Rouge, LA	✓						✓	
Madison, WI	✓	✓		✓	✓	✓	✓	✓
Pittsburgh, PA	✓			✓				
Spokane, WA	✓						✓	
St. Louis, MO	✓			✓				
Population 100-200K								
Charleston, SC	✓	✓				✓		
Chattanooga, TN	✓			✓				
Eugene, OR	✓		✓	✓	✓	✓	✓	✓
Fort Collins, CO	✓				✓	✓		
Salt Lake City, UT	✓			✓	✓	✓	✓	✓
Population < 100K								
Albany, NY	✓							
Bellingham, WA								
Boulder, CO	✓			✓		✓	✓	
Burlington, VT	✓						✓	
Davis, CA	✓	✓ (1)	✓			✓ (1)		✓
Missoula, MT	✓	✓		✓	✓	✓	✓	

Source: Midsized City Survey 2011/2012. **Notes:** Unanswered survey questions, or responses of "N/A" and "unknown," were taken to mean "no." All empty cells should be understood to be a "no" response. (1) Completed in 2013.

Charleston, Madison, and Missoula reporting the use of boulevards, and only Davis and Eugene reporting the use of woonerfs.

Eight cities indicated having colored bicycle lanes, and five reported having bike boxes. Cycle tracks, or protected bicycle lanes, and contraflow lanes have been installed in nearly half of the midsized cities (7 and 8, respectively). Bicycle traffic lights are more uncommon in these cities and can currently only be found in Madison, Eugene, Salt Lake City, and Davis. On the other hand, bicycle corrals are being used in 12 of the 17 midsized cities.

As the table to the right shows, public bike share programs are not only for the nation's large cities. Madison, Chattanooga, Fort Collins, Salt Lake City, and Boulder all have a public bike share program in place. Systems are currently in development in Baton Rouge, Pittsburgh, Charleston, Albany, Davis, and Missoula.

Bike Share Systems

Population > 200K	
Anchorage, AK	
Baton Rouge, LA	in progress
Madison, WI	✓
Pittsburgh, PA	in progress
Spokane, WA	
St. Louis, MO	
Population 100-200K	
Charleston, SC	in progress
Chattanooga, TN	✓
Eugene, OR	
Fort Collins, CO	✓
Salt Lake City, UT	✓
Population < 100K	
Albany, NY	in progress
Bellingham, WA	
Boulder, CO	✓
Burlington, VT	
Davis, CA	in progress
Missoula, MT	in progress

Source: Midsized City Survey 2011/2012.
Note: Unanswered survey questions, or responses of "N/A" and "unknown," were taken to mean "no." All empty cells should be understood to be a "no" response.

on the road

Austin, Texas:
Integrating Bicyclists into the Transportation Network

by Susan Wilcox, BikeTexas

Austin was similar to many other U.S. cities in 1990—less than 1% of commuters rode bikes, and bicycle infrastructure was scarce in the city. Bicycle advocates started working with city officials to push for bicycle and pedestrian growth in the Texas capital.

Throughout the 1990s, officials and advocates worked to make planning and street ordinances more amenable to building bicycle infrastructure, and to secure funding to improve the trails and bikeways already in place. The city also hired bicycle staff and began work on a Bicycle Master Plan.

In 1998, the city began planning a cross-town bicycle path. The Lance Armstrong Bikeway, a six-mile long combination of separated bicycle paths, on-street bicycle lanes, and signed bicycle routes, crosses the city center from MoPac Expressway to U.S. 183 and allows for east-to-west connectivity. Many local advocates, the city bicycle program, and the statewide advocacy organization, BikeTexas, worked to secure funding and plans for the bikeway. Meanwhile, on-street bicycle lanes continued to pop up around the city, with about 30 miles added to the network per year.

2007 was a big year for bicycling in Austin. The city began construction on the Lance Armstrong Bikeway, the city's bicycling mode share had increased to 1% citywide, and Bike Austin was instrumental in re-forming the city's Bicycle Advisory Council. Since then, advocacy groups have encouraged the city to work toward promised goals of increased bicycling in Austin. In 2009, the city updated Austin's Bicycle Plan to reflect new priorities for bicycling in the city.

Bicycle groups in Austin came together in 2010, along with other local partners like CapMetro, to secure $44 million for mobility projects, including bicycle and pedestrian projects. One of those projects, completing the Roy and Ann Butler Hike and Bike Trail on Lady Bird Lake by building a boardwalk

Austin, TX. Photo by effelar @Flickr

to close the loop on the southeast side of the lake, is underway and expected to be completed in spring 2014.

Also in 2010, CapMetro opened the commuter rail line. BikeTexas lobbied with CapMetro during the 2006 election cycle for funding of the rail line, with the understanding that bicycles would be accommodated on board the trains and at the stations, and that a multi-use trail would be built along the 32-mile line. Bicycle parking and accommodation on the trains were in place when the line opened, and a secure bicycle shelter opened at Kramer Station in 2012. Development of the next secure bicycle station along the line is underway, and the first link of the multi-use trail opened in 2013. Bike Austin worked with CapMetro to help decide where this first segment was most needed along the rail line, adding bicycling options for commuters and connecting neighborhoods in Central Austin.

Many new separated bicycle facilities have popped up in Austin in the past few years, including one near Barton Hills Elementary School. The school added bicycle parking before the beginning of the 2012–2013 school year in anticipation of an increase in bicycling and walking to school. The new bicycle boulevard and separated cycle track on Rio Grande Street provides easy, safe connectivity between downtown and the University of Texas campus area.

Also near the university, the Guadalupe Street cycle track provides a separated facility for the students and many others who travel on Guadalupe by bicycle every day. The new Mueller neighborhood development has recently installed separated bicycle lanes at the suggestion of state and local advocacy groups. Finally, the Pedernales cycle track, the first such facility in East Austin, opened in the autumn of 2013.

Austin, TX. Photo courtesy of BikeTexas

Austin, TX. Photo courtesy of BikeTexas

The city now has over 200 miles of bikeways crisscrossing the city, with no sign of bicycling development slowing down.

Austin was one of six cities chosen to participate in the Green Lane Project.

across borders

Freiburg, Germany:
Promoting Sustainable Transport While Reducing Car Use

by Maggie Melin, Alliance for Biking & Walking

Based on research by Ralph Buehler, Virginia Tech and John Pucher, Rutgers University
The full article (Buehler and Pucher, 2011) is available at:
www.Policy.Rutgers.edu/Faculty/Pucher/Freiburg_IJST_BuehlerPucher.pdf

Freiburg, a city of 220,000 inhabitants where cars once dominated transportation modes, is now considered one of Germany's most sustainable cities. Over the last 40 years, through a step-by-step process aimed at increasing the use of green modes of transport, Freiburg has seen car use decline, bicycle rates triple, and public transport rates double. Today, roughly 68% of trips in Freiburg are by bicycle, foot, or public transport.

During the 1950s and 1960s, Freiburg abandoned many of its streetcar lines and accommodated cars in its city center by turning the historic town square into a parking lot and building a highway connecting the city center to the Autobahn. However, in the 1970s, after much public discourse and citizen participation, a decision was made to resurrect the streetcar system. That policy shift steered public interest towards other modes of transport, and gradually, over the course of many years, steps were taken to strengthen bicycling, walking, and public transport.

The following are highlights of some of the integrated transport strategies Freiburg has initiated over the last few decades. Many of these ideas could be and have been applied successfully to cities in the United States.

Transport and Land-Use Planning

Freiburg's transport plans prioritize the concentration of new development around public transport stops and corridors. By 2006, 65% of residents and 70% of jobs were within 300 meters of a light rail stop. Compact, mixed-use development is given preference in order to allow for shorter trips, which are most easily made by foot or bicycle. Policies promote commercial hubs for small business, and big box retailers that encourage car use have been banned from the city.

Photo courtesy of City of Freiburg

Bicycle Integration

In 1972, Freiburg had 29km (18mi) of separated bicycle lanes and paths, and today it has over 682km (424mi) of a fully integrated bikeway network. This network includes 160km (99mi) of bicycle lanes, 120km (75mi) of bicycle paths, 400km (249mi) of traffic-calmed streets, and 2km (1.2mi) of bicycle streets.

Roughly 90% of residential streets have been traffic calmed, with speed limits under 30km (18mi) per hour. Over 180 residential neighborhood home zones have been created with speed limits of 7 km (4mi) per hour to give bicyclists, pedestrians, and playing children priority over motorists.

About half of the city's one-way streets have been converted into two-way streets for bicyclists, making bicycle trips shorter and more convenient.

The city center now has over 6,000 bicycle parking spaces, many of which are adjacent to public transport stops and stations. The main train station provides sheltered parking for 1,000 bicycles, as well as bicycle rentals and repairs, and most new building developments now require bicycle parking.

Pedestrian Integration

All streets in the city center were converted into a car-free zone. Cathedral Plaza, the main town square, was used as a car parking lot in the 1960s, but has been car-free since the 1970s and now hosts a lively open air market Monday through Saturday. Traffic calming on most residential streets has made it safer for pedestrians. The city's focus on compact, mixed-use development and land-use planning has made schools, workplaces, shopping, service establishments, and public transport stops more accessible to pedestrians.

Public Transport Integration

Light rail, regional trains, and buses have been expanded to connect neighborhoods with Freiburg's city center. A unified ticketing system links the transport options, and a monthly "environmental ticket" allows for unlimited, discounted travel throughout the region. Real-time travel information, bicycle parking at transit facilities, and traffic signals prioritizing buses and trains make public transport reliable, convenient, and fast.

Photo by Ralph Buehler

Car Restrictions

Freiburg's strategy to improve and integrate bicycling, walking, and public transport has also involved a strategy to make driving more expensive, slower and less convenient. Parking schemes have included limiting long-term parking and raising car parking fees. In the suburban neighborhood of Vauban, residents who desire a parking space must pay a fee of approximately $25,000, while residents who plan to live car-free pay only $5,000 to preserve an open space at the edge of the suburb. This scheme has significantly reduced car ownership in the neighborhood. The national government has likewise contributed to this strategy through high gasoline prices and sales taxes on automobiles.

Freiburg's gradual evolution into a leader in sustainable transportation has not always been easy, but the following lessons were learned from the city's 40-year evolution.

- Implementation works best in stages, especially for controversial policies. Transportation plans should be flexible and adaptable, with a long-term focus.
- If possible, incentives to increase bicycling, walking, and public transport use should be coupled with disincentives for driving.
- Land-use and transport planning should be integrated to help reduce trip lengths and encourage alternative transportation use.
- Citizen involvement and public discourse are important for moving sustainable ideas forward and keeping them growing over time.
- Federal policies and funding are needed to support and encourage sustainable transportation at the state and local levels.

Although much of this is already occurring in many U.S. cities, Freiburg provides some inspiring ideas and an example of what is possible through persistently taking gradual steps towards a goal of sustainable transport.

7

Connecting to Transit

The combination of walking, bicycling, and transit working together improves mobility options for travelers. Nearly every transit trip involves a walking trip at the beginning, the end or, often, both. Accommodating and encouraging bicyclist access to transit stations and stops further increases the number of people served by expanding the catchment area (the area served) and promotes transit use and the efficiency of transit. Incorporating bicyclist needs into transit stops and stations (for example, secure parking and easy access) expands travel options for the first or last mile of a transit trip.

Bicycle parking at transit stations and bicycle racks on buses have been shown to increase both bicycling and transit use (Dill et al., 2013). Bike share systems can even more effectively enhance public transportation as they provide multiple people access to bicycles and parking spaces day after day. Bikesharing further expands the catchment area of rail or bus by providing a consistently available connection with transit.

Many of the cities studied in this report are successfully integrating pedestrians and bicyclists with public transit. In this chapter, the Alliance for Biking & Walking partnered with the American Public Transportation Association (APTA) to examine some of the key elements that improve and maximize the opportunities for walking, bicycling, and transit.

Locating bike share stations near transit is a win-win combination providing increased first mile and last mile access to transit and wider trip access for bicyclists. Washington, D.C. Photo by Dan Reed @ Flickr

Closing the Gap

The First and Last Mile

The travel patterns involved in getting to a transit station (the first mile) and arriving at a destination point after getting off transit (the last mile) must be understood in order to better coordinate bicycle, pedestrian, and transit use. Understanding these patterns can inform decision makers on where bicycle and pedestrian improvements will be most effective. For example, placing a bike share station near transit lines, as well as near commercial and business centers, may greatly improve travel convenience for commuters and be mutually beneficial to transit and bike share systems.

Transit Catchment Areas

The distance to and accessibility of a transit station to an individual's origin and destination play a large role in determining transit ridership. Studies have shown that people who live within one-half mile of a transit station are between four and five times more likely to use transit (Cervero, 2007; Cervero, 1993). Making it easy and convenient for users to get to these stations is key to their use.

Transit catchment areas are those areas around transit stations that draw in riders and are often thought of as the distance people are willing to walk to take transit. Conventionally, transit catchment areas are considered the one-half mile radius around a transit station.

What is the Transit Catchment Area?

The American Public Transportation Association (APTA) defines transit area of influence as three types of spatial areas that form generally concentric areas around a transit stop or station.

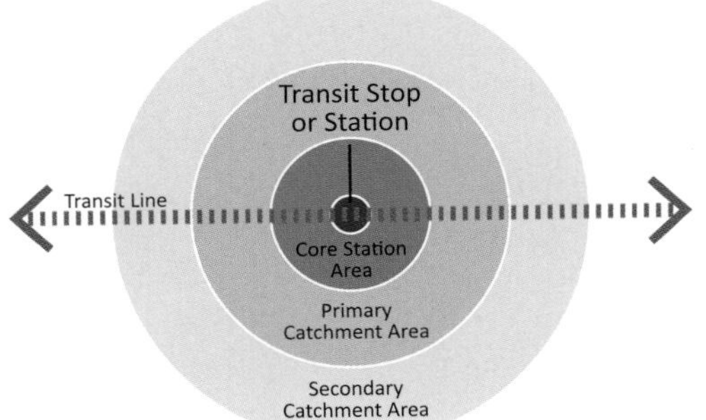

Core Station Area—The area around a transit stop or station within which land use and urban design features have a primary influence on transit ridership, and within which pedestrian access will generate a significant portion of transit trips to and from the stop or station.

Primary Catchment Area—The area within which land use and urban design features, and the ease and directness of access to the stop or station have a substantial impact on transit ridership, and within which pedestrian access will generate a significant portion of transit trips to and from the stop or station.

Secondary Catchment Area—The area around a transit stop or station within which ease and directness of access to the stop or station has the greatest influence on transit ridership, and within which the majority of all trips utilizing the stop or station are generated. Within this area, bicycle, feeder transit, and auto are the primary access modes to and from the stop or station.

Source: Reproduced and adapted from APTA publication "Defining Transit Areas of Influence" (SUDS-UD-RP-001-09, 2009). Used with permission.

Factors That Limit or Expand the Typical Catchment Area

Factor	Limit Catchment Area	Expansion of Catchment Area
Station infrastructure	Impediments to direct access to the station or stop (such as large surface parking lots or major bus intermodal facilities).	Integration of station or stop into surrounding community with direct access (such as connecting pathways or at-grade stations).
Street connectivity	Low intersection density, disconnected streets, and cul-de-sacs.	Connected street networks with frequent intersections and direct pedestrian paths.
Pedestrian environment	Poor pedestrian environments with blank ground floor walls, no buffer from automobiles, and unsafe, uncomfortable, or poorly lit pedestrian street crossings. Particularly relevant within the primary catchment area.	Pedestrian environments that include active ground floor commercial uses, high degrees of architectural interest and detail, and sufficient pedestrian lighting. Particularly relevant within the primary catchment area.
Bicycle environment	Poor bicycle environments, including high-speed automobile traffic, limited bicycle facilities, steep topography, poor pavement conditions, and lack of secure bicycle storage and/or ability to bring bicycles on transit vehicles. Particularly relevant in the primary and secondary catchment areas.	High-quality bicycle environments, including well-marked, direct, and safe bicycle routes; available and secure bicycle parking; and high established bicycle ridership levels. Particularly relevant in the secondary catchment area.
Wayfinding and orientation	Lack of wayfinding signage and difficult orientation.	Wayfinding signage and orientation maps assisting users in their journeys to and from the stop or station. Particularly relevant in the core transit area and the primary catchment area.
Safety/perception of safety	Physical safety concerns discourage pedestrian activity and create zones where transit-oriented land-use benefits will be reduced.	Good visibility and absence of safety concerns.
Transit parking availability	Large amounts of parking at transit stops limit the core transit area and primary catchment area by discouraging trips by pedestrians and bicyclists.	Small amounts of parking at transit stops expand the core transit area and primary catchment area by encouraging pedestrian and bicycle access.

Source: Reproduced and adapted from APTA publication "Defining Transit Areas of Influence" (SUDS-UD-RP-001-09, 2009). Used with permission.

Because transit users may additionally access the stations via bicycle, bus or car, a larger catchment area is sometimes useful to consider. The Federal Transit Administration, for example, provides grants for bicycle improvement projects within a three-mile radius of a transit stop and to pedestrian projects that fall within the standard one-half mile radius.

Improving bicycling and walking conditions within the transit catchment areas has great potential to reduce car trips. According to the American Public Transportation Association, conditions that can influence transit ridership include street connectivity, station infrastructure, and pedestrian and bicycle environments.

Within the catchment area, a street network ideally exists with frequent intersections and pedestrian paths that connect directly to the transit stations. Commercial activity, architectural interest, wayfinding signage, and lighting can improve the walking environment. Well-marked bicycle routes and lanes, and secure bicycle parking (both at the station and within the catchment area) improve the bicycling environment.

While transit ridership can benefit from bicycle and walking improvements, bicycling and walking levels can likewise be enhanced through transit improvements and network connectivity (such as intersecting transit lines).

Factors that limit transit accessibility and connectivity to the surrounding area for bicyclists and pedestrians can include large parking lots, freeways, disconnected streets, cul-de-sacs, warehouses, gated subdivisions, high-speed traffic, and poor pavement conditions.

Providing Relief for Peak-Period Demand on Transit Systems

In large cities, public transit can be congested at certain times of day. Increasing bicycling and walking opportunities can help relieve that daily spike in demand by offering alternative options for transportation.

A survey from the Mineta Transportation Institute studied the effects of bicycle sharing systems in four North American cities. The study found that the availability of a bike share system may impact transit ridership. On average, respondents reported that they used rail and bus less because of the bike share availability (43% and 38%, respectively) (Shaheen et al., 2012).(1)

This trend of shifting between public transportation modes (transit to bike share) was seen in the three cities with high density population and high public transit demand: Washington, DC; Toronto; and Montreal. In the Twin Cities, MN, which are generally lower density and have less public transit availability, 15% of bike share users surveyed actually increased their use of rail.

These findings illustrate the benefit of bike share systems in cities of various sizes; they offer an alternative to congested bus and rail systems in densely populated areas and make getting to rail and bus lines more appealing in less dense areas.

Note: (1) An additional study, still to be released, has found similar trends with the Capital Bikes program in Washington, DC (Buehler et al., Forthcoming).

Accommodating Bicyclists and Pedestrians on Transit Services

Contributions from Andrea Hamre, Virginia Tech

Investments to support nonmotorized access to transit typically involve less cost and are more sustainable and socially equitable than similar provisions for cars. Typical accommodations for bicyclists and pedestrians include secure bicycle parking, paths separated from car traffic, sidewalks, crosswalks, shelters with benches, on-board space for transporting bicycles, external bicycle racks on buses, bike share systems, and bicycle rental facilities near transit stations.

San Antonio, TX. Photo by Greg Griffin. Courtesy of www.pedbikeimages.org

Bike share and bicycle rental facilities near transit stations enable passengers to connect transit trips with short- and long-term bicycle rentals. Bikesharing enhances the public transportation system by providing consistent bicycle availability to multiple people every day.

Bicycle stations connect bicyclists directly with transit; provide the highest level of bike parking (sheltered, secure, monitored); and offer additional services, such as repair shops, air, and/or tools.

Washington, DC. Photo courtesy of Bikestation

Chicago, IL. Photo by Andrea Milne

Bicycle parking is the most common cycling-transit integration strategy globally, and costs less than a tenth as much as park-and-ride facilities for automobiles on a per-passenger basis. Secure bicycle racks can be greatly enhanced with shelter from the elements (roof and/or fully enclosed) or with bicycle lockers to better protect components on the bicycle from getting wet or stolen.

Seattle, WA. Photo by Sound Transit.
Courtesy of www.pedbikeimages.org

Roll-on bicycle service and on-board bicycle storage space on train cars enables bicyclists to ride their own bicycles at both ends of a transit trip. Bicycle racks on buses are common in North America (over 70% of U.S. and 80% of Canadian buses are equipped with racks). Bicycles are typically permitted on trains and light rail outside of peak travel hours.

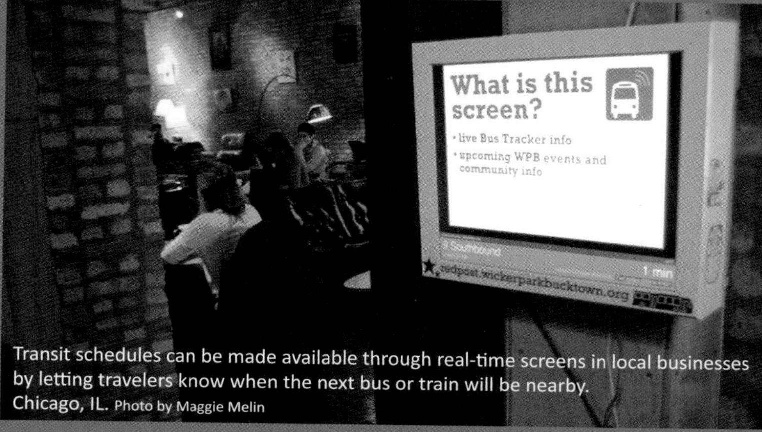

Transit schedules can be made available through real-time screens in local businesses by letting travelers know when the next bus or train will be nearby.
Chicago, IL. Photo by Maggie Melin

Charlotte, NC.
Photo by Laura Sandt. Courtesy of www.pedbikeimages.org

Shelters and benches at transit stops and stations provide refuge from the weather and increase traveler comfort. Heating, schedules, nighttime lighting, real-time traveler updates, maps, neighborhood wayfinding signage, and artistic designs all enhance the door-to-door traveler experience. In addition to station-area investments, some jurisdictions are experimenting with real-time transit screens at local businesses.

Separated paths and bicycle lanes, sidewalks, and crosswalks increase the safety and comfort of both bicyclists and pedestrians accessing transit stops and stations. Safe Routes to Transit programs, enhanced crosswalks, mid-crossing refuges, advanced signal timing for pedestrian crossings, and more prominent and separated bicycle lanes and cycle tracks are increasingly being implemented to increase the safety and comfort of bicyclists and pedestrians accessing transit stops and stations.

Austin, TX. Photo courtesy of PeopleForBikes

Accommodations for Bicycles on Public Transit

	% buses with bicycle racks	City Rail				
		local rail service?	# hours per week that trains run	# hours per week bicycles allowed roll-on access	% time bicycles are allowed on operating trains	# bikes allowed on a train car
Albuquerque	100%	✓	126	126	100%	8
Arlington, TX	(1)	(1)	(1)	(1)	(1)	(1)
Atlanta	100%	✓	145	145	100%	unlimited
Austin	100%	✓	74	74	100%	4
Baltimore	100%	✓	120	120	100%	unlimited
Boston	95%	✓	140	110	79%	2
Charlotte	100%	✓	137	137	100%	unlimited
Chicago	100%	✓	168	128	76%	2
Cleveland	100%	✓	154	154	100%	2
Colorado Springs	100%					
Columbus	100%					
Dallas	100%	✓	150	150	100%	-
Denver	100%	✓	168	168	100%	4
Detroit	(2)	(2)	(2)	(2)	(2)	(2)
El Paso	100%					
Fort Worth	97%	✓	103	103	100%	unlimited
Fresno	100%					
Honolulu	100%					
Houston	100%	✓	139	97	70%	unlimited
Indianapolis	100%					
Jacksonville	100%					
Kansas City, MO	100%					
Las Vegas	100%					
Long Beach	100%	✓	163	163	100%	unlimited
Los Angeles	100%	✓	137	137	100%	unlimited
Louisville	100%					
Memphis	100%	✓	168	168	100%	unlimited
Mesa	100%	✓	100	100	100%	
Miami	100%	✓	140	140	100%	unlimited
Milwaukee	100%					
Minneapolis	100%	✓	168	168	100%	unlimited
Nashville	75%	✓	55	55	100%	-
New Orleans	100%	✓	168	0	0%	folding bikes only
New York City	0%	✓	168	168	100%	unlimited
Oakland	100%	✓	140	120	86%	-
Oklahoma City	100%					
Omaha	100%					
Philadelphia	100%	✓	133	103	77%	2
Phoenix	100%	✓	140	140	100%	unlimited
Portland, OR	100%	✓	150	150	100%	14
Raleigh	100%					
Sacramento	100%	✓	136	136	100%	4
San Antonio	100%					
San Diego	100%	✓	168	168	100%	2
San Francisco	100%	✓	134	134	100%	unlimited
San Jose	100%	✓	139	139	100%	Caltrain 40/car, Light Rail 6/car
Seattle	100%	✓	131	131	100%	2
Tucson	100%					
Tulsa	100%					
Virginia Beach	100%					
Washington, DC	100%	✓	135	105	78%	4
Wichita	100%					
High	100%		168	168	100%	unlimited
Low	0%		55	0	0%	

Source: City Survey 2011/2012. **Notes**: Unanswered survey questions, or responses of "N/A" and "unknown," were taken to mean "no." All empty cells should be understood to be a "no" response. Cells with a dash (-) mean data were unavailable or not reported. (1) Arlington, TX does not have bus or rail service. (2) Detroit did not submit a survey for 2011/2012.

Commuting by Transit in Cities

In the 52 large U.S. cities surveyed for this report, 17% of commuters take public transportation to work, a consistent trend over the last decade. Of those commuters, approximately 52% are women and 48% are men. New York City has the highest transit commuting rate at 56%, followed by Washington, DC, at 38%, Boston at 33%, and San Francisco at 33%. All of the large cities surveyed for this report have bus service, except for Arlington, TX, and 31 cities have a local rail service.

Bicycle Racks on Buses

Buses equipped with bicycle racks have the potential to increase transit ridership and reduce car use. They offer the ability for bicycling commuters to take public transit when distances between a bus stop and a destination are too great for a convenient or comfortable walk. Many cities are aware of the benefits of bicycle racks on buses, with 46 cities reporting that 100% of their city buses have bicycle racks installed, up from 41 cities two years ago. New York City, with the country's largest transit system, remains the only large city in this report with no bicycle racks on buses.

Bicycle Access to Trains

Thirty-one of the large cities surveyed for this report have light rail systems. Twenty-four of these 31 cities (77%) allow bicycles on their trains 100% of the time while they are operational. Six of these cities allow bicycle access except during certain hours, in many cases during peak commuting hours. New Orleans only allows folding bikes on their rail system at any time. A slight majority of the 31 cities with light rail limit the number of bicycles per train car. Thirteen cities allow an unlimited number of bicycles, including Atlanta, Baltimore, Charlotte, Houston, Fort Worth, Los Angeles, Long Beach, Memphis, Minneapolis, Miami, New York City, Phoenix, and San Francisco.

Bicycle Parking Spaces near Transit

At transit stops, cities average 9.5 bicycle parking spaces for every 10,000 residents. Oakland tops the list with 111 bicycle parking spaces per 10,000 residents, followed by Portland with 24, Wichita with 20, and Chicago with 19 spaces per 10,000 people. New York City has the greatest number of bicycle parking spaces near transit at 8,332 spaces, but has less than four bicycle parking spaces per 10,000 residents.

Cicero, IL. Photo by Steve Vance @ Flickr

Accommodations for Bicycles Near Public Transit

	Transit Stops (1)				Transit Stations (2)					
	# bus stops	# city rail stops	# bicycle parking spaces at transit stops	# parking spaces per 10k population	# transit stations		# bicycle parking spaces		# parking spaces per 10k population	
					Bus	Rail	Bus	Rail	Bus	Rail
Albuquerque	100	15	-	-	-	-	-	-	-	-
Arlington, TX	(3)	(3)	(3)	(3)	(3)	(3)	(3)	(3)	(3)	(3)
Atlanta	5,350	24	213	4.9	-	38	-	180	-	4.2
Austin	2,900	7	150	1.8	26	9	156	36	1.9	0.4
Baltimore	3,633	27	-	-	-	89	-	148	-	2.4
Boston	4,000	78	-	-	17	255	16	6,005	0.3	96.1
Charlotte	3,800	15	-	-	4	19	51	86	0.7	1.1
Chicago	11,493	199	5,000	18.5	-	145	-	2,691	-	9.9
Cleveland	2,800	23	125	3.2	34	52	6	52	0.2	1.3
Colorado Springs	1,180	-	60	1.4	-	-	-	-	-	-
Columbus	4,939	-	604	7.6	5	-	30	-	0.4	-
Dallas	8,239	44	481	3.9	14	58	54	344	0.4	2.8
Denver	9,620	31	880	14.2	3	31	682	391	11.0	6.3
Detroit	(4)	(4)	(4)	(4)	-	13	-	5	-	0.1
El Paso	3,063	-	280	4.2	7	-	74	-	1.1	-
Fort Worth	1,947	4	35	0.5	6	5	22	30	0.3	0.4
Fresno	1,860	-	-	-	4	-	30	-	0.6	-
Honolulu	4,000	-	140	4.1	-	-	-	20	-	0.6
Houston	9,188	16	-	-	51	16	442	-	2.1	-
Indianapolis	4,000	-	40	0.5	-	-	-	-	-	-
Jacksonville	5,720	-	-	-	5	8	131	8	1.6	0.1
Kansas City, MO	4,013	-	51	1.1	5	-	18	-	0.4	-
Las Vegas	1,284	-	-	-	-	-	-	-	-	-
Long Beach	1,800	7	100	2.2	4	-	28	-	0.6	-
Los Angeles	15,115	45	-	-	37	135	680	2,922	1.8	7.6
Louisville	6,000	-	-	-	-	-	-	-	-	-
Memphis	5,500	36	75	1.2	4	36	82	20	1.3	0.3
Mesa	175	1	496	11.1	-	-	-	-	-	-
Miami	1,869	10	248	6.1	21	43	-	100	-	2.4
Milwaukee	3,755	-	-	-	-	-	-	-	-	-
Minneapolis	2,779	19	400	10.3	47	17	301	187	7.8	4.8
Nashville	-	3	-	-	2	-	-	-	-	-
New Orleans	2,113	174	10	0.3	-	-	-	-	-	-
New York City	15,000	468	8,332	3.4	30	467	8	-	0.01	-
Oakland	1,826	10	4,386	110.8	-	43	-	4,277	-	108.1
Oklahoma City	925	-	-	-	-	-	-	-	-	-
Omaha	4,000	-	-	-	-	-	-	-	-	-
Philadelphia	10,000	104	-	-	-	274	-	605	-	3.9
Phoenix	5,832	19	-	-	12	29	54	160	0.4	1.1
Portland, OR	3,634	96	1,403	23.6	6	89	462	1,773	7.8	29.8
Raleigh	1,430	-	-	-	-	-	-	-	-	-
Sacramento	-	-	-	-	-	-	-	-	-	-
San Antonio	8,081	-	336	2.5	11	-	60	-	0.4	-
San Diego	4,779	-	-	-	8	53	-	348	-	2.6
San Francisco	-	-	-	-	8	33	488	-	6.0	-
San Jose	1,812	39	562	5.8	16	62	259	242	2.7	2.5
Seattle	3,600	20	-	-	78	25	2,860	320	46.1	5.2
Tucson	1,800	-	60	1.1	29	-	59	-	1.1	-
Tulsa	174	-	16	0.4	-	-	-	-	-	-
Virginia Beach	452	-	26	0.6	-	-	-	-	-	-
Washington, DC	3,492	40	-	-	1	86	-	5,722	-	92.6
Wichita	-	-	762	19.8	-	-	-	-	-	-
High	15,115	468	8,332	110.8	78	467	2,860	6,005	46.1	108.1
Low	100	1	10	0.3	1	5	6	5	0.01	0.1

Sources: U.S. Census Bureau 2010 (land area), ACS 2011 (population-based averages are weighted), (1) City Survey 2011/2012, (2) APTA 2011 (unless noted). **Notes**: Cells with a dash (-) mean data were unavailable or not reported. APTA did not have data available for the following cities: Albuquerque, Colorado Springs, Indianapolis, Las Vegas, Louisville, Mesa, Milwaukee, New Orleans, Oklahoma City, Omaha, Raleigh, Sacramento, Tulsa, Virginia Beach, and Wichita. APTA 2010 data is used for the following cities because 2012 data was not available: Atlanta, Charlotte, Cleveland, Detroit, Fresno, Kansas City, Minneapolis, Oakland, Phoenix, and Tucson. APTA defines a transit station as "a passenger boarding/deboarding facility with a platform, a plaza flanked by several bus bays, or a dock." APTA data do not include not-station stops. (3) Arlington, TX, does not have bus or rail service. (4) Detroit did not submit a survey for 2011/2012.

Availability of Bike Share Systems

Bike share system available?	# operating stations	# bicycles available	# bicycles available per 100K population	
				Albuquerque
				Arlington, TX
✓ (1)	-	30	7	Atlanta
✓	40	400	49	Austin
✓ (1)	25	250	40	Baltimore
✓	72	1,064	170	Boston
✓	20	200	27	Charlotte
✓	400	4,000	148	Chicago
✓ (1)	-	-	-	Cleveland
				Colorado Springs
✓	30	300	38	Columbus
				Dallas
✓	80	800	129	Denver
(2)	(2)	(2)	(2)	Detroit
✓ (1)	-	-	-	El Paso
✓	30	300	39	Fort Worth
				Fresno
✓	-	-	-	Honolulu
✓	22	182	8	Houston
✓ (1)	-	-	-	Indianapolis
				Jacksonville
✓	12	90	18	Kansas City, MO
				Las Vegas
✓	25	400	86	Long Beach
✓ (1)	-	-	-	Los Angeles
✓ (1)	-	-	-	Louisville
✓ (1)	-	-	-	Memphis
✓ (1)	20	200	45	Mesa
✓ (1)	50	500	122	Miami
✓ (1)	25	250	42	Milwaukee
✓	170	1,500	387	Minneapolis
✓	31	290	48	Nashville
✓ (1)	-	-	-	New Orleans
✓	330	6,000	73	New York City
✓ (1)	-	-	-	Oakland
✓	7	95	16	Oklahoma City
✓	8	43	10	Omaha
✓ (1)	150	1,000	65	Philadelphia
✓ (1)	-	500	34	Phoenix
✓ (1)	75	750	126	Portland, OR
✓ (1)	-	-	-	Raleigh
✓ (1)	-	-	-	Sacramento
✓	52	450	33	San Antonio
✓ (1)	-	-	-	San Diego
✓	35	350	43	San Francisco
✓	16	150	16	San Jose
✓ (1)	220	2,200	35	Seattle
✓ (1)	-	-	-	Tucson
✓ (1)	-	-	-	Tulsa
				Virginia Beach
✓	300	2,500	405	Washington, DC
				Wichita
	400	6,000	405	High
	7	30	7	Low

Source: City Survey 2011/2012, ACS 2011 (population-based averages are weighted). **Notes**: Unanswered survey questions, or responses of "N/A" and "unknown," were taken to mean "no." All empty cells should be understood to be a "no" response. Cells with a dash (-) mean data were unavailable or not reported. (1) Bike share system is in development. (2) Detroit did not submit a survey for 2011/2012.

Photo courtesy of Alliance for Biking & Walking

Making Transit Connections in Midsized Cities

Most buses in the midsized cities studied for this report are equipped to carry bicycles. Fourteen of these 17 cities report that 100% of their bus fleet have bicycle racks. While all of the midsized cities have bus service, only Pittsburgh, St. Louis, and Salt Lake City have a local rail service. All three cities with local rail allow bicycles on train cars during all operating hours. St. Louis is the only city that allows an unlimited number of bicycles on the train.

As mentioned in Chapter 6, many small and midsized cities are implementing bike share systems. Five of the midsized cities included in this report have systems fully in place and six more are in development (see page 163). These systems provide new transportation options in areas that may not have access to other forms of public transit.

Accommodations for Bicycles on Trains

	local rail service?	# hours per week that trains run	# hours per week bicycles allowed roll-on access	# bicycles allowed in a train car
Pittsburgh, PA	✓	130	130	2
St. Louis, MO	✓	152	152	2 in front car, 4 in back car
Salt Lake City, UT	✓	138	138	16 on cars with bicycles racks, 4 on cars without bicycle racks

Source: Midsized City Survey 2011/2012

Accommodations for Bicycles on Buses

	% buses with bicycle racks
Population > 200K	
Anchorage, AK	100%
Baton Rouge, LA	100%
Madison, WI	100%
Pittsburgh, PA	100%
Spokane, WA	100%
St. Louis, MO	100%
Population 100-200K	
Charleston, SC	nearly 100%
Chattanooga, TN	100%
Eugene, OR	100%
Fort Collins, CO	100%
Salt Lake City, UT	100%
Population < 100K	
Albany, NY	100%
Bellingham, WA	100%
Boulder, CO	100%
Burlington, VT	100%
Davis, CA	0% intracity buses, 100% regional buses
Missoula, MT	80%
High value	
Midsized cities	100%
52 large cites	100%
Low value	
Midsized cities	80%
52 large cites	0%

Source: Midsized City Survey 2011/2012

on the road

TransForm: Providing Safe Routes to Transit

by Clarrissa Cabansagan, TransForm

Since 2005, the Safe Routes to Transit (SR2T) program has helped San Francisco Bay Area residents make crucial last-mile bicycle and pedestrian connections to regional transit. SR2T promotes bicycling and walking to transit stations by funding projects and plans that make nonmotorized trips easier, faster, and safer. The concept was inspired by successful programs in Japan, Germany, and the Netherlands that routinely link bicycling and walking improvements with transit operations.

Funded by a $1 bridge toll increase, the program has awarded over $16 million in four competitive grant cycles to projects, such as:

- Bulb-outs(1) at pedestrian crossings
- Wayfinding signage
- New or improved lighting
- Bicycle lanes
- Pedestrian tunnels
- Secure bicycle storage
- Bicycle stations
- Bicycle plans
- Station area plans

The Bay Area program has a lot of ground to cover: nine counties, 29 transit operators, and 101 cities. Each two-year cycle, TransForm has received about 30 applications, three times as many as funding can support.

Capital project awards can be as large as $500,000, while planning projects are smaller ($25,000–$100,000). TransForm encourages applicants to work together—maximum awards are 50–100% higher when agencies and other potential partners submit collaborative proposals. As more cities are embracing the Complete Streets framework, many projects have succeeded through a combination of SR2T grants and other funds.

Unique Funding Strategy

In 2002, California State Senator Don Perata approached TransForm and other key regional agencies, proposing a ballot measure to raise tolls on seven regional state-owned bridges, the funds of which would support public transportation. TransForm and allies quickly mobilized to develop top priorities for this nearly $4 billion opportunity and to build support for the toll increase.

Early on, TransForm teamed up with the East Bay Bicycle Coalition (EBBC)(2) to propose a $200 million SR2T program. After over a year of advocacy, the final ballot measure included a scaled back version at $22.5 million. Soon after, the measure garnered broad-based support of over 300 organizations, cities, and agencies, leading to voter approval in March 2004.

An unusual feature of the voter-approved ballot measure is that it specified TransForm and EBBC, a pair of nonprofits, to manage the SR2T grant program. The two groups manage the SR2T Advisory Committee of transit, bicycle, and pedestrian staff from public agencies

Oakland, CA. Photo Courtesy of AC Transit @ Flickr

Notes: (1) A bulb-out is a traffic calming element, built as a curb extension, shortening the distance a pedestrian needs to cross at an intersection, and improves visibility for both the pedestian and motorists on the road. (2) In early 2014, East Bay Bicycle Coalition was renamed Bike East Bay.

across the region. The committee scores and recommends applications for funding, and both groups monitor projects to completion. The Metropolitan Transportation Commission distributes funds to recipient agencies.

Goals

SR2T is the first competitive grant program of its kind. Projects must include connection to a bridge, and must demonstrate they will remove congestion on one or more state bridges by facilitating walking or bicycling to regional transit that serves trips between counties.

From its outset, the program has helped agency staff think big and try out new ideas. The program's launch event included representatives of several manufacturers of innovative products as well as bicycle and pedestrian experts. Project selection has rewarded innovative projects that provide benefits to low-income and minority households, incorporate new design features which can be replicated regionally, and boost the real and perceived safety of walking and bicycling to transit.

Results

Along the way, TransForm and EBBC have learned the benefits of allowing for longer grant timelines and additional flexibility for pilot projects. The first four grant cycles funded 40 projects, including two new bicycle stations, the reconfiguration of 54 rail cars to accommodate bicycles, 68 bicycle lockers, and hundreds of miles of marked crosswalks, bulb-outs, bicycle routes, lanes, and trails.

BART Bike Station in Downtown Berkeley

A bicycle station is a good solution when a rail station has high demand for bicycle parking, but little outdoor space for lockers. At Downtown Berkeley BART (Bay Area Rapid Transit), the old bicycle cage had bicycles hanging from cage walls and crowding in the aisles. The cage was also located inconveniently underground at the far end of the station. The new bicycle station now has street-level access, a retail/repair shop, and ample secure bicycle parking. The city of Oakland is now also planning to install a SR2T-funded bicycle station at its 19th Street BART Station.

Bay Area Bike Share
San Jose, CA
Photo by Richard Masoner / Cyclelicious @ Flickr

Regional Bike Share

SR2T initially funded the Santa Clara Valley Transportation Authority (VTA) for a pilot bike share project focused on bridging gaps from high-ridership Caltrain stations to popular nearby destinations. This was later combined with Bay Area Air Quality Management District funding to create a larger share. In August 2013, Bay Area Bike Share launched with 700 bicycles near transit in five cities from San Francisco to San Jose.

By maintaining an eye for innovation and flexibility in program management, SR2T has been able to have a regional impact.

SR2T projects are improving the travel experience for Bay Area pedestrians and bicyclists, and are giving commuters new options to leave their cars at home, living car-free or car-light. Regions, residents, and transit systems nationwide stand to benefit from increased access to transportation options through creative funding mechanisms like SR2T. TransForm and EBBC hope that word of SR2T allows for similar strategies to take root across the nation.

For more information visit TransForm's website: *www.TransFormCA.org/Campaign/SR2T*

8 Education and Encouragement

Both bicyclists and motorists need education on how to safely share the road and navigate traffic. Widespread education efforts can contribute to safer roadways for all. Encouragement is also needed to promote bicycling and walking as means of transport, recreation, and physical activity.

Many states and cities have implemented programs and events with these aims but have had no way to evaluate their success compared to others. This *Benchmarking Report* builds on data from the 2012 report to track progress of these efforts.

Photo courtesy of Alliance for Biking & Walking

Educating the Public

Making sure all roadway users understand their rights and responsibilities is a critical component of creating bicycle- and pedestrian-friendly communities. From share-the-road campaigns to driver's test questions, states and cities are working to promote the safety of the most vulnerable road users.

Driver Education

Driver education is a unique opportunity to instill knowledge about traffic laws and safety that individuals will use to form habits for years to come. For this report, the state survey collected information on whether bicycling is included in the state driver's manual and whether questions on sharing the roadway with bicyclists are included on the state driver's exam. All 50 states include information on bicycling in their state driver's manuals. Thirty-eight states include driver's license test questions on bicyclists, up from 33 states two years ago. Many states reported that their state's driver's license test randomizes questions, so a question about bicyclists does not appear on all tests taken.

Pedestrian and Bicyclist Education

Although nearly everyone must have some form of driver's education before receiving a license, there is no education requirement to ride a bicycle. Yet having knowledge and skills to properly handle a bicycle in traffic can improve safety for bicyclists and as some studies have shown, even make them better motorists. Bicycle education teaches youth and adults the rules of the road, how to properly handle a bicycle in traffic, and how to respectfully share the road with other users.

The Alliance survey on youth and adult bicycle education courses reveals that 50

Education and Encouragement in Large Cities

	Bicycle education course for youth	Bicycle education course for adults	Pedestrian education course for youth	Bike to Work Day events	Open Streets initiative	City-sponsored bicycle ride
Albuquerque	✓	✓	✓	✓		✓
Arlington, TX	✓	✓		✓		
Atlanta	✓	✓		✓	✓	✓
Austin	✓	✓	✓	✓	✓	
Baltimore	✓	✓		✓	✓	✓
Boston	✓	✓	✓	✓	✓	✓
Charlotte	✓	✓		✓		✓
Chicago	✓	✓	✓	✓	✓	✓
Cleveland	✓	✓		✓	✓	
Colorado Springs	✓	✓	✓	✓		✓
Columbus	✓	✓	✓	✓		✓
Dallas	✓	✓	✓	✓		✓
Denver	✓	✓		✓	✓	✓
Detroit	(1)	(1)	(1)	(1)	(1)	(1)
El Paso		✓		✓	✓	✓
Fort Worth	✓	✓	✓	✓	✓	✓
Fresno	✓	✓		✓		
Honolulu	✓	✓		✓	✓	✓
Houston	✓	✓		✓		✓
Indianapolis	✓	✓		✓	✓ (2)	✓
Jacksonville		✓		✓		
Kansas City, MO	✓	✓	✓	✓	✓	✓
Las Vegas		✓		✓	✓	
Long Beach	✓	✓	✓	✓		✓
Los Angeles	✓	✓	✓	✓	✓	✓
Louisville	✓	✓	✓	✓	✓	✓
Memphis	✓	✓	✓	✓	✓	✓
Mesa	✓	✓		✓	✓	✓
Miami	✓	✓	✓	✓	✓	✓
Milwaukee	✓	✓		✓		✓
Minneapolis	✓	✓	✓	✓	✓	✓
Nashville	✓	✓		✓		✓
New Orleans	✓	✓		✓	✓ (2)	
New York City	✓	✓	✓	✓	✓	✓
Oakland	✓	✓	✓	✓		
Oklahoma City		✓		✓		
Omaha	✓	✓		✓	✓ (2)	✓
Philadelphia	✓	✓	✓	✓	✓	
Phoenix	✓	✓		✓		✓
Portland, OR	✓	✓	✓	✓	✓	✓
Raleigh	✓	✓		✓		✓
Sacramento	✓	✓		✓		
San Antonio	✓	✓		✓	✓	✓
San Diego	✓	✓	✓	✓	✓ (2)	
San Francisco	✓	✓	✓	✓	✓	
San Jose	✓	✓	✓	✓	✓	✓
Seattle	✓	✓		✓	✓	
Tucson	✓	✓	✓	✓	✓	
Tulsa	✓	✓	✓	✓	✓	
Virginia Beach		✓		✓		✓
Washington, DC	✓	✓	✓	✓	✓	
Wichita	✓		✓	✓		
# of cities responding "yes"	46	50	26	51	32	33

Sources: City Survey 2011/2012 **Notes**: Unanswered survey questions, or responses of "N/A" and "unknown," were taken to mean "no." All empty cells should be understood to be a "no" response. (1) Detroit did not submit a survey for 2011/2012. (2) These cities started an Open Streets initiative in 2013, after surveys were submitted.

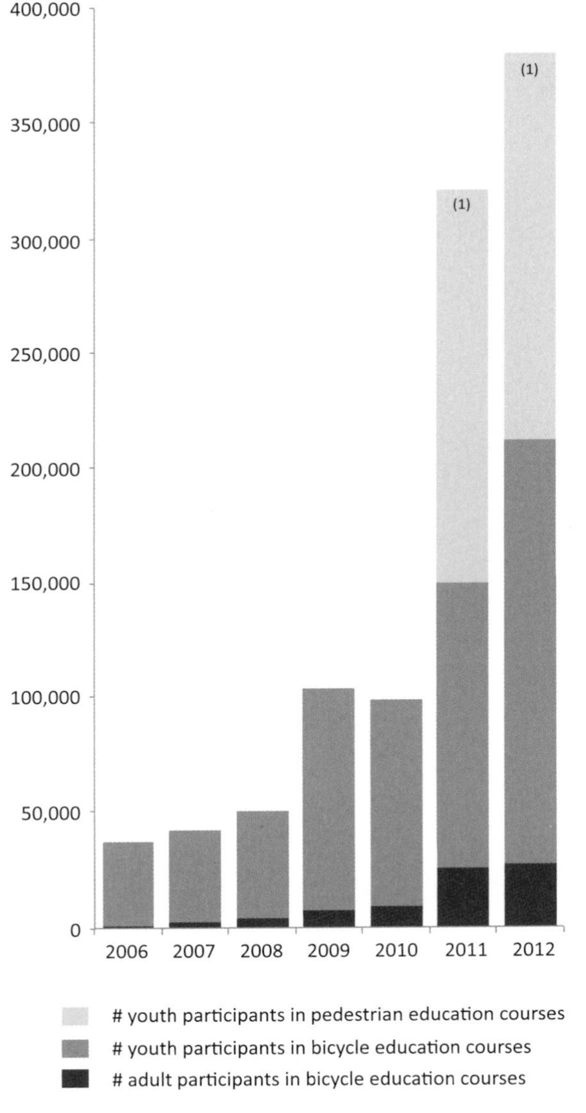

Sources: City Surveys: 2005/2006, 2007/2008, 2009/2010, and 2011/2012.
Note: (1) Youth pedestrian education courses were only reported for years 2011 and 2012.

cities (96% of cities surveyed, up from 41 cities two years ago) have adult bicycle education courses; and 46 cities, or 88% of cities surveyed, have youth bicycle education courses (up from 36 cities two years ago). These education courses vary in that some are sponsored by the local government, some by a local nonprofit or advocacy organization, some by local hospitals or local bicycle shops, and others are the result of partnerships between multiple agencies.

Surveys also reveal that city adult bicycle education courses averaged one participant per 800 adults in 2011 and 2012, a three-fold improvement from two years ago with one participant for every 2,363 adults. In 2012, Chicago reported the greatest participation rate of 10,000 adults, or one participant per 209 adult residents. Youth courses averaged one participant per 39 youth residents in 2011 and 2012, an improvement from one participant per 59 youth in 2009 and 2010. Long Beach and Austin had the greatest youth participation rates in 2012. Long Beach had nearly 37,000 youth education participants, or one participant per three youth in the city; and Austin had just over 47,000 youth participants, or one participant per four youth.

Photo courtesy of Alliance for Biking & Walking

In 2012, 50 large cities offered **bicycle education courses for adults** and had a total of 28,215 participants; 46 large cities offered **bicycle education courses for youth** and had a total of 183,243 participants; and 26 large cities offered **pedestrian education courses for youth** and had a total of 168,278 participants.

Statewide Education Efforts

	Share the Road campaign	Motorist/bicyclist interaction in state driver's manual	Driver's license test questions about bicyclists	State bicyclist manual	Annual statewide bike/ped conference	Bicycling enforcement taught in Police Officer Standards and Training (POST) course	Police academy curriculum for new officers includes bicycle enforcement training
Alabama		✓	✓				
Alaska	✓	✓	✓				
Arizona	✓	✓	✓	✓			
Arkansas		✓	✓			✓	✓
California	✓	✓	✓		✓	✓	✓
Colorado	✓	✓	✓	✓	✓ (1)	✓	✓
Connecticut		✓	✓		✓	✓	✓
Delaware	✓	✓		✓	✓		
Florida	✓	✓	✓	✓			
Georgia	✓	✓	✓	✓	✓ (1)	✓	
Hawaii	✓	✓	✓				✓
Idaho	✓	✓	✓	✓			
Illinois	✓	✓	✓	✓		✓	✓
Indiana		✓	✓			✓	✓
Iowa	✓	✓	✓	✓	✓	✓	✓
Kansas	✓	✓			✓		
Kentucky	✓	✓			✓		
Louisiana	✓	✓	✓			✓	✓
Maine	✓	✓	✓		✓	(2)	(2)
Maryland	✓	✓	✓	✓	✓ (1)	✓	
Massachusetts	✓	✓	✓		✓	✓	✓
Michigan	✓	✓	✓	✓	✓	✓	✓
Minnesota	✓	✓	✓		✓ (1)	✓	✓
Mississippi	✓	✓					
Missouri	✓	✓	✓			✓	✓
Montana	✓	✓				✓	✓
Nebraska		✓	✓			✓	✓
Nevada	✓	✓			✓		
New Hampshire		✓	✓			✓	✓
New Jersey	✓	✓	✓	✓	✓	✓	
New Mexico	✓	✓	✓				
New York	✓	✓					
North Carolina	✓	✓	✓	✓	✓ (1)		
North Dakota		✓					
Ohio	✓	✓		✓		✓	✓
Oklahoma	✓	✓	✓	✓	✓ (1)		
Oregon	✓	✓	✓	✓	✓	✓	✓
Pennsylvania		✓	✓	✓	✓	✓	✓
Rhode Island		✓				✓	✓
South Carolina	✓	✓	✓		✓ (1)	✓	
South Dakota		✓	✓		✓ (1)		
Tennessee	✓	✓			✓ (1)	✓	
Texas	✓	✓	✓	✓	✓	✓	
Utah	✓	✓	✓	✓	✓ (1)	✓	✓
Vermont	✓	✓	✓				
Virginia	✓	✓	✓				
Washington	✓	✓	✓	✓	✓	✓	✓
West Virginia		✓	✓				
Wisconsin	✓	✓	✓		✓		
Wyoming	✓	✓	✓				
# of states responding "yes"	39	50	38	19	26	27	22

Source: State Survey 2011/2012. **Notes**: Unanswered survey questions, or responses of "N/A" and "unknown," were taken to mean "no." All empty cells should be understood to be a "no" response. (1) Bicycle conference only. (2) Maine includes bicycling enforcement for officers in the general instruction for Title 29-A: Motor Vehicles.

Statewide Encouragement and Events

State-sponsored bicycling event to promote bicycling and physical activity	State-sponsored walking event to promote walking and physical activity	Bike to Work Day or commuter challenge	
			Alabama
		✓	Alaska
		✓	Arizona
		✓	Arkansas
✓		✓	California
✓		✓	Colorado
		✓	Connecticut
✓		✓	Delaware
		✓	Florida
			Georgia
		✓	Hawaii
✓	✓	✓	Idaho
✓	✓	✓	Illinois
		✓	Indiana
		✓	Iowa
		✓	Kansas
		✓	Kentucky
			Louisiana
✓		✓	Maine
		✓	Maryland
✓	✓	✓	Massachusetts
✓		✓	Michigan
✓		✓	Minnesota
		✓	Mississippi
✓	✓	✓	Missouri
		✓	Montana
		✓	Nebraska
✓	✓	✓	Nevada
		✓	New Hampshire
		✓	New Jersey
		✓	New Mexico
			New York
		✓	North Carolina
✓		✓	North Dakota
		✓	Ohio
		✓	Oklahoma
		✓	Oregon
		✓	Pennsylvania
		✓	Rhode Island
		✓	South Carolina
			South Dakota
✓		✓	Tennessee
✓	✓	✓	Texas
✓		✓	Utah
		✓	Vermont
		✓	Virgina
		✓	Washington
✓	✓	✓	West Virginia
✓	✓	✓	Wisconsin
		✓	Wyoming
17	8	45	# of states responding "yes"

Source: State Survey 2011/2012. **Note**: Unanswered survey questions, or responses of "N/A" and "unknown," were taken to mean "no." All empty cells should be understood to be a "no" response.

Share the Road Campaigns

"Share the Road" is perhaps the most common slogan used in bicycle education. Share the Road campaigns are widespread and can take many forms. Many states have Share the Road signs on roadways. Others have Share the Road bumper stickers. Some states have multi-media campaigns of public service announcements, including ads on buses, billboards, radio, and television. The basic message is always the same—encouraging bicyclists and motorists to obey traffic laws and show respect to other road users. Thirty-eight states, the same total as two years ago, report having a Share the Road or similar public safety campaign.

Police Training

Police officers without training in bicycle laws may not understand or uphold bicyclists' or pedestrians' rights in traffic crashes, may incorrectly stop or ticket bicyclists, or may set a bad example of the law for other motorists. Education of law enforcement in bicycle safety and laws pertaining to bicycling is critical to furthering bicycling safety and rights.

According to the Benchmarking Project state surveys, 23 states include bicycle enforcement training as a Police Academy requirement (up from 20 states two years ago), and 27 states include bicycle enforcement as part of a Police Officer Standards and Training (POST) course.

Professional Conferences

Bicycle and pedestrian professionals need opportunities for continuing education, networking, and collaboration. Many states now hold annual bicycle and pedestrian conferences or summits that provide bicycle and pedestrian professionals an opportunity for learning, networking, and planning. Sixteen states report having hosted a statewide bicycle and pedestrian conference, and another 10 have hosted a statewide bicycle-specific conference.

Programs and Events

Studies have shown that programs that promote bicycling and walking, such as Bike to Work days, Open Streets initiatives, and Safe Routes to School, have the ability to increase long-term healthy habits in participants (Dill et al., 2013). A study conducted in five states with Safe Routes to School programs concluded that active travel to school by bicycle or foot increased by 37% from 12.9 percent to 17.6 percent after implementation of the program (WSDOT, 2012).

Encouragement programs are activities that support and promote bicycling and walking. There are many different types of encouragement activities, but this *Benchmarking Report* looked at four specific types of common encouragement events: Bike to Work Day, Walk and Bike to School Day, city-sponsored bicycle rides, and Open Streets initiatives. This report also looked at participation levels in these efforts to establish benchmarks and baseline data to measure progress among cities in the future.

More than any other age group, young adults (ages 18–29) say they are more likely to bicycle if they have someone to ride with (LAB, 2013).

Promotional Bicycle Rides

Promotional bicycle rides are another popular encouragement activity that many states, cities, and advocacy organizations sponsor. While temporary in nature, these events can promote bicycling as a healthy and fun way to get around, and can raise awareness of local bicycle routes, issues, and groups. They are often an excellent entry point for new bicyclists who are not yet comfortable riding alone in traffic, but who will try out bicycling in a group ride setting. Promotional rides are also great opportunities for media coverage, and for forging new partnerships between bicycling organizations and other government and community groups.

Seventeen states and 33 cities report having government-sponsored rides to promote bicycling or physical activity (up from 31 cities reported in the *2012 Benchmarking Report*,

Number of Participants in Official City Bicycle Rides (2012)

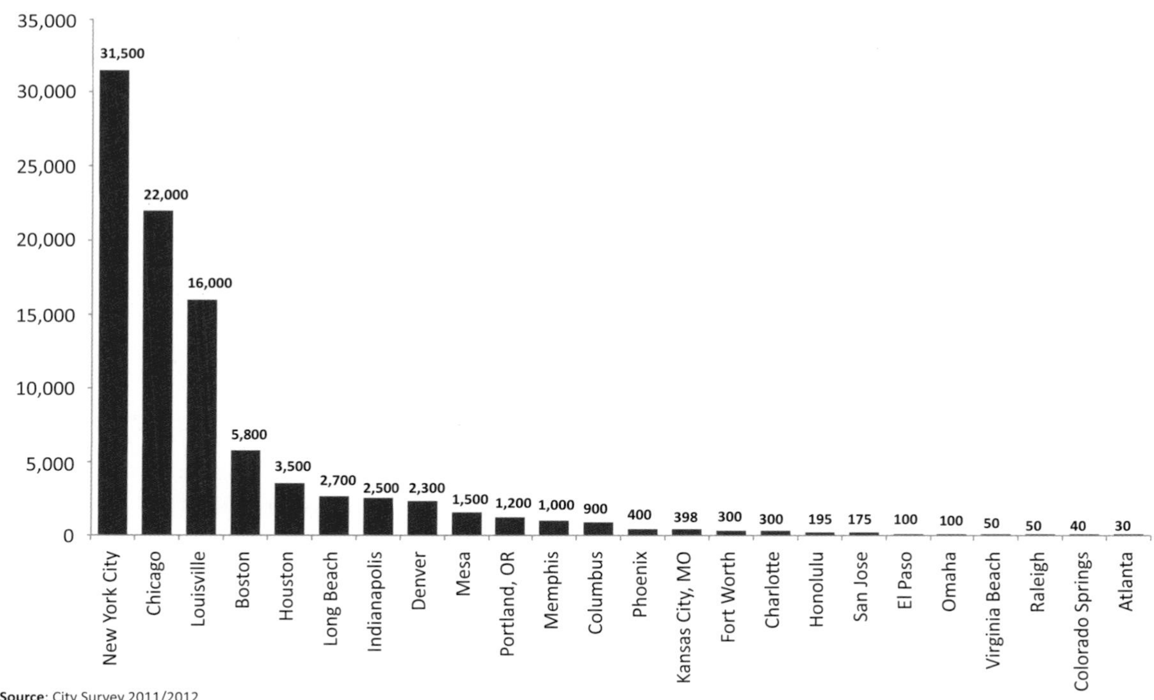

Source: City Survey 2011/2012

while the number of states stayed the same). Seven states reported hosting a Governor's ride, and eight states reported holding a state legislator's ride. New York City's city-sponsored ride (TD Bank Five Borough Bike Tour) attracts 31,500 bicyclists annually, more than any other city-sponsored ride. Louisville's Mayor's Healthy Hometown Hike and Bike attracts one participant for every 38 residents, making it the highest per capita participation of any city-sponsored ride in 2012.

Open Streets

Although a few cities—including Seattle, San Francisco, and New York City—have had regularly occurring car-free streets within parks for decades, a new sort of program has been spreading across North American in the last decade. These initiatives, called Open Streets, temporarily remove cars from the streets so that people may use them for healthy and fun physical activities like walking, jogging, bicycling, and dancing. See page 192 for a more detailed description of Open Streets initiatives.

Of the 52 large cities covered in this report, 32 hosted Open Streets initiatives in 2011/2012 (up from 20 large cities in 2009/2010). El Paso; Kansas City, MO; and Philadelphia each report hosting at least 52 Open Streets events per year. Four cities report having over 100,000 participants in 2012, up from only one city in 2010. San Francisco's Sunday Streets drew the most participants at 300,000, and New York City's Summer Streets drew in 256,000 in 2012. Los Angeles's Open Streets gathered 200,000 participants and events in Portland, OR, drew 103,000 people. These high turnouts demonstrate a large interest in, and latent demand for, safe places to bicycle and walk. Cities in North America continue to strive for more frequent Open Streets that occur at regular intervals.

More information on Open Streets is available at *OpenStreetsProject.org*.

Bike to Work Day

Bike to Work Day is an annual event held on the third Friday in May throughout most of the United States and Canada. Since the League of American Bicyclists organized the first Bike to Work Day in 1956, the day has been a rallying point for bicycle advocates to promote bicycling as a healthy and fun alternative to driving. Local advocacy organizations and government agencies across North America organize bicycling encouragement and promotion events around Bike to Work Day, including commuter challenges, organized rides, energizer stations (with coffee, breakfast treats, and bicycling literature), and more.

Bike to Work Day is the most common encouragement activity among major U.S. cities, with all 52 cities reporting some organized event around this day (up from 43 cities two years ago). Both government and nonprofit organizations sponsor these events. In 2012 and 2011, cities averaged one Bike to Work Day participant for every 394 adults. In 2010 and 2009, cities reported greater participation with one participant for every 306 adults. However, exact trends are difficult to determine because not every city was able to provide annual participation data. Of those cities that did report participation numbers in 2012, Washington, DC, and Portland, OR, had the greatest per capita participation, with one participant for 44 and 46 (respectively) city residents.

Walk and Bike to School Day

Walk and Bike to School Day is an annual international event held the first Wednesday in October to promote and encourage students bicycling and walking to school. The first Walk to School Day was in 1995 in Hertfordshire, England. By 2000, the first International Walk to School Day was held with events throughout Europe, Canada, and the United States. Communities can choose to celebrate International Walk to School Day for a day, a week, or an entire month. Events can range from simply encouraging parents and children to bicycle or walk to school, to an organized walk- or bicycle-to-school parade with refreshments and prizes for children who participate.

Photo by Barry Lewis. Courtesy of Alliance for Biking & Walking

In 2012, nearly 4,300 schools from all 50 states participated in Walk to School Day. This is a 20% increase from the *2012 Benchmarking Report*, with over 800 more schools participating compared to 2010. California topped the list with 495 Walk to School events in 2012. Portland, OR, and Nashville had more schools registered for Walk to School Day than any other major U.S. cities, with 67 and 50 registered schools, respectively. Memphis reported the highest number of students participating at 40,000 in 2012.

Savannah, GA. Photo courtesy of Savannah Bicycle Campaign

The first national Bike to School Day was held in May 2012. Forty-nine states participated, with South Dakota being the only state that did not have any registered events. Twenty-seven of the most populous cities reported at least one Bike to School event. Minneapolis held the most Bike to School events (18), followed by Washington, DC, with 16 events.

Impact of Education and Encouragement on Mode Share

Many advocacy organizations and government agencies sponsor education and encouragement efforts that influence mode share and safety. Although some baseline data were collected for the 2010 and 2012 *Benchmarking Reports*, as well as for this current report, there is still a severe deficiency in evaluation of these efforts. Because many cities and states could not provide data on participation levels, and many programs are brand new, potential relationships of data are difficult to explore. The Benchmarking Project will continue to collect data on education and encouragement efforts, and hopes to explore the relationship further in future reports.

Open Streets Across the U.S.

by Michael Samuelson, Alliance for Biking & Walking, Open Streets Project

Open Streets initiatives, also known as Ciclovías, Sunday Streets, and Sunday Parkways, temporarily close streets to motorized traffic and open them for walking, jogging, bicycling, dancing, playing, and just about any other physical activity. Today, there are nearly 100 Open Streets initiatives in the United States and Canada, up from only nine in 2005. These initiatives are located in all regions of the two countries.

Open Streets differentiate themselves from block parties and street fairs by promoting active living, and healthy lifestyle choices, and by connecting neighborhoods. The most successful Open Streets occur every week, opening up miles of streets and engaging hundreds of thousands of participants. While most initiatives happen during the warmer months, some initiatives are active throughout the year.

There are a variety of benefits associated with Open Streets. They provide a safe space to be physically active, promote local businesses, create an opportunity for community interaction and civic engagement, allow participants to explore new parts of their city, and encourage participants to consider incorporating walking and bicycling into their daily transportation routine.

These initiatives are also an excellent opportunity for advocates and officials to engage with new partners to promote bicycling and walking. Open Streets coalitions can include health partners, business leaders, environmentalists, community leaders, churches, transportation advocates, and more. Bicycling and walking advocates use Open Streets as a way to start conversations with individuals and organizations that are supportive of active transportation but have not found a way to engage in advocacy efforts in the past.

Although larger cities like New York and Los Angeles may dominate the headlines related to Open Streets, it is a phenomenon that has taken root in communities of all sizes. The definition of a successful Open Streets initiative varies greatly depending on the size of the community and the size of the space closed to car traffic. While some cities in Latin America close dozens of miles, North American cities tend to close between 1–10 miles for each initiative.

In association with The Street Plans Collaborative, the Alliance for Biking & Walking has created a central resource for information on Open Streets, the Open Streets Project. The Project includes a website (*www.OpenStreetsProject.org*) containing a collection of best practices (the *Open Streets Guide*), case studies on cities across the continent, a resources section, and news on the latest developments related to Open Streets.

The Open Streets Project offers technical assistance to interested communities, and held the first National Open Streets Training in August of 2013. For more information, contact Mike Samuelson, Open Streets Coordinator at:
Mike@PeoplePoweredMovement.org

Number of Large Cities with an Open Streets Initiative

Source: Benchmarking Project City Surveys

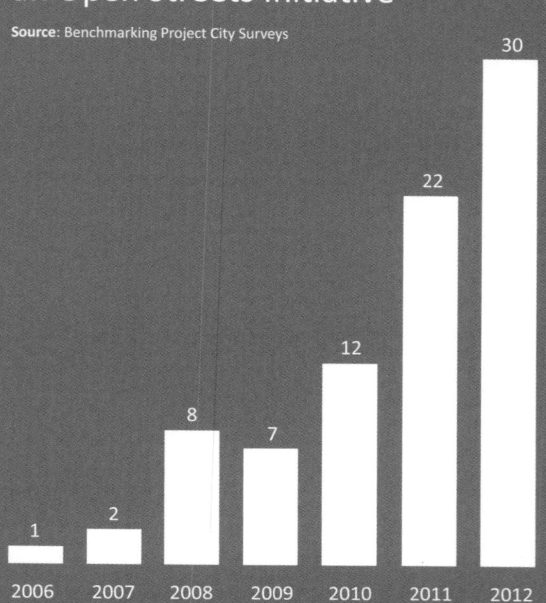

Existing Open Streets Initiatives in the Most Populous U.S. Cities

Sources: City Survey 2011/2012, Open Streets Project 2014
Note: See page 184 for a list of the most populous cities with Open Streets initiatives.

Open Streets initiatives are part of an ongoing, broader effort to:

encourage sustained **physical activity**,
redefine **public spaces**,
and increase **healthy transportation** options.

Minneapolis, MN. Photo by bradleypjohnson @ Flickr

Open Streets Model Types

While each Open Streets initiative is unique to the local context in which it is implemented, there are elements of all initiatives that tie them together. Several common models have emerged in the United States, based on an initiative's lead organizing entity (where funding is sourced), and the level of supporting activities offered. Supporting activities vary widely by city and may include classes (e.g. yoga, dance, zumba), bicycle education, playground games (e.g. hula hooping, jump-roping), and performances. Thus far, six model types have been identified, each named in honor of the city responsible for pioneering the model.

Cleveland Model

- Lead organization is a nonprofit
- Funding support is largely sourced from private business or charitable foundations
- Numerous supporting activities and initiatives are included along the route's trajectory

Kentucky Model

- Organized statewide by a coalition of public, private, and nonprofit entities
- Funded by public and private sector entities
- Substantial supporting activities

Portland (Oregon) Model

- Organization is in the hands of local government
- Funding is sourced from both public and private sources
- Various supporting initiatives and activities are included

San Francisco Model

- Organized by a coalition of nonprofits and public authorities
- Financial support sourced from private donations and public funds
- Wide scope of supporting activities
- The initiatives are often held in different parts of the city

Seattle Model

- The organization of the initiative is primarily in the hands of the local government
- Routes are chosen within parkways or alongside parks and other natural features where few intersections exist
- Funding is sourced from the state, county, and/or city government
- There are minimal or no supporting activities or related initiatives
- The initiatives typically occur on a regular basis

Savannah Model

- Organized by a coalition of public, private, and nonprofit entities
- Funded by private sector entities
- Substantial supporting activities

Winnipeg Model

- Organized by a nonprofit entity
- Funded by public and private sector entities
- Significant supporting activities and initiatives

Education and Encouragement Efforts in Midsized Cities

Over the last two years, the midsized cities surveyed for this report have been active in educating the public about bicycling and walking through special events and educational programs. In 2012, fourteen midsized cities had youth bicycle education courses, and nine cities had youth pedestrian education courses. During the same year, 15 of these cities reported the presence of an adult bicycle education course.

All 17 midsized cities participated in a Bike to Work Day event in 2012, and 15 of the cities also sponsored a public bicycle ride. Eight midsized cities currently host an Open Streets initiative.

Schools

Although only three midsized cities indicated that bicycle parking is required at public schools, ten reported having bicycle parking spaces at public schools, with Davis leading the count at 2,400 spaces. None of the midsized cities require bicycling and walking access for students and staff, but ten of the cities are enrolled in a city-sponsored Safe Routes to School program, and 16 of the cities reported participating in a Bike and Walk to School event during the 2011–2012 school year.

Education and Encouragement

	Bicycle education courses for youth		Pedestrian education courses for youth		Bicycle education courses for adults		Bike to Work Day events		City-sponsored Open Streets initiative		City-sponsored bicycle ride	
	2011	2012	2011	2012	2011	2012	2011	2012	2011	2012	2011	2012
Population > 200K												
Anchorage, AK					✓	✓	✓	✓				
Baton Rouge, LA	✓	✓			✓	✓	✓	✓			✓	✓
Madison, WI	✓	✓	✓	✓	✓	✓	✓	✓	✓	✓	✓	✓
Pittsburgh, PA			✓	✓			✓	✓				
Spokane, WA	✓	✓	✓	✓	✓	✓	✓	✓	✓	✓	✓	✓
St. Louis, MO	✓	✓			✓	✓	✓	✓	✓	✓	✓	✓
Population 100-200K												
Charleston, SC							✓	✓	✓	✓	✓	✓
Chattanooga, TN	✓	✓	✓	✓	✓	✓	✓	✓			✓	✓
Eugene, OR	✓	✓	✓	✓	✓	✓	✓	✓	✓	✓	✓	✓
Fort Collins, CO	✓	✓	✓	✓	✓	✓	✓	✓			✓	✓
Salt Lake City, UT	✓	✓	✓	✓	✓	✓	✓	✓		✓	✓	✓
Population < 100K												
Albany, NY	✓	✓			✓	✓		✓			✓	✓
Bellingham, WA	✓	✓	✓	✓	✓	✓	✓	✓			✓	✓
Boulder, CO	✓	✓			✓	✓	✓	✓	✓	✓	✓	✓
Burlington, VT	✓	✓			✓	✓	✓	✓			✓	✓
Davis, CA	✓	✓			✓	✓	✓	✓			✓	✓
Missoula, MT	✓	✓	✓	✓	✓	✓	✓	✓	✓	✓	✓	✓

Source: Midsized City Survey 2011/2012. **Note**: Unanswered survey questions, or responses of "N/A" and "unknown," were taken to mean "no." All empty cells should be understood to be a "no" response.

Red, Bike and Green

by Hamzat Sani; Red, Bike and Green

In her Oakland, CA, neighborhood, community leader Jenna Burton saw many people hopping on their bicycles to get around. However, many of these new bicyclists did not look like her or traditional Oaklanders. So, five years ago, she rounded up a small group of black bicyclists and went for a ride. That initial ride has turned into a multi-city movement of black bicyclists, called Red, Bike and Green.

"When you see fifty-plus black people on bikes in any neighborhood it's a symbol of black power," she says. "The rides are a way to make a space where black love and healthy black living is visible."

Red, Bike and Green (RBG) organizes around a three-pronged mission: improving health, economics, and the environment. With a motto like, "Its Bigger Than Bikes," RBG takes the approach that the bicycle is an increasingly powerful tool for building community. Through the monthly Community Ride, RBG provides a place for riders, young and old, to commune and commute together; to support black-owned businesses; and to highlight issues of safety, wellness, and access.

Red, Bike and Green is giving a voice to a growing contingent of black bicyclists and people of color around their commutes and the commutes of those they live with.

From its programming to its branding, Red, Bike and Green is revolutionary. The group borrows some ideals from the Pan-Africanist theories of Marcus Garvey, and has adopted the colors of the Pan-Africanist flag. The use of these colors gives a nod to the organization's efforts in predominantly black communities. While the group shares relationships with bicycling advocates both local and national, each chapter is hyper-local in its engagement, mission, and autonomy.

"If Red, Bike and Green's goal is to get more black folks bicycling, we must think less about the existing bicycling community and more about organizations invested in the on-the-ground livelihood of black people," says Eboni Hawkins, member of the group's Chicago chapter.

Propelled by its revolutionary aesthetic and a commitment to empowering local black bicyclists, the movement has spread to a number of cities across the country in just

2013 RBG Bike Tour. Photo courtesy of Red, Bike and Green

Oakland, CA. Photo courtesy of Red, Bike and Green

a few short years. In Oakland, the group curates its own traveling art exhibit with images featuring blacks and their bicycles. In Chicago, Hawkins, the ride leader, has partnered with the Pioneers Bicycling Club and Active Transportation Alliance to host rides, educate youth on safe bicycling and maintenance, and call for a fair distribution of transportation resources.

In Atlanta, RBG has advocated for bicycle lanes in communities of color, pushed for greater engagement between black businesses and bicyclists, and even starred in their own movie. This year, RBG-New York hosted riders in the first annual RBG Bike Tour from Washington, DC, to Brooklyn, NY, featuring a stop at the AfroPunk Festival. With its newest chapter, which opened in Indianapolis in the fall of 2013, RBG continues expanding its reach to cities across the U.S.

To learn more about Red, Bike and Green, visit: *www.RedBikeandGreen.com*

Photo courtesy of Red, Bike and Green

The Netherlands: Bicycle Education in Schools

by Tijs Buskermolen, Goshen College

The Ministry of Education in the Netherlands has made traffic education a required subject for students in kindergarten and primary school. The main goals of traffic education are:

- to teach children about traffic signs and traffic rules, so that they know and are able to apply them as they participate in traffic, and
- to teach children to safely participate in traffic as pedestrians, bicyclists, and passengers.

The main organization that provides learning materials for traffic education is Veilig Verkeer Nederland (Save Traffic Netherlands), or VVN, a non-profit organization that is run mainly by volunteers. The organization gets funding from donations and government grants and charges small fees to schools for the usage of their products.

Once a year VVN holds a national theory exam to test students' knowledge of traffic signs, rules, safety, and participation. The organization provides teaching materials and a complete framework of lessons to schools that organize a practical bicycling exam. VVN also offers schools free insurance for students participating in the exam, so if something happens to one of the students during the exam, the VVN insurance will pay for the expenses. Teachers and volunteers create the specific exam and route for their own school. Schools are not required to participate in these exams, but the government recommends it.

The practical exam has two parts; the first part is a bicycle check. A couple days before the exam, students' bicycles are checked by volunteers to make sure that they will be safe to use in traffic. A student's bicycle must pass the check in order for them to participate in the practical exam.

The second part of the exam is a riding course that has been organized by the teachers and volunteers. VVN has developed a set of standards, identifying what must be included for a course to be qualified. For example, the route must include multiple traffic situations. The course is around two miles long, and volunteers observe students at different points along the route. The volunteers record whether or not students participate safely in traffic, and if they follow the traffic rules. After the exam, the teacher and volunteers conduct a review with the students and address the most common mistakes made during the exam. A student must score above 80% to successfully pass the practical exam. If a student fails the exam, the student will be able to retake it at another time.

The expenses to administer the exam are low, and most local governments will cover the cost if the school communicates with them. About 60–70% of schools in the Netherlands participate in the exams yearly.

Children practicing bicycling skills. Photo by Jeff Miller

Image examples from the Veilig Verkeer Nederland (Save Traffic Netherlands) workbooks.

My personal experience with bicycle education started when I entered kindergarten. My teachers engaged me in small activities, games, songs, and drawings related to participating in traffic.

In second grade, we received a workbook-like magazine from VVN, called *Stap Vooruit* (*Step Forward*). *Stap Vooruit* is published eight times a year, and is filled with fun learning exercises, pictures, and activities, which we would complete during class time.

In third and fourth grades, we received a different workbook/magazine that was a little more challenging. *Op de Voet en Fietsen* (*On Feet and Biking*) is also published eight times a year. After working through each magazine, we completed a short quiz about the information covered.

We received *Jeugd VerkeersKrant* (*Youth Traffic Newspaper*) in fifth and sixth grades. The main goal of this magazine was to prepare us for the theory exam (described earlier), which we took in sixth grade. A couple of weeks after the theory exam, my school organized a practical exam. The whole class biked the exam route together a couple of days before the real exam, and we were allowed to practice it by ourselves ahead of time. I passed my exam with one of the allowed three mistakes. Two students in my class of 25 did not pass the exam; however, both passed the exam on their second try a couple of weeks later.

VVN was started more than 80 years ago, and had its first big success in 1959 when the government required traffic education for elementary schools. Data from the European Cyclists' Federation show that The Netherlands has seen a 45% increase in bicycling and a 58% decrease in traffic-related fatalities between 1980 and 2005 (ECF, 2012). VVN's actions have likely had an effect on these positive developments in bicycling safety.

The government and VVN have encouraged the Dutch population to adopt the philosophy that bicyclists are not the danger on the road, but cars and car drivers are. Therefore, car drivers should take the responsibility for avoiding collisions with bicyclists. The government has enacted a law that makes car drivers almost always liable in a collision with a bicycle. This law, as well as the traffic education efforts, has made the Netherlands one of the safest and most bicycle-friendly countries in the world.

People Powered Movement

Bicycle and pedestrian advocacy is on the rise. When the Alliance for Biking & Walking was formed in 1996 as the North American coalition of grassroots bicycle and pedestrian advocacy organizations, there were just 12 member organizations. Today the Alliance includes over 200 state and local advocacy organizations in 49 U.S. states, five Canadian provinces, and two Mexican states.

These organizations work to educate, inspire, and hold accountable community leaders and decision makers, transforming our communities into more vibrant, healthy, and livable places. Both the presence and the capacity of these organizations are indicators of the growing prominence of bicycling and walking in communities across the U.S.

And these advocate voices are being heard. Government staff and advisory committees at the local, state, and national levels are working to improve policy and implement projects that make communities more bicycle- and pedestrian-friendly.

Salt Lake City, UT. Photo by Salt Lake City Bike Party / Alliance for Biking & Walking

Advocacy Organizations

Grassroots advocacy is one of the most certain ways for communities to become better places to bicycle and walk. Advocacy groups understand the issues on the ground, and are often best able to stir up community support and offer creative solutions to some of the barriers that often limit governments. Their presence in both large and small communities is crucial.

The presence and strength of advocacy organizations in states and cities have been used as indicators to measure the state of bicycling and walking. Strong advocacy organizations are often necessary to local jurisdictions that have hopes of passing and implementing progressive policies for bicycling and walking. Government and elected officials passionate about these issues often work with emerging advocates, recognizing the need for increased citizen involvement in the public policy discourse.

Measuring the capacity of advocacy organizations is not an easy thing to do. Some organizations with strong leaders and a dedicated base can and do win great victories for bicycling and walking with few financial resources. However, in the Alliance's experience, organizations with sustainable revenue sources and budgets to employ full-time staff are the most self-sustaining, and are able to accomplish more in the long term. More staff means greater capacity, more growth, and greater results.

Organizations are represented in this chapter by the state or city they serve. In the cases where more than one advocacy organization serves a particular state or city, the organizations are combined to show the capacity within the city or state. Appendix 4 contains the list of all 50 states and 52 cities studied in this report and identifies Alliance member organization(s) in each city or state. Only organizations who completed the 2013 Alliance member survey are included in the analyses of this chapter.

Membership and Engagement

A strong membership base is often a critical component for successful advocacy organizations. Members provide a volunteer pool, means for political leverage, and donors. In 2013, statewide organizations averaged one member per 3,220 residents. This is an increase from 2011, when states averaged one member per 4,975 people. Vermont and Oregon have the highest rate of members to population with one member for every 294 Vermont and 516 Oregon residents.

Organizations serving cities have also seen an increase in membership and, on average, have higher membership rates than states. Overall, these locally-focused organizations have one member per 404 residents (previously one member per 1,522 residents in 2011). Seattle has the highest membership rate with one member for every 41 residents. San Francisco ranks second with one member for every 64 residents, followed by Portland, OR, with one member for every 79 residents.

Alliance Member Organizations in States and Large Cities

Source: Alliance for Biking & Walking 2013

Alliance Member Organizations Representing States and Large Cities in this Chapter

Statewide Organizations

Alabama	Alabama Bicycle Coalition
Arkansas	Bicycle Advocacy of Central Arkansas
California	California Bicycle Coalition California Walks
Colorado	Bicycle Colorado
Connecticut	Bike Walk Connecticut
Delaware	Bike Delaware
Florida	Florida Bicycle Association
Georgia	Georgia Bikes!
Hawaii	PATH—Peoples Advocacy for Trails Hawaii (1) Hawaii Bicycling League
Idaho	Idaho Pedestrian and Bicycle Alliance
Illinois	League of Illinois Bicyclists
Indiana	Bicycle Indiana
Iowa	Iowa Bicycle Coalition
Maine	Bicycle Coalition of Maine
Maryland	Bike Maryland
Massachusetts	MassBike
Michigan	League of Michigan Bicyclists
Minnesota	Bicycle Alliance of Minnesota
Montana	Bike Walk Montana (1)
Nevada	Nevada Bicycle Coalition
New Hampshire	Bike-Walk Alliance of NH
New Jersey	New Jersey Bike + Walk Coalition
New York	New York Bicycling Coalition
North Carolina	North Carolina Active Transportation Alliance
Oregon	Bicycle Transportation Alliance
South Carolina	Palmetto Cycling Coalition
Tennessee	Bike Walk Tennessee
Texas	Bike Texas
Utah	Bike Utah
Vermont	Vermont Bicycle & Pedestrian Coalition
Virginia	Virginia Bicycling Federation (1) Bike Virginia
Washington	Washington Bikes (formerly Bicycle Alliance of Washington)
Wisconsin	Bicycle Federation of Wisconsin
Wyoming	Wyoming Pathways (1) Teton Valley Trails and Pathways

Notes: The organizations represented in this chapter are Alliance member organizations who completed the annual member survey in 2013. Data reported are for 2012. Where more than one organization completed a survey for a state or large city, data for all organizations are combined. (1) Organization was not included in the *2012 Benchmarking Report*.

City-Focused Organizations

Albuquerque	BikeABQ
Atlanta	Atlanta Bicycle Coalition
Austin	Bike Austin (1) Austin Cycling Association (1)
Baltimore	Bikemore (1)
Boston	Boston Cyclists Union Green Streets Initiative (1) Walk Boston LivableStreets
Chicago	The Chainlink Community LLC (1) Active Transportation Alliance
Cleveland	Bike Cleveland
Columbus	Consider Biking Yay Bikes!
Dallas	BikeDFW
Denver	BikeDenver
Fort Worth	BikeDFW
Fresno	Bike Happy (1)
Honolulu	Hawaii Bicycling League
Houston	BikeHouston (1)
Indianapolis	INDYCOG Alliance for Health Promotion
Kansas City, MO	BikeWalkKC Revolve Kansas City Metro Bike Club
Long Beach	Los Angeles County Bicycle Coalition
Los Angeles	Los Angeles County Bicycle Coalition C.I.C.L.E. (1) Los Angeles Walks (1)
Louisville	Bicycling for Louisville
Memphis	Livable Memphis
Mesa	Not One More Cyclist Foundation (1)
Milwaukee	Bicycle Federation of Wisconsin
Minneapolis	Midtown Greenway Coalition St. Paul Smart Trips Minneapolis Bicycle Coalition
New Orleans	Bike Easy
New York City	Recycle-A-Bicycle (1) Transportation Alternatives
Oakland	East Bay Bicycle Coalition* Walk Oakland Bike Oakland
Omaha	Mode Shift Omaha (1)
Philadelphia	Bicycle Coalition of Greater Philadelphia
Portland, OR	Bicycle Transportation Alliance Community Cycling Center
Sacramento	WalkSacramento
San Diego	Bike San Diego (1)
San Francisco	San Francisco Bicycle Coalition Walk San Francisco
San Jose	Silicon Valley Bicycle Coalition
Seattle	Cascade Bicycle Club Undriving and Urban Sparks Feet First Bike Works
Tucson	Living Streets Alliance
Tulsa	Tulsa Hub
Washington, DC	Washington Area Bicyclist Association
Wichita	Bike/Walk Alliance (Bike Walk Wichita) (1)

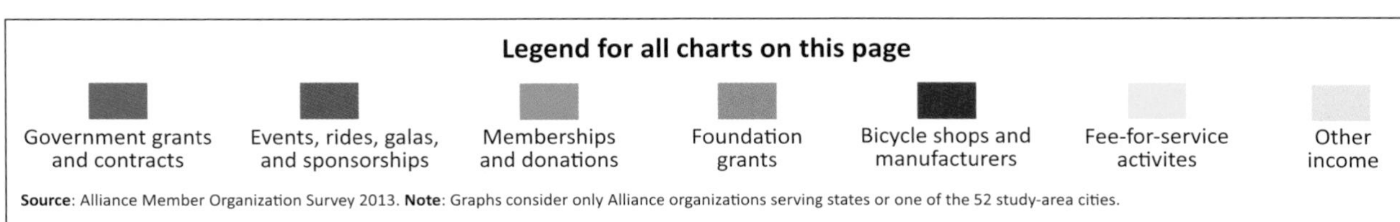

Breakdown of Every Dollar Earned by Alliance Organizations

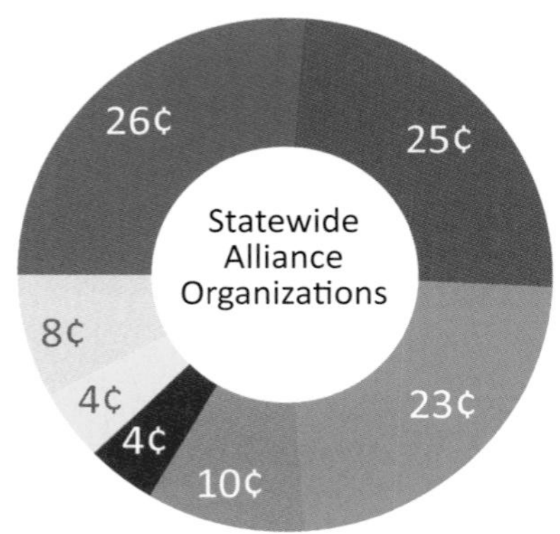

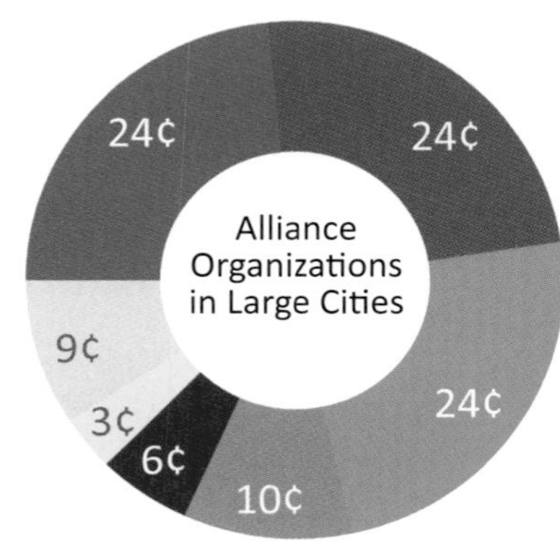

Revenue Sources of Alliance Organizations

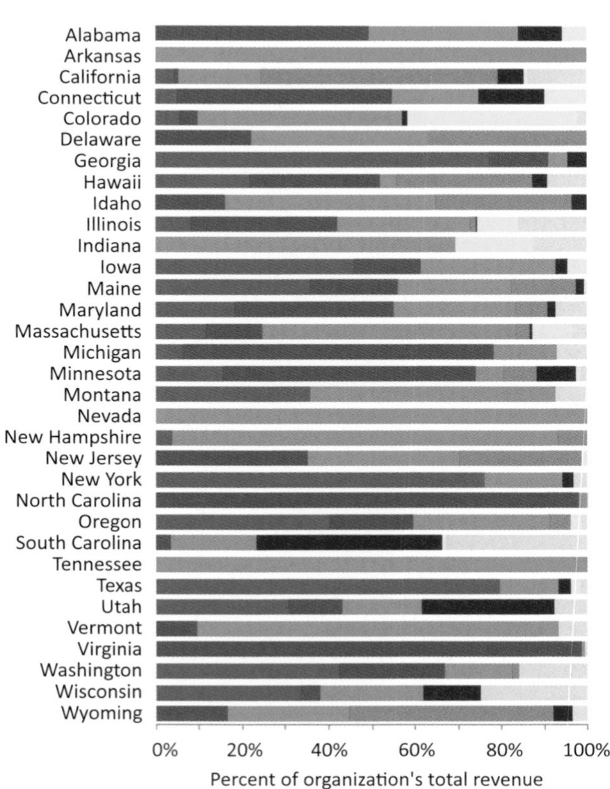

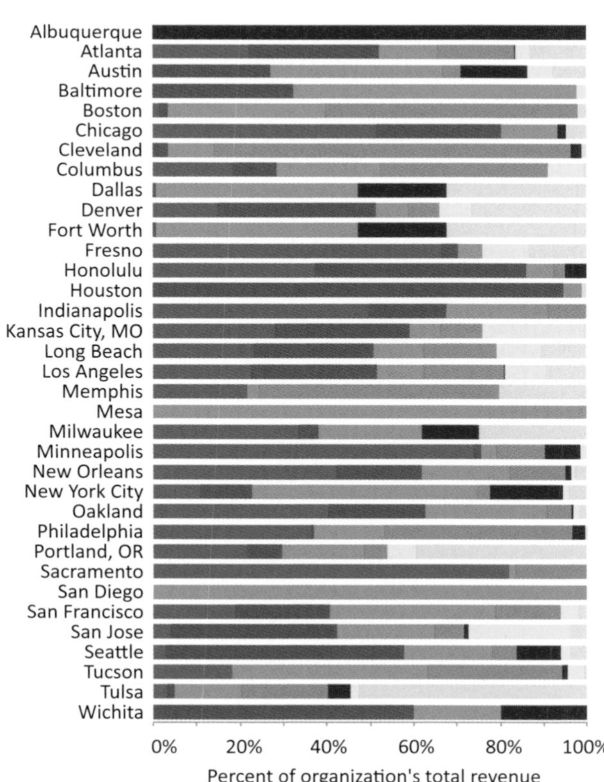

Along with membership, number of contact addresses indicate the reach an organization potentially has within the community. Both state and local organizations reported more mail contacts, on average, than email contacts for the *2012 Benchmarking Report*. However, for this update, only three organizations reported mail contacts, likely in response to the shifting preference for electronic communication. Statewide organizations average one email contact for every 804 residents (1,663 residents in 2010). Local organizations average one email contact for every 108 residents (299 residents in 2010).

Funding Advocacy Organizations

The Alliance for Biking & Walking asked its member organizations for their revenue sources from the most recent budget year. Data indicate that, on average, statewide Alliance organizations operate on 4 cents per capita, an increase from 2 cents per capita in 2010. The state with the highest per capita income for advocacy is Hawaii, with a budget of 52 cents per capita, followed by Maine with a budget of 42 cents per capita.

Organizations that represent cities have significantly higher incomes per capita than statewide organizations, and have also seen an increase in recent years. On average, Alliance organizations representing cities earned 69 cents per capita in 2012[(1)], compared to just 15 cents per capita in 2010. Seattle ranks highest in per capita earnings of all cities surveyed at $7.87 per capita (combining the revenue of four local advocacy organizations).

The range is wide among states and cities in part because some advocacy organizations are new and are being compared to longer-established organizations. Also, some organizations have full-time staff for fundraising, while others do not.

In addition to increases in revenue overall, state- and city-focused Alliance organizations are also operating with more diversified revenue sources. About a quarter of the combined income is from memberships and donations, another quarter from program fees and events, and another quarter from government grants and contracts. The final quarter of revenue is split between income from bicycle shops and manufacturers, foundation grants, fee-for-service activities, and other income.

This is an improvement in revenue diversity since 2010, when states were relying more heavily on membership fees and donations (36%) and government grants and contracts (28%). Citywide organizations were relying more heavily on income from events and programs (33%) and government grants and contracts (27%) (Alliance for Biking & Walking, 2012).

Note: (1) This average includes all organizations/cities that responded to the 2013 Alliance member organization survey. Organizations in Seattle and Portland, OR, reported very high incomes per capita. Removing the organizations in these cities brings the average per capita income down to $0.50. Removing Seattle organizations alone brings the average per capita income down to $0.56.

Capacity of Statewide Alliance Organizations

	Gross income 2012	Per capita total gross income 2012	# of staff (FTE) 2012	# of staff per 1 million residents	# of members 2012	# of state residents per:	
						member	e-mail contact
Alabama	$18,000	$0.00	1.0	0.2	150	32,018	11,015
Arkansas	$5,000	$0.00	0.0	0.0	50	58,760	2,099
California	$679,871	$0.02	4.0	0.1	30,000	1,256	370
Colorado	$728,887	$0.14	7.0	1.4	9,043	566	569
Connecticut	$81,166	$0.02	1.0	0.3	238	15,045	942
Delaware	$24,447	$0.03	1.0	1.1	150	6,048	861
Florida	$200,000	$0.01	2.8	0.2	1,300	14,660	9,529
Georgia	$110,000	$0.01	1.0	0.1	80	122,690	3,926
Hawaii	$720,243	$0.52	7.0	5.1	650	2,115	509
Idaho	$16,787	$0.01	0.5	0.3	372	4,261	4,354
Illinois	$240,000	$0.02	2.1	0.2	2,000	6,435	-
Indiana	$107,000	$0.02	1.0	0.2	3,800	1,715	1,629
Iowa	$300,000	$0.10	3.0	1.0	1,550	1,976	1,730
Maine	$566,797	$0.43	6.0	4.5	500	2,656	190
Maryland	$270,000	$0.05	3.0	0.5	200	29,141	224
Massachusetts	$293,689	$0.04	4.1	0.6	-	-	927
Michigan	$375,000	$0.04	3.0	0.3	1,216	8,122	9,711
Minnesota	$541,600	$0.10	6.0	1.1	1,678	3,185	677
Montana	$14,250	$0.01	1.0	1.0	20	49,910	2,936
Nevada	-	-	-	-	5	544,664	5,447
New Hampshire	$17,700	$0.01	1.0	0.8	90	14,647	1,318
New Jersey	$14,200	$0.00	1.0	0.1	300	29,404	3,835
New York	$103,400	$0.01	1.5	0.1	325	59,893	12,977
North Carolina	$29,100	$0.00	0.0	0.0	235	41,091	-
Oregon	$1,087,844	$0.28	14.0	3.6	7,500	516	605
South Carolina	$94,000	$0.02	2.0	0.4	500	9,358	-
Tennessee	$7,880	$0.00	0.0	0.0	79	81,055	53,361
Texas	$1,036,783	$0.04	13.0	0.5	1,000	25,675	1,895
Utah	$65,000	$0.02	0.8	0.3	300	9,391	3,522
Vermont	$51,645	$0.08	0.8	1.2	2,130	294	218
Virginia	$610,007	$0.08	4.5	0.6	110	73,605	666
Washington	$676,000	$0.10	6.5	1.0	1,660	4,114	2,021
Wisconsin	$1,134,405	$0.20	12.0	2.1	5,300	1,078	122
Wyoming	$133,197	$0.23	2.5	4.4	1,087	523	631
State total	$10,353,898		114.0		73,618		
State average	$304,526	$0.04	3.5	0.5	2,231	3,220	804
State median	$133,197	$0.02	2.1	0.5	500	9,358	1,629
High	$1,134,405	$0.52	14.0	5.1	30,000	544,664	53,361
Low	$5,000	$0.00	0.0	0.0	5	294	122

Source: Alliance Member Organization Survey 2013, ACS 2011 (population-based averages are weighted). Cells with a dash (-) mean data were unavailable or not reported.

On average, there is **one member** of an Alliance city-focused organization for every **404 residents in large cities**. There is one member of an Alliance statewide organization for every **3,220 people in the U.S.**

Capacity of Alliance Organizations Serving Large Cities

Gross income 2012	Per capita total gross income 2012	# of staff (FTE) 2012	# of staff per 1 million residents	# of members 2012	# of city residents per: member	# of city residents per: e-mail contact	
$0	$0.00	1.0	1.8	220	2,513	2,513	Albuquerque
$344,332	$0.80	3.5	8.1	1,123	385	101	Atlanta
$154,742	$0.19	4.0	4.9	1,522	539	97	Austin
$3,110	$0.01	1.0	1.6	-	-	885	Baltimore
$322,584	$0.52	10.0	16.0	2,341	267	48	Boston
$3,955,195	$1.46	35.0	12.9	6,800	398	146	Chicago
$185,345	$0.47	1.0	2.5	336	1,172	246	Cleveland
$298,232	$0.37	4.3	5.3	527	1,510	159	Columbus
$12,152	$0.01	0.0	0.0	60	20,390	1,151	Dallas
$226,485	$0.37	2.7	4.3	250	2,480	207	Denver
$12,152	$0.02	-	-	60	12,679	716	Fort Worth
$10,135	$0.02	3.0	6.0	-	-	151	Fresno
$400,000	$1.17	5.0	14.7	650	525	487	Honolulu
$42,558	$0.02	0.0	0.0	80	26,824	4,769	Houston
$279,419	$0.34	3.0	3.6	350	2,355	278	Indianapolis
$423,000	$0.91	6.0	13.0	1,553	298	116	Kansas City, MO
$650,715	$1.40	10.0	21.5	1,424	327	72	Long Beach
$731,989	$0.19	11.5	3.0	1,424	2,682	448	Los Angeles
$20,000	$0.03	0.0	0.0	200	3,010	2,007	Louisville
$184,000	$0.28	2.0	3.1	160	4,075	513	Memphis
$23,791	$0.05	0.0	0.0	-	-	1,941	Mesa
$1,134,405	$1.90	12.0	20.1	5,300	113	13	Milwaukee
$660,780	$1.70	6.0	15.5	655	592	50	Minneapolis
$123,000	$0.34	3.0	8.3	397	909	113	New Orleans
$3,371,837	$0.41	36.0	4.4	11,009	749	824	New York City
$516,800	$1.31	5.4	13.6	4,330	91	48	Oakland
$0	$0.00	0.0	0.0	-	-	2,005	Omaha
$845,852	$0.55	10.5	6.8	4,765	322	192	Philadelphia
$2,580,844	$4.34	39.0	65.5	7,500	79	15	Portland, OR
$442,203	$0.94	7.0	14.8	-	-	1,889	Sacramento
$4,748	$0.00	2.0	1.5	300	4,421	3,315	San Diego
$1,690,008	$2.08	16.0	19.7	12,676	64	30	San Francisco
$597,000	$0.62	7.0	7.2	1,200	806	342	San Jose
$4,886,366	$7.87	52.0	83.7	15,214	41	9	Seattle
$59,204	$0.11	2.3	4.3	485	1,085	572	Tucson
$150,001	$0.38	1.0	2.5	-	-	-	Tulsa
$900,000	$1.46	11.5	18.6	5,200	119	19	Washington, DC
$1,000	$0.00	-	-	15	25,629	3,844	Wichita
$26,243,984		310.6		88,126			Large cities total
$690,631	$0.69 (1)	8.6	8.3	2,753	404	108	Large cities average
$288,826	$0.38	4.1	5.7	889	778	246	Large cities median
$4,886,366	$7.87	52.0	83.7	15,214	26,824	4,769	High
$0	$0.00	0.0	0.0	15	41	9	Low

Source: Alliance Member Organization Survey 2013, ACS 2011 (population-based averages are weighted) **Note**: Cells with a dash (-) mean data were unavailable or not reported.
(1) Organizations in Seattle and Portland, OR, reported very high incomes per capita. Removing the organizations in these cities brings the average per capita income down to $0.50. Removing Seattle organizations alone brings the average per capita income down to $0.56.

Smart Phone Users Can Help

Besides those who are hired to work on implementing bicycling and walking improvements, everyday bicyclists and pedestrians are a part of encouraging change as well. Mobile phone apps now offer an easy way for people on the road to identify unsafe bicycling and walking conditions. *WalkScore.com* released a smart phone application that allows users to map a location of concern or enjoyment by taking a photo and adding commentary.

See Appendix 5 for more information about the Walk Score Project.

The Impact of Advocacy

The Alliance's coalition of grassroots advocacy organizations is constantly influencing public policy and helping to create more bikeable and walkable communities.

A look at organizational capacity (mainly, membership and funding levels) suggests a connection to bicycling and walking levels. Besides using these data to illustrate their effectiveness, Alliance leaders can also learn where they are successful and which areas need greater attention, thus refocusing limited resources for the greatest impact.

This *Benchmarking Report* compares per capita income (organization revenue/city population) and staffing levels of organizations to levels of bicycling and walking. Results indicate a positive correlation between levels of bicycling and walking to work,

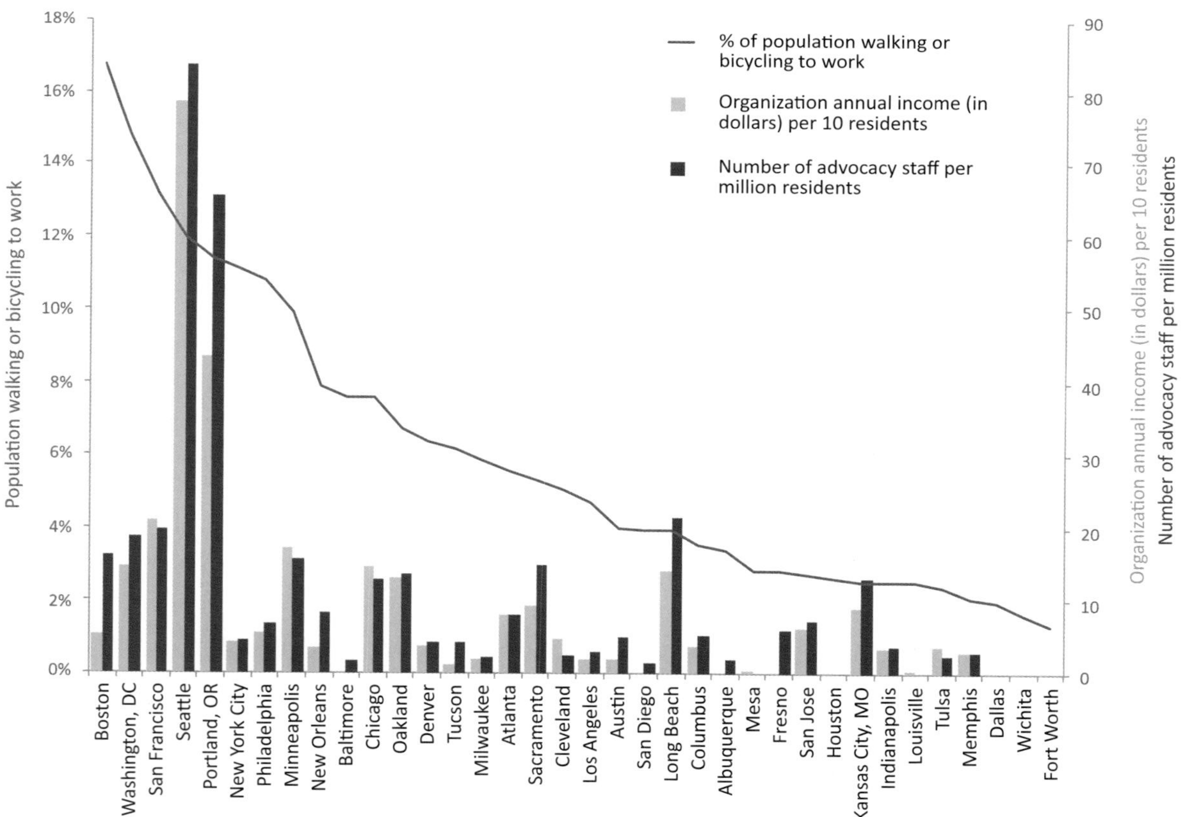

Sources: ACS 2009–2011, Alliance Member Organization Survey 2013. **Notes**: r = 0.51 (organization annual income per 10 residents / % population walking or bicycling to work), r = 0.49 (organization staffing per million residents / % population walking or bicycling to work)

and the standardized income (r = 0.51) and staffing levels (r = 0.49) of Alliance organizations. Although one cannot assume that advocacy capacity and bicycling/walking levels are causally related, comparing the two at least suggests that the presence of a strong advocacy organization can be an indicator of a city's bicycling and walking levels. Causation could go in either direction. Cities with higher bicycling and walking rates are likely to have more people supportive of advocacy, and cities with strong advocacy organizations are likely to experience growth in bicycling and walking

People Power in Government

State and Municipal Staff

The number of Full Time Equivalent (FTE) staff working in each city ranges between zero and 33 FTE and in each state between one and 32.9 FTE. San Francisco had an average of 33 FTE in 2011 and 2012, followed by Portland, OR, with 23.2 FTE. Michigan leads the states with 32.9 full time staff hours working on bicycling and walking, followed by Maryland, Massachusetts, and Texas with an average of 28.1, 25.9, and 25 FTE respectively.

Advisory Committees

In many states and cities, bicycle and pedestrian advisory committees assist with the planning, development, prioritizing, and implementation of bicycling and walking programs and facilities. These committees are typically comprised of volunteer community stateholders such as concerned citizens, bicycle and running club leaders, bicycle shop owners, and advocacy leaders. Groups typically meet monthly or quarterly to review and make recommendations to city or state staff and planners about facilities, programs, and issues relating to bicycling and walking in their state/community. Twenty-one cities and 19 states that were surveyed report having a combined bicycle and pedestrian advisory committee. Twenty-two cities have a separate bicycle advisory committee, as do six states. Missouri and 11 cities report having a standalone pedestrian advisory committee.

State Staff Working on Bicycling and Pedestrian Projects

	State staff working on bike/ped	
	Average FTE in 2011/2012	# of staff per 1 million population
Alabama	11.5	2.1
Alaska	4.0	5.5
Arizona	10.0	1.5
Arkansas	5.0	1.7
California	-	-
Colorado	10.0	2.0
Connecticut	9.0	2.5
Delaware	8.5	7.7
Florida	11.0	0.6
Georgia	5.5	0.6
Hawaii	2.0	1.5
Idaho	2.8	1.9
Illinois	5.5	0.4
Indiana	2.3	0.4
Iowa	5.0	1.6
Kansas	2.5	1.4
Kentucky	3.2	0.7
Louisiana	5.0	1.1
Maine	7.0	5.3
Maryland	28.1	4.8
Massachusetts	25.9	2.6
Michigan	32.9	3.6
Minnesota	16.5	2.9
Mississippi	6.5	2.4
Missouri	8.0	1.3
Montana	2.0	2.0
Nebraska	1.5	0.8
Nevada	6.0	2.2
New Hampshire	3.0	2.3
New Jersey	(1)	(1)
New Mexico	2.0	1.0
New York	4.0	0.2
North Carolina	2.5	0.2
North Dakota	3.0	4.4
Ohio	4.0	0.4
Oklahoma	4.7	1.4
Oregon	13.9	3.5
Pennsylvania	9.9	0.7
Rhode Island	3.0	2.9
South Carolina	5.0	1.1
South Dakota	1.0	1.2
Tennessee	5.3	0.8
Texas	25.0	1.0
Utah	11.0	3.6
Vermont	12.0	19.2
Virgina	7.0	0.9
Washington	15.0	2.2
West Virginia	1.8	0.8
Wisconsin	16.0	2.8
Wyoming	2.0	3.5
State total	388.0	
State average	8.1	1.5
State median	5.4	1.7
High	32.9	19.2
Low	1.0	0.2

Sources: State Survey 2011/2012, ACS 2011 (population-based averages are weighted). **Note**: States were asked to report how many state employees, expressed in FTE (full-time equivalent), work on bicycle and/or pedestrian issues as detailed in their work description in the last two years (including Safe Routes to School and regular contract hours). An FTE of 1.0 means that the person is equivalent to a full-time worker, while an FTE of 0.5 indicates that the worker is only half-time. Cells with a dash (-) mean data were unavailable or not reported. (1) New Jersey FTE data could not be verified.

City Staff Working on Bicycling and Pedestrian Projects

	City staff working on bike/ped		Staff on bicycles			Staff on foot		
	Average FTE in 2011/2012	# staff per 100k population	Average FTE in 2011/2012	% police on bicycles	% other staff on bicycles	Average FTE in 2011/2012	% police on foot	% other staff on foot
Albuquerque	-	-	-	35%	-	-	-	-
Arlington, TX	4.0	0.7	-	-	0%	-	-	-
Atlanta	4.0	1.1	50.0	100%	-	-	-	-
Austin	15.0	3.5	53.0	60%	40%	0.4	100%	0%
Baltimore	2.5	0.3	43.0	100%	0%	-	-	-
Boston	12.0	1.9	11.0	60%	40%	-	-	-
Charlotte	3.3	0.5	26.0	92%	8%	-	-	-
Chicago	9.0	1.2	-	-	-	-	-	-
Cleveland	4.0	0.2	4.0	100%	0%	0.0	100%	0%
Colorado Springs	5.5	1.4	-	100%	0%	-	-	-
Columbus	19.0	4.5	111.0	52%	48%	0.5	0%	100%
Dallas	6.0	0.8	35.0	100%	0%	-	-	-
Denver	7.0	0.6	18.5	50%	50%	0.5	0%	100%
Detroit	(1)	(1)	(1)	(1)	(1)	(1)	(1)	(1)
El Paso	4.0	0.6	125.0	100%	0%	0.0	0%	100%
Fort Worth	1.0	0.2	7.5	1%	1%	0.0	0%	0%
Fresno	2.0	0.3	-	-	-	-	-	-
Honolulu	2.0	0.4	45.0	100%	0%	-	-	-
Houston	4.0	1.2	-	-	-	-	-	-
Indianapolis	1.5	0.1	-	-	-	-	-	-
Jacksonville	22.0	2.7	22.0	55%	45%	0.5	100%	0%
Kansas City, MO	3.0	0.4	10.0	100%	0%	0.0	100%	0%
Las Vegas	2.6	0.6	16.0	2%	0%	0.0	-	-
Long Beach	3.0	0.5	-	-	-	-	-	-
Los Angeles	9.0	1.9	375.0	53%	47%	-	-	-
Louisville	1.5	0.0	90.0	90%	10%	0.1	100%	0%
Memphis	2.0	0.3	50.0	100%	0%	-	-	-
Mesa	2.0	0.3	3.5	0%	100%	1.0	0%	0%
Miami	5.0	1.1	55.0	50%	0%	0.0	20%	0%
Milwaukee	5.0	1.2	-	-	-	-	-	-
Minneapolis	10.0	1.7	-	-	-	-	-	-
Nashville	4.0	1.0	-	-	-	-	-	-
New Orleans	2.4	0.4	-	-	-	-	-	-
New York City	-	-	-	-	-	-	-	-
Oakland	15.0	0.2	5.5	100%	0%	0.0	100%	0%
Oklahoma City	1.0	0.3	9.0	100%	100%	-	-	-
Omaha	1.0	0.2	8.0	100%	-	-	-	-
Philadelphia	-	-	-	-	-	-	-	-
Phoenix	3.5	0.2	-	100%	0%	-	-	-
Portland, OR	23.2	1.6	41.5	15%	85%	0.9	22%	78%
Raleigh	2.5	0.4	12.0	100%	-	-	-	-
Sacramento	-	-	-	-	-	-	-	-
San Antonio	3.0	0.6	104.0	54%	46%	-	-	-
San Diego	-	-	-	-	-	-	-	-
San Francisco	33.0	2.5	-	-	-	-	-	-
San Jose	4.5	0.6	2.0	0%	100%	-	-	-
Seattle	12.0	1.2	-	-	-	-	-	-
Tucson	1.3	0.2	10.0	95%	0%	0.0	100%	-
Tulsa	3.0	0.6	1.0	0%	0%	-	-	-
Virginia Beach	1.0	0.3	-	-	-	-	-	-
Washington, DC	7.0	1.6	5.0	-	-	-	-	-
Wichita	0.0	0.0	-	-	-	-	-	-
Large Cities Total	288.1		1,348.5			3.8		
Large Cities Average	6.3	0.7	45.0	69%	25%	0.3	53%	29%
Large Cities Median	4.0	0.6	20.3	92%	0%	0.0	61%	0%
High	33.0	4.5	375.0	100%	100%	1.0	100%	100%
Low	0.0	0.0	1.0	0%	0%	0.0	0%	0%

Sources: City Survey 2011/2012, ACS 2011 (population-based averages are weighted). **Notes**: Cities were asked to report how many city employees, expressed in FTE (full-time equivalent), work on bicycle and/or pedestrian issues as detailed in their work description in the last two years (including Safe Routes to School and regular contract hours). An FTE of 1.0 means that the person is equivalent to a full-time worker, while an FTE of 0.5 indicates that the worker is only half-time. Cells with a dash (-) mean data were unavailable or not reported. (1) Detroit did not submit a survey for 2011/2012.

Who Makes it Happen in Midsized Cities

Each of the midsized cities included in this report are represented by an Alliance organization. Eleven of the cities have locally-focused Alliance member organizations, and seven have statewide or regionwide organizations. Salt Lake City is represented by both a city-focused organization and a statewide organization.

Compared to the major U.S. cities, the midsized cities have significantly more staff working on bicycle and pedestrian issues. For the large cities studied in this report, the average number of bicycling ad walking staff per 100,000 residents is 0.6, while the average for the midsized cities is 2.5. Burlington and Boulder lead the way with 31.8 staff per 100,000 and 15.8 staff per 100,000 respectively.

Of the 17 midsized cities, 16 have some type of bicycle or pedestrian advisory council. Eleven of these cities have a combined bicycle/pedestrian advisory council and the remaining five have only a bicycle advisory council. Three of these cities additionally have a Safe Routes to School council.

Alliance Member Organizations

	Advocacy organization	Focus area	Website
Population > 200K			
Anchorage, AK	Bicycle Commuters of Anchorage	city	*BicycleAnchorage.org*
Baton Rouge, LA	Baton Rouge Bike Club	city	*www.BatonRougeBikeClub.com*
	Bike Baton Rouge/Baton Rouge Advocates for Safe Streets	city	*www.BikeBR.org*
Madison, WI	Bicycle Federation of Wisconsin	state	*WisconsinBikeFed.org*
Pittsburgh, PA	Bike Pittsburgh	city	*BikePGH.org*
Spokane, WA	Bicycle Alliance of Washington	state	*WABikes.org*
St. Louis, MO	Trailnet	region	*www.Trailnet.org*
Population 100-200K			
Charleston, SC	Charleston Moves	city	*CharlestonMoves.org*
	FestiVELO de Charleston	city	*hwww.FestiVelo.org*
Chattanooga, TN	Bike Chattanooga	city	*www.BikeChattanooga.org*
Eugene, OR	GEARs - Greater Eugene Area Riders	city	*EugeneGears.org*
Fort Collins, CO	Bicycle Cooperative of Fort Collins	city	*www.FCBikeCoop.org*
	Bike Fort Collins	city	*BikeFortCollins.org*
Salt Lake City, UT	Bike Utah	state	*www.BikeUtah.org*
	Salt Lake Bicycle Collective	city	*www.BicycleCollective.org*
Population < 100K			
Albany, NY	New York Bicycling Coalition	state	*www.NYBC.net*
Bellingham, WA	Bicycle Alliance of Washington	state	*WABikes.org*
Boulder, CO	Community Cycles	city	*CommunityCycles.org*
Burlington, VT	Local Motion	state	*www.LocalMotion.org*
Davis, CA	Davis Bicycles!	city	*www.DavisBicycles.org*
Missoula, MT	Bike/Walk Alliance for Missoula	city	*www.BikeWalkMissoula.org*
	Missoula In Motion	city	*www.MissoulaInMotion.com*

Source: Midsized City Survey 2011/2012

City Staff Working on Bicycling and Pedestrian Projects

	Average FTE in 2011/2012	# staff per 100k population	Advisory committees: Combined bicycle and pedestrian advisory council	Advisory committees: Standalone bicycle advisory council	Advisory committees: Standalone pedestrian advisory council	Advisory committees: Safe Routes to School (SRTS) advisory council
Population > 200K						
Anchorage, AK			✓			
Baton Rouge, LA	1.0	0.4	✓			✓
Madison, WI	3.5	1.5	✓			
Pittsburgh, PA	3.0	1.0				
Spokane, WA	1.0	0.5	✓			
St. Louis, MO	0.5	0.2	✓	✓		
Population 100-200K						
Charleston, SC	1.5	1.2	✓			✓
Chattanooga, TN	4.0	2.4	✓			
Eugene, OR	2.6	1.7		✓		✓
Fort Collins, CO	2.5	1.7	✓	✓		
Salt Lake City, UT	5.5	2.9	✓			
Population < 100K						
Albany, NY	0.5	0.5	✓			
Bellingham, WA	2.0	2.5		✓		
Boulder, CO	15.5	15.8		✓		
Burlington, VT	13.5	31.8		✓		
Davis, CA	2.3	3.4		✓		
Missoula, MT	4.8	7.2	✓			
High value						
Midsized cities	15.5	31.8				
52 large cites	33.0	4.5				
Low value						
Midsized cities	0.5	0.2				
52 large cites	0.0	0.0				
Large cities average	6.3	0.7				

Sources: Midsized City Survey 2011/2012, ACS 2011 (population-based averages are weighted)

Advocacy Organizations: Making it Happen!

by Mary Lauran Hall, Alliance for Biking & Walking

Local Spokes (New York City, NY)

Comprised of nine organizations working on various issues—including Alliance members Transportation Alternatives and Recycle-A-Bicycle—Local Spokes has shown the power of starting conversations without an agenda and letting community members lead the way.

The coalition works in New York City's Chinatown and the Lower East Side, two of the city's most economically challenged and ethnically diverse neighborhoods. The area represents a large population of public housing residents, boasts a large foreign-born population, and registers a median income of $35,000. Parts of the neighborhoods lack public transit access and see heavy traffic congestion, leading to poor air quality. Importantly, the city has invested in substantial bicycle infrastructure in these neighborhoods and throughout the city, and the new Citi Bike bike share system is centered in this vibrant area.

Local Spokes engages local residents in planning and actualizing the neighborhood's bicycling future, breaking down barriers to bicycling through its work as a coalition of diverse neighborhood interests. In addition to transportation advocacy and planning groups, the nine-organization coalition includes Good Old Lower East Side, a housing and preservation organization; Asian Americans for Equality, a social service and development group; Green Map System, a civic engagement mapping platform; and Two Bridges Neighborhood Council, a local neighborhood association.

The coalition spent several years working to "engage, understand and advocate for the community's various perspectives on bicycling through multilingual outreach,

Local Spokes Youth Ambassadors created artwork which was installed along bike paths and greenways in Lower East Side and Chinatown New York City, NY. Photo courtesy of Local Spokes

public participation activities, and a Youth Ambassadors program" (Local Spokes, 2013).

Each year, coalition members worked with ten Youth Ambassadors—high school students who live or attend school in the Lower East Side or Chinatown. The students explored their neighborhoods by bicycle, met people who were involved in designing New York City's streets, and learned the power of their own voices through conversations about urban planning and transportation.

Local Spokes also held visioning workshops and community events, and distributed 1,200 surveys in their two focus neighborhoods. During these sessions, local residents shared their ideas and visions for their neighborhoods. The coalition then distilled community members' ideas into a Neighborhood Action Plan. Released in May of 2012, the plan serves as a blueprint and resource for ongoing neighborhood advocacy.

Local Spokes' fearless approach to creating community partnerships has forged a successful model for transportation advocates and community organizations across North America. The coalition distilled their experiences in community-led planning into a downloadable toolkit, which advocates hope will spur similar initiatives in other cities.

For more information, and to download the toolkit, visit *LocalSpokes.org*.

Georgia Bikes

Georgia Bikes has built a comprehensive network of savvy local advocates and riders who have accumulated an impressive number of statewide legislative and policy wins.

The organization's very first victory, soon after its 2003 founding, was creating "Share the Road" license plates. Revenue from the plates fed a fund for bicycle safety education and outreach, enabling the group to hire Brent Buice as its first Executive Director in 2009. Under Buice's leadership, the organization spent its first staffed year building relationships with two-dozen local advocacy groups and riding clubs around the state.

Laying a grassroots foundation proved to be hugely important. In 2011, Georgia Bikes championed a bundle of pro-bicycling legislation, including a 3-foot passing law. Every state representative and senator heard from at least one constituent in favor of the legislation, allowing the bill to pass both chambers seamlessly and earn a quick signature from the governor.

Since then, Georgia Bikes has been on a roll, racking up policy wins in both proactive and defensive battles.

The organization's first major legislative challenge came from State Senator Butch Miller,

Elected officials riding in the 2012 annual "Georgia Rides to the Capitol" Atlanta, GA. Photo by Timothy J Carroll @Flickr

who introduced a single-file bill that would have made it illegal for bicyclists to ride two abreast. Georgia Bikes responded immediately. The group lined up parents and bike shop owners to testify against the bill in committee, while also engaging with Miller's staff behind the scenes. In short order, the bill was dropped, and Senator Miller agreed to work with the advocates to craft a state Complete Streets policy.

The winning didn't stop there. A few weeks later at Georgia Bikes' annual Ride to the Capitol, the chief engineer of the Georgia Department of Transportation found himself surrounded by bicycle advocates chanting, "Complete the streets!"

In response to the surge of public support and Senator Miller's stated intentions, Georgia Department of Transportation (GDOT) decided to take a proactive approach towards Complete Streets. Advocates worked with the agency to create GDOT's own Complete Streets policy, earning Georgia Bikes the Alliance's 2012 Campaign of the Year award. GDOT has since worked with advocates to address Complete Streets implementation on routine resurfacing projects.

Georgia's new policy is paying off. In April of 2013, a Georgia Bikes board member successfully worked to incorporate bidirectional bicycle lanes on a new bridge in the Atlanta suburbs.

Yet, Georgia Bikes' most public accomplishment lay in exhibiting leadership during an unexpected statewide surge of outrage about an anti-bicycling bill. The legislation, introduced in 2013, would have instituted bicycle registration and would have banned bicycling from some roads. During the outcry, Georgia Bikes positioned itself as the expert entity fighting for bicyclists' rights. Legislators facing angry calls from constituents quickly realized that they had kicked a hornets' nest, and Georgia Bikes tripled their membership and racked up hundreds of new social media followers.

Visit *www.GeorgiaBikes.org* to learn more about Georgia Bikes.

Walkers in the 2013 Annual Walk Boston, MA. Photo by Carla Osberg. Courtesy of WalkBoston

WalkBoston

Despite their name, WalkBoston reaches far beyond Massachusetts' biggest metropolis. From consulting with planners and commenting on proposed designs to leading walking audits and creating walking maps, WalkBoston advocates will go the extra mile to make sure that public spaces throughout the Bay State are designed with people in mind.

"I think of our work as being a bridge between neighborhood groups and municipal or state agencies," said Executive Director Wendy Landman. "We speak both languages."

As part of their work to improve community walkability, WalkBoston advocates often hold workshops and presentations for municipal staff and facilitate public input forums for community members.

But the most effective work is often done out on the street. Advocates bring municipal staff out of the office, onto their communities' streets to experience and identify challenges for pedestrians. These "walkability assessments" are a powerful tool: in the transportation field where planning is often done from a desk, pounding the pavement can help city staff understand how their policies and plans impact peoples' everyday experiences traveling through the community.

WalkBoston advocates have focused particularly on former industrial cities where incomes are lower and people of color and new immigrants make up much of the population. In one such community, design plans for a new school prioritized parking lot access over walkability even though over 85% of students walked to school. Advocates intervened by making recommendations to the design teams about how to better protect students walking to school. Advocates also regularly help communities develop and deepen Safe Routes to School programs.

At the state level, WalkBoston is deeply involved in helping the state implement pro-walking policies. "Massachusetts has been putting in place some terrific policies around modes of travel other than driving," Landman explained. "We've been working with the state and with lots of other organizations to set the stage for change in the coming years."

In 2012, the Massachusetts Department of Transportation set a goal to triple the number of walking, bicycling, and transit trips by 2030. And in 2013, the Secretary of Transportation issued the Healthy Design Directive, stipulating that state transportation projects must take walking and transit into account. Advocates at WalkBoston are working with other organizations to make sure that these plans are implemented with every new project.

"We're hopeful that the 10,000 foot big-picture policies, like the modeshift goal and the healthy transportation compact, will be pulled down into the department and will change the way the department works, and then be further extended to municipal public works and engineering departments" said Landman.

WalkBoston posts downloadable maps of walking routes on their website at *WalkBoston.org/Resources/Maps.*

Members of the RSST gather to survey a multi-jurisdictional freeway overpass popular with bicyclists.
Photo courtesy of Silicon Valley Bicycle Coalition

Silicon Valley Bicycle Coalition

The counties south of San Francisco that make up Silicon Valley are not just home to some of the world's most booming tech companies; they are also fertile ground for bicycling. And the region's growing population of riders is lucky that Silicon Valley Bicycle Coalition is there to work across the region to advocate for more bicycle-friendly policies and improvements.

Silicon Valley Bicycle Coalition, or SVBC, is pioneering a highly collaborative Vision Zero campaign to find solutions to some of the tough problems the area faces. While other organizations around the country have taken on Vision Zero campaigns—initiatives that aim to eliminate fatal bicycle crashes—SVBC's initiative stands out for the unique ways in which it involves stakeholders from across disciplines and jurisdictions.

The idea emerged when the Coalition hosted a summit on traffic safety with Stanford Hospital & Clinics Trauma Center. Staff at the clinic were concerned about the number of people who were involved in fatal or life-altering crashes while bicycling. In response, SVBC worked with the Hospital to convene a diverse cross-section of stakeholders to discuss the issues around serious crashes. Conversation at the summit was so rich that the event's key stakeholders agreed to continue convening as a lasting group to stop fatal crashes.

The stakeholders organized as the Vision Zero Roadway Safety Solutions Team (RSST). Team members are diverse in both discipline and local origin: the RSST includes city councilmembers, planners, and engineers; DMV staff; AAA representatives; staff from California's Department of Transportation; first responders; law enforcement officials; and public health department staff from throughout Silicon Valley. The RSST is working to encourage safer infrastructure, develop behavior-changing public messaging, and institute better bicycle and motorist education.

"We've really built, over the last two years, a collaborative," said Corinne Winter, executive director of Silicon Valley Bicycle Coalition. "It's just been phenomenal to watch."

The Vision Zero initiative is already having a positive effect on how public officials approach safe street design. Small towns within Silicon Valley's counties that previously had contradictory active transportation policies have begun to coordinate their bicycle and pedestrian design standards to ensure a smooth ride from point A to B. Transportation planners, armed with knowledge about locations of bike crashes in recent years, have held numerous site visits and targeted the most dangerous areas for safety treatments.

Involving stakeholders from many different professions related to bicycling has been essential, said Winter. "The law enforcement guys have a very different perspective on what happens on the roadways than the public works folks do."

Learn more about Vision Zero at *www.VisionZeroInitiative.com/Concept* and Silicon Valley Bicycle Coalition at *BikeSiliconValley.org*

Hedding Street Bikeway. San Jose, CA
Photo by Richard Masoner / Cyclelicious @ Flickr

across borders

Belo Horizonte, Brazil:
Creating Change Through People Power

by Colin Hughes, Institute for Transportation and Development Policy

While many of the picture postcards from Rio de Janeiro show off Copacabana's beachside bicycle path, the reality of bicycling in Brazil's largest cities is far less sunny. Bicycle lanes have been rare in Brazilian cities, and bicycle mode share in Brazil was estimated to average less than 1% of all trips in cities with over one million people just ten years ago (BIANCO, 2003).

However, the pedals are beginning to turn, particularly in Belo Horizonte, home to 2.5 million people in southeastern Brazil. Fifty kilometers (31 miles) of new bicycle lanes were installed last year, and 300 additional kilometers (186 miles) and a bike share system are planned for installation by 2016. Several streets in the city center have also been redesigned to be pedestrian-friendly, and walking and bicycling as a mode share is growing.

These changes did not happen easily. Dedicated, forward-thinking city staff and advocates led the way.

Bike Anjo (Bike Angel). Belo Horizonte, Brazil
Photo by upslon @ Flickr (CC BY-SA)

BHTrans, the city transportation agency, stands out among major Brazilian cities, not just in building bicycle and pedestrian infrastructure and encouraging people to bicycle and walk, but also in the way it is conducting long-range transportation planning and community outreach.

While the value of planning is well-accepted in the U.S., in Brazil it is largely ignored. Manager of Mobility at BHTrans, Marcelo Cintra do Amaral, knew Belo Horizonte needed to change its ways and plan for the future. He guided the development of a plan to integrate a multi-modal transport system in Belo Horizonte.

Completed in 2012, the plan envisioned large investments in bus rapid transit, bicycling, and walking. The plan was not only Belo Horizonte's first transportation plan, but also the first such plan in Brazil. It was so warmly received that the Brazilian National Congress passed a National Mobility Law shortly after, requiring all cities in Brazil to write their own mobility plan, using Belo Horizonte as a model.

Eveline Prado Trevisan was not much of a bicyclist when she took her job as Project Manager of Pedela BH, the city's bicycling program. Yet, when she leaves her office on Fridays, she does not go home. Instead, she meets up with a diverse group of bicyclists for a regular Friday night ride around the city. She rides with the bicyclists, young and old, in spandex and in denim, to better understand the needs of bicyclists. Bicycle lane design standards are not well established in Brazil, and some lessons in Belo Horizonte have been learned the hard way.

Riding the new bicycle lanes in Belo Horizonte, one encounters a mix of both well-designed lanes and some that are too narrow, or too close

Friday night bicycling group. Belo Horizonte, Brazil. Photo by Colin Hughes

to traffic and car doors. Many lanes still require revision and improvement. But Prado and BHTrans have maintained a strong relationship with city bicyclists. They are listening to bicyclists, both informally and through surveys, about what currently works and what does not, and are developing a list of improvements to tackle. In addition, they are researching new design standards to adopt, with the goal of constantly improving the city for bicycling.

Bicycling advocates are also active in the city and include recreational bicycling groups like Mountain Bike BH, urban cycling advocacy groups like BH Cycle, community bicycle shops like Cicloficina, and gatherings like Critical Mass. Twenty-one-year-old Augosto Schmidt is active in bicycle advocacy in Belo Horizonte and works with another bicycling promotion program called Bike Angels. Bike Angels exposes new people to bicycling through the use of a loaner bike, instruction on city bicycling, and help finding safe commuting routes in the city.

Thanks to the work of individuals like Marcelo Cintra do Amaral, Eveline Prado, and Augosto Schmidt, Belo Horizonte is not only on its way to becoming a great place to walk and ride a bicycle, it is leading a new approach to sustainable mobility for the whole country of Brazil.

10 What's Next for Bicycling and Walking?

In recent decades, communities across the U.S. have increasingly recognized the value of integrating bicycling and walking into the transportation system. As research continues to reveal the health, safety, social, and economic benefits of active transportation, communities are prioritizing funding and policy change at higher levels. The Alliance for Biking & Walking supports these improvements and offers the following recommendations for continued growth.

Portland, OR. Photo by Greg Raisman

Diversify the Approach

As more and more people seek to incorporate active transportation into their daily lives, cities and states of all sizes are realizing that transportation is a multi-modal system that affects public health, workforce productivity, and economic development. Walking and bicycling are essential elements of the transportation mix. Our streets are "complete" when they accommodate people of all abilities and ages traveling on foot, on bicycle, in transit, and in cars; when our streets are complete, they create safe, comfortable, and vibrant communities (Chapters 3 & 6). Increased pedestrian and bicyclist traffic improves local economies, boosts public health, improves air quality, and helps improve the transportation system's efficiency for everyone (Chapters 3 & 4).

United States transportation planning over the last half century has prioritized automobile connectivity, often at the expense of making transportation more difficult for the third of Americans who do not drive (FHWA, 2014). Significant transportation challenges exist in low-income communities where residents often cannot afford cars. Hispanic and Black Americans are more likely to be fatally injured while bicycling or walking than their white, non-Hispanic peers (Chapter 3). Twenty-one percent of the U.S. population is too young to drive; many more people are either unable to drive or choose not to. Ensuring that the road network is comfortable and accessible for pedestrians and bicyclists helps make the streets navigable for all people.

- The Alliance recommends that state and city governments adopt policies and street designs that improve bicycling and walking for all people, in all communities. Public officials have the opportunity to institute policies and street designs that make it possible—and easy—to get around without a car (Chapters 5 & 6). These improvements benefit whole communities, especially people of color, people with low-income, youth, senior citizens, and people with disabilities.
- The Alliance recommends that data collected on bicycling and walking include representation of people from different racial and ethnic groups, income levels, genders, and abilities. Improving bicycling and walking for all people requires understanding who is currently bicycling and walking, and who is deterred from these modes of transportation.

Integrate Accessibility

Building a bicycle path or installing a pedestrian crosswalk does not, by itself, accomplish transportation accessibility. Improved mobility means thinking about the transportation network from pedestrian and bicyclist perspectives. Engineering public space from a motorized vehicle perspective has been the go-to approach in the U.S. since the 1950s—and remains pervasive and ingrained. Today, we realize that such planning causes multiple problems and often fails to match community values, support local economies, and keep travelers safe.

Elected officials, agency staff, and advocates are working together to put the needs of citizens first when planning and redeveloping the transportation network. As a result, many communities now integrate bicycling and walking more successfully. Great neighborhoods for bicycling and walking boast streets, paths, and networks with signage, safety elements, and traffic pattern considerations for all users. By taking a Complete Streets approach when building and updating roads, communities can ensure that improvements for motorized traffic do not inadvertently make existing bicycle and pedestrian routes more dangerous or disconnected (Chapter 5 & 6).

Improving accessibility to transportation education is another approach to making transportation systems safe and comfortable for all. All travelers—people riding bicycles, people walking, transit operators, and drivers—

Chicago, IL. Photo by Andrea Milne

can be educated about how various modes of transportation work together to create a complete, safe, and efficient system. Drivers must understand bicyclists' rights. Bicyclists must understand their own rights and responsibilities, as well as the rights of motorists and pedestrians. Pedestrians, too, must understand their own rights and responsibilities on the street, and the rules of the road for all other modes of transportation they will encounter.

Ultimately, good design will help improve safe behavior by all. State and city leaders can make this type of education accessible for everyone through on-street signage; bicyclist and pedestrian courses in schools through programs such as Safe Routes to School; driver education, including bicycle and pedestrian safety; consistent police enforcement; and correction programs that send road users to the classroom following a citation or warning (Chapter 5 & 8).

- The Alliance recommends that advocates, agencies, and elected officials work together to leverage all eligible funding at the federal, state, and local levels to fulfill the public desire for safe and well-designed bicycling and walking infrastructure. Advocacy Advance, a partnership of the Alliance and the League of American Bicyclists, provides resources, technical assistance, and trainings to help educate all community and state leaders about eligible funding and successful examples from other states, regions, and cities. See *www.AdvocacyAdvance.org*

- The Alliance recommends that city leaders work with advocates and community organizations to implement initiatives like Open Streets, Rides and Walks with the Mayor, and other opportunities to encourage bicycling and walking. While some communities organize such initiatives as one-time events, there is increasing evidence that these encouragement initiatives lead to higher levels of bicycling and walking on a daily basis.

Standardize the Data

The Benchmarking Project improves the national movement to collect previously unavailable data on bicycling and walking. This project's continuation is essential to tracking new trends and progress. Because the Benchmarking Project draws available data on bicycling and walking from many different sources, it highlights the difficulties associated with variations in available data. In order to better understand the extent and impacts of bicycling and walking, researchers, agencies, and policymakers need standardized methodologies for data collection.

Some data are collected equally across all states and municipalities for federal programs, yet definitions and reporting methods differ from agency to agency. While leadership on data standards is preferred at the federal level, the Alliance for Biking & Walking welcomes standard-setting by professional associations, such as the National Association of City Transportation Officials (NACTO) and the American Association of State Highway and Transportation Officials (AASHTO).

- The Alliance recommends that a standardized methodology be developed to track modes of transportation for all purposes and demographics at the city level. The National Household Travel Survey (NHTS) provides infrequent (every 5–7 years) estimates of trip mode share from small sample sizes, leaving many cities and states with incomplete and outdated data at the local level. The American Community Survey (ACS) tracks mode of transportation annually at the local state and city level, but only for people commuting to work. Both of these surveys could be improved by coordinating efforts.

  Many states and cities have already begun tracking bicycle and pedestrian trips. However, there is great disparity in quality, frequency, and methodology of these data (Chapter 2). Consistent counting methods will provide a more accurate image of bicycling and walking in the U.S.

- The Alliance recommends that the Federal Highway Administration (FHWA) set standards for coding transportation projects so that spending on bicycling and walking can be more accurately tracked. All state departments of transportation report to FHWA their federal funds spent on bicycling and walking improvement projects. However, variations in project coding methods often make data on funding inaccurate or incomparable between states.

  For example, one location may not code a larger project as a bicycle and pedestrian project even if it includes bicycle and pedestrian subcomponents. Another location may take the opposite approach by breaking the project into its parts (Chapter 5). Furthermore, differences in coding can make it difficult to identify which projects took place in which cities. Some projects are coded by county, some by standard place code, and some by urbanized area. If projects that spanned a county also included codes for the cities affected by the project, it would be easier to obtain accurate spending data at the local level.

- The Alliance recommends that FHWA develop a more uniform method of tracking federal safety funding. Specifically, the agency could develop a tracking method to determine what percentage of federal safety funds each state uses for bicycle and pedestrian projects. With great disparities between bicycle and pedestrian mode share and fatality rates, it is essential that officials and advocates push for safety funding for bicycle and pedestrian facilities that is proportional to bicycle and pedestrian fatalities (Chapter 5).
- The Alliance recommends that FHWA develop a framework for best practices that states and local jurisdictions can reference to conduct audits and report on bicycle and pedestrian facilities every one to two years. Many states and cities were unable to provide complete data on existing bicycle and pedestrian infrastructure, such as miles of sidewalks, bicycle lanes, trails, and number of bicycle racks. FHWA could collaborate with the Federal Transit Administration (FTA) to audit access to—and gaps in—public transit facilities (Chapters 6 & 7).
- The Alliance recommends that state and city governments produce a report every one to two years indicating the shortfall in funding needed to complete their bicycle and pedestrian system. This would provide vital data on cost needs—something that has existed for highways and bridges but not for bicycle and pedestrian facilities (Chapter 5).
- The Alliance recommends that state and city governments work with advocates and community organizations to track participation levels and other outcomes associated with bicycle and pedestrian encouragement and education initiatives. Tracking participation levels in education and encouragement events is sparse, even though evaluation is a key component to measuring the success or impact of these efforts. For example, a city could report on how many people participated in Bike to Work Day and, through a survey sample, could ask what influence this event had on participants' intentions to bicycle to work in the future. These measurements, tracked over time, could help evaluate the program's effectiveness.

Keep it Going!

The Alliance initiated the Benchmarking Project over a decade ago because we knew "what isn't counted, doesn't count." With this 4th *Benchmarking Report* and the data we have compiled through the years, we know that much progress has been made and much more progress remains to be made. We urge advocates, agency staff, elected officials, and media to utilize this report to its fullest (see page 32) and work together to help make our communities better and safer places to bicycle and walk.

Visit *www.BikeWalkAlliance.org/Benchmarking* to follow the Benchmarking Project and progress of bicycling and walking initiatives across the U.S.

Portland, OR. Photo by Greg Raisman

OVERVIEW OF DATA SOURCES

Source	Description	Method of Data Collection	Frequency of Data Collection	Last Date Available[1]
ACS	American Community Survey: a survey conducted by the U.S. Census Bureau that collects year-round data, and releases new data annually	Similar to Census long form; (about three million households)	Continuous	2011
APTA	American Public Transportation Association—Public Transportation Vehicle Database: collects and summarizes data on transit agency vehicles	Data are from the National Transit Database (NTD) report published by the U.S. Federal Transit Administration (FTA). APTA supplements these data with special surveys.	Yearly	2012
BLS	Bureau of Labor Statistics	Average annual expenditures and characteristics for MSAs, Consumer Expenditure Survey, 2010–2011	Yearly	2010/11
BRFSS	Behavioral Risk Factor Surveillance System: from Centers for Disease Control and Prevention (CDC); statewide health information	Telephone health survey	Continuous	2010 (cities) 2011 (states)
BTS RITA	Bureau of Transportation Statistics: Research and Innovative Technology Administration	State Transportation Statistics 2011, a statistical profile of transportation in the 50 states and the District of Columbia.	Yearly	2011
Census	From U.S. Census Bureau	Mailed forms, and house visit for nonresponders	Every 10 years	2010
FARS	Fatality Analysis Reporting System: federal database of the National Highway Traffic Safety Administration (NHTSA) of vehicle injuries and fatalities	FARS analyst from each state collects data from governments	Yearly	2011
FHWA - FMIS	Federal Highway Administration (FHWA) Fiscal Management Information System (FMIS)	Data reported to FHWA from state and local government agencies	Continuous	2012
GHSA	Governors Highway Safety Association tracks distracted driving laws on cell phone use and texting while driving	Data collected from the Insurance Institute for Highway Safety and State Highway Safety Offices	Continuous	2013
LAB	League of American Bicyclists: Bicycle Friendly State program surveys collect information on statewide policies, education, enforcement, and other efforts aimed at bicycle promotion	Online surveys sent to state bicycle and pedestrian coordinators	Yearly	2013
NCSRTS	National Center for Safe Routes to School: (Walk To School Day Participation) tracks numbers of schools signed up to participate (Safe Routes to School [SRTS] National Program): Quarterly SRTS Program Tracking Brief provides information about state SRTS programs	(Walk to School Day): online form completed by event organizer (SRTS National Program): questionnaires to state Safe Routes to School Coordinators	(Walk to School Day): Continuous (SRTS National Program): Quarterly	2013

(1) Latest date of availability, presented in this report, as of June 2013.

Source	Description	Method of Data Collection	Frequency of Data Collection	Last Date Available[1]
NCSC	National Complete Streets Coalition: tracks and assists with Complete Streets policies	Monitors adoption of policies through network, media, etc.	Continuous	2013
NHTS	National Household Travel Survey: inventory of daily and long-distance travel; NHTS is a national survey, and analysis below the national level have problems with small samples; also, NHTS data is reported by metropolitan areas so data shown for cities are estimates only	Survey of 26,000 households (additional 44,000 from nine "add-on" areas); collected by the FHWA	Every 5–7 years since 1969	2009
NOAA	National Oceanic and Atmospheric Administration, US Climate Normals	Precipitation and temperature data archived at the National Climatic Data Center from various sources including weather satelites, radars, airport weather stations, National Weather Service cooperative observers, etc.	Continuous	1971–2000
NTEC	National Transportation Enhancements Clearinghouse: sponsored by the FHWA and Rails-to-Trails Conservancy, reports on funded projects	Information comes from funded Transportation Enhancement (TE) projects	Yearly	2012
RTC	Rails-to-Trails Conservancy: tracks current information about the trails movement and rail-trail use at the national and state level	Monitors rail trails through media, interviews with trail managers, and network	"Periodically"	2013
SRTSNP	Safe Routes to School National Partnership: monitors and collects benchmarking data on the national Safe Routes to School program and produces quarterly "State of the States" report	Secondary data collection: from the Federal Highway Administration and other sources	Quarterly	2012
STN	School Transportation News: inventory of U.S. transportation data elements on a state-by-state basis, specifically including student enrollment and school bus information	Surveys to the pupil transportation section of state departments of education	Yearly	2013
USDOE	US Dept of Education: National Center for Education Statistics (2010–2011)	Public Elementary and Secondary School Student Enrollment and Staff Counts From the Common Core of Data: School Year 2010–2011	Yearly	2010/11
USHCN	United States Historical Climatology Network: daily and monthly meteorological data	1,000 observing stations	Continuous	2004–2005
WISQARS	Web-based Injury Statistics Query and Reporting System. Center of Disease Control's online database that provides fatal and nonfatal injury, violent death, and cost of injury data.	Data are from the National Electronic Injury Surveillance System—All Injury Program (NEISS-AIP) operated by the U.S. Consumer Product Safety Commission with CDC's NCIPC.	Yearly	2011

CHALLENGES WITH TRIP DATA

Determining how many people bicycle or walk is not easily answered with the limited data available. Currently, the most reliable source of data comes from the U.S. Census Journey to Work data and the annual American Community Survey. However, Census figures are limiting and inaccurate for a number of reasons. The Census Bureau only collects data on the main mode of transportation to work. This measure excludes trips of individuals not in the workforce, such as children, retirees, and other unemployed people.

Moreover, other trip purposes, such as shopping and recreational outings, are not captured. The Census Bureau only reports the main mode of transportation to work, thus excluding many walking and bicycling trips used for shorter segments of commutes. Trips to transit stops, between a parking garage and the office, or a walk down the street for lunch are all missed in this data set. It also misses people who walk or bicycle to work one or two days a week.

Comparing Census and ACS Data

It is also not completely accurate to compare data from the decennial Census to the annual American Community Survey. While the decennial Census is taken only in April, ACS data are collected throughout the year. The time of year the Census data are collected might influence reported bike and walk share of work trips. This is particularly true in cities such as Minneapolis and Boston, which can still be cold in April. Although the decennial Census has a larger sample size, in this case, the ACS may more accurately reflect bicycle travel because it is collected throughout the year.

The biggest difference in the surveying between the ACS and the Census is that the ACS is done every year instead of every decade. However, the Census provides detailed socioeconomic data and for much smaller areas. There are differences in the ACS and the Census when it comes to residence rules, universes, and reference periods. However, comparisons can generally be made for most population and housing subjects. For some categories such as disability, income, and employment status, the U.S. Census Bureau recommends not comparing, or comparing with caution. But according to the Bureau, the category "means of transportation to work" is comparable from the ACS to the Census and between the different years of the ACS.

Travel Data for All Trip Purposes

The National Household Travel Study (NHTS) is another source of data on daily travel, sponsored by the Bureau of Transportation Statistics and the Federal Highway Administration. The NHTS attempts to collect data on all trips, not just trips to work. However, because it is a national survey, analysis below the national level has problems with small sample sizes. It is also difficult to extract data for cities from this source as it uses Metropolitan Statistical Areas (MSAs), which often stretch beyond city boundaries. Also, the NHTS is only collected every 5 to 7 years. Due to these limitations, NHTS data on city and state levels should be considered as rough estimates for walking and bicycling in these areas.

The NHTS methodology includes a brief phone survey that gathers basic demographic information and asks the person if he or she is willing to keep a travel diary for a day to record all trips by members of the household, including children. Travel diaries are mailed to the household and NHTS officials follow up to answer any questions. Survey participants then receive a follow-up call from NHTS to collect information from the travel diary. They are asked a number of questions on their travel behavior during their assigned travel day and during the last week including such questions as how many times they went for a walk or bike ride, how long did they spend bicycling or walking, and (if they drive) how many minutes it takes them to walk from where they park to their workplace.

Other Trip Count Efforts

Because of the serious gap in reliable data on bicycling (and walking) trips, there have been numerous efforts to create a more reliable means to measure travel. Barnes and Krizek (2005) developed a formula for determining total bicycling trips by multiplying the commute share by 1.5 and adding 0.3%. Some cities have done their own travel counts in an attempt to determine the share of all bicycle trips. See Chapter 1, page 57, for an overview of the counting initiatives reported by cities and states in the benchmarking survey.

The National Bicycle and Pedestrian Documentation Project (NBPD), a joint effort of Alta Planning & Design and the Institute of Transportation Engineers Pedestrian and Bicycle Council, sets detailed standards and guidelines and provides tools for performing bicycle and pedestrian counts and surveys. See page 56 for more information on this nationwide initiative to improve mode share count data.

Applications

Improved collection of bicycling and walking data would assist transportation planners, public health officials, and elected officials in making informed decisions. Transportation planners would receive information regarding the impact of bicycling and walking facilities, and be able to put information on injuries in perspective with information on the levels of bicycling and walking. A robust data collection system could help public health officials target and assess community-level interventions for physical activity and injury prevention efforts. Elected officials would have access to the same types of data that exist for motor vehicles, including information on the cost of the projects and the subsequent effect on bicycling and walking.

The World Health Organization Regional Office for Europe has developed a promising tool, the Health Economic Assessment Tool (HEAT) for bicycling. This tool informs decisions about bicycling and walking infrastructure by providing an estimate of the economic value of positive health effects of bicycling. HEAT for bicycling requires information on the number of trips taken by bicycle and the average trip distance. The economic savings that result from reduced mortality due to the regular physical activity of bicycling to work can then be estimated based on these inputs and best-evidence default values.

Tools, like HEAT, can help estimate the value of health effects of current levels of bicycling, calculate the health-related economic benefits when planning new bicycling infrastructure, or provide input into more comprehensive cost-benefit analyses. When bicycling and walking data collection is as robust as other modes of transportation, it assists professionals and the public in making more informed decisions about the design of their communities.

CITY SURVEY TOOL

The Benchmarking Project hopes to expand the availability of bicycling and walking data to cities of all sizes. The following is a list of the survey questions sent to the 52 most populous cities in October 2012. Cities are invited to use this tool to collect local data for further research. Please credit the Alliance for Biking & Walking, Benchmarking Project with any use of this tool.

NOTE: Throughout this survey, the term "city" refers to within the official city limits. Please do not include data from the surrounding suburbs or metropolitan area.

For which city are you completing this survey?
(dropdown menu with city names)

BICYCLE AND PEDESTRIAN MODESHARE

1. Does your city conduct household travel surveys for all trips taken? Yes/No/Unknown

If yes, please answer the following questions:
a) Does the survey specifically include pedestrian trips? Yes/No/Unknown
b) Does the survey specifically include bicyclist trips? Yes/No/Unknown
c) What year was the most recent survey conducted?
d) What percentage of all trips surveyed were by foot?
e) What percentage of all trips surveyed were by bicycle?

2. Does your city conduct counts of bike/ped commuting? Yes/No/Unknown

If yes, please answer the following questions:
a) Does the survey specifically include pedestrian trips? Yes/No/Unknown
b) Does the survey specifically include bicyclist trips? Yes/No/Unknown
c) What year was the most recent survey conducted?
d) How many walking commuters were counted? What percentage of all modes counted did pedestrians represent?
e) How many bicycling commuters were counted? What percentage of all modes counted did bicyclists represent?

3. Does your city conduct Cordon counts?
Definition: Cordon counts are conducted by counting vehicles and/or people who cross a selected location within a specified timeframe.

If yes, please answer the following questions:
a) Does the count specifically include pedestrian trips? Yes/No/Unknown
b) Does the count specifically include bicyclist trips? Yes/No/Unknown
c) What year was the most recent survey conducted?
d) How many pedestrians were counted? What percentage of all modes counted did pedestrians represent?
e) How many bicyclists were counted? What percentage of all modes counted did bicyclists represent?

4. Does your city conduct any other method of count?

If yes, please answer the following questions:
a) Briefly, what was the methodology of these counts?
b) Does the survey specifically include pedestrian trips? Yes/No/Unknown
c) Does the survey specifically include bicyclist trips? Yes/No/Unknown
d) What year was the most recent survey conducted?
e) How many pedestrians were counted? What percentage of all modes counted did pedestrians represent?
f) How many bicyclists were counted? What percentage of all modes counted did bicyclists represent?

FUNDING BIKING AND WALKING

5. Does your city have an overall bicycle and pedestrian spending target? Yes/No/Unknown

If yes, please answer the following questions:
a) What is the current target as a percentage of the city's transportation budget?
b) What is the timeline to reach the target? (eg. how many months or years?)

6. How much did your city spend on bicycle and pedestrian programs (infrastructure and education, including things such as sidewalk improvements, bike lanes, curb cuts, trails, classroom education, safety, literature, etc.) in the last two years?
a) Dedicated city budget funds to bike/ped in 2011:
b) Dedicated city budget funds to bike/ped in 2012

7. How much did your city spend on transportation in total
a) in 2011?
b) in 2012?

8. Please tell us about any unique bicycling or pedestrian funding activities in your city.

STAFFING

9. Expressed in FTE, how many city employees work on bicycle and/or pedestrian issues as detailed in their work description in the last two years (including Safe Routes to School and regular contractor hours)?

10. Does your city fund staff on bikes (for example, police and EMTs)? Yes/No/Unknown

If yes, please answer the following questions:
a) How many total FTE staff on bikes were funded in 2011?
b) How many total FTE staff on bikes were funded in 2012?
c) Approximately what percentage of these FTE were police on bikes?
d) Approximately what percentage of these FTE were other staff on bikes (eg. EMT)?

11. Does your city fund staff on foot (for example, police and EMTs)? Yes/No/Unknown

If yes, please answer the following questions:
a) How many total FTE staff on foot were funded in 2011?
b) How many total FTE staff on foot were funded in 2012?
c) Approximately what percentage of these FTE were police on foot?
d) Approximately what percentage of these FTE were other staff on foot (eg. EMT)?

12. On average, what percentage of FTE city-funded police are on patrol on bike or foot at one time?

13. Please tell us about any unique staffing circumstances that have aided in bike/ped initiatives in your city.

EXISTING BICYCLE AND PEDESTRIAN FACILITIES

14. How many miles of each of the following does your city currently have in place? Do not include bicycle boulevards or cycle tracks in your calculations here. These are included in the next question.
 a) Lane miles of on-street bike lanes
 Count both directions when bike lanes are on both sides of the street (i.e. two miles of bike lanes on both sides of the two-way street = 4 miles of bike lanes)
 b) Miles of multi-use paths and dedicated bike paths
 These are paths that may be next to, but are physically separated from roads
 c) Miles of on-road signed bike routes
 Signed routes are on roads, but not marked as separate lanes
 d) Miles of sidewalks
 Count both directions when sidewalks are on both sides of the street

15. Which of the following innovative bike/ped infrastructure has your city implemented? Check all that apply

SHARED LANE MARKINGS: Such as sharrows
 How many lane miles?

BICYCLE TRAFFIC LIGHTS
 How many intersections?

BIKE BOXES: Advanced stop lines. For more information, see http://nacto.org/cities-for-cycling/design-guide/intersection-treatments/bike-boxes/.
 How many?

BIKE CORRALS: On-street bike parking. For more information, see http://www.sfbike.org/?corrals
 How many corrals?
 How many bike spaces?

COLORED BIKE LANES: Such as green lanes

CONTRA FLOW LANES FOR BIKES: Bike lanes permitting two-way bike travel on one-way streets. See http://www.bicyclinginfo.org/bikesafe/case_studies/casestudy.cfm?CS_NUM=209 for more information.
 How many lane miles?

BICYCLE BOULEVARDS / NEIGHBORHOOD GREENWAYS: Low-volume streets optimized for bicycle travel through traffic calming and diversion, signage, pavement markings, and intersection crossing treatment. For more information, see www.bicyclinginfo.org/faqs/answer.cfm?id=3976
 How many lane miles?

CYCLE TRACKS / PROTECTED BIKE LANES: An exclusive bicycle facility that combines the user experience of a separated path with the on-street infrastructure of a conventional bike lane. Uses barriers, bollards or paint to distinguish bike lane from motorized traffic lane. For more information, see http://nacto.org/cities-for-cycling/design-guide/cycle-tracks/
 How many lane miles?

HOME ZONE / WOONERFS: An area, usually residential, where motorists and other users share the street without boundaries, such as lanes and curbs. For more information, see http://streetswiki.wikispaces.com/Woonerf
 How many designated locations?
 What is the average width of the area(s)?
 What is the total length in miles?

16. Does your city currently have a public bike-sharing program? Yes / No, but one is currently being developed / No, and there are no plans to develop a program / Unknown

If yes, please answer the following questions:
 a) Who leads implementation of this program? Check all that apply: Government/Nonprofit organization/Unknown/Other: please specify
 b) Does your city government provide financial sponsorship for this program? Yes/No/Unknown
 c) How many bicycles are made available to the public at any given time?
 d) How many stations are in operation?
 e) How many total docking spaces are there?
 f) Are the number of bike share check-outs tracked? Yes/No/Unknown

 If yes, please answer the following questions:
 i. How many total check-outs were there in 2011?
 ii. What was the average daily check-out rate in 2011?
 iii. How many total check-outs were there in 2012?
 iv. What was the average daily check-out rate in 2012?

17. Please tell us about any unique bicycling or pedestrian infrastructure in your city.

PLANNED BICYCLE AND PEDESTRIAN INFRASTRUCTURE

18. Does your city have published goals to increase bicycle facilities? Yes/No/Unknown

19. Does your city have published goals to increase pedestrian facilities? Yes/No/Unknown

20. How many miles of planned bicycle facilities does your city currently have? Include those published in local transportation plans

21. Over how many years are these bicycle facilities planned? What is your planning horizon - e.g. over the next 5 years, over the next 25 years, etc.?

22. How many miles of planned pedestrian facilities does your city have? Include those published in local transportation plans.

23. Over how many years are these pedestrian facilities planned? What is your planning horizon - e.g. over the next 5 years, over the next 25 years, etc.?

BIKE-TRANSIT INTEGRATION

24. Does your city have bus service? Yes/No/Unknown

If yes, please answer the following questions:
 a) What percent of buses servicing your city have bike racks?
 b) How many bus stops are within your city?

25. Does your city have local rail service? Yes/No/Unknown

If yes, please answer the following questions:
 a) How many hours per week do the trains run? (0-168 hours)
 b) How many hours per week are bikes allowed roll-on access? (0-168 hours)
 c) What are the legal limits for how many bikes can board a train car?
 d) How many rail stops are within your city?

26. How many bike parking spaces are at transit stops (bus and/or rail) within your city?

27. Please tell us about any unique efforts to improve biking and transit integration in your city.

BICYCLING AND WALKING POLICIES & PLANNING

28. Does your city have a published goal to
   a) increase walking? Yes/No/Unknown
   b) increase biking? Yes/No/Unknown
   c) increase physical activity? Yes/No/Unknown
   d) decrease pedestrian fatalities? Yes/No/Unknown
   e) decrease bicyclist fatalities? Yes/No/Unknown

29. Does your city enforce drivers not yielding to pedestrians and cyclists when nonmotorized traffic has the right-of way?

   If yes, what is the fine and/or penalty associated with this enforcement?

30. Does your city enforce bicyclist violations of road rules? Yes/No/Unknown

31. Does your city enforce pedestrian violations of road rules? Yes/No/Unknown

32. Has your city adopted
   a) the NACTO Urban Bikeway Design Guide for facility design standards? Yes/No/Unknown
   b) a combined bicycle and pedestrian master plan? Yes/No/Unknown
   c) a stand-alone bicycle master plan? Yes/No/Unknown
   d) a stand-alone pedestrian master plan? Yes/No/Unknown
   e) a trails master plan? Yes/No/Unknown
   f) a mountain bike master plan? Yes/No/Unknown
   g) a policy setting minimum spending levels for bicycling and pedestrian facilities and programs? Yes/No/Unknown
   h) infrastructure project selection criteria that include physical activity? Yes/No/Unknown
   i) performance measures that include increasing biking? Yes/No/Unknown
   j) performance measures that include increasing walking? Yes/No/Unknown

33. Does your city have a policy that requires
   a) a MINIMUM number of car parking spaces for new developments? Yes/No/Unknown
   b) a MAXIMUM number of car parking spaces for new developments? Yes/No/Unknown
   c) bike parking in buildings or parking garages? Yes/No/Unknown
   d) bike parking for new developments? Yes/No/Unknown
   e) secure or valet parking at public events (such as festivals, ball games, concerts, etc)? Yes/No/Unknown

34. Does your city have a plan for reducing carbon emission? Yes/No/Unknown

   If yes, please answer the following questions:
   a) Does it include bicycle use?
   b) Does it include pedestrian use?

35. Does your city have a bicycle, pedestrian, and/or Safe Routes to School advisory council that meets regularly? Check all that apply.
   Combined bicycle/pedestrian advisory council
   Standalone bicycle-focused advisory council
   Standalone pedestrian-focused advisory council
   Safe Routes to School advisory council
   None of the above

   If your city has one or more of the above advisory councils, please answer the following questions:

   a) How often does each council meet?
   Choose one: annually, quarterly, monthly, or not applicable
      Combined bicycle/pedestrian advisory council
      Standalone bicycle-focused advisory council
      Standalone pedestrian-focused advisory council
      Safe Routes to School advisory council

   b) Is there interagency participation in these councils?
   Choose one: yes, no, or not applicable
      Combined bicycle/pedestrian advisory council
      Standalone bicycle-focused advisory council
      Standalone pedestrian-focused advisory council
      Safe Routes to School advisory council

   c) Is there user group representation on these councils?
   Choose one: yes, no, or not applicable
      Combined bicycle/pedestrian advisory council
      Standalone bicycle-focused advisory council
      Standalone pedestrian-focused advisory council
      Safe Routes to School advisory council

   d) How is council membership determined?
   Choose one: appointment, nomination/election, open invitation, or not applicable
      Combined bicycle/pedestrian advisory council
      Standalone bicycle-focused advisory council
      Standalone pedestrian-focused advisory council
      Safe Routes to School advisory council

36. Please tell us about any unique bicycling or pedestrian policies and planning initiatives in your city.

SAFE ROUTES TO SCHOOL (SRTS)

37. How many pupils (grades K-12) attend public schools in your city?

38. How many bike parking spaces are at public schools in your city?

39. Does your city have a policy that requires minimum acreage for school siting? Check with Department of Education staff. Yes/No/Unknown

   If yes, what is the requirement in acres?

40. Does your city have a policy
   a) that places children in schools for any reason other than proximity to residence? Check with Department of Education staff.
   b) that requires biking and walking access for students and staff?
   c) that requires bike parking at schools?

41. Does your city sponsor a SRTS program? Yes/No/Unknown

42. What percentage of schools in your city participates in a SRTS program?

43. How many students in your city are served by a SRTS program?

44. How is the program funded? Check all that apply
- Federal funds
- Local funds
- Regional funds
- Private funds
- Unknown
- Not applicable
- Other: Please specify

45. Please tell us about any unique efforts to create safe routes to school in your city.

EDUCATION AND ENCOURAGEMENT

46. Have schools in your city participated in a Bike and/or Walk to School event in the past two school years? Yes/No/Unknown

If yes, please answer the following questions:
a) What percentage of schools in your city participated in this event in the 2010/2011 school year?
b) How many students participated in the 2010/2011 school year?
c) What percentage of schools in your city participated in this event in the 2011/2012 school year?
d) How many students participated in the 2011/2012 school year?

47. Were youth bicycle education courses available in your city in the past two years? ("Youth" refers to ages <18)
Yes/No/Unknown

If yes, please answer the following questions:
a) Who leads implementation of these courses?
Check all that apply
- Government
- Nonprofit organization
- Unknown
- Other: Please specify

b) Does your city government provide financial sponsorship for these courses?
c) How many youth participated in these courses in 2011?
d) How many youth participated in these courses in 2012?

48. Were youth pedestrian education courses available in your city in the past two years? ("Youth" refers to ages <18)
Yes/No/Unknown

If yes, please answer the following questions:
a) Who leads implementation of these courses?
Check all that apply
- Government
- Nonprofit organization
- Unknown
- Other: Please specify

b) Does your city government provide financial sponsorship for these courses?
c) How many youth participated in these courses in 2011?
d) How many youth participated in these courses in 2012?

49. Were adult bicycle education courses available in your city in the past two years? Yes/No/Unknown

If yes, please answer the following questions:
a) Who leads implementation of these courses?
Check all that apply
- Government
- Nonprofit organization
- Unknown
- Other: Please specify

b) Does your city government provide financial sponsorship for these courses?
c) How many adults participated in these courses in 2011?
d) How many adults participated in these courses in 2012?

50. Were Bike to Work Day events hosted in your city in the past two years? Yes/No/Unknown

If yes, please answer the following questions:
a) Who leads implementation of these courses?
Check all that apply
- Government
- Nonprofit organization
- Unknown
- Other: Please specify

b) Does your city government provide financial sponsorship for these courses?
c) How many adults participated in these courses in 2011?
d) How many adults participated in these courses in 2012?

51. Did your city sponsor an Open Streets initiative (also known as "ciclovia," "Sunday Streets," or "Saturday Parkways") in the past two years, where streets are closed to cars and opened to people to promote biking, walking, and other physical activity? Yes/No/Unknown

If yes, please answer the following questions:
a) How many Open Streets events occurred in 2011?
b) How many Open Streets events occurred in 2012?
c) How many people participated in these events in 2011?
d) How many people participated in these events in 2012?

52. Did your city sponsor a bike ride in the past two years to promote bicycling, walking, and physical activity?
Yes/No/Unknown

If yes, please answer the following questions:
a) How many people participated in these events in 2011?
b) How many people participated in these events in 2012?

53. Please tell us about any unique bicycling or pedestrian education and encouragement efforts in your city.

ECONOMIC IMPACT

54. Has your city studied the economic impact of the following? Check all that apply
- Bicycling
- Walking
- Trails
- Car-free zones in city centers
- None

55. If your city has completed an economic impact study, please briefly describe the results. Include a link, if available, and/or the date when the study was published.

ADVOCACY ORGANIZATIONS AND STUDY AREA MATCHES

States and Cities Represented in Advocacy Analyses (Chapter 9)

Alliance Member Statewide Organizations

* = Alliance member organization is newly represented in advocacy analyses since the *2012 Benchmarking Report*

◊NRO = No Representative Organization—state is not included in advocacy analyses:
Statewide Alliance member organization(s) present, but did not complete a 2013 Alliance Member Organization Survey

NRO = No Representative Organization—state is not included in advocacy analyses:
State is not represented by an Alliance statewide organization (as of December 2013)

Alabama	Alabama Bicycle Coalition
Alaska	NRO
Arizona	◊NRO
Arkansas	Bicycle Advocacy of Central Arkansas
California	California Bicycle Coalition, California Walks
Colorado	Bicycle Colorado
Connecticut	Bike Walk Connecticut
Delaware	Bike Delaware
Florida	Florida Bicycle Association
Georgia	Georgia Bikes!
Hawaii	PATH—Peoples Advocacy for Trails Hawaii*, Hawaii Bicycling League
Idaho	Idaho Pedestrian and Bicycle Alliance
Illinois	League of Illinois Bicyclists
Indiana	Bicycle Indiana
Iowa	Iowa Bicycle Coalition
Kansas	◊NRO
Kentucky	◊NRO
Louisiana	NRO
Maine	Bicycle Coalition of Maine
Maryland	Bike Maryland
Massachusetts	MassBike
Michigan	League of Michigan Bicyclists
Minnesota	Bicycle Alliance of Minnesota
Mississippi	◊NRO
Missouri	◊NRO
Montana	Bike Walk Montana*
Nebraska	NRO
Nevada	Nevada Bicycle Coalition
New Hampshire	Bike-Walk Alliance of NH
New Jersey	New Jersey Bike + Walk Coalition
New Mexico	◊NRO
New York	New York Bicycling Coalition
North Carolina	North Carolina Active Transportation Alliance
North Dakota	NRO
Ohio	◊NRO
Oklahoma	◊NRO
Oregon	Bicycle Transportation Alliance
Pennsylvania	◊NRO
Rhode Island	◊NRO
South Carolina	Palmetto Cycling Coalition
South Dakota	◊NRO
Tennessee	Bike Walk Tennessee
Texas	Bike Texas
Utah	Bike Utah
Vermont	Vermont Bicycle & Pedestrian Coalition
Virginia	Virginia Bicycling Federation*, Bike Virginia
Washington	Washington Bikes (formerly Bicycle Alliance of Washington)
West Virginia	◊NRO
Wisconsin	Bicycle Federation of Wisconsin
Wyoming	Wyoming Pathways*, Teton Valley Trails and Pathways

Alliance Member City-Focused Organizations

* = Alliance member organization is newly represented in advocacy analyses since the *2012 Benchmarking Report*

◊NRO = No Representative Organization—city is not included in advocacy analyses:
City-focused Alliance member organization(s) present, but did not complete a 2013 Alliance Member Organization Survey

NRO = No Representative Organization—city is not included in advocacy analyses:
City is not represented by an Alliance city-focused organization (as of December 2013)

City	Organization(s)
Albuquerque	BikeABQ
Arlington, TX	NRO
Atlanta	Atlanta Bicycle Coalition
Austin	Bike Austin*, Austin Cycling Association*
Baltimore	Bikemore*
Boston	Boston Cyclists Union, Green Streets Initiative*, Walk Boston, LivableStreets
Charlotte	◊NRO
Chicago	The Chainlink Community LLC*, Active Transportation Alliance
Cleveland	Bike Cleveland
Colorado Springs	◊NRO
Columbus	Consider Biking, Yay Bikes!
Dallas	BikeDFW
Denver	BikeDenver
Detroit	NRO
El Paso	NRO
Fort Worth	BikeDFW
Fresno	Bike Happy*
Honolulu	Hawaii Bicycling League
Houston	BikeHouston*
Indianapolis	INDYCOG, Alliance for Health Promotion
Jacksonville	NRO
Kansas City, MO	BikeWalkKC, Revolve, Kansas City Metro Bike Club
Las Vegas	◊NRO
Long Beach	Los Angeles County Bicycle Coalition
Los Angeles	Los Angeles County Bicycle Coalition, C.I.C.L.E.*, Los Angeles Walks*
Louisville	Bicycling for Louisville
Memphis	Livable Memphis
Mesa	Not One More Cyclist Foundation*
Miami	◊NRO
Milwaukee	Bicycle Federation of Wisconsin
Minneapolis	Midtown Greenway Coalition, St. Paul Smart Trips, Minneapolis Bicycle Coalition
Nashville	◊NRO
New Orleans	Bike Easy
New York City	Recycle-A-Bicycle*, Transportation Alternatives
Oakland	East Bay Bicycle Coalition*, Walk Oakland Bike Oakland
Oklahoma City	NRO
Omaha	Mode Shift Omaha*
Philadelphia	Bicycle Coalition of Greater Philadelphia
Phoenix	NRO
Portland, OR	Bicycle Transportation Alliance, Community Cycling Center
Raleigh	NRO
Sacramento	WalkSacramento
San Antonio	NRO
San Diego	Bike San Diego*
San Francisco	San Francisco Bicycle Coalition, Walk San Francisco
San Jose	Silicon Valley Bicycle Coalition
Seattle	Cascade Bicycle Club, Undriving and Urban Sparks, Feet First, Bike Works
Tucson	Living Streets Alliance
Tulsa	Tulsa Hub
Virginia Beach	NRO
Washington, DC	Washington Area Bicyclist Association
Wichita	Bike/Walk Alliance (Bike Walk Wichita)*

OTHER BENCHMARKING EFFORTS IN THE U.S.

The Alliance for Biking & Walking's Benchmarking Project is the only focused effort to set benchmarks for bicycling and walking in the United States using data from all 50 states and the 50 most populous cities. Other benchmarking efforts from abroad and within the United States have provided examples and inspiration for this project.

Bicycle Friendly America℠
www.BikeLeague.org/BFA

The League of American Bicyclists (LAB) has created a system for assessing "bicycle-friendliness." Communities, universities, and businesses interested in receiving a "Bicycle Friendly" designation submit an application to the League's Bicycle Friendly America℠ (BFA℠) program. As of early 2014, 292 communities, 654 businesses, and 68 universities are recognized as bicycle-friendly. All 50 states are ranked annually.

A national panel of bicycling experts scores BFA applications in consultation with local bicyclist reviewers. Award levels are determined based on a score received in five categories: engineering, education, encouragement, enforcement, and evaluation. The BFA program has inspired a spirit of competition among communities to be designated "Bicycle Friendly." The program also requires communities to complete an in-depth application, which gives them an opportunity to evaluate where they stand and causes them to gather data on bicycling in their community.

Walk Friendly Communities
www.WalkFriendly.org

In 2010, the Pedestrian and Bicycle Information Center launched the Walk Friendly Communities (WFC) program, modeled after the League of American Bicyclists' BFA program described above. WFC is a national recognition program developed to encourage U.S. communities to support safer walking environments. The WFC program recognizes places that are working to improve conditions for walking, including safety, mobility, access, and comfort. As of October 2013, 44 communities have received a WFC award.

State-level Policies and Practices
www.BikeWalk.org/pdfs/NCBWpubthereyet0203.pdf

The National Center for Bicycling and Walking (NCBW) conducted a one-time study between December 2002 and February 2003 to evaluate state Departments of Transportation (DOTs) accommodating bicycles and pedestrians. "The Benchmarking Project" focused on data from questionnaires sent to the Bicycle and Pedestrian Coordinator of each state DOT. NCBW identified four benchmarks: presence of statewide long-range plan for bicycle/pedestrian elements, accommodating bicycles into all transport projects, accommodating pedestrians into all state highway projects, and other special programs.

NCBW identified national standards for these benchmarks and assessed how each state measured up. Results were reported as "Yes" or "No" for each state meeting all or part of the benchmark, and summarized by benchmark. The report concluded that most state DOTs did not meet the benchmarks they identified for bicycle and pedestrian planning, accommodation (design), and special programs.

Walkability and Bikeability Checklists
www.PedBikeInfo.org/Community/Walkability.cfm

The Pedestrian and Bicycle Information Center's Walkability and Bikeability checklists are another means of evaluating conditions for bicycling and walking. These checklists are community tools that allow individuals to subjectively score their communities. The document invites individuals to go for a walk or bicycle ride, survey in hand, and to rate their experience on a scale of 1 to 5 while checking off potential problems. The document then goes through each question and offers potential solutions to common problems and also provides a list of resources at the end. This survey could be useful for community stakeholders wishing to gain insight into "bikeability" or "walkability." It could also be used by advocates in coordinated education efforts or to raise public perception of a problem area.

National Bicycle and Pedestrian Documentation Project

BikePedDocumentation.org

Although not a benchmarking project per se, the National Bicycle and Pedestrian Documentation Project (NBPD) is addressing a critical component of all benchmarking efforts for bicycling and walking: trip counts. NBPD provides guidance on measuring bicycling and walking trips using visual counts and intercept surveys. All resources for the methodology are freely available on the project's website (*BikePedDocumentation.org*).

Since the project's beginning in 2002, over 60 U.S. communities have conducted counts using the NBPD methodology in more than 500 locations. NBPD requests that communities using the documentation methodology submit data back to project facilitators to be stored in a nationwide database. Cities of all sizes have sent in their count data. See page 56 of this report for more information.

Scoring Walkability and Bikeability

www.WalkScore.com

Walk Score®, launched in July 2007, calculates and scores the walkability and bikeability of a street address or city. Walkability is determined by distance to amenities, such as stores, restaurants, schools, and parks, as well as population density and road metrics, such as block length and intersection density. Points are awarded for closeness to amenities; locations within 0.25 mile (about a 5-minute walk) receive the maximum number of points allowed. A Walk Score is in a range from 0 ("car-dependent") to 100 ("walker's paradise").

Bikeability is calculated using data for on-street and off-street bicycle paths, topography, distance and access to amenities, and bicycle commuting mode share. A Bike Score is in a range from 0 ("somewhat bikeable") to 100 ("biker's paradise"). Details on the Bike Score methodology is available at: *www.WalkScore.com/bike-score-methodology.shtml*

The Walk Score® system also provides Transit Score, which determines how well a location is served by public transportation.

ADDITIONAL RESOURCES

Advocacy Organizations:

State and Local Advocacy Organizations

• See *www.BikeWalkAlliance.org* to find your state or local bicycle and pedestrian advocacy organization

National Advocacy Organizations

• Adventure Cycling Association: *http://www.AdventureCycling.org*
• Alliance for Biking & Walking: *http://www.BikeWalkAlliance.org*
• America Bikes: *http://www.AmericaBikes.org*
• American Public Health Association: *http://bit.ly/d5iw6O*
• American Trails: *http://www.AmericanTrails.org/*
• America Walks: *http://www.AmericaWalks.org*
• Association of Pedestrian and Bicycle Professionals: *http://www.APBP.org*
• PeopleForBikes: *http://www.PeopleForBikes.org*
• International Mountain Bicycling Association: *http://www.IMBA.com*
• League of American Bicyclists: *http://www.BikeLeague.org*
• National Center for Bicycling and Walking: *http://www.BikeWalk.org*
• National Complete Streets Coalition: *http://www.CompleteStreets.org*
• Rails-to-Trails Conservancy: *http://www.RailsToTrails.org*
• Safe Routes to School National Partnership: *http://www.SafeRoutesPartnership.org*

Economic Impact:

• The Hidden Health Costs of Transportation: *http://bit.ly/cMo7HI*
• Economic Benefits of Bicycle Infrastructure:
http://www.AdvocacyAdvance.org/site_images/content/Final_Econ_Update%28small%29.pdf
• Economic Impact of Road Riding Events:
http://www.PeopleForBikes.org/resources/entry/road-riding-events-survey
• How Bicycling Investments Affect Real Estate: *http://www.bikesbelong.oli.us/Resources/Real_estate.pdf*
• Economic Value Walkability: *http://www.vtpi.org/walkability.pdf*
• Economic Statistics (PeopleForBikes): *http://www.PeopleForBikes.org/statistics/category/economic-statistics*
• Economic Impact of U.S. Bike Route: *http://www.adventurecycling.org/routes-and-maps/us-bicycle-route-system/implement-a-us-bike-route/benefits-and-building-support/economic-impact/*
• Health Economic Assessment Tool (World Health Organization): *http://www.heatwalkingcycling.org/*
• Employment Impacts of Pedestrian and Bicycle Infrastructure:
http://www.peri.umass.edu/fileadmin/pdf/published_study/PERI_ABikes_October2011.pdf

Economic Impact Studies

• Colorado: *http://www.atfiles.org/files/pdf/CObikeEcon.pdf*
• Florida, California, and Iowa (trails): *http://bit.ly/qaepVb*
• Maine: *http://live-active.org/yahoo_site_admin/assets/docs/ME_biketourismexecsumm.172150329.pdf*
• Maryland/Pennsylvania: *http://www.atatrail.org/docs/GAPeconomicImpactStudy200809.pdf*
• Minnesota: *http://bit.ly/c1YuLK*
• New York (trails): *http://nysparks.com/recreation/trails/statewide-plans.aspx*.; Statewide Trails Plan. Appendix C – Every Mile Counts – An Analysis of the 2008 Trail User Surveys.
• North Carolina (Outer Banks): *http://ncdot.gov/bikeped/download/bikeped_research_EIAoverview.pdf*
• Portland (cost:benefit): *http://bit.ly/nC5nY9*
• Portland (bike industry): *http://bit.ly/kMQih4*
• San Francisco (bike lanes): *http://www.sfbike.org/download/bikeplan/bikelanes.pdf*
• Virginia (trail): *http://atfiles.org/files/pdf/VACstudy04.pdf*
• Wisconsin: *http://www.dot.wisconsin.gov/business/econdev/docs/impact-bicycling.pdf*

Education:

• Blueprint for a Bicycle Friendly America:
http://www.bikeleague.org/sites/lab.huang.radicaldesigns.org/files/bfa_blueprint_0.pdf
• State Bike Summit Guide:
http://www.bikeleague.org/sites/lab.huang.radicaldesigns.org/files/state_bike_summit_guide.pdf

Share the Road

• Colorado (3-2-1 Courtesy Code): *http://bicyclecolo.org/page.cfm?PageID=1030*
• Maine (Share the Road): *http://www.maine.gov/mdot/bikeped/safety/*
• Minnesota (Share the Road): *http://www.sharetheroadmn.org*
• New York City (Give Respect/Get Respect): *http://bit.ly/6tp1C*
• San Francisco (Coexist): *http://www.sfbike.org/?coexist*
• South Carolina (Safe Streets Save Lives): *http://www.safestreetssavelives.org*
• South Carolina (Share the Road): *http://www.pccsc.net/sharetheroad.php*

Model Bicycle Education Programs

• Arizona Bike Safety Classes: *http://www.dot.pima.gov/tpcbac/SafetyClasses.htm*
• Arizona Education Guides: *http://www.azbikeped.org/education.asp*
• Delaware: *http://bit.ly/mBFKZ*
• Connecticut: *http://www.bikewalkct.org/bike-education.html*
• Florida: *http://www.floridabicycle.org/programs/education.html*
• Illinois: *http://www.bikelib.org/*
• Indiana: *http://www.bicycleindiana.org/educate.php*
• Kansas: *http://www.ksdot.org/burRail/bike/*
• Maine: *http://www.bikemaine.org/what-we-do/education*
• Michigan: *http://www.lmb.org*
• Minnesota: *http://www.bikemn.org/education*
• New York: *http://www.bikenewyork.org/education/*
• Oklahoma: *http://okbike.org/index.php?option=com_content&task=section&id=6&Itemid=35*
• Oregon: *http://btaoregon.org/get-involved/walkbike-education/*
• Texas: *http://www.biketexas.org/en/education*
• Vermont: *http://www.vtbikeped.org/ resources/basics-of-bicycle-commuting/basics.html*
• West Virginia: *http://www.wvcf.org/home/*

Encouragement:

• Blueprint for a Bicycle Friendly America:
http://www.bikeleague.org/sites/lab.huang.radicaldesigns.org/files/bfa_blueprint_0.pdf

Bike to Work Day Events

• Baltimore: *http://www.baltometro.org/bicycle/bike-to-work-day*
• Cleveland: *http://www.bikecleveland.org/btwd/*
• Denver: *http://biketowork2013.org/*
• Louisville: *http://www.louisvilleky.gov/BikeLouisville/biketoworkday.htm*
• San Francisco: *http://www.sfbike.org/?btwd and http://www.youcanbikethere.com/*
• San Jose: *http://bikesiliconvalley.org/btwd*
• Washington, DC: *http://www.biketoworkmetrodc.org/*

Open Streets/Ciclovias/Sunday Parkways

• See the current info on over 60 Open Streets initiatives at: *http://www.OpenStreetsProject.org*
• Baltimore: *http://www.baltimorespokes.org/article.php?story=20070821100331287*
• Chicago: *http://www.activetrans.org/openstreets*
• Los Angeles: *http://www.ciclavia.org/*
• Miami: *http://bikemiamiblog.wordpress.com/*
• New York City: *http://www.nyc.gov/html/dot/summerstreets/html/home/home.shtml*

- Oakland: *http://oaklavia.org/*
- Portland: *http://www.portlandoregon.gov/Transportation/46103*
- San Francisco: *http://sundaystreetssf.com/*
- Seattle: *http://www.seattle.gov/transportation/summerstreets.htm*

Promotional Rides

- Chicago's MB Financial Bike the Drive: *http://www.bikethedrive.org*
- Iowa's Register's Annual Great Bicycle Ride Across Iowa: *http://ragbrai.com*
- Louisville's Mayor's Healthy Hometown Hike and Bike:
http://www.louisvilleky.gov/HealthyHometown/HikeandBikeMHHM/

Public Bike Sharing

- Chicago: *http://divvybikes.com/*
- Denver: *http://www.denverbikesharing.org/*
- Minneapolis: *https://www.niceridemn.org/*
- Nashville: *http://www.nashvillebikeshare.org/*
- Washington, DC: *http://www.capitalbikeshare.com/*

Engineering:

- Blueprint for a Bicycle Friendly America:
http://www.bikeleague.org/sites/lab.huang.radicaldesigns.org/files/bfa_blueprint_0.pdf

Bicycle Parking

- APBP's Bicycle Parking Guidelines: *http://www.apbp.org/?page=Publications*
- Minneapolis: *http://www.ci.minneapolis.mn.us/bicycles/parking*
- Stolen Bicycle Registry: *http://www.stolenbicycleregistry.com*

Bicycle and Pedestrian Facility Design

- Bicycle Facility Design: *http://www.pedbikeinfo.org/planning/facilities.cfm*
- Outdoor Developed Areas (recreational trails): *http://www.access-board.gov/outdoor/index.htm*
- Pedestrian Facility Design: *http://www.pedbikeinfo.org/planning/facilities.cfm*
- Public Rights of Way: *http://www.access-board.gov/guidelines-and-standards/streets-sidewalks/public-rights-of-way*
- Shared Use Paths: *http://www.access-board.gov/sup.htm*
- Urban Bikeway Design Guide: *http://nacto.org/cities-for-cycling/design-guide/*

Environment:

Climate Change/Air Quality

- Climate Change and Bicycling: *http://www.advocacyadvance.org/docs/climate_change_bicycling.pdf*
- Congestion Mitigation and Air Quality Improvement Program: *http://bit.ly/r15wxM*

Funding:

- America Bikes Funding Fact Sheet: *http://www.americabikes.org/federal_investments_in_biking_and_walking*
- Congestion Mitigation and Air Quality Improvement Program: *http://bit.ly/r15wxM*
- Federal Funding for Bicycling and Pedestrian Improvements:
http://www.fhwa.dot.gov/environment/bicycle_pedestrian/guidance/
- Federal Highway Administration MAP-21 website: *http://www.fhwa.dot.gov/MAP21/*
- Highway Safety Improvement Program: *http://bit.ly/r8vwB8*
- Highway Safety Improvement Program Case Studies: *http://bit.ly/pnKSLG*
- Recreational Trails Program: *http://www.fhwa.dot.gov/environment/recreational_trails/*
- Rescissions: *http://www.advocacyadvance.org/site_images/content/Rescissions_FAQs.pdf*
- Transportation Alternatives Program: *http://www.fhwa.dot.gov/environment/transportation_alternatives/*
- Transportation Enhancements (archived, as of September 2013): *http://www.enhancements.org*

Infrastructure:

- Bicycles on Bridges: *http://www.advocacyadvance.org/docs/Bridge_Access_Report.pdf*
- Economic Benefits of Bicycle Infrastructure: *http://bit.ly/rchKVd*

Sharrows

- San Francisco: *https://www.sfmta.com/getting-around/bicycling/bike-lanes*
- Seattle: *http://www.cityofseattle.net/transportation/sharrows.htm*

Healthy and Active Living:

- American Public Health Association: *http://bit.ly/d5iw6O*
- Active Living Research: *http://www.activelivingresearch.org/*
- Centers for Disease Control and Prevention: *http://www.cdc.gov/HealthyYouth/index.htm*
- Health Economic Assessment Tool: *http://www.heatwalkingcycling.org/*
- Healthy Places (CDC): *http://www.cdc.gov/healthyplaces*
- Fact Sheets: *http://www.cdc.gov/healthyplaces/factsheets.htm*
- Healthy Community Design: *http://www.cdc.gov/healthyplaces/healthy_comm_design.htm*
- Health Impact Assessment: *http://www.cdc.gov/healthyplaces/hia.htm*
- Images: *http://www.cdc.gov/healthyplaces/images.htm*
- Increasing Physical Activity: *http://www.cdc.gov/healthyplaces/healthtopics/physactivity.htm*
- Reducing Injury: *http://www.cdc.gov/healthyplaces/healthtopics/injury.htm*
- Kaiser Permanente's Thrive Campaign: *http://share.kaiserpermanente.org/article/kaiser-permanentes-thrive-campaign-showcases-the-benefits-of-the-organizations-integrated-health-care-delivery-system/*
- National Environmental Public Health Tracking: *http://www.cdc.gov/nceh/tracking/*
- Robert Woods Johnson Foundation Active Living by Design: *http://www.activelivingbydesign.org*

Health Impact Assessments

- Oregon (Crook County): *http://1.usa.gov/p0hUcx*
- Sacramento: *http://www.ph.ucla.edu/hs/health-impact/docs/WalktoschoolSummary.pdf*
- Washington (Clark County): *http://bit.ly/r54yTu*

International Organizations:

- Denmark Cycling Embassy: *http://www.cycling-embassy.dk/*
- European Cyclists Federation: *http://www.ecf.com/*
- Fietsberaad: *http://www.fietsberaad.nl/*

Maps:

- Arizona: *http://www.dot.pima.gov/tpcbac/Publications.html#map and http://www.azbikeped.org/maps.asp*
- Austin: *http://www.austintexas.gov/service/bicycle-route-map*
- Colorado: *http://bicyclecolo.org/page.cfm?PageID=626*
- Delaware: *http://bit.ly/2yvA13*
- Denver: *http://www.bikedenver.org/maps/*
- Illinois: *http://www.gettingaroundillinois.com/gai.htm*
- Louisville: *http://www.louisvilleky.gov/BikeLouisville/IWantTo/existingbikelanes.htm*
- Maine: *http://www.exploremaine.org/bike/search-bike.shtml*
- Michigan: *http://bit.ly/caNrl*
- Milwaukee: *http://city.milwaukee.gov/maps4460.htm*
- Minneapolis: *http://www.minneapolismn.gov/bicycles/maps/index.htm*
- Minnesota: *http://www.dot.state.mn.us/bike/maps.html*
- New Hampshire: *http://www.nh.gov/dot/programs/bikeped/maps/index.htm*
- New Jersey: *http://www.njbikemap.com/*
- New York: *http://www.nycbikemaps.com/*
- North Carolina: *http://www.ncdot.gov/travel/mappubs/bikemaps/default.html*

- Ohio: *http://www.noaca.org/index.aspx?page=209*
- Oklahoma: *http://oklahomabicyclesociety.com/route-maps/*
- Oregon: *http://www.oregon.gov/ODOT/HWY/BIKEPED/maps.shtml*
- Philadelphia: *http://www.bicyclecoalition.org/resources/maps*
- Portland: *http://bit.ly/lEzWp*
- San Francisco: *http://www.sfbike.org/?maps*
- Seattle: *http://www.cityofseattle.net/transportation/bikemaps.htm*
- Washington, DC: *http://www.waba.org/resources/maps.php*
- Wisconsin: *http://www.dot.wisconsin.gov/travel/bike-foot/bikemaps.htm*

Master Plans:

Bicycle & Pedestrian Master Plans

- Arizona: *http://www.azbikeped.org/statewide-bicycle-pedestrian.asp*
- Arlington, TX: *http://www.arlingtontx.gov/planning/HikeandBike.html*
- Atlanta: *http://bit.ly/pmYIYp*
- Las Vegas: *http://www.rtcsnv.com/cycling/non-motorized-alternative-mode-plan/*
- Nashville: *http://mpw.nashville.gov/IMS/stratplan/PlanDownload.aspx*
- Sacramento: *http://www.sacog.org/bikeinfo/download_bike_ped_trails_mp.cfm*

Bicycle Master Plans

- Austin: *http://www.austintexas.gov/department/bicycle-program-0*
- Baltimore: *http://1.usa.gov/rkgyvT*
- Chicago: *http://bike2015plan.org/*
- Columbus: *http://www.altaprojects.net/columbus/*
- Dallas: *http://dallascityhall.com/public_works/bikePlan/*
- Davis: *http://bicycles.cityofdavis.org/beyond-platinum-bicycle-action-plan*
- Delaware: *http://bit.ly/1qfa1T*
- Denver: *http://bit.ly/kH56Mf*
- Fresno: *http://bit.ly/11E7HM*
- Hawaii: *http://hidot.hawaii.gov/highways/bike-plan-hawaii-master-plan/*
- Honolulu: *http://www1.honolulu.gov/dts/oahu+bike+plan.htm*
- Los Angeles: *http://planning.lacity.org/cwd/gnlpln/transelt/NewBikePlan/TOC_BicyclePlan.htm*
- Long Beach: *http://bit.ly/vFOTi*
- Louisville: *http://www.louisvilleky.gov/BikeLouisville/bikefriendly/*
- Minneapolis: *http://www.ci.minneapolis.mn.us/bicycles/projects/plan*
- Nevada: *http://www.bicyclenevada.com/bikeplan03.htm*
- New York City: *http://www.nyc.gov/html/dcp/html/bike/mp.shtml*
- Oakland: *http://bit.ly/njCGb2*
- Portland, OR: *http://bit.ly/17AeXX*
- Raleigh: *http://www.raleighnc.gov/business/content/PWksTranServices/Articles/BicycleProgram.html*
- Sacramento County: *http://www.sacog.org/bikeinfo/download_bike_ped_trails_mp.cfm*
- San Diego: *http://bit.ly/1271Kl*
- San Francisco: *http://www.sfmta.com/projects-planning/projects/2009-san-francisco-bicycle-plan*
- Seattle: *http://www.cityofseattle.net/transportation/bikemaster.htm*

Pedestrian Master Plans

- Austin: *http://www.austintexas.gov/department/pedestrian*
- Kansas *City: http://bit.ly/p8E8hn*
- Louisville: *http://www.louisvilleky.gov/HealthyHometown/activeliving/pedmasterplan/*
- Minneapolis: *http://www.minneapolismn.gov/pedestrian/projects/pedestrian_pedestrian-masterplan*
- Oakland: *www.oaklandnet.com/government/pedestrian/PedMasterPlan.pdf*
- Portland, OR: *http://www.portlandoregon.gov/transportation/article/90244*
- San Diego: *http://bit.ly/WsW5r*
- San Francisco: *http://www.sf-planning.org/index.aspx?page=2568*

• Seattle: *http://www.seattle.gov/transportation/pedestrian_masterplan*
• Washington, DC: *http://www.dc.gov/DC/DDOT/On+Your+Street/Bicycles+and+Pedestrians/Pedestrians/Pedestrian+Master+Plan/Pedestrian+Master+Plan+2009*

Policies:

Advisory Committees

• Arlington Bicycle Advisory Committee: *http://www.nctcog.org/trans/committees/bpac/index.asp*
• California Bicycle Advisory Committee: *http://www.dot.ca.gov/hq/tpp/offices/bike/cbac.html*
• California Pedestrian Advisory Committee: *http://saferoutescalifornia.org/2011/05/10/california-pedestrian-advisory-committee-may-meeting/*
• Caltrans District 4 Pedestrian Advisory Committee: *http://www.dot.ca.gov/dist4/transplanning/pedcomm/*
• City of Columbus Bikeway Advisory Committee: *http://bit.ly/nRJhhi*
• Denver Bicycling Advisory Committee: *http://bit.ly/QUqTZ*
• Fresno Bicycle/Pedestrian Advisory Committee: *http://bit.ly/1yWDmp*
• Fort Worth Bicycle and Pedestrian Advisory Committee: *http://bit.ly/4oErlO*
• Houston Pedestrian and Bicycle Committee: *http://www.h-gac.com/community/qualityplaces/pedbike/subcommittee.aspx*
• Los Angeles Bicycle Advisory Committee: *http://labac.tumblr.com/*
• Los Angeles Pedestrian Advisory Committee: *http://ladot.lacity.org/WhatWeDo/Safety/PedestrianSafety/PedestrianAdvisoryCommittee/index.htm*
• Maryland Bicycle and Pedestrian Advisory Committee: *http://bit.ly/jcQ1Q*
• Miami-Dade Bicycle Pedestrian Advisory Committee: *http://www.miamidade.gov/mpo/committees/m13-committees-bpac.htm*
• Minneapolis Bicycle Advisory Committee: *http://www.ci.minneapolis.mn.us/bicycles/bac*
• Nashville Bicycle Pedestrian Advisory Committee: *http://www.nashville.gov/Mayors-Office/Priorities/Health/Bicycle-Pedestrian-Advisory-Committee.aspx*
• Nevada: *http://www.nevadadot.com/About_NDOT/NDOT_Divisions/Planning/BikePed/BikePedBoard.aspx*
• Oakland Bicycle Advisory Committee: *http://bit.ly/oXsjIh*
• Omaha Bicycle Advisory Committee: *http://bit.ly/o9llI*
• San Antonio Bicycle Mobility Advisory Committee: *http://www.sametroplan.org/Committees/BMAC/*
• San Francisco Bicycle Advisory Committee: *http://www.sfgov3.org/index.aspx?page=579*
• San Francisco Pedestrian Safety Advisory Committee: *https://www.sfmta.com/ko/about-sfmta/organization/committees/pedestrian-safety-advisory-committee-psac*
• San Jose Bicycle Pedestrian Advisory Committee: *https://www.sanjoseca.gov/index.aspx?NID=3448*
• Tucson Bicycle Advisory Committee: *http://biketucson.pima.gov/*

Complete Streets

• Advice on Complete Streets campaigns: *http://www.BikeWalkAlliance.org/Contact*
• The latest Complete Streets news: *http://www.completestreets.org*
• Guide to Complete Streets Campaigns: *http://www.BikeWalkAlliance.org/Publications*
• Examples of Complete Streets Policies and Guides: *http://bit.ly/5Iy15q*
• Federal policy: *https://www.fhwa.dot.gov/publications/publicroads/10julaug/03.cfm*
• California: *http://www.smartgrowthamerica.org/documents/cs/policy/cs-ca-legislation.pdf*
• Connecticut: *http://www.cga.ct.gov/current/pub/chap_238.htm#sec_13a-153f*
• Delaware: *http://governor.delaware.gov/orders/exec_order_06.shtml#TopOfPage*
• Hawaii: *http://www.smartgrowthamerica.org/documents/cs/policy/cs-hi-legislation.pdf*
• Illinois: *http://www.smartgrowthamerica.org/documents/cs/policy/cs-il-legislation.pdf*
• Louisiana: *http://www.smartgrowthamerica.org/documents/cs/policy/cs-la-resolution.pdf*
• Louisville: *http://www.louisvilleky.gov/BikeLouisville/Complete+Streets/*
• Massachusetts: *http://bit.ly/pVDsBQ*
• Minnesota: *http://www.smartgrowthamerica.org/documents/cs/policy/cs-mn-legislation.pdf*
• New Jersey: *http://www.smartgrowthamerica.org/documents/cs/policy/cs-nj-dotpolicy.pdf*
• North Carolina: *http://www.smartgrowthamerica.org/documents/cs/policy/cs-nc-dotpolicy.pdf*
• Oregon: *http://www.smartgrowthamerica.org/documents/cs/policy/cs-or-legislation.pdf*

- Rhode Island: *http://www.rilin.state.ri.us/statutes/title31/31-18/31-18-21.HTM*
- Wisconsin: *http://www.smartgrowthamerica.org/documents/cs/policy/cs-wi-legislation.pdf*

Police on Bicycles
- International Police Mountain Biking Association: *http://www.ipmba.org*

Safe Passing Laws
- 3FeetPlease.com: *http://www.3feetplease.com/*
- Safely Passing Bicyclists: *http://www.ncsl.org/research/transportation/safely-passing-bicyclists.aspx*
- Arizona: *http://azbikelaw.org/articles/ThreeFoot.html*
- Austin: *http://austintexas.gov/page/bicycle-laws-codes*
- Delaware: *http://delcode.delaware.gov/title21/c041/sc03/index.shtml*
- Georgia: *http://www.legis.ga.gov/legislation/en-US/Display.aspx?Legislation=32251*
- Louisiana: *http://www.legis.la.gov/Legis/Law.aspx?d=670621*
- Maine: *http://www.mainelegislature.org/legis/statutes/29-a/title29-asec2070.html*
- New Hampshire: *http://www.gencourt.state.nh.us/rsa/html/XXI/265/265-143-a.htm*
- Oklahoma City: *http://bit.ly/46paAG*
- Tennessee: *http://www.tennessee3feet.org/*

Mandatory Helmet Laws
- Bicycle Helmet Safety Institute: *http://www.helmets.org/mandator.htm*
- Arguments/Case Study Against Mandatory Bicycle Helmet Laws: *http://www.cycle-helmets.com/*
- LAB Helmet Law Position: *http://www.bikeleague.org/content/topics*
- Arguments Against Mandatory Helmet Laws: *http://www.bellboycott.com/cached/www.kenkifer.com/bikepages/advocacy/mhls.htm*

Staffing
- Why Communities & States Need Bicycle and Pedestrian Staff: *http://bit.ly/o5Kjel*

Retailers/Industry:

- PeopleForBikes: *http://www.peopleforbikes.org*
- National Bicycle Dealers Association: *http://www.nbda.com*

Safety:

- Distracted Driving: *http://www.advocacyadvance.org/docs/distracted_driving_league_report.pdf*
- Highway Safety Improvement Program: *http://bit.ly/r8vwB8*
- Highway Safety Improvement Program Case Studies: *http://bit.ly/pnKSLG*
- Proven Safety Countermeasures: *http://safety.fhwa.dot.gov/provencountermeasures/*
- Traffic Safety Fact Sheets: *http://bit.ly/wrKo0*
- State Traffic Safety Information: *http://bit.ly/d3EzmD*

Safe Routes to School:

- Safe Routes to School National Partnership: *www.saferoutespartnership.org*
- The National Center for Safe Routes to School: *http://www.saferoutesinfo.org*
- Progress Reports: *http://www.saferoutesinfo.org/resources/tracking-reports.cfm*
- State of the States: *http://www.saferoutespartnership.org/state/stateofstates*
- EPA School Siting Guidelines: *http://www.epa.gov/schools/siting/*

Sample Safe Routes to School Programs
- Boston: *http://www.walkboston.org/work/safe_routes.htm*
- California: *http://saferoutescalifornia.org/*
- Colorado: *http://www.coloradodot.info/programs/bikeped/safe-routes*
- Connecticut: *http://www.ctsaferoutes.ct.gov/*

- Delaware: *http://deldot.gov/information/community_programs_and_services/srts*
- Denver: *http://www.denvergov.org/infrastructure/PolicyandPlanning/CurrentProjects/SafeRoutestoSchool/tabid/442763/Default.aspx*
- Florida: *http://www.dot.state.fl.us/safety/2A-Programs/Safe-Routes.shtm*
- Illinois: *http://www.dot.il.gov/saferoutes/saferouteshome.aspx*
- Indiana: *http://www.in.gov/indot/2355.htm*
- Iowa: *http://www.iowadot.gov/saferoutes/*
- Kansas: *http://www.ksdot.org/burTrafficEng/sztoolbox/default.asp*
- Louisiana: *http://www.dotd.louisiana.gov/planning/highway_safety/safe_routes/*
- Maine: *http://www.bikemaine.org/what-we-do/maine-safe-routes-to-school-program*
- Massachusetts: *http://www.commute.com/schools*
- Michigan: *http://www.saferoutesmichigan.org/*
- Minnesota: *http://www.dot.state.mn.us/saferoutes/*
- Mississippi: *http://www.mdottrafficsafety.com/Programs/Pages/safeRoutestoSchool.aspx*
- Missouri: *http://mobikefed.org/content/missouri-safe-routes-school-information*
- Montana: *http://www.bikewalkmontana.org/resources/srts/*
- Nebraska: *http://www.saferoutesne.com/*
- New Jersey: *http://www.state.nj.us/transportation/community/srts/*
- New Mexico: *http://www.dot.state.nm.us/content/dam/nmdot/planning/NMSRTS_Handbook.pdf*
- New York: *https://www.dot.ny.gov/divisions/operating/opdm/local-programs-bureau/srts*
- North Carolina: *https://connect.ncdot.gov/projects/BikePed/Pages/Safe-Routes-To-School.aspx*
- Oklahoma: *http://www.okladot.state.ok.us/srts/index.php*
- Portland: *http://www.portlandonline.com/TRANSPORTATION/40511*
- South Carolina: *http://www.scdot.org/getting/saferoutes.aspx*
- Texas: *http://www.txdot.gov/government/funding/safe-routes.html*
- Wisconsin: *http://www.dot.wisconsin.gov/localgov/aid/saferoutes.htm*

Statistics/Studies:

General Information

- Advocacy Advance: *http://www.advocacyadvance.org*
- Alliance Benchmarking Project: *http://www.BikeWalkAlliance.org/Benchmarking*
- PeopleForBikes: *http://www.peopleforbikes.org/statistics*
- Federal Highway Administration: *http://www.fhwa.dot.gov/environment/bicycle_pedestrian/*
- Fietsberaad (Netherlands): *http://www.fietsberaad.nl/index.cfm?lang=en§ion=Kennisbank*
- League of American Bicyclists: *http://www.bikeleague.org/content/bicycle-commuting-data*
- National Highway Traffic Safety Administration Traffic Safety Fact Sheets: *http://bit.ly/wrKo0*
- Pedestrian and Bicycle Information Center: *http://www.pedbikeinfo.org*
- Rails-to-Trails Conservancy: *http://www.railstotrails.org/ourWork/advocacy/activeTransportation*
- Victoria Transport Policy Institute: *http://www.vtpi.org/*
- National Environmental Public Health Tracking: *http://www.cdc.gov/nceh/tracking/*

Mode Share (Bicycle and Pedestrian Counts)

- Commuter Trends: *http://www.bikeleague.org/content/bicycle-commuting-data*
- National Bicycle and Pedestrian Documentation Project: *http://bikepeddocumentation.org*

Trainings:

- Navigating MAP-21 Workshops: *http://www.advocacyadvance.org/trainings*
- Membership Development Training: *http://bit.ly/2Rrx7Q*
- Safe Routes to School: *http://www.saferoutestoschools.org/Programs/Workshops.htm* and *http://www.saferoutesinfo.org/events-and-training/national-course*
- Winning Campaigns Trainings: *http://www.BikeWalkAlliance.org/WCTraining*

CORRECTIONS TO 2012 BENCHMARKING REPORT

The Alliance for Biking & Walking and our project team of advisors makes every effort to ensure the accuracy of data contained in this report. The self-reported nature of state and city data can lead to discrepancies from year to year, especially as respondents may change and interpret questions differently. In our effort to ensure accurate tracking and reporting of data, a number of responses to the surveys reported in the *2012 Benchmarking Report* have been updated. These corrections are reflected in the data analysis contained in this report. Below is a complete list of all corrections to the initial printed version of the 2012 report released in January 2012. Corrections are organized by chapter and page number.

Chapter 2: Levels of Bicycling and Walking

Page 43:

Ethnicity of People Who Walk to Work pie chart—Percentage of "Blacks" who walk to work corrected to 10.5% and percentage of "Asians" who walk to work corrected to 6.5%

Chapter 4: Policies

Page 68:

Published goals to increase bicycling—Response corrected to "no": Florida, Virginia; Response corrected to "unknown": Ohio

Published goals to increase walking—Response corrected to "no": Mississippi, Nevada, Virginia; Response corrected to "unknown": Ohio

Published goals to decrease bicycling fatalities—Response corrected to "no": Delaware, Kansas

Published goals to decrease walking fatalities—Response corrected to "no": Kansas

Mountain bike master plan adopted—Response corrected to "no": Kansas, Virginia

Trail master plan adopted—Response corrected to "no": Hawaii, Oklahoma, North Carolina, South Dakota

Page 69:

Published goals to increase bicycling—Response corrected to "no": Las Vegas

Published goals increase walking—Response corrected to "no": Atlanta, Las Vegas, Long Beach

Published goals to decrease bicycling fatalities—Response corrected to "no": Las Vegas, Long Beach, San Francisco

Published goals to decrease walking fatalities—Response corrected to "no": Las Vegas, Long Beach

Bike & pedestrian master plan adopted—Response corrected to "no": Atlanta, El Paso

Pedestrian only master plan adopted—Response corrected to "no": San Francisco

Mountain bike master plan adopted—Response corrected to "no": Fresno

Trail master plan adopted—Response corrected to "no": El Paso

Page 73:

Maximum number of car parking for new developments—Response corrected to "no": Kansas City, MO; Philadelphia

Bike parking in buildings/garages—Response corrected to "no": Columbus, Oakland, Philadelphia

Bike parking in new developments—Response corrected to "no": Honolulu, Omaha

Secure/valet bike parking at public events—Response corrected to "no": Jacksonville

Page 76:

Safe Routes to School participation—Response corrected to "unknown": Hawaii

Policy requiring minimum acreage for school siting—Response corrected to "no": Alabama, Alaska, Arizona, Maine, Mississippi, Missouri, Ohio, Oklahoma, Rhode Island, Utah, Virginia, Washington; Response corrected to "yes": Arkansas, Illinois, Iowa, Michigan

Provides additional SRTS funding—Response corrected to "no": North Dakota

Page 77:

Minimum acreage for school siting—Response corrected to "no": Fresno; Kansas City, MO; Response corrected to "unknown" for Las Vegas

A policy that places children in schools for any reason other than proximity to residence—Response corrected to "no": Fresno; Kansas City, MO; Omaha; Response corrected to "unknown" for Las Vegas

Page 86:

State spending target for bicycling and walking—Response corrected to "no": Iowa

Page 87:

City spending target for bicycling and walking—Response corrected to "no": Honolulu, Las Vegas, San Francisco

Page 99:

Current miles of on-street bicycle lanes per square mile (total miles)—Chicago total miles unknown; El Paso corrected to 0.10 miles per square mile (26 miles); Houston total miles unknown; Jacksonville corrected to 0.30 miles per square mile (224 miles); Philadelphia corrected to 2.94 miles per square mile (393.67 miles); Portland, OR, total miles unknown

Current miles of multi-use paths per square mile (total miles)—Arlington, TX, corrected to 0.44 miles per square mile (42 miles); Chicago corrected to 0.18 miles per square mile (42 miles); El Paso corrected to 0.009 miles per square mile (2.19 miles); Jacksonville corrected to 0.04 miles per square mile (30 miles); Virginia Beach corrected to 0.30 miles per square mile (74.7 miles)

Current miles of on-road signed bicycle routes per square mile (total miles)—Arlington, TX, corrected to 0 miles per square mile (0 miles); Atlanta total miles unknown; Dallas total miles unknown; Los Angeles total miles unknown; New Orleans corrected to 0.006 per square mile (1 mile); Portland, OR, corrected to 0 miles per square mile (0 miles); Raleigh corrected to 0.70 miles per square mile (100 miles)

Miles of sidewalks—Atlanta total miles unknown; Columbus total miles unknown; Dallas total miles unknown; Louisville total miles unknown; San Antonio corrected to 4500 miles

Miles of planned bicycle facilities—Las Vegas total miles unknown

Adopted goals to increase pedestrian facilities—Response corrected to "no": Baltimore, Long Beach

Page 104:

Existing miles of shared lane markings—Fort Worth corrected to 0 miles; Kansas City, MO, corrected to 4.8 miles; San Francisco total miles unknown

Woonerfs—Philadelphia corrected to 20 miles; Portland, OR, corrected to "no"

Bicycle Boulevards—Response corrected to zero: Las Vegas

Page 109:

Percentage of buses with bike racks—Las Vegas percentage unknown

Chapter 5: Education and Encouragement

Page 113:

Info on bicycling in driver's manual—Response corrected to "no" for Rhode Island

Page 114:

Youth pedestrian education courses—Response corrected to "unknown": Las Vegas

City-sponsored bike ride—Response corrected to "no": San Francisco

Page 123:

Number of Schools Participating in Bike and/or Walk to School Day—Response corrected to "unknown": Las Vegas

BIBLIOGRAPHY

Adventure Cycling Association. (2010, February 3).U.S. Bicycle Route System 101 [web log comment]. Retrieved from http://blog.adventurecycling.org/

Akar, G., Clifton, K. (2009). The influence of individual perceptions and bicycle infrastructure on the decision to bike. Transportation Research Record, 2140, 165–172.

Alliance for Biking & Walking. (2007). Bicycling and Walking in the U.S.: Benchmarking Report 2007. Retrieved from http://www.peoplepoweredmovement.org/site/index.php/site/memberservices/2007_benchmarking_report/

Alliance for Biking & Walking. (2010). Bicycling and Walking in the United States: 2010 Benchmarking Report. Retrieved from http://www.peoplepoweredmovement.org/site/index.php/site/memberservices/C529

Alliance for Biking & Walking. (2012). Bicycling and Walking in the United States: 2012 Benchmarking Report. Retrieved from http://www.peoplepoweredmovement.org/benchmarking

Alta Planning and Design. (2008, September). The Value of the Bicycle-Related Industry in Portland. Retrieved from http://www.altaplanning.com/App_Content/files/fp_docs/2008%20Portland%20Bicycle-Related%20Economy%20Report.pdf

American Automobile Association. (2013). Your Driving Costs: 2013 Edition. Retrieved from http://newsroom.aaa.com/wp-content/uploads/2013/04/YourDrivingCosts2013.pdf

America Bikes and League of American Bicyclists. (2011). Rescissions FAQ. Retrieved from http://www.advocacyadvance.org/site_images/content/Rescissions_FAQs.pdf

American Public Health Association. (2011). Health Impact Assessments: A tool to ensure that health and equity are considered in transportation policy and systems. Retrieved from http://www.apha.org/NR/rdonlyres/1CD24FFB-37FB-4576-86A1-6D68A1C5DBAF/0/APHAHIAFactsheetJan2011.pdf

Andersen, T., Bredal, F.,Weinreich, M., Jensen, N., Riisgaard-Dam, M. & Kofod Nielsen, M. (2012). Collection of Cycle Concepts. Retrieved fromhttp://www.cycling-embassy.dk/2013/08/01/cycle-concepts2012/

APTA. (2009). Standards Development Program Recommended Practice: Defining Transit Areas of Influence (APTA SUDS-UD-RP-001-09). Retrieved from http://www.apta.com/resources/standards/Documents/APTA%20SUDS-UD-RP-001-09.pdf

APTA. (2011). 2010 Public Transportation Vehicle Database. Retrieved from http://www.apta.com/resources/statistics/Pages/OtherAPTAStatistics.aspx

APTA. (2014). 2012 Public Transportation Infrastructure Database. Retrieved from http://www.apta.com/resources/statistics/Pages/OtherAPTAStatistics.aspx

Association of Pedestrian and Bicycle Professionals. (2010). Bicycle Parking Guidelines (2nd ed.). Retrieved from http://www.apbp.org/?page=publications

Aultman-Hall, L., Hall, F.L.,& Baetz, B.B. (1998). Analysis of bicycle commuter routes using geographic information systems: Implications for bicycle planning. Transportation Research Record, 1578, 102–110.

Barnes, G. & Krizek, K. (2005, December). Tools for Predicting Usage and Benefits of Urban Bicycle Network Improvements. Report prepared for Minnesota Department of Transportation, Research Services Section. Retrieved from http://www.lrrb.org/media/reports/200550.pdf

Bassett, D., Pucher, J., Buehler, R., Thompson, D., & Crouter, S. (2008, November). Walking, Cycling, and Obesity Rates in Europe, North America, and Australia, Journal of Physical Activity and Health, 5(6), 795-814.

Behan, D. F. &Cox,S.H. (2010, December). Obesity and its Relation to Mortality and Morbidity Costs, Society of Actuaries. Report sponsored by Committee on Life Insurance Research Society of Actuaries. Retrieved from http://www.soa.org/Files/Research/Projects/research-2011-obesity-relation-mortality.pdf

Bell, J., & Cohen, L. (2009). Health Effects of Transportation Policy. Healthy Equitable Transportation Policy Recommendations and Research. S. Malekafzali (Ed.) Retrieved from http://www.aarp.org/content/dam/aarp/livable-communities/plan/transportation/healthy-equitable-transportation-policy-aarp.pdf

Bergström, A. & Magnusson, R. (2003). Potential of transferring car trips to bicycle during winter. Transportation Research Part A: Policy and Practice, 37(8), 649–666.

Berrigan, D, Carroll, D. D., Fulton, J. E., Galuska, D. A., Brown, D. R., Dorn, J. M., Armour, B., &P. Paul. (2012, August 10). Vital Signs: Walking Among Adults," Morbidity and Mortality Weekly Report, Retrieved from http://www.cdc.gov/mmwr/preview/mmwrhtml/mm6131a4.htm?s_cid=mm6131a4_w

Bicycle Federation of Wisconsin. (2012) 2011 Wisconsin Bicycling Benchmarking Report. Retrieved fromhttp://wisconsinbikefed.org/wp-content/uploads/2012/03/2011-Wisconsin-Bicycling-Benchmarking-Report-FINAL.pdf

Bicycle Transportation Alliance. (2002) The Bicycle-Friendly Communities Report Card: A Comparative Look at the Quality of Bicycling in Oregon's Cities. Retrieved from http://www.thunderheadalliance.org/site/images/uploads/BTA_reportcard.pdf

Bikes Belong. (2009, November). Bikes Belong Survey: The Size and Impact of Road Riding Events. Retrieved from http://www.issuelab.org/click/download1/road_riding_events

Bikes Belong. (2011). The Federal Investment in Bicycling: 10 Success Stories. Retrieved from http://www.aarp.org/content/dam/aarp/livable-communities/learn/transportation/federal-investment-in-bicycling-10-success-stories.pdf

BikeTexas. (2010). BikeTexas Benchmark Study. Retrieved from http://www.biketexas.org/en/infrastructure/benchmark-study

Bodea, T. D., Garrow, L.A., Meyer, M.D. &Ross, C.L. (2009). Sociodemographic and built environment influences on the odds of being overweight or obese: The Atlanta experience. Transportation Research Part A: Policy & Practice, 43(4), 430–444.

Borgman, F. (2003). The Cycle Balance: Benchmarking local cycling conditions. Retrieved from http://media.fietsersbond.nl/Engels/Information%20about%20the%20Cycle%20Balance.pdf

Bradley, J. (2008, October 8). A Small-town or Metro Nation. Brookings Institute. Retrieved from http://www.brookings.edu/research/articles/2008/10/08-smalltowns-katz

Brons, M., Givoni, M., & Rietveld, P. (2009).Access to railway stations and its potential in increasing rail use. Transportation Research Part A: Policy and Practice,43(2), 136–149.

Buck, D., Buehler, R. Happ, P., Rawls, B. Chung, P., & Borecki, N. (2014). Are Bikeshare Users Different from Regular Cyclists? First Look at Short-Term Users, Annual Members, and Area Cyclists in the Washington, D.C., Region. Transportation Research Record, forthcoming. Retrieved from http://docs.trb.org/prp/13-5029.pdf

Buehler, R. (2012). Determinants of Bicycle Commuting in the Washington, D.C. Region: The Role of Bicycle Parking, Cyclist Showers, and Free Car Parking at Work. Transportation Research Part D: Transport and Environment, 17(7), 525-531.

Buehler, R. & Pucher, J. (2011). Sustainable transport in Freiburg: Lessons from Germany's environmental capital. International Journal of Sustainable Transportation, 5, 43–70.

Buehler, R. & Pucher J. (2012). Cycling to work in 90 large American cities; new evidence on the role of bike paths and lanes. Transportation,39(2); 409-432.

Buehler, R., Pucher, J., Merom, D., & Bauman, A. (2011, September). Active Travel in Germany and the USA: Contributions of Daily Walking and Cycling to Physical Activity. American Journal of Preventive Medicine, 40(9), 241–250.

BYPAD. (2003). Bicycle Policy Audit Retrieved on February 17, 2014 from http://www.bypad.org

Campos Inc. (2009, August 7). The Great Allegheny Passage Economic Impact Study (2007-2008). Report for The Progress Fund, Laurel Highlands Visitors Bureau, and Allegheny Trail Alliance. Retrieved from http://www.atatrail.org/docs/GAPeconomicImpactStudy200809.pdf

Casagrande, S. L. (2011). Association of walkability with obesity in Baltimore City, Maryland. American Journal of Public Health, 101 (Suppl 1), S318–S324.

Caulfield, B. & Leahy, J. (2011). Learning to cycle again: examining the benefits of providing tax-free loans to purchase new bicycles, Research in Transportation Business & Management, 2, 42–47.

Ceder, J. (2012, September 25). Walkability Experts Use New Walk Score App to Audit Neighborhood [Web log comment]. Retrieved from http://blog.walkscore.com/2012/09/walkability-experts-use-walk-score-to-audit-neighborhood/

Centers for Disease Control and Prevention. (2013). Social Determinants of Health, Frequently Asked Questions. Retrieved from http://www.cdc.gov/socialdeterminants/FAQ.html

Cervero, R. (2007). Transit-oriented development's ridership bonus: a product of self-selection and public policies. Environment and Planning A, 39(9), 2068–2085.

Chaddock, L., Erickson, K.I., Prakash, R.S. et al.(2010). Basal Ganglia Volume Is Associated with Aerobic Fitness in Preadolescent Children. Developmental Neuroscience, 32, 249–256.

Charity Walk. (2014). Table 2013 Visitor industry charity walk statistics. About Us. Retrieved February 13, 2014 from http://www.charitywalkhawaii.org

Clifton, K., Muhs, C., Morrissey, S., et al. (2013). Examining Consumer Behavior and Travel Choices. Retrieved from http://www.otrec.us/project/411

City of Copenhagen. (2009, August). Copenhagen City of Cyclists: Bicycle Account 2008. Retrieved from http://cphbikeshare.com/files/Bicycle%20Account%202008.pdf

City of Copenhagen. (2011). Copenhagen City of Cyclists Bicycle Account 2010. Retrieved from http://www.cycling-embassy.dk/wp-content/uploads/2011/05/Bicycle-account-2010-Copenhagen.pdf

Cortright, J. (2009, August). Walking the Walk: How Walkability Raises Home Values in U.S. Cities. Retrieved from http://www.ceosforcities.org/research/walking-the-walk/

Cortright, J. (2010, April). New York City's Green Dividend. Retrieved from http://www.nyc.gov/html/dot/downloads/pdf/nyc_greendividend_april2010.pdf

Cosgrove, L., Chaudhary, N., & Reagan, I. (2011). Four High-Visibility Enforcement Demonstration Waves in Connecticut and New York Reduce Hand-Held Phone Use, National Highway Traffic Safety Administration. Retrieved from http://www.distraction.gov/files/for-media/2011/508-research-note-dot-hs-811-845.pdf

Cradock, A., Troped, P., Fields, B., Melly, S., Simms, S., Gimmler, F., & Fowler, M. (2009). Factors associated with federal transportation funding for local pedestrian and bicycle programming and facilities. Journal of Public Health Policy 30, S38–S72.

Cradock, A., Fields, B., Barrett, J., & Melly, S. Program practices and demographic factors associated with federal funding for the Safe Routes to School program in the United States. Health & Place 18 (2012) 16-23.

Deichmeister, J., Dows, B., & Perry, K.L. (2009, September 2). Biking and Walking Resources in Virginia: Part I. Report for BikeWalk Virginia. Retrieved from http://community.railstotrails.org/media/p/2247.aspx

deGeus, B., de Bourdeaudhuij, I., Jannes, C., & Meeusen, R. (2008). Psychosocial and environmental factors associated with cycling for transport among a working population. Health Education Research 23, 697–708.

DeMaio, P. (2009). Bike-sharing: History, impacts, models of provision, and future. Journal of Public Transportation 14(4), 41–56.

Department of Transport. (2009). A Sustainable Transport Future: A New Transport Policy for Ireland 2009 - 2020. Retrieved from http://smartertravel.ie/sites/default/files/uploads/pdfs/NS1264_Smarter_Travel_english_PN_WEB.pdf

Dill, J. & Carr, T. (2003). Bicycle commuting and facilities in major US Cities: If you build them, commuters will use them. Transportation Research Record, 1828, 116–123.

Dill, J. (2009). Bicycling for transportation and health: The role of infrastructure. Journal of Public Health Policy, 30, S95–S110.

Dill, J., Handy, S., & Pucher, J. (2013). How to Increase Bicycling for Daily Travel. Report funded by the Robert Wood Johnson Foundation. Retrieved from http://activelivingresearch.org/files/ALR_Brief_DailyBikeTravel_May2013.pdf

Dougherty, C. (2009, July 1). Cities Grow at Suburbs' Expense During Recession. The Wall Street Journal. Retrieved from http://online.wsj.com/news/articles/SB124641839713978195

ECMT(2004).National Policies to Promote Cycling. European Conference of the Ministers of Transport. Retrieved from http://internationaltransportforum.org/pub/pdf/04Cycling.pdf

Ecoplan. (2010). World City Bike Cooperative: Public Bike System Inventory. Retrieved from http://www.ecoplan.org/wtpp/citybike_index.htm.

Elvik, R. (2009). The non-linearity of risk and the promotion of environmentally sustainable transport. Accident Analysis and Prevention, 41, 849–855.

Emond, C., Tang, W., & Handy, S. (2009). Explaining gender difference in bicycling behavior. Transportation Research Record, 2125, 16–25.

Encyclopedia, Victoria Transport Policy Institute. (March, 2007). Evaluating Nonmotorized Transport: Techniques for Measuring Walking and Cycling Activity and Conditions," Transportation Demand Management (TDM). Retrieved from http://www.vtpi.org/tdm/tdm63.htm#*Toc121444872

European Cycling Federation. (n.d.) Safety in number: Fact sheet. Retrieved from http://www.ecf.com/wp-content/uploads/ECF_FACTSHEET4_V3_cterree_SafetyNumb.pdf

Federal Highway Administration. (n.d) Section 402 Highway Safety Funds. Retrieved from http://safety.fhwa.dot.gov/policy/section402/

Federal Highway Administration. (2012, April). Report to the U.S. Congress on the Outcomes of the Nonmotorized Transportation Pilot Program: SAFETEA-LU Section 1807. Retrieved from http://www.fhwa.dot.gov/environment/bicycle_pedestrian/ntpp/2012_report/page00.cfm

Federal Highway Administration. (2014, January). Highway Statistics 2012: Licensed Drivers By Sex And Ratio To Population. Retreived from https://www.fhwa.dot.gov/policyinformation/statistics/2012/dl1c.cfm

Fietsberaad. (2010). Bicycle Policies of the European Principals: Continuous and Integral. Retrieved from http://www.fietsberaad.nl/library/repository/bestanden/Fietsberaad_publicatie7_Engels.pdf

Flusche, D. (2011, May 3). US Mayors Want More Bicycle and Pedestrian Investments, League of American Bicyclists [Web log comment]. Retrieved from http://www.bikeleague.org/blog/2011/05/us-mayors-want-more-bicycle-and-pedestrian-investments/

Fort Worth South, Inc. (2011). Near Southside Dashboard, Second Half 2011. Retrieved from http://www.fortworthsouth.org/wp-content/uploads/2012/02/Dashboard-FWSI-2H-2011.pdf

Fort Worth South, Inc. (2009). Near Southside Dashboard, Second Half 2009. Retrieved from http://www.fortworthsouth.org/wp-content/uploads/2012/02/Dashboard-FWSI-2H-2009.pdf

Frank, L. D., Engelke, P.,& Schmid, T.L. (2003). Health and community design: The impact of the built environment on physical activity. Washington, DC: Island Press.

Frank L.D., Andresen, M.A., & Schmid, T.L. (2004). Obesity relationships with community design, physical activity, and time spent in cars. American Journal of Preventive Medicine, 27(2):87–96.

Frank, L., T. Schmid, Sallis, J., et al. (2005). Linking Objectively Measured Physical Activity with Objectively Measured Urban Form: Findings from SMARTRAQ. American Journal of Preventive Medicine 28(2S2): 117-125.

Furth, P. (2012). Bicycling Infrastructure for Mass Cycling: A Transatlantic Comparison. In Pucher, J., Buehler, R. (Eds.), City Cycling (105-139). Cambridge, MA: MIT Press.

Garrard, J., Rissel, C., Bauman, A. (2012). Health Benefits of Cycling. In Pucher, J., Buehler, R. (Eds.), City Cycling (31-56). Cambridge, MA: MIT Press.

Garrard, J., Dill, J., Handy, S. (2012). Women and Cycling. In Pucher, J., Buehler, R. (Eds.), City Cycling (211-234). Cambridge, MA: MIT Press.

Garrard, J., Rose, G., Lo, S.K. (2008). Promoting transportation cycling for women: The role of bicycle infrastructure. Preventive Medicine, 46, 55–59.

Garrett-Peltier, H. (2010, December). Estimating the Employment Impacts of Pedestrian, Bicycle, and Road Infrastructure Case Study: Baltimore. Retrieved from http://www.downtowndevelopment.com/pdf/baltimore_Dec20.pdf

Gatersleben, B. & Appleton, K. (2007). Contemplating cycling to work: Attitudes and perceptions in different stages of change. Transportation Research Part A: Policy and Practice, 41(4), 302–312.

Givoni, M & Rietveld, P. (2007). The access journey to the railway station and its role in passengers' satisfaction with rail travel. Transport Policy 14, 357–365.

Glickman, D., Parker, L., Sim, L., et al. (2012). Accelerating Progress in Obesity Prevention: Solving the Weight of the Nation. Report for the Committee on Accelerating Progress in Obesity Prevention, Food and Nutrition Board, Institute of Medicine of the National Academies. Retrieved from http://www.iom.edu/Reports/2012/Accelerating-Progress-in-Obesity-Prevention.aspx

Global Ideas Bank. (2012, August 1). Groningen, the car-free city for bikes. Retrieved from http://archive.is/ifH8

Goldberg, D., et al. (2007, January). New Data for a New Era: A Summary of the SMARTRAQ Findings Linking Land Use, Transportation, Air Quality, and Health in the Atlanta Region. Retrieved from http://www.smartgrowthamerica.org/documents/SMARTRAQSummary_000.pdf

Gomez, L., Sarmiento, O., Lucimi, D., Espinosa, G., Forero, R., & Bauman, A. (2005). Prevalence and factors associated with walking and bicycling for transport among young adults in two low-income localities of Bogotá, Colombia. Journal of Physical Activity and Health 2, 445–449.

Gordon-Larsen P., J. Boone-Heinonen, S. Sidney, B. Sternfeld, D.R. Jacobs, Jr., C.E. Lewis (2009). Active commuting and cardiovascular disease risk: The CARDIA study. Archives of Internal Medicine, 169(13), 1216-1223.

Gotschi, T. & Mills, K. (2008). Active Transportation for America: The Case for Increased Federal Investment in Bicycling and Walking, Rails-to-Trails Conservancy. Retrieved from http://www.railstotrails.org/atfa

Gotschi, T. (2011). Costs and Benefits of Bicycling Investments in Portland. Oregon Journal of Physical Activity and Health. 8(S1), S49-S58.

Grabow, M., Hahn, M., & Whited, M. (2010). Valuing Bicycling's Economic and Health Impacts in Wisconsin. Retrieved from http://www.sage.wisc.edu/igert/download/bicycling_final_report.pdf.

Green Ribbon Committee on Environmental Sustainability. (June 2009). Together Making Nashville Green. Retrieved from http://www.nashville.gov/Portals/0/SiteContent/Sustainability/GRC_Report_090701.pdf

Guide to Community Preventive Services. (2013, October 25). Environmental and policy approaches to increase physical activity: Community-scale urban design land use policies. Retrieved from www.thecommunityguide.org/pa/environmental-policy/communitypolicies.html

Hallal, P.C., Andersen, L.B., Bull, F.C., Guthold, R., Haskell, W., & Ekelund, U. (2012, July 21). Global physical activity levels: Surveillance progress, pitfalls, and prospects. The Lancet, 380 (9838), 247-257. doi:10.1016/S0140-6736(12)60646-1.

Hamer, M & Chida, Y. (2008). Active commuting and cardiovascular risk: A meta-analytic review. Preventive Medicine 46(1):9–13.

Harris, M., C. Reynolds, M. Winters, et al. (2012, February 14). Comparing the effects of infrastructure on bicycling injury at intersections and non-intersections using a case-crossover design. Injury Prevention. Retrieved from http://injuryprevention.bmj.com/content/early/2013/02/13/injuryprev-2012-040561.full.pdf

Heart and Stroke Foundation. (2005, February 10). Report Card on Canadians' Health—Has the Suburban Dream Gone Sour? [Press Release]. Retrieved from www.heartandstroke.ca

Heath, G., Brownson, R., Kruger, J. et al. (2006). The Effectiveness of Urban Design and Land Use and Transport Policies and Practices to Increase Physical Activity: A Systematic Review. Journal of Physical Activity and Health, 3 (Suppl 1) S55-S76.

Hegger, R. (2007). Public transport and cycling: Living apart or together? Public Transport International 2, 38–41.

Heinen, E., Van Wee, B.,Maat, K. (2010). Bicycle use for commuting: A literature review. Transport Reviews 30(1), 105–132.

Hillman, C.H., Castelli, D.M., & Buck, S.M. (2005). Aerobic fitness and neurocognitive function in healthy preadolescent children. Medicine and Science in Sports and Exercise, 37:1967–1974.

Hopkinson, P. & Wardman, M.(1996). Evaluating the demand for new cycle facilities. Transport Policy 3(4), 241–249.

Howard, C. & Burns, E. (2001). Cycling to work in Phoenix: Route choice, travel behavior, and commuter characteristics. Transportation Research Record 1773, 39–46.

Hunt, J. & Abraham, J. (2007). Influences on bicycle use. Transportation, 34, 453–470.

Institute of Transportation Engineers Pedestrian and Bicycle Council. (2005, August). National Bicycle and Pedestrian Documentation Project: Description. Retrieved from http://bikepeddocumentation.org/

Interim Program Guidance. (2006, October 31). The Congestion Mitigation and Air Quality (CMAQ) Improvement Program under the Safe, Accountable, Flexible, Efficient Transportation Equity Act: A Legacy for Users. Retrieved from http://www.fhwa.dot.gov/environment/cmaq06gd.pdf.

Jacobsen, P. & Rutter, H. (2012). Cycling Safety. In Pucher, J., Buehler, R. (Eds.), City Cycling (141-156). Cambridge, MA: MIT Press.

Jacobsen, P.L. (2003). Safety in Numbers: More Walkers and Bicyclists, Safer Walking and Bicycling. Injury Prevention, 9, 205–209.

Jensen, S. (2008). How to obtain a healthy journey to school. Transportation Research Part A: Policy and Practice 42(3), 475–486.

Johnson, S., Sidebotttom, A., & Thorpe, A. (2008). The Problem of Bicycle Theft (Guide No. 52). Retrieved from http://www.popcenter.org/problems/bicycle_theft

Jones, M.G., Ryan, S., Donlon, J., Ledbetter, L. & Ragland, D.R. (2010). Seamless Travel: Measuring Bicycle and Pedestrian Activity in San Diego County and Its Relationship to Land Use, Transportation, Safety, and Facility Type. Retrieved from http://www.altaplanning.com/App_Content/files/Seamless-Final-Report-June-2010.pdf

Knoch, C. & Tomes, P. (2006). Pine Creek Rail Trail 2006 User Survey and Economic Impact Analysis, Rails-to-Trails Conservancy. Retrieved from http://atfiles.org/files/pdf/PineCreeksurvey.pdf

Knoch, C. (2007). Heritage Rail Trail County Park 2007 User Survey and Economic Impact Analysis. Report prepared for York County Department of Parks and Recreation. Retrieved from http://conservationtools.org/libraries/1/library_items/1084-Heritage-Rail-Trail-County-Park-2007-User-Survey-and-Economic-Impact-Analysis

League of American Bicyclists (2011). Bicycle Friendly America: Bicycle Friendly Community Master List. Retrieved from http://www.bikeleague.org/programs/bicyclefriendlyamerica/

League of American Bicyclists & Sierra Club. (2013). The New Majority: Pedaling Towards Equity. Retrieved from https://www.bikeleague.org/content/equity-reports-and-resources

Lankford, S. et al. (2008). The Economic Impact & Spectator Characteristics of RAGBRAI. Report prepared for the Des Moines Register for RAGBRAI. Retrieved from http://www.uni.edu/step/reports/STEP_RAGBRAI.pdf

Larson, J. & El-Geneidy, A. (2010). A travel behavior analysis of urban cycling facilities in Montréal, Canada. Transportation Research Part D: Transport and Environment, 16(2), 172–177.

Lawrie, J., Guenther, J., Cook, T., Meletiou, M.P. & O'Brien, S.W. (2004). Pathways to Prosperity: The Economic Impact of Investments in Bicycle Facilities. Report for the North Carolina Department of Transportation. Retrieved from http://www.ncdot.gov/bikeped/downloadbikeped_research_eiafulltechreport.pdf

The Leadership Conference Education Fund. (2011, May). Where We Need to Go: A Civil Rights Roadmap for Transportation Equity. Retrieved from http://www.civilrights.org/transportation/where-we-go.html

Liberles, J. (2010, November 3). Money talks, UCI3 Harbin Park event brings $200,000 to community. CXmagazine.com. Retrieved from http://www.cxmagazine.com/uci3-harbin-park-economic-impact-2010

Local Spokes. (2013). Retrieved September 25, 2013 from http://www.localspokes.org/

Karadeniz, D. (2008). The Impact of the Little Miami Scenic Trail on Single Family Residential Property Value (Master Thesis). University of Cincinnati School of Planning. Retrieved from http://www.americantrails.org/resources/economics/littlemiamipropvalue.html

Living Streets. (2012). Walk to School Campaign History. Retrieved from: http://www.walktoschool.org.uk/

Local Government Commission. (2000). The Economic Benefits of Walkable Communities.Retrieved from http://www.lgc.org/wordpress/docs/freepub/community_design/focus/walk_to_money.pdf

Lusk, A.C., Furth, P.G., Morency, P. et al. (2011). Risk of injury for bicycling on cycle tracks versus in the street. Injury Prevention. Retrieved from http://grist.files.wordpress.com/2011/02/risk-of-injury-study.pdf

Making the Grade 2009: T.A.'s 12th Annual Bicycling Report Card. (2009). Reclaim Magazine. Winter Edition, 5-8. Retrieved from http://transalt.org/news/magazine/2009/winter

Mapes, J. (2009). Pedaling Revolution: How Cyclists are Changing American Cities. Corvalis, OR: Oregon State University Press.

Martens, K. (2004). The bicycle as a feedering mode: Experiences from three European countries. Transportation Research Part D: Transport and Environment, 9, 281–294.

Maus, J. (2006, June 15). Portland bicycle industry worth $63M. BikePortland.org. Retrieved from http://bikeportland.org/2006/06/15/survey-says-bicycle-industry-nears-63m-1476

McClintock, H. & Cleary, J. (1996). Cycle facilities and cyclists' safety—experience from Greater Nottingham and lessons for future cycling provision. Transport Policy, 3, 67–77.

McCann, B. & Handy, S. Regional Response to Federal Funding for Bicycle and Pedestrian Projects. Journal of the American Planning Association, 77(1), 23-38.

McDonald, N.C. (2007). Active Transportation to School: Trends Among U.S. Schoolchildren, 1969–2001. American Journal of Preventive Medicine, 32(6), 509–516.

McDonald, N., A. Aalborg (2009). Why parents drive children to school: Implications for safe routes to school programs. Journal of the American Planning Association, 75(3): 331–342.

McDonald, N. (2011). U.S. School Travel, 2009: An Assessment of Trends. American Journal of Preventive Medicine, 41(2): 146-151.

McDonald, N. (2012). Children and Cycling. In Pucher, J., Buehler, R. (Eds.), City Cycling (235-256). Cambridge, MA: MIT Press.

Menghini, G., Carrasco, N., Schüssler, N., Axhausen, K. (2010). Route choice of cyclists in Zurich. Transportation Research Part A: Policy and Practice (9), 754–765.

Metropolitan Nashville Planning Department (2012, March 22). Implementing Complete Streets: Major and Collector Street Plan of Metropolitan Nashville. Retrieved from http://www.nashville.gov/Portals/0/SiteContent/Planning/docs/trans/MajorCollectorStreetPlanMar2012.pdf

Millennials say they are driving less. (2010, November 22). UPI. Retrieved from http://www.upi.com/Business_News/2010/11/22/Millennials-say-they-are-driving-less/UPI-73481290485950

Moudon, A., Lee, C., Cheadle, A., Collier, C., Johnson, D., & Schmid, T. (2005). Cycling and the built environment, a US perspective. Transportation Research Part D: Transport and Environment, 10, 245–261.

Nankervis, M. (1999). The effect of weather and climate on bicycle commuting. Transportation Research Part A: Policy and Practice, 33(6), 417–431.

Nashville Area Metropolitan Planning Organization. (2010, December 15). 2035 Regional Transportation Plan. Retrieved from http://www.nashvillempo.org/plans_programs/rtp/2035_rtp.aspx

National Association of Realtors. (2011, March).The 2011 Community Preference Survey. Retrieved from http://www.realtor.org/reports/2011-community-preference-survey

National Center for Safe Routes to School. History of Safe Routes to School. Retrieved from www.saferoutesinfo.org

National Center for Health Statistics. (2006, November). Health, United States, 2006: With Chartbook on Trends in the Health of Americans (DHHS Publication No. 2006-1232). Hyattsville, MD.

National Center for Safe Routes to School. (2009, June). Summer 2009 SRTS Program Tracking Brief. Retrieved from http://www.saferoutesinfo.org/resources/tracking-reports.cfm

National Center for Safe Routes to School. (2011, August). Federal Safe Routes to School Program: Progress Report. Retrieved from http://www.saferoutesinfo.org/sites/default/files/resources/

progress%20report_FINAL_web.pdf

National Center for Safe Routes to School. (2011, November). How Children Get to School: School Travel Patterns From 1969 to 2009. Retrieved from http://www.saferoutesinfo.org/program-tools/

NHTS-school-travel-1969-2009

National Complete Streets Coalition. (2010). Examples of Complete Streets Policies and Guides. Retrieved from http://www.completethestreets.org

National Conference of State Legislatures. (2014, January) Safely Passing Bicyclists. Retrieved February, 2014 from http://www.ncsl.org/research/transportation/safely-passing-bicyclists.aspx

National Governors Association. (2006, August). Investing in America's Health. Retrieved from http://www.nga.org/files/live/sites/NGA/files/pdf/0608HEALTHYREPORTNATIONAL.PDF

National Prevention Council (2011). National Prevention Strategy: America's Plan for Better Health and Wellness. Retrieved from http://www.surgeongeneral.gov/initiatives/prevention/strategy/introduction.pdf

National Transportation Alternatives Clearinghouse. (2013, May). Transportation Enhancements Spending Report, FY 1992 - FY 2012. Retrieved from http://www.ta-clearinghouse.info/action/document/download?document_id=194.

Nelson, A. & D. Allen, D.(1997). If you build them, commuters will use them. Transportation Research Record, 1578, 79–83.

NHTS. National Household Travel Survey, U.S. Department of Transportation and Federal Highway Administration, 2001, 2009.

North Carolina Department of Transportation NCDOT. (2004). The Economic Impact of Investments in Bicycle Facilities; A Case Study of the Northern Outer Banks. Retrieved from http://ncdot.gov/bikeped/download/bikeped_research_EIAoverview.pdf

NYCDOT. (2012). Measuring the Street: New Metrics for 21st Century Streets. Retrieved fromhttp://www.nyc.gov/html/dot/downloads/pdf/2012-10-measuring-theived retr-street.pdf.

Ogden, C., Lamb, M., Carroll, M. & Flegal. K. (2010). Obesity and socio-economic status in adults: United States, 2005-2008. NCHS Data Brief (50):1-8.

Ogden, C. & Carroll, M. (2008). Prevalence of Obesity Among Children and Adolescents: United States, Trends 1963–1965 through 2007–2008. National Center for Health Statistics. Retrieved from http://www.cdc.gov/nchs/data/hestat/overweight/overweight_adult.htm

Ogden, C. & Carroll, M. (2010). Prevalence of Overweight, Obesity, and Extreme Obesity Among Adults: United States, Trends 1960–1962 Through 2007–2008. National Center for Health Statistics. Retrieved from http://www.cdc.gov/nchs/data/hestat/obesity_adult_07_08/obesity_adult_07_08.pdf

Oja, P., Titze, S., Bauman, A., de Geus, Krenn, B. P., Reger-Nash, B., Kohlberger, T. (2011). Health benefits of cycling: A systematic review. Scandinavian Journal of Medicine and Science in Sports, 21, 496-509.

Parkin, J., Wardman, M. &Page, M. (2008). Estimation of the determinants of bicycle mode share for the journey to work using census data.Transportation,35, 93–109.

Partnership for a Walkable America. Walkability Checklist: How walkable is your community? Retrieved from www.walkableamerica.org/checklist-walkability.pdf

PBIC &FHWA. (2010, May). The national walking and bicycling study: 15-year status report. Retrieved from http://drusilla.hsrc.unc.edu/cms/downloads/15-year_report.pdf

Pedestrian and Bicycle Information Center. (n.d) Bikeability Checklist—How bikeable is your community? Retrieved from http://www.pedbikeinfo.org/pdf/bikeability_checklist.pdf

PolicyLink. (2009, August). All Aboard! Making Equity and Inclusion Central to Federal Transportation Policy. Retrieved from http://www.policylink.org/atf/cf/%7B97C6D565-BB43-406D-A6D5-ECA3BBF35AF0%7D/all_aboard.pdf

PolicyLink. (2009, July). The Transportation Prescription: Bold New Ideas for Healthy, Equitable Transportation Reform in America. Retrieved from http://www.policylink.org/atf/cf/%7B97C6D565-BB43-406D-A6D5-ECA3BBF35AF0%7D/transportationRX_final.pdf

Pucher, J., de Lanversin, E., Suzuki, T., & Whitelegg, J. (2012). Cycling in Megacities: London, Paris, New York, and Tokyo. In Pucher, J., Buehler, R., (Eds.), City Cycling (319-346). Cambridge, MA: MIT Press.

Pucher, J., & Dijkstra, L. (2003, September). Promoting Safe Walking and Cycling to Improve Public Health: Lessons from The Netherlands and Germany. American Journal of Public Health, 93 (9), 1509-1506.

Pucher, J., & Renne, J.L. (2003) Socioeconomics of Urban Travel: Evidence from the 2001 NHTS. Transportation Quarterly, 57(3), 49–77.

Pucher, J. & Buehler, R. (2006). Why Canadians cycle more than Americans: A Comparative Analysis of Bicycling Trends and Policies. Transport Policy, 13, 265–279.

Pucher, J. & Buehler, R. (2007, December). At the Frontiers of Cycling: Policy Innovations in the Netherlands, Denmark, and German. World Transport Policy and Practice, 13(3), 8–57.

Pucher, J. & Buehler, R. (2008). Making Cycling Irresistible: Lessons from the Netherlands, Denmark, and Germany. Transport Reviews, 28(4), 95–528.

Pucher, J. &Buehler, R. (2009). Integration of Bicycling and Public Transport in North America. Journal of Public Transportation, 12(3), 79–104.

Pucher, J. & R. Buehler (2010). Walking and Cycling for Healthy Cities. Built Environment, 36(5), 391-414.

Pucher, J. & Buehler, R. (2012). Integration of Cycling with Public Transport. In Pucher, J., Buehler, R. (Eds.), City Cycling (157-182). Cambridge, MA: MIT Press.

Pucher, J., Buehler, R., Bassett, D. &Dannenberg, A. (2010). Walking and Cycling to Health: Recent Evidence from City, State, and International Comparisons, American Journal of Public Health, 100(10), 1986-1992.

Pucher, J., Buehler, R.,& Seinen, M. (2011). Bicycling Renaissance in North America? An Update and Re-Assessment of Cycling Trends and Policies. Transportation Research Part A: Policy and Practice, 45(6), 451-475.

Pucher, J., Buehler,R., Merom, D., & Bauman, A. (2011). Walking and Cycling in the United States, 2001-2009: Evidence from the National Household Travel Surveys, American Journal of Public Health, 101(10), S310-S317.

Pucher, P., Buehler, R., Merom, D., &Bauman, A. (2011, September). Active Travel in Germany and the USA: Contributions of Daily Walking and Cycling to Physical Activity. American Journal of Preventive Medicine, 40(9), 241-250.

Pucher, J., Dill, J. & Handy, S. (2010). Infrastructure, Programs and Policies to Increase Bicycling: An International Review. Preventive Medicine, 50(S1), S106-S125.

Pucher, J., Garrard, J. &Greaves, S. (2011b). Cycling down under: a comparative analysis of bicycling trends and policies in Sydney and Melbourne. Journal of Transport Geography 19(2), 332–345.

Pucher, J., Thorwaldson, L., Buehler, R., &Klein, N. (2010). Cycling in New York: policy innovations at the urban frontier. World Transport Policy and Practice 16(2), 7–50.

Rails to Trails Conservancy. (2011). Active Transportation Beyond Urban Centers: Walking and Bicycling in Small Towns and Rural America. Retrieved from http://www.railstotrails.org/resources/documents/ourWork/reports/BeyondUrbanCentersReport.pdf

SFMTA. (2008). Report Card on Bicycling: San Francisco 2008. Retrieved from http://www.sfbike.org/?reportcard

Revenue. (2011). Tax Rates and Tax Bands. Retrieved on January 21, 2011 from http://www.revenue.ie/en/tax/it/leaflets/it1.html#section3

Reynolds, C., Harris, M., Teschke, K., Cripton, P., & Winters, M. (2009). The impact of transportation infrastructure on bicycling injuries and crashes: A review of the literature. Environmental Health,8(47).Doi: 10.1186/1476-069X-8-47

Ridgway, D. (2010). Kansas City Regional Tiger Application Appendix D: KC Bicycle/Pedestrian Project. Retrieved fromhttp://www.marc.org/Recovery/assets/tiger/APPENDIX_D_Bicycle_Pedestrian.pdf.

Rietveld, P. (2000). The accessibility of railway stations: the role of the bicycle in The Netherlands. Transportation Research Part D: Transport and Environment5(1), 71-75.

Rietveld, P. & Daniel, V. (2004). Determinants of bicycle use: Do municipal policies matter? Transportation Research Part A: Policy and Practice, 38(7), 531–550.

Rojas-Rueda, D., Nazelle, A.,Tainio, M., & Nieuwenhuijsen, M. (2011, August 4). The health risks and benefits of cycling in urban environments compared with car use: Health impact assessment study. British Medical Journal, 343:d4521.

Rose, G. & H. Marfurt. (2007). Travel behaviour change impacts of a major ride to work day event. Transportation Research Part A: Policy and Practice, 41(4), 351–364.

Roux, Larissa et al. (2008). Cost Effectiveness of Community-Based Physical Activity Interventions. American Journal of Preventive Medicine 35(6), 578–588.

Saelens, B.E. &Handy, S.L. (2008). Built environment correlates of walking: a review. Medicine and Science in Sports and Exercise, 40(S7), S550–S566.

Sælensminde, K. (2004). Cost-benefit analyses of walking and cycling track networks taking into account insecurity, health effects and external costs of motorized traffic. Transportation Research Part A: Policy and Practice,38(8), 593-606.

Safe Routes to School National Partnership. (2012). Safe Routes to School Federal Program: State of the States. As of December 31, 2012. Retrieved from http://www.saferoutespartnership.org/sites/default/files/pdf/State-of-the-States-December-2012-FINAL.pdf

Safe Routes to School National Partnership. (n.d.). Creating Your Action Plan: The 5E's for Safe Routes to School. Retrieved from http://www.saferoutespartnership.org/local/4191/4219?tid=2184

Safe Routes to School National Partnership. (n.d.). I Walk The Official Website of International Walk to School: About the Walk. Retrieved February 18, 2014 from http://www.walktoschool-usa.org

Sarmiento, O., Torres, A., Jacoby, E., Pratt, M., Schmid, T., & Stierling, G. (2010). The Ciclovía—recreativa: A mass recreational program with public health potential. Journal of Physical Activity and Health (S2), S163–S180.

Sehatzadeh, B., Noland, R.B., & Weiner, M.D. (2011). Walking Frequency, Cars, Dogs, and the Built Environment. Transportation Research Part A: Policy and Practice, 45(8), 741-754.

Shafizadeh, K. & Niemeier,D. (1997). Bicycle journey-to-work: Travel behavior characteristics and spatial analysis. Transportation Research Record 1578, 84–90.

Shaheen, S., Guzman, S., & Zhang, H. (2010). Bikesharing in Europe, the Americas, and Asia: Past, present, and future. Paper presented at the 89th Annual Meeting of the Transportation Research Board, Washington, DC.

Shaheen, S., Guzman, S., & Zhang, H. (2012). Bikesharing across the Globe. In Pucher, J., Buehler, R., (Eds.), City Cycling (183-210). Cambridge, MA: MIT Press.

Shaheen, S., Martin, E., Cohen, A., & Finson, R. (2012, June). Public Bikesharing in North America: Early Operator and User Understanding (Report 11-26). San Jose, CA: Mineta Transportation Institute. Retrieved from http://transweb.sjsu.edu/PDFs/research/1029-public-bikesharing-understanding-early-operators-users.pdf

Shephard R. (2008). Is active commuting the answer to population health? Sports Medicine 39(9), 751-758.

Shoup, Donald. (2005). High cost of free parking. Washington, DC: Chicago, IL: American Planning Association.

Sierra Club. (2012). Pedaling to prosperity: Pedaling will save Americans $4.6 Billion in 2012. Retrieved from http://www.sierraclub.org/pressroom/downloads/BikeMonth_Factsheet_0512.pdf

Singh, A., Uijtdewilligen, L., Twisk, J.W.R., et al. (2012). Physical Activity and Performance at School. Archives of Pediatrics and Adolescent Medicine, 166(1):49-55.

Smart, M. (2010). US immigrants and bicycling: Two-wheeled in autopia. Transport Policy 17(3), 153–159.

Staunton, C., Hubsmith, D., & Kallins, W. (2003). Promoting safe walking and biking to school: The Frequency of bicycle commuting: Internet-based survey analysis Marin County success story. American Journal of Public Health 93(9), 1431–1434.

Stinson, M. &Bhat, C. (2004). Frequency of bicycle commuting: Internet-based survey analysis. Transportation Research Record, 1878 (1)122–130. doi:10.3141/1878-15

Su, J., Winters, M., Nunes, M., & Brauer, M. (2010). Designing a route planner to facilitate and promote cycling in Metro Vancouver, Canada. Transportation Research Part A: Policy and Practice, 44(7), 495–505.

TEA-21. (1998, September 14) Surface Transportation Program Fact Sheet. Retrieved from http://www.fhwa.dot.gov/Tea21/factsheets/stp.htm

Texas Department of Health State Services. (2010, May). Texas Overweight and Obesity Statistics. Retrieved from www.dshs.state.tx.us/obesity/pdf/txobesitydata.pdf

Tilahun, N., Levinson, D.,&Krizek, K. (2007, May). Trails, lanes, or traffic: Valuing bicycle facilities with an adaptive stated preference survey. Transportation Research Part A: Policy and Practice, 41(4), 287–301.

Timperio, A., Ball, K., Salmon, J., Roberts, R., Giles-Corti, B., Baur, C., & Crawford, D. (2006). Personal, family, social, and environmental correlates of active commuting to school. American Journal of Preventive Medicine, 30 (1), 45–51.

Toole Design Group and The Pedestrian and Bicycle Information Center. (2012). Bike Sharing in the United States: State of the Practice and Guide to Implementation Retrieved from http://www.bicyclinginfo.org/promote/bikeshareintheus.pdf

Toronto Coalition for Active Transportation. (2008, April 25). Benchmarking Toronto's Bicycle Environment: Comparing Toronto to other World Cities. Retrieved from http://www.cleanairpartnership.org/files/

TCAT%20Benchmarking%20Toronto%20Bicycle%20Environment.pdf

Transportation for America. (2011) Dangerous by Design 2011. Retrieved from http://www.aarp.org/content/dam/aarp/livable-communities/learn/transportation/dangerous-by-design-2011-aarp.pdf

Transportation Research Board Institute of Medicine. (2005) Does the Built Environment Influence Physical Activity: Examining the Evidence (TRB Special Report 282). Retrieved from http://onlinepubs.trb.org/onlinepubs/sr/sr282.pdf

Transport and Travel Research, Ltd. (2006). The Urban Transport Benchmarking Initiative: Year Three Final Report, Cycling Scotland. Retrieved from http://www.transportbenchmarks.eu.

Tour of Missouri. (2010). Tour of Missouri Set to Cancel for 2010, May 27, 2010. http://mobikefed.org/content/tour-missouri-set-cancel-2010

U.S. Census Bureau. (1980-2011). Population Estimates. Historical Data. Retrieved from http://www.census.gov/popest/data/historical/index.html

U.S. Department of Health and Human Services. (2013, August 28). Healthypeople.gov 2020 Topics and Objective: Environmental Health Retrieved February 19, 2014 from http://www.healthypeople.gov/2020/topicsobjectives2020/objectiveslist.aspx?topicId=12

U.S. Department of Transportation. (2011, July 11). New Research Shows Enforcement Cuts Distracted Driving: Pilot Programs in Syracuse, NY, and Hartford, CT, Significantly Curb Texting and Cell Phone Use Behind the Wheel [press release]. Retrieved from http://www.nhtsa.gov/About+NHTSA/Press+Releases/2011/New+Research+Shows+Enforcement+Cuts+Distracted+Driving

U.S. Environmental Protection Agency. (2013, April 12). Inventory of U.S. Greenhouse Gas Emissions and Sinks: 1990-2011 (Report No. EPA 430-R-13-001). Retrieved from http://www.epa.gov/climatechange/ghgemissions/usinventoryreport.html

Vandenbulcke, G., Dujardin, C., Thomas, I., de Geus, B., Degraeuwe, B., Meeusen, R., & IntPanis, L. (2011). Cycle commuting in Belgium: Spatial determinants and 're-cycling' strategies. Transportation Research Part A: Policy and Practice, 45(2), 118–137.

Vandenbulcke, G., Thomas,I., de Geus, B., Degraeuwe, B., Torfs, R., Meeusen, R., IntPanis, L. (2009). Mapping bicycle use and the risk of accidents for commuters who cycle to work in Belgium. Transport Policy, 16(2), 77–87.

Vélo Mondial. (2005, May 7). National Cycling Benchmark Policies. Retrieved from http://www.velomondial.net/page_display.asp?pid=14

Vélo Québec. (2010). Bicycling in Québec in 2010. Retrieved from http://www.velo.qc.ca/en/Bicycling-in-Quebec

Venegas, E. (2009, November). Economic Impact of Recreational Trail Use in Different Regions of Minnesota. Report prepared for University of Minnesota Tourism Center. Retrieved from http://www.tourism.umn.edu/prod/groups/cfans/@pub/@cfans/@tourism/documents/asset/cfans_asset_167538.pdf

Vernez-Moudon, A., Lee, C., Cheadle, A.D., Collier, C.W., Johnson, D., Schmid, T.L., &Weather, R.D. (2005). Cycling and the built environment, a US perspective. Transportation Research Part D: Transport and Environment, 10(3), 245–261.

Victoria Department of Transport (2009). Walking and Cycling International Literature Review. Report prepared by K. Krizek, A. Forsyth & L. Baum. Retrieved from http://www.transport.vic.gov.au/__data/assets/pdf_file/0004/31369/WalkingCyclingLiteratureReview.pdf

Victoria Transport Policy Institute. (2011, February 1). Economic Value of Walkability. Victoria Transport Policy Institute. Report by T. Litman. Retrieved from http://www.vtpi.org/walkability.pdf

Vinther, E. (2008,Nomber 30). Children who walk to school concentrate better. Science Nordic. Retrieved from from http://sciencenordic.com/children-who-walk-school-concentrate-bette

Washington State Department of Transportation. Moving Forward: Safe Routes to School Progress in Five States (WA-RD 743.3). Report by A. Vernez Moudon and O. Stewart. Retrieved from http://www.wsdot.wa.gov/research/reports/fullreports/743.3.pdf

Walk Score. How Walk Score Works. Retrieved from http://www.walkscore.com/how-it-works.shtml

Walker, J. (2010, July 5). The State of Walking in London, Walk21 [PDF Document]. Retrieved from http://www.walk21.com/uploads/File/WC%20conference%20London%20100507.pdf

Wang, G., Macera, C.A., Scudder-Soucie, B., Schmid, T., Pratt, M., & Buchner, D. (2005). A Cost-Benefit Analysis of Physical Activity Using Bike/Pedestrian Trails. Health Promotion Practice, 6(2), 174-179.

Wang, X., Lindsey, G., Schoner, J., & Harrison, A. (2012, August 1). Modeling bike share station activity: The effects of nearby business and jobs on trips to and from stations. Paper presented at the Transportation Research Board 92nd Annual Meeting. Paper retrieved from http://b.3cdn.net/bikes/3eaf6daa97fd203fbd_uim6brbur.pdf

Wardman, M., Tight, M., & Page, M.(2007).Factors influencing the propensity to cycle to work. Transportation Research Part A: Policy and Practice, 41(4), 339–350.

Winters, M., M. Friesen, M. Koehoorn, K. Teschke. (2007). Utilitarian bicycling: A multilevel analysis of climate and personal influences. American Journal of Preventive Medicine, 32, 52–58.

Witlox, F. & Tindemans, H. (2004). Evaluating bicycle-car transport mode competitiveness in an urban environment: An activity-based approach. World Transport Policy and Practice, 10(4), 32–42.

Wray, H. (2008). Pedal Power: The Quiet Rise of the Bicycle in American Public Life. Boulder, CO: Paradigm Publishers.

Bicycling and Walking in the United States: 2014 Benchmarking Report

Finding Your Angle Factsheet/Worksheet

LEVELS of BIKING & WALKING to WORK (2009–2011)

Share of commuters who bike to work (page 43)

American Community Survey (ACS) 2011 (national average), 2009–2011 (cities and states)

Average of U.S. states: 0.6% Your state: ________ %
High: 2.3% (Oregon)
Low: 0.1% (Alabama, Arkansas, Mississippi, Tennessee, and West Virginia)

Average among large U.S. cities: 1.0% Your city: ________ %
High: 6.1% (Portland, OR)
Low: 0.1% (Arlington, TX, and Fort Worth)

Share of commuters who walk to work (page 43)

ACS 2011 (national average), 2009–2011 (cities and states)

Average of U.S. states: 2.8% Your state: ________ %
High: 7.9% (Alaska)
Low: 1.2% (Alabama)

Average among large U.S. cities: 5.0% Your city: ________ %
High: 15.0% (Boston)
Low: 1.2% (Fort Worth)

Percent of bicycle commuters who are women (page 47)

ACS 2011 (national average), 2009–2011 (cities and states)

Average of U.S. states: 27% Your state: ________ %
High: 42% (Wyoming)
Low: 15% (Nevada)

Average among large U.S. cities: 29% Your city: ________ %
High: 41% (Fresno)
Low: 4% (El Paso)

Percent of walking commuters who are women (pages 48–49)

ACS 2011 (national average), 2009–2011 (cities and states)

Average of U.S. states: 46% Your state: ________ %
High: 51% (Massachusetts and New Hampshire)
Low: 37% (North Carolina)

Average among large U.S. cities: 50% Your city: ________ %
High: 55% (Honolulu and Philadelphia)
Low: 28% (Virginia Beach)

Bicycling and Walking in the United States: 2014 Benchmarking Report

Finding Your Angle Factsheet/Worksheet

SAFETY (2009–2011)

Percent of traffic fatalities that are bicyclists (pages 83 and 85)
Fatality Analysis Reporting System (FARS) 2009–2011

Average of U.S. states: 1.9% Your state: ________ %
High: 4.3% (Florida)
Low: 0.2% (Maine)

Average among large U.S. cities: 3.4% Your city: ________ %
High: 9.5% (Fresno)
Low: 0.0% (Arlington, TX, and Wichita)

Percent of traffic fatalities that are pedestrians (pages 82 and 84)
FARS 2009–2011

Average of U.S. states: 12.9% Your state: ________ %
High: 25.5% (New York)
Low: 2.6% (Wyoming)

Average among large U.S. cities: 27.8% Your city: ________ %
High: 55.0% (New York City)
Low: 10.0% (Colorado Springs)

Bicyclist fatality rate (fatalities per 10K bicyclists) (page 79)
FARS 2009–2011, ACS 2009–2011

Average of U.S. states: 8.5 Your state: ________ %
High: 70.4 (Mississippi)
Low: 1.0 (Montana)

Average among large U.S. cities: 4.9 Your city: ________ %
High: 41.9 (Fort Worth)
Low: 0.0 (Arlington, TX, and Wichita)

Pedestrian fatality rate (fatalities per 10K pedestrians) (page 79)
FARS 2009–2011, ACS 2009–2011

Average of U.S. states: 11.0 Your state: ________ %
High: 38.6 (Florida)
Low: 2.2 (Vermont)

Average among large U.S. cities: 8.3 Your city: ________ %
High: 41.6 (Jacksonville)
Low: 0.9 (Boston)

Bicycling and Walking in the United States: 2014 Benchmarking Report

Finding Your Angle Factsheet/Worksheet

HEALTH (2011)

Percent of adults who met recommended minimum weekly aerobic physical activity (pages 73–74)

Behavioral Risk Factor Surveillance System (BRFSS) 2011

Average of U.S. states: 51.1% Your state: ________ %
High: 61.8% (Colorado)
Low: 39.0% (Tennessee)

Average among large U.S. cities: 52.3% Your city: ________ %
High: 62.4% (Oakland and San Francisco)
Low: 37.8% (Memphis)

Percent of adults who are obese (pages 73–74)

BRFSS 2011

Average of U.S. states: 27.7% Your state: ________ %
High: 34.9% (Mississippi)
Low: 20.7% (Colorado)

Average among large U.S. cities: 26.4% Your city: ________ %
High: 36.8% (Memphis)
Low: 18.6% (San Francisco and Oakland)

FUNDING (2009–2011)

Percent of federal transportation dollars to biking and walking (pages 126–127)

Federal Highway Administration (FHWA) Fiscal Management Information System (FMIS) 2009–2012
Cities and states listed here have an overall positive obligation of funds.

Average of U.S. states: 2.1% Your state: ________ %
High: 3.7% (Delaware)
Low: 0.7% (North Dakota and West Virginia)

Average among large U.S. cities: 3.3% Your city: ________ %
High: 39.6% (Louisville)
Low: 0.03% (Indianapolis)

Per capita funding to biking and walking (pages 126–127)

FHWA FMIS 2009–2012, ACS 2011
Cities and states list here have an overall positive obligation of funds.

Average of U.S. states: $3.10 Your state: ________ %
High: $12.05 (Alaska)
Low: $1.18 (Maryland)

Average among large U.S. cities: $2.78 Your city: ________ %
High: $14.22 (Miami)
Low: $0.002 (Indianapolis)